Rudolf Sachs / Birgit Abegg

Commercial Correspondence

Englische Handelskorrespondenz
für die Berufspraxis

New Edition

Hueber

Grundlage dieser Neubearbeitung durch Birgit Abegg ist Rudolf Sachs, *Commercial Correspondence: Einführung in die moderne englische Handelskorrespondenz*. 2. aktualisierte Auflage Ismaning: Hueber, 1993 (ISBN: 3-19-002336-0).

Ⓡ Dieses Werk folgt der seit dem 1. August 1998 gültigen Rechtschreibreform.

€ 3. 2. 1. | Die letzten Ziffern
2005 04 03 02 01 | bezeichnen Zahl und Jahr des Druckes.
Alle Drucke dieser Auflage können, da unverändert, nebeneinander benutzt werden.
1. Auflage

Umschlaggestaltung: Christiane Gerstung, München
Zeichnungen: Daniela Eisenreich, München; Reinhard Blumenschein, München (S. 112)
Layout und Satz: Christiane Gerstung, München
Muttersprachliche Beratung: John Stevens, Bad Münstereifel
Verlagsredaktion: Dr. Astrid Krake, München
Herstellung: Astrid Hansen
Druck und Bindung: J. P. Himmer GmbH & Co. KG, Augsburg
Printed in Germany
ISBN 3-19-002708-0

Vorwort

Seit Erscheinen der ersten Auflage wurde „Commercial Correspondence“ mehrfach revidiert und den modernen Gegebenheiten angepasst.

In den letzten Jahren erfuhr die Berufspraxis des Exports in zunehmendem Maß Neuheiten und Veränderungen. Der internationale Handelsverkehr hat sich gewandelt und erweitert, die Europäische Union schreibt eigene Gesetze und führte den Euro ein, der Siegeszug der E-Mail und des E-Commerce hat begonnen. Das internationale Büro hat sich durch den Einzug des Computers und den Nachrichtenverkehr über Kabel und Satellit völlig verändert, neue Geschäftsformen bahnen sich an, die internationale Struktur von Unternehmen wurde und wird erneuert, Begriffe wie „Freundliche oder Feindliche Übernahmen“ oder „Shareholder Value“ werden zu Alltagsvokabular.

Um diesen Neuerungen auch im internationalen Schriftverkehr Rechnung zu tragen, wurde „Commercial Correspondence“ einer völligen Überarbeitung unterzogen. Die von meinem Kollegen, Herrn Rudolf Sachs, wertvollen, gültig gebliebenen und jahrelang erfolgreich erprobten Teile sind beibehalten, auch die Aufteilung der einzelnen Kapitel erfolgt weiterhin in der bewährten, von ihm kreierten Form. Geändert oder ergänzt wurden alle Teile, die den heutigen Gegebenheiten nicht mehr entsprechen. So sind etwa neue Vorschriften wie die Incoterms 2000 und andere Neuheiten berücksichtigt worden.

Diese Neuausgabe soll Schülerinnen und Schülern sowie Studierenden an Handels- und Sprachenschulen, Lehranstalten und Hochschulen, Auszubildenden in kaufmännischen Ausbildungsberufen und allen, die beruflich mit Wirtschaftsenglisch zu tun haben, ein umfassendes Grundwissen im Bereich der schriftlichen Kommunikation in Handel und Wirtschaft vermitteln. Da es sich bei allen Dokumenten um geringfügig abgeänderte Originale aus der Wirtschaftspraxis handelt, ist das Material besonders für Berufspraktiker im Exportbereich von Interesse.

Die Verordnung über die Berufsausbildung des Kaufmanns/der Kauffrau im Groß- und Außenhandel der IHK in der Bundesrepublik Deutschland sieht in ihrem Prüfungsfach „Abschlussprüfung in der Fachrichtung Außenhandel“ die „fremdsprachliche Bearbeitung eines Falles aus dem Bereich des Außenhandelsgeschäftes“ vor. Hierfür ist dieses Lehrbuch besonders geeignet, da es Mitarbeitern im Außenhandel das notwendige Fachwissen in der Fremdsprache Englisch vermittelt.

Das Lehrbuch gliedert sich in ein Einleitungskapitel mit Informationen über die äußere Form heutiger Geschäftsbriefe, Faxe und E-Mails sowie weitere 17 Korrespondenz-Kapitel. Jedes Kapitel trägt einem bestimmten Bereich des kaufmännisches Schriftverkehrs Rechnung und wurde gegenüber der alten Ausgabe erheblich erweitert. Die ersten 10 Kapitel behandeln die klassischen Formen des kaufmännischen Briefverkehrs; ab Kapitel 11 werden etwa Vertretungen, Joint Ventures und Lizenzverträge behandelt. Ein Novum ist Kapitel 13; es trägt der steigenden Bedeutung des Bankwesens in Exportgeschäften Rechnung. Die weiteren Kapitel beschäftigen sich mit dem Transport- und Speditionswesen sowie Versicherungen, Handelsmessen und Ausstellungen. Ebenfalls neu ist der Bereich der Bürokommunikation, der sich zu einem eigenständigen Gebiet entwickelt hat. Das letzte Kapitel behandelt Bewerbungen nach britischem und amerikanischen Muster. Den Kapiteln schließen sich ein ausführliches Vokabelverzeichnis und ein Glossar der wichtigsten kaufmännischen Fachbegriffe an.

Jedes Korrespondenzkapitel folgt einem bestimmten Muster:
1. eine englische Einleitung mit Erläuterungen und kaufmännischem Grundwissen zum Thema;
2. Musterbriefe, Faxe und E-Mails nach englischem und amerikanischem Vorbild;
3. Ausdrücke und Satzbeispiele aus englischsprachiger Korrespondenz mit deutschen Übersetzungen;
4. ein Übungsteil zur Übersetzung (Brief, Fax oder E-Mail);
5. ein Übungsteil mit Stichwortbrief-Aufgaben, die wahlweise als Brief, Fax oder E-Mail abgefasst werden können. Diese Aufgaben entsprechen in Inhalt und Form den Prüfungsaufgaben der Industrie- und Handelskammern in der Bundesrepublik für die Prüfungen „Zusatzqualifikation Fremdsprache für Auszubildende“, „Fremdsprachenkorrespondent/in Englisch“, „Fremdsprache im Beruf“ und „Übersetzer/in für Handelsenglisch“, in deren Prüfungsausschüssen die Bearbeiterin als Prüferin tätig ist.

Mein besonderer Dank gilt Herrn Diplom-Sparkassenbetriebswirt Wilfried Röth, Stadtsparkasse Köln, der mir einen gesamten Akkreditiv-Vorgang mit allen Dokumenten zur Verfügung stellte; Herrn Diplom-Kaufmann Wolfgang Freitag, Düsseldorf, der mir einen Vertreter-Vertrag sowie ein „Letter of Intent“ mit Kauforder überließ; Herrn Speditionskaufmann Thomas Dünnwald, Düsseldorf für die Überlassung von Speditions- und Versicherungsdokumenten; der Lloyds TSB Bank plc, London für die Überlassung von Bankvordrucken; dem Verlag Macmillan Publishers Ltd, Oxford für die Bereitstellung von Rechnungen; meinem Mann, Peter Abegg, Exportkaufmann, für die kaufmännische Beratung bei Briefen und Übersetzungsübungen und die Überlassung von Originalbriefen; Herrn Dr. Richard Hooton und Herrn John Stevens für die muttersprachliche Beratung und nicht zuletzt der Lektorin des Max-Hueber-Verlags, Frau Dr. Astrid Krake, für die redaktionelle Betreuung dieser Neuausgabe.

Der überwiegende Teil der Namen und Anschriften ist frei erfunden. Mögliche Ähnlichkeiten sind zufällig.

Birgit Abegg

Contents

0. The Form of the Business Letter

0.1 Essential parts

The essential parts of a business letter are:

- Letterhead
- Reference and date
- Inside address
- Salutation
- Body of the letter
- Complimentary close
- Signature, name, position
- Enclosures
- Postscriptum

0.1.1 Letterhead

The letterhead is printed at the top of the letter sheet. There is no set rule as to what a letterhead should look like, but it contains at least the firm's name, logo, postal address, its telephone and fax number as well as its e-mail address. Some companies indicate their website.
Certain additional information may be required by law to be given on letter sheets. For example, a British limited company has to indicate the names of its directors, the address of its registered office, the place of registration and the registered number. Many letterheads include printed words indicating the space reserved for references (*Your ref., our ref.*).

0.1.2 Reference and date

The reference consists of the initials of the person dictating the letter, followed by those of the typist. Letters and numbers indicating the writer's department or section, file numbers or the like, may also be used for reference purposes. (In British letters the reference is usually placed above the date, in American letters it appears in the left-hand lower corner of the letter sheet).
Example: JDS/MB or JDS/mb or jds/mb.
(Dictator's name: *J D Smith*; typist's name: *Mary Brown*)

The date may be written in various different ways.

In Britain, the usual order is day, month and year:
12 August 20..
or
12th August 20..

Americans usually put the month first, followed by day and year:
August 12, 20..

In any case, it is no longer necessary to write 1st, 2nd, 3rd etc. Commas can be left out, too. It is, however, still possible to include them, if desired, eg: August 12th, 20..

All-numeric forms, as recommended by the International Standards Organization (ISO), should be in the order year, month and day, eg: 20..-8-12. However, since numeric dates may also be written in a different order in other countries, it is recommended that the month be written out as a word or at least its abbreviated form (eg *Aug.*) to avoid confusion. If you wrote, for example, 12-8-20.. or 8-12-20.. or 20..-12-8, nobody would know if 12 August or December 8 was meant.

0.1.3 Inside address

The inside address consists of the addressee's name and postal address.

0.1.3.1 Name

Individuals have a surname (last name) and one or more forenames (first names). Business firms have their distinct firm names.

A sole-trader enterprise (in the United States called sole proprietorship) may be carried on under a personal name (the name of the founder or owner) or an impersonal one (such as *Protect Your Environment Store*).

There may be partnership names like *Smith & Johnson, Solicitors; Brown & Co., Accountants*; *Baker & Son*; *Green Bros*. Some partnerships have impersonal names, eg *The Bristol Squash Club*.

The names of British public limited companies include the abbreviation PLC (plc), those of private limited companies the word Limited (Ltd). American corporations have names ending with Company (Co.), Corporation (Corp) or Incorporated (Inc). Pty Ltd (proprietary limited) designates private limited companies in Australia and South Africa, Pte Ltd is the abbreviation used by private limited companies in Singapore.

0.1.3.2 Titles

Women are addressed by Ms (married or unmarried), *Mrs* (married), or *Miss* (unmarried – only used if the ladies insist on being addressed in this way).

Men are addressed by *Mr* for one man and *Messrs* for two or more men. If writing to a partnership whose company name consists of names of either only male or both male and female partners, you also use *Messrs*. Registered companies and partnerships having impersonal names should not be addressed in this manner. (In the United States it is not customary to preface the names of partnerships by *Messrs*.)

Examples:

	Messrs Smith & Co
but:	The South Kensington Polo Club
or:	Smith & Co. Ltd

Courtesy titles or academic degrees, eg those of doctors and professors, are to be indicated in the address,

eg: The Honourable James Donovan
Dr Henry Green
Professor John Edwards

Titles designating a person's office or position, such as Managing Director, President, Secretary and Sales Manager, are placed below or after the name,

eg: Mr J D Carpenter
Managing Director
or: Mr Henry A. Swift, President

Registered companies and other corporate bodies are often addressed through an official whose name is not mentioned,

eg: The Manager
Lloyds Bank

The Company Secretary
Baker & Green plc

0.1.3.3 Postal address

The postal address consists of house number and street name. Since American houses often have suite or apartment numbers, this number is usually written after the street name. In the next line American addresses show the name of the city, town or village, followed by the abbreviation of the state and the ZIP code. In British addresses the name of the city, town or village is written in capital letters, and the postcode (also in capital letters) follows on a separate line.

In foreign mail, the name of the country of destination has to be added (in the language of the sender's country). Should the addressee have a post-office box, the POB number is substituted for the house number and street. When a letter is sent to a person's temporary address (or a private letter to the person's business address), the abbreviation *c/o* (*care of*) is used.

Examples:

UK address:	*USA address:*
Johnson & Quick Ltd	Software Incorporated
38 Leadenhall Street	115 Crestmont Drive, Suite 810
LONDON	Laurel, MD 20708
EC1 4WW	USA
England	

The postal address may also include special instructions to the post office and/or the addressee:

(By) Air Mail	(Mit) Luftpost
Registered (Mail)	Einschreiben
Express Delivery, Special Delivery (AE)	Durch Eilboten
By courier	Durch Kurier
Poste Restante, To be called for	Postlagernd
Printed matter	Drucksache
If undelivered, return to ...	Falls unzustellbar, bitte zurück an ...
Urgent	Eilt
Personal	Persönlich
Confidential	Vertraulich

0.1.4 Salutation

In letters to individuals, the following salutations are used (listed in order of decreasing formality): *Sir or Madam; Dear Sir or Madam; Dear Mr Baker, Dear Ms White, Dear Mrs Smith, Dear Miss Brown; Dear Jim, Dear Mary.*

Sir/Madam is highly formal and therefore used only in specific cases. *Dear Sir/Dear Madam* is also quite formal; it is appropriate when the addressee is not personally known to the writer. In circulars and similar letters, a combined form such as *Dear Sir/Madam* may be used. *Dear Mr/Ms, Mrs, Miss* is a suitable salutation when the correspondents are personally known to each other or when the writer wishes to establish a friendly relationship with the addressee. Where appropriate, *Mr/Ms, Mrs, Miss* may be replaced by another title (eg *Dr, Professor*).

In a letter to two or more men, a business firm or other organization, the salutations *Dear Sirs* and *Gentlemen* are used. The former is preferred in Britain, the latter in the United States.

In the United States you sometimes use *Ladies* when writing to two or more women, or to a firm or organization consisting entirely of women.

There is not yet an accepted English salutation which, like the German *Sehr geehrte Damen und Herren*, takes account of the fact that a firm or organization consists of both men and women. In Britain, you increasingly find the singular form *Dear Sir or Madam or Dear Sir / Madam*, in America the salutation *Ladies and Gentlemen* or *Gentlemen and Ladies* is gradually replacing the older term *Gentlemen*. But in many cases the salutation *Dear Sirs* (in Britain) and *Gentlemen* (in the U.S.) is still used.

0.1.5 Body of the letter

The body of the letter contains the message. It always starts with a capital letter. If letters are longer than one page, they continue on a continuation sheet (see below).

0.1.6 Complimentary close

The complimentary close must be consistent with the salutation. In Britain, the appropriate close for letters beginning with *Dear Sir / Dear Madam, Dear Sirs* is *Yours faithfully*. It is *Yours sincerely* if the recipient's name was used in the salutation (eg *Dear Mr Smith, Dear Ms Robert, Dear Jack, Dear Susan*). In friendly letters the complimentary close can be preceded by *With best regards* or *With kind wishes*.

In American business letters, the close *Sincerely* or *Sincerely yours* is used in all cases. The formerly used close *Yours (very) truly* or *(Very) Truly yours* has become obsolete. Letters beginning with an informal salutation can also be closed with the above-mentioned phrases *With kind regards, With best wishes* or with *Cordially yours, Yours cordially, Cordially*.

0.1.7 Signature

After the complimentary close it is customary to indicate the name of the firm sending the letter. This name is followed by the sender's signature. Since signatures are often difficult to read, the name of the person signing the letter is usually typed below.

If the signatory signs on behalf of another person, *pp* (meaning *per procurationem*) or *for and on behalf of* can be typed before the signature.

Examples:

Johnson & Reefs Ltd
Michael Harvard
Michael Harvard
General Manager

or:

Johnson & Reefs Ltd
Michael Harvard
pp Michael Harvard
General Manager

British and American business letters bear only one signature. Double signatures, as in Germany, are not customary.

A secretary signing a letter in her boss's absence may use the following mode:

Ajax Manufacturing Co Ltd

P R Baker
Production Manager

Signed in Mr Baker's absence

Jane Smith

Jane Smith (Mrs)
Secretary to Mr P R Baker

0.2 Optional parts

A business letter may also include the following optional parts, which are included only when needed:

- Attention line
- Subject line
- Enclosures and carbon copies
- Postscript
- Continuation-sheet heading

0.2.1 Attention line

The attention line is used to bring a letter addressed to a business firm or other organization to the attention of a particular person or department; it is typed below the inside address.

Example:
Ferris Electronics plc
15 Lothian Square
EDINBURGH
ED6 6HL

<u>For the attention of Mr Lewis</u>

The attention line may also read *Attention: Mr Lewis* or *Attention: Sales Manager*. The word "Attention" may be abbreviated *Att.* or *Attn.*

0.2.2 Subject line

The subject line is an optional feature which serves the reader's convenience. In Britain it is usually placed below the salutation, but it may also appear above it. In America, it is placed before the salutation and can be preceded by an introductory word (*Subject* or *Re*). The subject line can be put in bold print, capitalized or underlined.

0.2.3 Enclosures and carbon copies

When enclosures are sent with the letter, or when another person, a branch office, etc is to receive a copy, this is indicated in the left-hand lower corner of the letter.

Examples:

Enclosure(s) *or:* Enc(s) *or:* Enc:
1 pro forma invoice

The abbreviation "cc" is still used to indicate that a copy of the letter is to be sent to another person or persons named.

Example:

cc Ms Gabriella Robinson, Personnel Manager
Mr Graham Jones, Sales Manager

0.2.4 Postscript

The postscript has practically disappeared from modern business correspondence since anything can be inserted into a letter written on a computer. It may, however, sometimes be added to inform a reader of a last-minute development or to emphasize an important point.

0.2.5 Continuation-sheet heading

Continuation sheets should bear the page number, the date and the recipient's name, eg:

Mr Jonathan Hall	*or:*	Miller & Bridges plc
30 June 20..		2 January 20..
Page 2		Page 5

0.3 Envelope

The envelope bears two addresses, the address of the addressee and that of the sender. Normally a window envelope is used, so the inside address also serves as the envelope address.

0.4 Layout and punctuation

All business letters today are written in block form. This means that all relevant details, such as the date, the inside address, the salutation, the lines of each paragraph, the complimentary close and the signature begin with the left-hand margin.

Punctuation in the body of the letter is, of course, the same as in any other written text. With regard to the other parts of the letter, there is the possibility of open or closed punctuation. In a letter with closed punctuation, punctuation marks can be placed after the date, the salutation and the complimentary close. In American letters a colon is put after the salutation. When open punctuation is used, these punctuation marks are omitted. This also applies to full stops after abbreviations (*eg, ie, etc, pm, A L Baker, No 25*).

0.4.1 Samples of business letters

Example of the layout of a British business letter

MANAGEMENT STRATEGIES PLC, Eaglesham Road 430, East Kilbridge G75 8EA,
Tel. no.: ++ 44 (13 55) 40 9176, Fax no.: ++ 44 (13 55) 40 91 86, E-mail address: management.exp@strat.uk

GHS/pr

27 September 20..

Ms E. Jaeger
Jaeger & Holler AG
Parkstr. 12–16
01589 Riesa
Germany

Dear Ms Jaeger

Your PORTFOLIO for the 21st century

We would like to introduce you to our new programme "PORTFOLIO – Marketing Strategies for EU companies in the 21st century".

As you are certainly aware of, huge global changes in business-to-business marketing are taking place, and we are meeting an ever-increasing need to encounter our competition through management expertise.

Our programme offers an unrivalled opportunity to enhance skills in formulating and implementing marketing strategies; to review, follow up and upgrade existing marketing knowledge; and to test ideas through our newly developed methods.

Please find enclosed a brochure detailing our new programme. We hope you are interested in learning more about it. Please contact us at any time.

We look forward to the pleasure of hearing from you in the near future.

Yours sincerely
MANAGEMENT STRATEGIES PLC

Humprey L. Gates

Humprey L. Gates
Chief Sales Coordinator

Encl.

Directors: L S Templeton (Managing), R S O´Brien, H. Francis, L A Peters • Registered No 01 65 90 83, England

Example of the layout of an American business letter

Worldwide Shopping Inc.
549 East Chicago Avenue
Chicago, Illinois 60611
Tel. ++ 1-312-40 91 03
Fax: ++ 1-312-40 91 04
e-mail: worldwide.shop@northwestern.us

September 10, 20..

Rupert L. Miller
Purchasing Manager
Miller & Jones Inc.
18730 Market Ave., Suite 254
Baltimore, MD21202
U.S.A.

Re: Your Enquiry of September 4, 20..

Dear Mr. Miller:

Thank you for your above-mentioned enquiry for our internet shopping facilities program. As an attachment please find an application form as well as a complete program of all our services.

Should you wish to become a regular customer of our Worldwide Shopping System, please return the completed application form. You will then receive a Worldwide Shopping Card which entitles you to buy direct from our internet address. You simply have to indicate your Worldwide Shopping Card number for every purchase.

We would be extremely happy to serve you in the best possible way. Welcome to Worldwide Shopping Incorporated!

Sincerely yours,

Peter J. Brown

Peter J. Brown
Customer Service Manager

Encl.: Catalog
Membership application form

0.4.2 Fax

A fax (facsimile) does not have a fixed layout. A company is free to choose its own heading for a fax. All faxes should, however, indicate the fax number of the recipient, the sender's address, fax, telephone numbers etc, the date and subject matter. It is important to give the number of pages since sometimes the fax transmission may be interrupted and the recipient then does not know whether pages are missing.

In some countries faxes are not yet accepted as legally binding, so it may be necessary to confirm a fax in a binding form.

A fax is often addressed to *FAO*. This stands for *For the attention of*.

Example of a fax:

fax

FAO: Ms Lydia Hammerschmidt
Purchase Department
Immobilienbau GmbH
Düsseldorf, Germany

Fax No: 00 49 (2 11) 54 09 28

From: Helen F. Peterson
Sales Division
Computer Software Limited
P.O. Box 30459
London SE1 7RT
Great Britain

Date: 3 June 20..

Subject: Your order of 31 May 20..

Total Pages: 1

Dear Lydia

Thank you so much for your order for our software package VX 3090. We have mailed it to you today, so you should receive it in the course of the next few days.

Our invoice will be sent separately.

I hope that it works to your entire satisfaction. If you have any queries, please ring me up immediately.

Kindest regards

Helen

0.4.3 E-mail

E-mails are very easily written on the screen of a computer and usually their structure is prescribed by the computer program itself. So the form can vary according to the computer program used. In general, e-mails contain the e-mail address of the recipient, a subject line, a line for "cc" (*carbon copies*), where the persons who are to receive a copy of the e-mail are indicated, and a line "attachment" for files which are to be sent with the respective e-mail. The advantage is that all kinds of files can be enclosed in an e-mail, ie graphics, texts, etc.

Since e-mails are very quickly and easily sent everywhere worldwide and, in addition, are much cheaper than any other form of written communication, they have started to replace a lot of other written messages such as letters sent by mail. But, as in the case of faxes, binding messages for the time being still have to be confirmed in traditional written form afterwards.

Example:

e-mail

Mail to: schroeder.moden@netcom.de
from: Holz.Jaeger@ing.de cc:
Subject: Your hotel booking of Jan. 5, 20..
Attachment:

Dear Schroeder Moden

This is to confirm your a. m. hotel booking for one night Jan. 10 to Jan. 11 for one single room with bath, TV, telephone and internet connection in the name of Dr Juergen Rademacher. Price 85 pounds plus VAT. Thank you for choosing to stay with us.

Yours sincerely
The Star Hotel Bristol
Alexandra Smith
Booking Department Officer

1. Enquiries

Looking for suppliers or customers; enquiries and requests for quotations

1.1 Introduction

Looking for suppliers or customers. Firms looking for foreign suppliers or customers (or wishing to establish other business contacts abroad, for example with potential agents, distributors, or licencees) can address enquiries (inquiries) to various sources of information, both at home and abroad (eg chambers of commerce, banks, embassies and consulates).

These sources will provide the enquirers (inquirers) with names and addresses, so as to enable them to write directly to the firms in question; they may also refer their enquiry to interested parties.

Browsing through the internet is another way to get the addresses of potential customers. Many manufacturers offer their goods and/or services on home pages, where they can be contacted at any time of day or night. Others have call centres which answer oral or written general or specific enquiries via telephone or the internet.

Another possibility for firms seeking business contacts in foreign countries is to advertise in international trade papers or magazines and on bulletin boards, or to respond to such advertisements.

In this connection, mention should also be made of the invitations to tender issued by foreign government agencies wishing to place contracts for the supply of equipment, the performance of construction work, etc.

Enquiries and requests for quotations. The enquiries dealt with in this chapter are those asking for names and addresses of potential customers or suppliers and those asking for details about goods, terms, delivery dates, etc. The latter are addressed to manufacturers or dealers by firms interested in doing business with them. Often the enquirer merely asks the supplier to furnish descriptive literature, a price list, samples or patterns. If the prospective buyer wants a detailed offer, he sends the supplier a request for a quotation, which has to include full details of his requirements. Enquiries and requests for quotations are without obligation for the enquirer.

For credit enquiries see Chapter 5. Enquiries are also included in Chapters 11, 12, and 14.

1.2 Model correspondence

1.2.1 Enquiry for ball bearings

BECKWORTH BEARINGS LTD
80–85 Harlow Street
Norwich, NR6 4AN

JDM/EMX

17 September 20..

The Secretary
Industrie- und Handelskammer
Düsseldorf
Postfach 4429
D-40001 Düsseldorf

Dear Sir/Madam

BALL AND ROLLER BEARINGS

Our local chamber of commerce has given us your address.

We are manufacturers and exporters of anti-friction bearings and are looking for an opportunity to do business with Germany. Our product range includes bearings for ships and aircraft, road vehicles, agricultural and textile machinery, machine tools and other kinds of equipment. We also supply miniature bearings and bearings designed and manufactured for particular applications.

We would be grateful if you could bring our company and its products to the attention of those firms among your members who are importers/distributors or large-scale users of bearings.

We look forward to receiving enquiries from firms in Germany and thank you for your kind assistance in this matter.

Yours faithfully
Beckworth Bearings Ltd

J D Mayall

J D Mayall
Managing Director

1.2.2 American company asks for information about plywood and veneers

e-mail

Mail from: Atkinson.golloway@inc.amex.us
to: Holz.Jaeger@ing.de **cc:**
Subject: Request for leaflets and price lists
Attachment:

Dear Holz Jaeger GmbH

We got your e-mail address from a local publication about European plywood and veneer manufacturers and would very much appreciate your sending us descriptive literature on your complete product range including a recent export price list.

Please send your price list by e-mail to our a. m. address and illustrated brochures to the following address:

Atkinson & Golloway Inc.
115 Crestmont Drive
Laurel, Md. 20708

Cordially
Atkinson & Golloway Inc.
George L. Atkinson
Vice President

1.2.3 British company asks for new software program

FAO: Ms Gabriele Mehltau
Computer-Box GmbH
Postfach 34 09 10
72191 Nagold

Fax No.: 00 49 (74 52) 38 97 41

From: Robert M. Jones
Purchasing Department
Littleton & Hammersmith plc
48 Jeremy Street

Date: 18 November 20..

Subject: Your computer software program SW 109/60

Total Pages: 1

Dear Gabriele Mehltau

We saw your ad for the new software package program SW 109/60 on your home page on the internet and are very interested in receiving further details. Could you please tell us how this program can rationalize our in-house computer work (our program is MSK 502/3). Is it compatible with British company standards?

Please get in touch with the undersigned as soon as possible. Thanks in advance.

Regards

Peter M. Jones

Peter M. Jones
Purchasing Department

1.2.4 Request for quotation by German company's agents in the U.K.

Dear Sirs

Warner Kitchenware Company Ltd, Birmingham

Please quote best price and indicate earliest date of delivery for the following:

25 sets of kitchen units as per your catalogue no. TX 312 A, of which:

10 sets in colour yellow 24
20 sets in colour light green 814
5 sets in black with white frames colour 18.

All sets are to be built in ready-made kitchens into new turn-key town houses according to the enclosed drawings and plans.

The kitchens are urgently required, because the houses for which they are intended are already under construction.

The sizes of all kitchens are identical, they only differ in colour.

Our customer is a well-known property development company, so we think it is worthwhile granting an attractive trade discount.

If our prices are competitive, we can count on substantial orders in the future.

Please tell us as soon as possible what your shortest delivery time is.

Kind regards

Enc

1.2.5 American company asks for quotation

Ladies and Gentlemen:

We saw your advertisement for a new type of digital watch in *The Herald Tribune* and are very interested in receiving a detailed quotation for this type of watch.

Could you indicate your best wholesale price for quantities between 100 and 150 units each, both men's and women's, including packing suitable for air transport, DDU New York Airport.

Before we place a trial order for the above-mentioned quantity, we would like to receive a sample each for test purposes. How soon can a sample be delivered? Please also send us a detailed leaflet covering your whole production range. Can you indicate an American wholesaler or agent that has your watches in stock? This would be interesting for follow-up orders.

We look forward to receiving your quotation as soon as possible.

Sincerely yours

1.2.6 Tender notice

Perusahaan Umum Listrik Negara
Agency of the Ministry of Mines and Energy of The Government
of the Republic of Indonesia

Invitation to Tender

Tenders for the Turbine Generator and Ancillary Plant Contract for Suralaya steam power plant Units 3 and 4 as the extension of Suralaya steam power plant Units 1 and 2 currently under construction near the town of Merak in West Java will be received at or before 10:00 hours on 1st February 20.., for public opening at 11:00 hours on the same date at the head office of Perusahaan Umum Listrik Negara, Jalan Trunojoyo Blok MI/135, Kebayoran Baru, Jakarta Selatan, Indonesia.

The Turbine Generator and Ancillary Plant Contract comprises the design, manufacture, supply, erection and commissioning of 2 × 400 MW units.

Beginning 7th November 20.., the tender documents may be examined and collected personally by prospective tenderers or by their authorised representative in Jakarta upon cash payment of the non-refundable amount of US$1,200 at the following address:

Perusahaan Umum Listrik Negara
Directorate of Planning
Jolan Trunojoyo Blok MI/135
Kebayoran Baru, Jakarta Selatan
Indonesia

To qualify for an award, tenderers (individual or consortium) must demonstrate that they have successfully executed contracts for at least two turbine generators of the same or larger capacity than that specified, with each plant having a minimum of three years' successful commercial operation.

Tenders will be received from qualified tenderers or their authorised representatives.

Perusahan Umum Listrik Negara has applied for a loan from the International Bank for Reconstruction and Development and will apply the proceeds of this loan for payment under this contract.

Only tenderers / manufacturers residing in member countries of the International Bank for Reconstruction and Development and Switzerland and Taiwan are eligible to tender.

Perusahaan Umum Listrik Negara reserves the right to reject any or all tenders and may waive minor irregularities and informalities.

Jakarta, November 20..
Perusahaan Umum Listrik Negara

1.3 Terms and phrases

1.3.1 Reference to source of address, advertisement, etc

We have been referred to you by …	*… hat uns an Sie verwiesen.*
We have been given your address / fax / e-mail address by …	*Wir verdanken Ihre Anschrift / Fax- / E-Mail-Adresse …*
… has kindly given us your address / fax / e-mail address.	*… hat uns freundlicherweise Ihre Anschrift / Fax- / E-Mail-Adresse zur Verfügung gestellt.*
We have received your address / fax / e-mail address from …	*Wir haben Ihre Anschrift / Fax- / E-Mail-Adresse von … erhalten.*
We have been informed by … that you are manufacturers of …	*Wir haben von … erfahren, dass Sie … herstellen.*
We saw your name / products … at the … exhibition / fair.	*Wir haben Ihren Namen / Ihre Produkte … auf der … Ausstellung / Messe gesehen.*
We got your name from your home page / an online publication.	*Wir haben Ihren Namen Ihrer Homepage / einer Internet-Publikation entnommen.*
You have been mentioned to us as …	*Sie wurden uns als … genannt.*

1.3.2 Reasons for enquiring

We are interested in …	*Wir interessieren uns für …*
We need … / We require … / We are in the market for …	*Wir benötigen … / Wir haben Bedarf an …*
We have received many enquiries from customers for … and …	*Da wir viele Anfragen von Kunden für … erhalten haben, …*
Our stock of … is very low / running low / is nearly exhausted / has to be replenished.	*Unser Lagerbestand an … geht zur Neige / ist beinahe erschöpft / muss wieder aufgefüllt werden.*

1.3.3 Requests for information, quotation, etc

Please inform us / let us know on what terms you can supply …	*Bitte teilen Sie uns mit, zu welchen Bedingungen Sie … liefern können.*
We would appreciate / be pleased to receive your information on … / your latest catalogue / descriptive literature / an online presentation.	*Wir wären Ihnen für die Übersendung Ihrer Informationen über … / Ihres neuesten Katalogs / Prospektmaterials / einer Internetpräsentation dankbar.*
Please quote your lowest / keenest prices for …	*Bitte nennen Sie uns Ihre äußersten Preise für …*
Please quote us for … / Please send us a quotation for …	*Bitte machen Sie uns ein (Preis)Angebot über …*
Please state your earliest delivery date.	*Bitte nennen Sie uns Ihr frühestes Lieferdatum.*
Please let us know whether you can supply from stock.	*Bitte teilen Sie uns mit, ob Sie ab Lager liefern können.*
Please give us details on your terms of payment and delivery.	*Bitte teilen Sie uns Einzelheiten über Ihre Zahlungs- und Lieferbedingungen mit.*

1.3.4 Giving references

Information on / about our company can be obtained from … / For information on our company please refer to … / write to … / contact …	*Auskünfte über unsere Firma können von … eingeholt werden.*
Should you wish to make any enquiries about us, please refer to …	*Sollten Sie Erkundigungen über uns einziehen wollen, wenden Sie sich bitte an …*
For references please click our home page on the internet www …	*Falls Sie Referenzen wünschen, klicken Sie bitte unsere Homepage im Internet unter www … an.*

First-class trade and bank references can be provided on / upon request.	*Erstklassige Handels- und Bankreferenzen können auf Wunsch geliefert werden.*
The company ... will be pleased to give you any reference you may want to obtain.	*Die Firma ... wird Ihnen gern jede Referenz geben, die Sie haben möchten.*

1.3.5 Suggesting future business

If your prices are competitive, / favourable, / reasonable, ...	*Wenn Ihre Preise konkurrenzfähig / günstig / angemessen sind, ...*
If your products are of first-class quality, ...	*Wenn Ihre Erzeugnisse von erstklassiger Qualität sind, ...*
If the quality of the goods is satisfactory / comes up to our expectations / meets our requirements, ...	*Wenn die Qualität der Waren zufriedenstellend ist / unseren Erwartungen / unserem Bedarf entspricht, ...*
If the samples / patterns / specimen find / meet with our customers' approval, ...	*Wenn die Muster / Proben unseren Kunden zusagen, ...*
... we would be prepared to place a (trial) order.	*... wären wir bereit, einen (Probe)Auftrag zu erteilen.*
... we would be able to place substantial orders.	*... wären wir in der Lage, größere Aufträge zu erteilen.*
... your products should sell well / readily in this market.	*... dürften sich Ihre Produkte auf dem hiesigen Markt gut verkaufen lassen.*
... should find / meet with a ready market.	*... dürften Ihre Erzeugnisse guten Absatz finden.*
... there will certainly be no problem to sell your products / services over here.	*... ist es sicher kein Problem, Ihre Produkte / Dienstleistungen hier zu verkaufen.*
... we are sure that we would be able to distribute your goods in this area.	*... sind wir sicher, dass wir Ihre Waren in diesem Gebiet vertreiben können.*

1.4 Exercises
Please translate:

1.4.1 E-Mail von Modehaus Küfer, Düsseldorf (küfer.moden@com.de) an Mc Donald & Co. Ltd Glasgow (donald.fashion@spencer.com.uk)

Letztes Jahr haben wir bei Ihnen einen Posten Cashmere- und Lambswool-Pullover zu sehr günstigen Preisen gekauft, die wir erfolgreich absetzen konnten.

Wir sind im Begriff, unsere Herbst-/Winterkollektion für nächstes Jahr zusammenzustellen. Bitte schicken Sie uns daher Ihr diesjähriges Angebot für den Großhandel.

Lieferbedingung wie immer FOB London. Sind Sie bereit, uns jetzt ein Zahlungsziel zu gewähren?
Beste Grüße,
Gundula Küfer
Chefeinkäuferin

1.4.2 Bauer & Co., Im Hilgenfeld 27, 59077 Hamm (Westf) an Taylor & Brown plc, 48 Gordon Square, London WC1 8PF, Großbritannien

Wir besuchten Ihren Stand auf der letzten Hannover-Messe und erfuhren dabei von Ihrem Verkaufsleiter, Mr Mills, dass Sie auch Spezialanfertigungen übernehmen.

Wir benötigen bis spätestens 1. März eine vollautomatische Bohrmaschine nach beiliegender Zeichnung. Bitte teilen Sie uns mit, ob Sie die Maschine bis zu diesem Termin liefern können. Wir bitten ebenfalls um Mitteilung des Preises und Ihrer Verkaufsbedingungen.

Falls Sie Referenzen über uns wünschen, wenden Sie sich bitte an die Birmingham Lathe Company Ltd in Birmingham, P.O. Box 24903, Birmingham B69 HG4, von der wir bereits mehrere Maschinen bezogen haben.

Please draft letters, faxes or e-mails from the following particulars:

1.4.3 Geschäftsfall:

Sie arbeiten für die Firma Sprachenstudio Heitkamp GmbH, Von-Hymmen-Platz 4, 53121 Bonn, Fax-Nr.: +49 (2 28) 39 76 91, E-Mail-Adresse: sprachen.heitkamp@ptx.de.

Auf der Homepage der Firma Internet Trade Ltd, Cambridge House, Pannells Court, Guildford, Surrey GU1 4EU, GB, Fax-Nr.: +44 (14 83) 27 09 84 2, E-Mail-Adresse: int.trade.ltd@com.uk, haben Sie eine Anzeige für ein neues computergestütztes Lernprogramm für die englische Sprache gesehen.

Aufgabe: Schreiben Sie an die Marketingabteilung der britischen Firma eine E-Mail oder ein Fax und berücksichtigen Sie dabei die folgenden Punkte:

- Bezug auf Anzeige im Internet
- Interesse an neuem Programm
- Bitte um Vorabinformation per E-Mail
- Weiteres Informationsmaterial per Post

- Da Sie vorhaben, ein solches Programm bei Eignung einem größeren Kundenstamm zugänglich zu machen, Bitte um besonders günstige Bedingungen
- Kann ein solches Programm vor dem Kauf getestet werden?
- Wo wird ein solches Programm vorgeführt?
- Ist es ggf. möglich, einen Trainer nach Deutschland zu schicken, der das Programm vor Ort einführt?
- Bitte um Referenzen, wo das Programm sich schon bewährt hat.

1.4.4 Geschäftsfall:

Ihre Firma, die Arnold & Busch GmbH, Weender Str. 110, 37073 Goslar, ist in der Radio-, Fernseh-, Phono- und Videobranche tätig. Einer Ihrer Mitarbeiter war kürzlich in den Vereinigten Staaten auf der Electronics Fair in New York und brachte einen Katalog der Scott Electronics Inc, 1240 New York Avenue NW, Washington, DC 20577, USA, mit.

Aufgabe: Schreiben Sie an die amerikanische Firma eine Anfrage und schließen Sie folgende Punkte ein:

- Bezugnahme auf Messebesuch
- Sie haben in dem Katalog das Videogerät Scott DT 2400 gesehen, das Sie besonders interessiert.
- Bitte um eine genaue Beschreibung dieses Geräts
- Ist es für den europäischen/deutschen Markt geeignet und mit den europäischen/deutschen Bandbreiten kompatibel?
- Entspricht es den EU-Normen?
- Bitte um Preise für größere Abnahmemengen
- Wie schnell kann geliefert werden?
- Nachbestellungen möglich?
- Probelieferung von 10 Stück innerhalb von 14 Tagen nach Bestellung möglich?

1.4.5 Geschäftsfall:

Ihre Firma, die Textil-Import KG, Postfach 33 08 57, 45054 Düsseldorf, hat auf der Igedo-Modemesse in Düsseldorf den Stand der Textiles Export Inc, P.O. Box 12500, GPO 10490 Penang, Malaysia, besucht und dort mehrere Ballen Seide besichtigt.

Aufgabe: Schreiben Sie an die malaysische Firma eine Anfrage folgenden Inhalts:

- Bezugnahme auf Messebesuch und inspizierte Ware
- Ihnen wurde zugesagt, dass jedes Kleidungsstück daraus gefertigt werden kann
- Sie schicken mehrere Zeichnungen von Damenkleidern mit, die Sie in den Größen 36–42 in den Mustern der Seide „Blue Dragon“, „White Angel“ und „Silver Whale“ jeweils 50 × fertigen lassen möchten.
- Bitten Sie um ein detailliertes Angebot
- Lieferzeit: 8 Wochen nach Auftragserteilung
- Bei günstigen Bedingungen stellen Sie regelmäßige Aufträge in Aussicht.

2. Offers

Replies to enquiries; offers and sales letters

2.1 Introduction

Replies to enquiries. In a reply to an enquiry, the seller gives the information requested, sends the price list, catalogue, etc the prospective customer asked for, or submits a detailed offer.

If a delay in answering the enquiry is inevitable (eg a technical specification has to be worked on), the seller should send the enquirer a brief acknowledgement, saying that the enquiry is receiving attention. Sometimes the seller has to ask for additional details before answering the enquiry. Should the enquiry have to be referred to an agent or distributor, both the enquirer and the agent or distributor are notified.

If sellers are unable to quote, they should inform the enquirer immediately, suggesting, if possible, other sources of supply from which the latter is likely to obtain the goods required.

Offers. By submitting an offer (also known as a *quotation, quote, bid,* or *proposal*), sellers declare their willingness to sell certain goods at certain prices and on certain terms.

Offers may be submitted in answer to an enquiry (*solicited offers*) or on the seller's own initiative in an effort to create new business (*unsolicited* or *voluntary offers*). Unless otherwise indicated, the person making the offer (offeror) is expected to keep it open for a reasonable time (*firm offer*)[1].

Since legislation in the various EU countries also differs and a general law embracing this question has not yet been enforced, it is in any case recommendable for the offerors to include in their offers a reservation clause that releases them from the obligation to keep their offer open longer than they originally wanted. They may do so by indicating a fixed time for acceptance (eg *We are keeping this offer open for two weeks* or *This offer is valid for two weeks*) or by stating that their offer is *without engagement* or *subject to confirmation*. Clauses that are frequently used in this context are: *Our goods are subject to prior sale or to being unsold*, or *Our prices are subject to change without notice*, or *Our offer is valid as long as stocks last*.

If the offer is accepted by the person to whom it is made (offeree) before it has lapsed, a contract is concluded between the two parties.

[1] According to English law (in contrast to Scottish and American law), the offeror can revoke an offer at any time before it has been accepted, though there may have been a promise not to revoke it. Such a promise is binding only if based on a separate contract.

Since the arrival of online advertising, many offers are made in this way. Special laws are applicable for the validity of such offers which can usually be revoked within a legally stipulated period of time.

An offer should include the following essential points:
- Nature and quality of the goods or services
- Quantity of goods or period of time for services rendered
- Prices and discounts (if discounts are granted)
- Delivery date
- Terms of delivery and payment.

If necessary, the offer is supplemented by printed material, illustrations, samples or patterns. Should it fail to produce a response, follow-up letters may be sent.

Sales letters or circulars. These are usually unsolicited. They do not necessarily ask for orders; their purpose may be to stimulate enquiries, to prepare the ground for a salesperson or to promote goodwill.

Online sales offers. Many offers are made via the internet. They are usually unsolicited offers and made by the supplier without obligation.

2.2 Model correspondence

2.2.1 Brief acknowledgement – enquiry is receiving attention

e-mail

Mail from: dba.engineering@exec.us
to: Scharrenberg.GmbH@online.com cc:
Subject: Your enquiry of 22nd Jan 20..

Dear Scharrenberg GmbH:

Thank you for your enquiry.

It will probably take a few days until our engineer has prepared the necessary technical data. As soon as this information is available, we will send you our quotation.

Cordially
DBA Engineering Incorporated
John Miller
Sales Manager

2.2.2 Request for additional information

fax

FAO: Mr Helge Panther
Software Importwaren KG
Merowinger Straße 110
40223 Düsseldorf

Fax No.: 00 49 (2 11) 28 95 04

From: Peter Graham Carter
Sales Manager
Computer Games Ltd
40 Old Burlington Street
London W 1X 1LA

Date: 3rd August 20..

Subject: Your enquiry for computer games of 2nd August 20..
Total number of pages: 2

Dear Helge

Thank you for your recent enquiry which will be attended to as soon as possible.

Before we can, however, proceed to working out a detailed quotation, we still need to know several details about the specific software you require for the computer games in question.

We enclose a form which we would ask you to fill in and return to us by fax. On receipt of this information we will quote for the games in question.

We await your reply with interest.

Kind regards

Peter Graham Carter

Peter Graham Carter
Sales Manager

Enc

2.2.3 Enquiry referred to distributor

Gentlemen:

Thank you for your recent inquiry regarding laboratory equipment.

We are asking our distributors in your area, Gernot & Koch KG, Hamburg, to see that descriptive literature is made available to you at the earliest possible date.

Should you desire additional information on specific applications of this equipment, please do not hesitate to contact them at any time.

Your interest in our products is appreciated.

Sincerely yours

2.2.4 Supplier unable to quote

Dear Sirs

Thank you for your letter of 10th February. We regret to inform you, however, that we cannot quote for the equipment you require, as it is not included in our line. We would suggest that you write to BELCO Ltd, Plymouth, who will, no doubt, be able to submit the quotation requested.

We enclose some literature giving you an outline of the complete range of our products and will be glad to hear from you whenever you are in the market for any of the equipment manufactured by us.

Yours faithfully

Encs

2.2.5 Distributor sends literature

Dear Ms Russell

Small-capacity milling machine

Thank you for your letter of 20 February.

As sole distributors for Maschinenfabrik Müller AG in Hanau, Federal Republic of Germany, we are delighted to offer you our services.

The enclosed brochure gives information about our principal's range of milling machines, and the leaflet also attached describes the smallest machine of the range, the RM 16A, which is ideally suited to cover your requirements. This machine is available in several designs as shown in the enclosure. Prices vary from approx. £5,000 to £15,000, ex works Hanau.

We trust the above information will enable you to send us drawings of a representative selection of components to be milled, so that we can prepare a detailed proposal.

Yours sincerely

Enc

2.2.6 Quotation (pro forma invoice)

e-mail

Mail from: Warwick.textiles@wbs.com.uk
to: schneider.import@back.aol.de cc:
Subject: Import of textiles
Attachment:

Dear Schneider Import GmbH
We herewith confirm your urgent e-mail of this morning and submit the following quotation as follows:

400 yds	cat.no. 1040 wine	
300 yds	cat.no. 3876 marine	
200 yds	cat.no. 5407 white	
900 yds at £...		£...
less 5 % special discount		£...
	Total:	**£...**

Payment: £... to be remitted by banker's transfer as soon as your order is placed, balance cash against documents.

It is understood that the deposit will become forfeited should the documents not be taken up on first presentation.

Please place your order as soon as possible and confirm per e-mail or fax when remittance has been made as we can only start production of the special material after receiving this confirmation.

Thank you for your confidence. We await your order asap to be able to serve you with the usual speed and accuracy.

Yours sincerely

2.2.7 Letter accompanying quotation

Revell

Revell Computer Furniture Limited
Cambridge House, London Road
Bath, BA 1 6AY
telephone: (+44) 12 25 36 07 76
fax: (+44) 12 25 36 07 77

Our ref. ET/sh

8th December 20..

The Purchasing Manager
Herr Werner Mann
Computermöbel GmbH
Kastanienweg 44
D-30457 Hannover
Germany

Dear Herr Mann

As we have learned from our representative for Germany, Herr Schmidt, with whom you have already held discussions, you are looking for a special type of computer desk to fit the latest model of your computer range MALTA 3000 for companies in the electronics industry in Germany and Eastern Europe.

We are pleased to inform you that we are specialists in this kind of furniture and therefore submit you enclosed our quotation for our special desk "Computer-Assistant LT 403". It fits all computers of the sizes Mr Schmidt mentioned to us and is adjustable both in height and length to all modern computers. We have already sold this desk to thousands of UK and American customers and are beginning to distribute it on the Continent, too. We enclose a reference list for your information.

Together with the quotation and the reference list please find enclosed a brochure which will give you all the details you may need. You will note that the brochure describes various desk options. We have included in our quotation the option N, which is the normal one. All other options can, of course, also be offered.

The prices in our quotation are FOB UK port, export packing included. Delivery can be effected in 4–5 weeks. Payment is to be made in £ Sterling, in the following manner:

a. 30 % of the invoice amount by banker's transfer to our account with National Westminster Bank, Shaftsbury Avenue, London, W1V 8AL, not later than 30 days from the date of signing the contract.

b. The remaining 70 % of the invoice amount by irrevocable letter of credit, to be opened in our favour not later than 30 days from the date of contract and confirmed by National Westminster Bank. All bank charges, including those incurred in the UK, will be for the opener's account. The letter of credit is to be valid for 30 days after despatch of the furniture.

In case of regular orders we are certainly prepared to grant you open account terms. Mr Schmidt's staff will, of course, assist you with the installation of the desks, should this prove necessary.

We would be pleased to hear from you in the near future and remain at your service for any additional questions you may have.

Yours sincerely

C. G. Lewis
Sales Manager

Encs

Directors
D. C. McMinn, MA, MBIM (Chairman), D. A. Owen, C. Eng., MIEE (Managing),
C. G. A. Bailey, A. B. Cornell, S. W. Laughton, C. G. Lewis, T. B. Norton (USA), J. Pedre M. Inst.M.
Registered number: 880721 England

2.2.8 Detailed quotation

norpak

our ref JMC/DW
your ref
date 12 January 20..

Norpak Plastics Ltd

D. S. Elton (Pty.) Ltd
167 Cosgrave Street
Collingwood
Victoria 3066
Australia

288 Harrogate Road
Bradford West Yorkshire
BD2 3SP
England
Telephone (+44) 274 63 18 11
Fax (+44) 274 63 18 12

Packaging and Mailing Machinery
Packaging and Allied Materials
Polythene Envelopes and Film

Dear Sirs,

We refer to our previous correspondence and are pleased to submit our quotation on the terms set out below and our General Conditions of Sale printed on the back (the latter being valid to the extent that they are not superseded by the former).

Quotation No. X-001-002

ONE – Norpak In-line Wrapper, Model ILW, as described in the attached specification, to wrap your products in polyethylene film	£
ONE – Shuttle Feeder	£
ONE – Insert Feeder	£
Spares	£
Ex works	£
FOB and delivery costs	£
Total	£

Installation: Engineer's cheapest air fare and living expenses

Terms of payment

Deposit of 30 % of ex works price with order. 60 % payable after shipment by irrevocable confirmed letter of credit on presentation of the mate's receipt or bill of lading.
The balance of 10 % plus FOB and installation costs payable 30 days after installation and successful testing of the equipment on your premises.

FOB and delivery costs

The charges quoted include crating, seaworthy packaging, UK inland freight to docks and documentation.

.../2

Directors
Terence L Parry, John M Cayton

Registered in England No 948863
Registered office as above

Page 2

Delivery
We would expect to have the equipment ready for delivery within 10–12 weeks. This would be subject to confirmation at the time your order was placed and would date from receipt of such confirmation, deposit payment, opening of the Letter of Credit, provision of test supplies by a date to be specified, and clarification of all technical details.

Product description and dimensions
A4 magazines, with inserted address sheet (samples of which have been submitted).

Machine speed
On the basis of the type of film recommended, we would expect to obtain a machine sealing speed of 100 cycles per minute.

Type of final pack
Pillowpack, sealed at both ends, with a long seam on the overlap. Can be shrunk, if required.

Customer responsibilities
(a) To pay freight and insurance from UK port to final destination, bill of lading charges (if a B/L should have to be presented under the Letter of Credit), local port charges, clearance costs, customs duties and all other charges.
(b) To arrange, at its expense, the off-loading, de-crating and positioning of all equipment on site ready for installation.
(c) To provide electric power on site and connection to the equipment (380/440 volt, 3 phase, 50 cycles).
(d) To provide the means of presenting product to the infeed and removal of final packs from take-off.
(e) To provide adequate supplies of product and wrapping material when requested both at Bradford and on site for machine testing.

This quotation is valid until 9th March 20...

We look forward to hearing from you soon.

Yours faithfully,
Norpak Machines Ltd

John M. Clayton

John M. Clayton
Director

Enc

2.2.9 Quotation form

DECKEL

Deckel Limited
Maybrook Industrial Estate
Birmingham Road
Stratford-on-Avon
Warwickshire CV37 0BT

Telephone: (+44) 7 89 69 21 71
Fax: (+44) 7 89 69 21 73

Quotation:

Your enquiry of | Our ref | Date

Thank you very much for your enquiry. We are plased to submit our quotation which is subject to our attached Terms and Conditions of Trading.

Prices quoted are:	Ex Works Stratford-on-Avon unless otherwise stated.
	Subject to VAT at the rate ruling at time of supply.
	To an exchange rate of €... = £1.00
	Subject to currency adjustment as per paragraph 2(b) of our attached Terms and Conditions of Trading.
	Valid for a period of 60 days from the above date unless oherwise specified.
Payment terms:	One third deposit with order.
	A further third on notification of despatch.
	Invoice will be presented on delivery for payment within 28 days.
Delivery time:	

Description:	Prices:

Registered in England No. 1176967

2.2.10 Follow-up to quotation

Dear Sirs

With our letter of 2nd August 20.. we submitted a quotation for our "Rivonia Design" travel goods including our special flexible frame protecting laptop travel bags on the basis of your enquiry of 30th July 20...

Since we have not heard anything from you, we would like to ask whether any decision has yet been made or will be forthcoming in the near future.

If any further information is required in addition to the details already given, please let us know.

Yours faithfully

2.2.11 Unsolicited offer of services

Gentlemen:

We have seen your home page on the internet and understand that you are one of the leading German finance and marketing companies for logistics.

We are a well-known American producer of general management programs in the field of manufacturing and logistics and can offer customer-designed programs for individual company needs. We are proud to say that we count the most important logistics companies in the world among our clients.

We enclose illustrated literature about the range of our services as well as our recently published reference list. We also enclose a special customer form which you only need to fill out and return to us.

Upon receipt of this form, we can send you a detailed offer tailor-made to your company's requirements.

Don't hesitate to contact us! We will answer your letter / e-mail / fax immediately.

Thank you for your early reply.

Yours faithfully,

Encs

2.2.12 Sales letter

THE MOBILE PHONE NEWSLETTER LTD

Eaglesham Road
East Kilbridge
G75 8EA
Tel. no.: 00 44-13 55-82 09 64
Fax no.: 00 44-13 35-82 09 65
e-mail address: mobile.news@net.uk
Our mobile phone no.: 0 77 15-4 91-6 43 07

Dear prospective customer

May we introduce ourselves: We are the only company worldwide to be able to supply the whole world with the MOBILE PHONE NEWSLETTER.

Every day, thousands of people use the services of mobile phone companies.
We serve you by providing up-to-date information on the services they provide and use worldwide. We inform you about the most modern, the most up-to-date, the most up-market end-to-end mobile internet solutions. We bring together network operators and application developers to serve the local markets with solutions in the field of news services, games, on-line shopping facilities, music etc.

We inform both companies and individuals about innovations and the new services in the world of mobile telephony. And the future possibilities in this field are practically endless!

Please contact us for details how to subscribe to this wonderful new
MOBILE PHONE NEWSLETTER!

Yours faithfully

G. Terence Hall

G. Terence Hall
European Marketing Manager

2.3 Terms and phrases

2.3.1 Openings

Thank you for your enquiry of …	*Vielen Dank für Ihre Anfrage vom …*
We were pleased to receive your enquiry of …	*Über Ihre Anfrage vom … haben wir uns sehr gefreut.*
We are pleased to note from your letter / fax / e-mail of … that you are interested in …	*Ihrem Schreiben / Fax / Ihrer E-Mail vom … entnehmen wir gerne, dass Sie sich für … interessieren.*
We have seen your address on the internet and take pleasure in sending you attached descriptive literature about our company.	*Wir haben Ihre Anschrift aus dem Internet und freuen uns, Ihnen in der Anlage Prospektmaterial über unsere Firma zu senden.*
As requested, / As desired, we are sending you enclosed / by e-mail / under separate cover / by parcel post …	*Wunschgemäß senden wir Ihnen in der Anlage / per E-Mail / mit getrennter Post / als Postpaket …*
We appreciate your interest in our new … (description of product) and will be glad to arrange a demonstration on your premises.	*Wir freuen uns über Ihr Interesse an unserem/r neuen … (Beschreibung des Produkts) und veranlassen gern eine Vorführung in Ihrem Hause.*
We have learned from … that you are looking for … (description of services) and take this opportunity to send you our latest catalogue / brochure / leaflet on the range of services offered by us.	*Wir haben von … erfahren, dass Sie nach …. (Beschreibung von Dienstleistungen) suchen und nehmen diese Gelegenheit wahr, um Ihnen unsere(n) neueste(n) Katalog / Broschüre / Prospekt über die von uns angebotene Dienstleistungs-palette zu senden.*
We refer to your enquiry of … and are glad to quote as follows / to submit the following quotation: …	*Wir beziehen uns auf Ihre Anfrage vom … und bieten Ihnen gerne wie folgt an / unterbreiten Ihnen gerne folgendes Angebot: …*

2.3.2 Prices and discounts

Our prices are / are to be understood / quoted FOB London.	*Unsere Preise verstehen sich FOB London.*
packing included	*einschließlich Verpackung*
packing at cost	*Verpackung zum Selbstkostenpreis*
gross for net	*brutto für netto*
A cash discount of 2½% is allowed / can be granted for settlement within one month.	*Für Zahlung innerhalb eines Monats gewähren wir 2½% Skonto.*

On orders for at least ... (quantity) a discount of ... % will be granted.	*Für Aufträge von mindestens ... (Menge) wird ein Nachlass von ... % gewährt.*
The quantity discounts indicated in our price list vary according to the size of the order.	*Die in unserer Preisliste angegebenen Mengenrabatte richten sich nach der Größe Ihrer Bestellung.*
We grant a trade discount of ... % on our list prices.	*Auf unsere Listenpreise gewähren wir einen Händlerrabatt von ... %.*
Our catalogue prices are subject to a special discount of ... %.	*Auf unsere Katalogpreise gewähren wir Ihnen einen Sonderrabatt von ... %.*
We grant an initial / introductory discount of ... %.	*Wir gewähren einen Einführungsrabatt von ... %.*
If your order is received here by ..., we are prepared to grant you an early-order discount of ... %.	*Wenn Ihr Auftrag bis zum ... hier eingeht, sind wir bereit, Ihnen einen Frühdispositionsrabatt von ... % zu gewähren.*

2.3.3 Terms of delivery as issued by the International Chamber of Commerce in Paris in 2000

Group E
Departure
(goods are available to the buyer at the seller's own premises)

EXW	Ex works	*Ab Werk*

Group F
Main carriage unpaid
(the seller is called upon to deliver goods to a carrier appointed by the buyer)

FCA	Free carrier	*Frei Frachtführer*
FAS	Free alongside ship	*Frei Längsseite Seeschiff*
FOB	Free on board	*Frei an Bord*

Group C
Main carriage paid
(the seller has to contract for carriage, but without assuming risk of loss or damage to the goods or additional costs)

CFR	Cost and freight	*Kosten und Fracht*
CIF	Cost, insurance and freight	*Kosten, Versicherung und Fracht*
CPT	Carriage paid	*Frachtfrei*
CIP	Carriage and insurance paid	*Frachtfrei versichert*

Group D
Arrival
(the seller has to bear all costs and risks up to country of destination)

DAF	Delivered at frontier	*Geliefert Grenze*
DES	Delivered ex ship	*Geliefert ab Schiff*
DEQ	Delivered ex quay	*Geliefert ab Kai (verzollt)*
DDU	Delivered duty unpaid	*Geliefert unverzollt*
DDP	Delivered duty paid	*Geliefert verzollt*

Other terms of delivery

Franco domicile	*Frei Haus*
Carriage paid / freight prepaid	*Fracht bezahlt*
Carriage forward / freight collect	*Unfrei*

2.3.4 Delivery

The goods can be delivered immediately on receipt of your order.	*Die Waren können sofort nach Eingang Ihrer Bestellung geliefert werden.*
Delivery will be effected as soon as possible / at the earliest possible date.	*Die Lieferung erfolgt so bald wie möglich.*
Machines made to specification can be delivered within 4–6 months.	*Die Lieferzeit für Maschinen, die nach gesonderter Spezifikation hergestellt werden, beträgt 4–6 Monate.*
Our time of delivery is ... days / weeks / months.	*Unsere Lieferzeit beträgt ... Tage / Wochen / Monate.*
We cannot promise delivery within the period stated in your enquiry unless we receive your order by ...	*Wir können Lieferung innerhalb der in Ihrer Anfrage genannten Frist nur dann zusagen, wenn wir Ihren Auftrag bis ... erhalten.*

2.3.5 Terms of payment

cash in advance	*Vorauszahlung*
cash with order (CWO)	*Barzahlung bei Auftragserteilung*
payment on receipt of invoice / payment on invoice	*Zahlung bei Rechnungserhalt*
payment by bank draft on London against pro forma invoice	*Zahlung durch Bankscheck auf London nach Eingang der Proforma-Rechnung*
one-third with order, one-third on delivery, and one-third within two months after delivery	*⅓ bei Auftragserteilung, ⅓ bei Lieferung und ⅓ innerhalb von zwei Monaten nach Lieferung*

cash on delivery (COD)	*gegen Nachnahme*
payment on receipt of goods	*Zahlung bei Erhalt der Waren*
payment within 60 days from date of invoice	*Zahlung innerhalb von 60 Tagen nach Rechnungsdatum*
30 days net	*30 Tage netto*
two months' credit	*2 Monate Ziel*
strictly net, net cash	*rein netto, netto Kasse*
3 % for cash	*3 % Skonto bei Barzahlung*
10 days 2 %, 30 days net	*bei Zahlung innerhalb von 10 Tagen 2 % Skonto, netto bei Zahlung innerhalb von 30 Tagen*
... less 2 % cash discount for payment within ... days	*... abzüglich 2 % Skonto für Zahlung innerhalb von ... Tagen*
2 % E.O.M. (end of month) / R.O.G. (receipt of goods)	*2 % Skonto für Zahlung innerhalb 10 Tagen nach dem Ende des Liefermonats / nach Erhalt der Waren*
against three months' acceptance	*gegen Dreimonatsakzept*
by bill of exchange 30 / 60 / 90 days after sight	*durch 30 / 60 / 90 Tage-Wechsel nach Sicht*
by cheque	*per Scheck*
by banker's draft	*per Bankscheck*
by banker's transfer	*per Banküberweisung*
documents against payment (D/P) / cash against documents (CAD)	*Kasse gegen Dokumente*
documents against acceptance (D/A)	*Dokumente gegen Akzept*
by (ir)revocable and (un)confirmed documentary (letter of) credit	*durch (un)widerrufliches und (un)bestätigtes Dokumentenakkreditiv*

2.3.6 Validity of offer

This offer is firm subject to immediate acceptance, otherwise without engagement.	*Dieses Angebot ist fest bei sofortiger Annahme, sonst freibleibend.*
Our offer is firm / valid subject to:	*Unser Angebot ist fest / gültig vorbehaltlich:*
acceptance by ...	*bei Annahme bis ...*
... your confirmation	*... Ihrer Bestätigung*
... change without notice	*... einer Änderung ohne Benachrichtigung*
Our prices are subject to:	*Unsere Preise unterliegen:*
... market fluctuations	*... Marktschwankungen*
... prior sale / being unsold	*... Zwischenverkauf vorbehalten*
Our offer is without engagement and only valid while / as long as stocks last.	*Unser Angebot ist freibleibend und nur gültig, solange der Vorrat reicht.*

2.3.7 Instructions

Please inform us by fax / e-mail / telephone if you intend to place an order.	*Bitte teilen Sie uns per Fax / E-Mail / Telefon mit, ob Sie einen Auftrag erteilen wollen.*
If you wish to place an order, please use the attached order form.	*Wenn Sie einen Auftrag erteilen wollen, benutzen Sie bitte das beigefügte Auftragsformular.*
When placing your order, please indicate our ref. no. / catalogue no. / model no.	*Wenn Sie Ihre Bestellung aufgeben, nennen Sie bitte unsere Ref. Nr. / Katalog-Nr. / Modell-Nr.*

2.3.8 Endings

If / Should you require any further information, please do not hesitate to contact us.	*Wenn / Sollten Sie noch weitere Informationen benötigen, so teilen Sie uns dies bitte mit.*
Please let us know your requirements soon / in due course.	*Bitte teilen Sie uns bald / zu gegebener Zeit Ihren Bedarf mit.*
We hope that our favourable conditions will help you decide to place the order with us.	*Wir hoffen, dass unsere günstigen Bedingungen Ihnen die Entscheidung erleichtern, uns den Auftrag zu erteilen.*
We look forward to receiving your (trial) order in the near future.	*Wir freuen uns, Ihren (Probe)Auftrag in Kürze zu erhalten.*
As prices are expected to rise, we would advise you to take advantage of this favourable offer.	*Da ein Anziehen der Preise erwartet wird, möchten wir Ihnen raten, von diesem günstigen Angebot Gebrauch zu machen.*
We assure you that your order will be given our prompt and careful attention.	*Wir versichern Ihnen, dass Ihr Auftrag prompt und sorgfältig ausgeführt wird.*
A trial order will convince you of the efficiency of our service.	*Ein Probeauftrag wird Sie von unserer Leistungsfähigkeit überzeugen.*
As we have not had the pleasure of doing business with you before, please indicate the usual references when sending your order.	*Da wir bisher mit Ihnen noch nicht in Geschäftsverbindung standen, bitten wir Sie bei Auftragserteilung um Angabe der üblichen Referenzen.*
If you need additional information before placing your order, please do not hesitate to contact us.	*Falls Sie vor Auftragserteilung zusätzliche Informationen benötigen, zögern Sie bitte nicht, uns dies mitzuteilen.*

2.4 Exercises
Please translate:

2.4.1 E-Mail von Jakowetz Electronics GmbH, Langenfeld (electronics.de@eu.com) an Jeremy Inc., New York (jeremy.inc@tel.us.com)

Vielen Dank für Ihre E-Mail vom ... Als Attachment senden wir Ihnen die gewünschte Adressenliste mit der Bitte, sich unmittelbar mit den genannten Firmen in Verbindung zu setzen.

Die Liste erhebt keinen Anspruch auf Vollständigkeit. Wir überlassen Sie Ihnen kostenlos, werden uns aber ggf. wieder an Sie wenden, wenn wir eine ähnliche Liste benötigen.

Wir hoffen, Ihnen hiermit geholfen zu haben.

2.4.2 Fax von Laseroptik AG, Jena (Fax-Nr.: +49-3641-265403) an Optical Instruments Ltd, Dublin, Irland (Fax-Nr.: +357-1-2766993)

Vielen Dank für Ihre Anfrage vom 03.04.

Als Anlage erhalten Sie unseren Laser-Optik-Katalog für dieses Jahr mit Preisliste. Die Preise verstehen sich ausschließlich für den Fachhandel.

Die weiteren Bedingungen sind wie folgt:

Preisstellung:	Ab Werk
Liefertermin:	Bis 100 Stück pro Position ab Lager, andernfalls nach Vereinbarung
Verpackung:	Ist in den Preisen eingeschlossen
Zahlung:	14 Tage 2 %, 30 Tage netto Bei einem Auftragswert von über € 3.000,– kann ein längeres Zahlungsziel vereinbart werden

Für eventuelle Rückfragen steht Ihnen jederzeit unser Exportsachbearbeiter für Großbritannien, Herr Jörg Rüttger, zur Verfügung.
Wir freuen uns auf einen Auftrag.

2.4.3 Strahler & König KG, Ludwigshafen, an Cooper & Co. Ltd, Birmingham

Wir danken Ihnen für Ihre Anfrage vom 30.08. und fügen das gewünschte Prospektmaterial über unsere Maschine XC 840 bei.

Sollten Sie eine Konstruktion nach gesonderter Spezifikation vorsehen, wäre es ohne weiteres möglich, diese Maschine entsprechend abzuändern oder Ihren Bedürfnissen anzupassen. Hierfür müssten wir natürlich Ihre besonderen technischen Einzelheiten erfahren.

Wir stehen Ihnen jederzeit unter der Fax-Nr. +49-7141-23168, der Tel. Nr. +49-7141-23189 oder der E-Mail-Adresse Strahlkoe@aol.de für weitere Auskünfte zur Verfügung.

2.4.4 **Optische Werke GmbH, Braunschweig, an Mukerjee & Co., Bombay**

Wie danken Ihnen für Ihr Schreiben vom 10. 2. und freuen uns, dass Sie sich für unsere Overheadprojektoren interessieren.

Als Drucksache senden wir Ihnen Prospektmaterial über alle Geräte, die wir zur Zeit liefern. Die Prospekte enthalten Abbildungen und Beschreibungen sowie die Maße und Gewichte der einzelnen Geräte.

Die Preise sind in der beiliegenden Exportpreisliste enthalten. Sie verstehen sich FOB deutscher Hafen oder Flughafen, einschließlich Verpackung. Preisänderungen behalten wir uns vor.

Unsere Zahlungsbedingungen lauten: Bei Erstaufträgen Eröffnung eines unwiderruflichen Akkreditivs zu unseren Gunsten, auszahlbar bei der Dresdner Bank in Braunschweig; bei Nachbestellungen und Angabe von Referenzen Kasse gegen Dokumente durch eine Bank in Bombay.

Gegenwärtig benötigen wir für alle unsere Geräte eine Lieferzeit von 6–8 Wochen. Mit Auskünften über Verschiffungsmöglichkeiten, Frachtsätzen usw. sowie mit Proforma-Rechnungen zur Einholung von Importlizenzen stehen wir Ihnen auf Wunsch gerne zur Verfügung.

Wir sind seit 1950 auf die Herstellung von Projektoren spezialisiert. Unsere Geräte haben sich aufgrund ihrer Präzisison und Zuverlässigkeit im In- und Ausland einen guten Namen gemacht.

Wir hoffen, bald einen Probeauftrag von Ihnen zu erhalten, den wir prompt und sorgfältig erledigen werden.

Anlage

Please draft letters, faxes or e-mails from the following particulars:

2.4.5 **Geschäftsfall:**

Sie arbeiten für die Firma Mettendorff KG, Postfach 3789, 74351 Besigheim, Fax-Nr.: +49-7143-239086, E-Mail-Adresse: info@Mettendorff.de.

Vor ca. 2 Wochen erhielten Sie von der Brown Strategic Software plc, P.O. Box 23 980 11, Oxford OX2 3NY, GB, Fax-Nr.: +44-1865-422961, E-Mail-Adresse: brownsoft@oxford.uk, eine Anfrage für die neue Software EXL 2005, für die Sie auf Ihrer Homepage im Internet geworben hatten.

Aufgabe: Schicken Sie der Brown Strategic Software plc ein Angebot unter Berücksichtigung folgender Punkte:

- Dank für Anfrage
- In der Anlage erhält die Firma eine nähere Beschreibung in englischer Sprache.
- Mit getrennter Post ist Ihr Spezialkatalog für die neue Software unterwegs.
- Da die Einführung der Software besonders schwierig ist, würden Sie bei Interesse einen Fachmann nach Oxford schicken, der die Installation und Einführung übernimmt.

- Der Preis der Software richtet sich nach der Anzahl der Anwendungen im Unternehmen, kann aber auf Wunsch vorab errechnet werden, wenn der potentielle Kunde die Fragen auf dem ebenfalls beigefügten Fragebogen ausfüllt.
- Eine Referenzliste englischer Firmen, die die neue Software bereits besitzen, ist ebenfalls beigefügt.

2.4.6 **Geschäftsfall:**

Die Maschinenfabrik Georg Mössner GmbH, Lyoner Str. 18, 60528 Frankfurt/M, Fax-Nr: +49-69-89 37 49, E-Mail-Adresse: mössner.gmbh@technik.com, erhält von der Máquinas de México S.A., Apdo. Postal 5-593, México, D. F. 06600, México, E-Mail-Adresse: maquinas.mexico@cgiar.com, eine Anfrage in englischer Sprache wegen der Anfertigung einer Spezialmaschine nach beiliegender Zeichnung.

Aufgabe: Arbeiten Sie ein Angebot nach folgenden Punkten aus:
- Preis der Maschine: € 33.000,–
- Lieferung: FOB deutscher Hafen, einschl. seemäßige Verpackung
- Lieferzeit: 3 Monate nach Auftragserteilung, Haftung bei Streik oder höherer Gewalt wird ausgeschlossen
- Zahlung: Gegen unwiderrufliches, bestätigtes Dokumentenakkreditiv, zahlbar bei Ihrer Bank in Frankfurt/Main
- Montage: Durch Ihre Techniker auf Kosten des Kunden
- Garantie: ein Jahr auf technische Fehler an der Maschine
- Gerichtsstand: Frankfurt/Main

2.4.7 **Geschäftsfall:**

Sie sind Cynthia (Heinrich) Bottermann und arbeiten für die Jakob Müller GmbH, Nauheimer Str. 11, 14197 Berlin, Fax-Nr.: +49-30-20 80 99, Tel.-Nr.: +49-30-20 80 10, E-Mail-Adresse: jakob.müller@dgh.de.

Aufgabe: Sie möchten Ihr Sommerlager an Bademoden und Mode für junge Leute räumen und schicken an Ihre Kundschaft in ganz Europa ein Rundschreiben in englischer Sprache unter Berücksichtigung der folgenden Punkte:
- Grund Ihres unverlangten Angebots
- Bezugnahme auf erfolgreiche Geschäfte in der Vergangenheit
- Rigoroser Lagerabbau mit bis zu 50 % Rabatt
- Als Attachment ist ein Angebot der Hauptprodukte mit den jeweiligen Nachlässen angegeben
- Lieferung sofort ab Lager
- Wer zuerst bestellt, wird zuerst bedient
- Lieferung nur solange der Vorrat reicht
- Geben Sie Tel.-, Fax-Nr. und E-Mail-Adresse an

3. Orders

Letters in response to offers; orders; order cancellations

3.1 Introduction

Letters in response to offers. If the seller's offer is acceptable, the buyer places an order. An order following a firm offer, provided it is placed on time and without any qualifications, results in a contract. An order placed on the basis of an offer without engagement does not have this effect: there is no contract unless (and until) the buyer's order is accepted by the seller.

Sometimes certain points of the offer have to be clarified, or additional information has to be obtained from the seller, before an order can be placed. If the buyer does not agree to the prices or terms proposed by the seller, (s)he may try to obtain concessions from the seller or make a counter-offer. A buyer who finds an offer unsuitable should, out of courtesy, send the seller a refusal.

Orders. Orders are placed either in response to an offer, as mentioned above, or on the buyer's own initiative, without a preceding offer. In the latter case, the prospective buyer makes an offer to buy, which leads to a contract if accepted by the seller. An order which opens business between two firms is called a *first* or *initial order*. A further order for the same kind of goods is a *repeat* or *subsequent order*. A *trial order* is an order for a small quantity for testing purposes. It gives the buyer an opportunity to test the quality and marketability of the goods before placing a larger order. *Advance orders* are those placed ahead of the time when delivery is desired. A *standing order* calls for goods to be delivered in specified quantities at certain intervals until further notice. The buyer may also request quantities as they are needed (*merchandise on call*). Today it has become quite customary to place last-minute orders for urgently required goods. Storage times are getting shorter and shorter, so goods are often ordered for *"just-in-time delivery"*.

An order to buy goods placed by a foreign importer with an exporter acting as buying agent is called an *indent*. It may be open or closed, depending on whether it specifies the supplier or leaves the choice of the supplier to the exporter. (Many companies refer to all their foreign orders as indents.)

Order cancellations. Sometimes unforeseen circumstances force the buyer to cancel an order. The buyer is entitled to cancel an order at any time before it has been accepted by the seller. If an order is to be cancelled after acceptance, this is a matter for negotiation. (The buyer has, of course, the right to cancel an order after acceptance if the seller fails to perform contractual obligations.)

Orders placed online. The internet has paved the way for a completely new method of placing orders. An increasing number of companies today have a website, which in certain cases allows the customer to place a direct order. It usually suffices to indicate the buyer's credit card number, or a regular buyer receives a *PIN* (*Personal Identification Number*), which is kept confidential to prevent fraud. This method applies, however, to *B2C* (*business to consumer*) and not to *B2B transactions* (*business to business*). In the latter case the customer has to register with the supplier before internet business can take place.

As in the case of faxes, orders placed via the internet may need to be confirmed in writing, since many countries do not yet accept virtual signatures in legal proceedings.

3.2 Model correspondence

3.2.1 Request for a sample

e-mail

Mail from: Tower.ramsey@ocra.com
to: hkl-beratung@t-online.de **cc:**
Subject: Your offer for pump THG for water treatment
Attachment:

Dear hkl-beratung,

Thank you for your a. m. offer of 22 July this year. Before making a decision as to whether we should place an order for several of the pumps THG, we would like to ask you to send us one sample pump at the offered price of 450 euros including packing and transport costs free our premises. As soon as we have tested the suitability of your pump for the application we have in mind, we will let you know.

Regards,
Jonathan P. Morley
Purchasing Coordinator

3.2.2 Prospective customer asks for price concession

BRISCOE ELECTRONICS LTD
17 Granger Street Cardiff CF5 2LQ
Tel.: +44 (29) 13 75 68-0
Fax: +44 (29) 13 75 68-33

25 July 20..

Hofer GmbH & Co. KG
D- 67655 Kaiserslautern
Germany

Dear Sir / Dear Madam

Thank you for your offer of 16 July for Electrical Switches and the sample switches you sent us by airmail.

We are favourably impressed by the quality of your products, but feel that the prices are rather high. The prices quoted by other suppliers are, on average, 10 % lower. However, in view of the high quality of your switches, we are quite prepared to do business with you if you re-examine your prices. The switches are to be incorporated into devices destined for export to a market where competition is very keen, and we are therefore forced to cut our own prices to remain competitive.

If you reduce your prices by 5 %, we shall place an order for some 20,000 switches. We trust that in view of the size of the order you will see your way to making this concession.

Yours faithfully

Briscoe Electronics LTD

3.2.3 Refusal of quotation

FAO: Ms Jeannette Hansen
Wolf & Bitter KG
Postfach 40 78 192
10004 Berlin

Fax No.: +49 (30) 2 08 93 56 60

From: Helen Richardson
20488 Prince William St.
MD 21908
USA

Date: 8 January 20..

Subject: Your offer of 2 January 20..

Dear Ms Hansen:

Thank you for your offer of 2 January for 2,000 hand-made cuckoo-clocks "Schwarzwald 400 A". We regret to inform you, however, that we cannot make use of your quotation, because your prices are far too high and the delivery time is too long. We have meanwhile ordered the cuckoo-clocks from another supplier.

Sincerely,

3.2.4 Confirmation of order placed by telephone

Dear John:

We enclose Purchase Order No. 1787 in confirmation of the order we placed with you by telephone this morning, signed by our Purchasing Manager.

Please make sure that the delivery time of 4 weeks is strictly adhered to and our order is executed promptly and in accordance with our instructions.

Sincerely yours,

Encl.

3.2.5 Confirmation of order in reply to e-mail received (see 2.2.6)

e-mail

Mail from: schneider.import@back.aol.de
to: Warwick.textiles@wbs.com.uk **cc:**
Subject: Import of textiles
Attachment:

Dear Mr Webster

Thank you for replying to our urgent e-mail so quickly.

We have pleasure in placing a first trial order as follows:

400 yds	your cat.no. 1040 wine	
300 yds	your cat.no. 3876 marine	
200 yds	your cat.no. 5407 white	
900 yds at £20.00		£1,800.00
less 5 % special discount		£90.00
Total:		**£1,710.00**

Payment: £210,00 will be remitted by banker's transfer in the course of the next few days.

It is understood that the deposit will become forfeited should the documents not be taken up on first presentation.

We have advised our bank to inform you by e-mail or fax as soon as they have remitted the amount to your account to enable you to start production.

Please ensure that our order is executed with the utmost care and within the shortest possible time. If the material turns out to our customers' satisfaction, we will be pleased to place further orders with you.

Yours sincerely

3.2.6 Cancellation of order

Dear Mr Gollohan

On 12 October 20.. we placed an order with you for your application software for the location of cargo via the internet. You promised to let us have this software for a test period of 2 months. Unfortunately, it has turned out that this software may be excellent for an ordinary transport agency with the usual day-to-day transport business, but our company has to monitor such a diverse and complicated transport system that we found your software inadequate for our purposes.

We are confident that we will be able to compensate you for the loss of this order, as you will presumably have other software programs coming up in the near future which may be suitable for our requirements.

Please confirm the above cancellation.

Yours sincerely

3.2.7 Letter accompanying order

R L HARRIS & CO PLC
Harris House
780 Walker Street
London SW1A 8JD

AHB/jdm

15 February 20..

Mr Georg Schwarz
Alpha Data GmbH
Bahnhofstrasse 10
D-82131 Gauting
Germany

Dear Mr Schwarz

Thank you for your recent visit to Harris House and the demonstration of your AP-1500 Printer, which you kindly arranged together with your representative in London, Mr Murphy, and the head of your local sales team, Mr Holton.

On the basis of your Quotation of 22 January, the results of the demonstration, and your assurance that the AP-1500 Printer will meet our specifications for

- quality,
- speed,
- dependability and long life,

the Board of R L Harris & Co PLC have decided to buy the printer. I am therefore pleased to enclose Order No 1245/457, which includes the prices and terms mutually agreed upon.

Could you please confirm that the maintenance charges commence after the 60-day warranty period has expired and that your company has a target of less than four hours from the notifications of a "down" condition of the AP-1500 Printer to the arrival of an Alpha Data service engineer at Harris House, with due allowance for the normal working hours of 9.00 am to 5.00 pm, Monday to Friday (excluding public holidays), of the Alpha Data service team.

Yours sincerely
R L Harris & Co PLC

A H Brooks

A H Brooks
EP Manager

Enc.: order No 1245/457

3.2.8 Order for printer

R L HARRIS & CO PLC
Harris House
780 Walker Street
London SW1A 8JD

ORDER NO 1245/457

15 February 20..

Alpha Data GmbH
Bahnhofstrasse 10
D-82131 Gauting
Germany

Please supply the following, subject to the conditions as specified:
ONE (1) AP-1500 printer with the optional features outlined in your quotation of 22 January.

Delivery: Two months from receipt of order.

Price:

Ex works, incl. packing	€00,000.00
Transfer to airport, air freight to London, delivery to Harris House and installation by Alpha Delta engineers	€00,000.00
Total	**€00,000.00**

Payment:
The purchase price will be due and payable when
- the printer has been delivered to Harris House, London, and installed there;
- the printer operates to a sufficient standard to produce the quality of printing as documented by the sample attached;
- the printer operates to the standard outlined above for a 24-hour period maintaining the speed.

The invoice amount will be remitted to Alpha Data's account with Deutsche Bank, Gauting Branch, Account No 122/347.

Operating Environment:

Alpha Data have

- inspected the Harris House computer room and accept it as a suitable environment in which to operate an AP-1500;
- inspected the ACM computers and their accessories in the Harris House computer room and find them suitable to the operation of an AP-1500 Printer;
- discussed the technical relationship between the ACM computers and the AP-1500 Printer with the Engineering manager of ACM London (suppliers to R L Harris of the ACM computers) and found that the AP-1500 is a suitable printer for the ACM computers.

Warranty and Maintenance:

R L Harris's requirements call for a printer to operate

- at the speeds mentioned in your quotation;
- at a quality equal to the sample attached;
- in two eight-hour shifts, seven days per week, for a period of no less than five years.

Alpha data will provide

- a full warranty for a period of 60 days from the day that all the conditions mentioned in the Section "Payment" have been fulfilled;
- an ongoing Maintenance Agreement which will maintain the machine in a condition necessary to meet the requirements outlined above.
- The Maintenance Agreement is to be subject to the terms outlined in Alpha Data's Quotation of 22 January.

R L Harris & Co PLC

L H Kennan

L H Kennan
Director

3.2.9 Indent

GANDASURIA & CO
Export and Import Merchants
157 Raja Matraman
Jakarta, Indonesia

3 rd June, 20..

Sanderson & Smith LTD
216 Bedford Street
London
WC2E 9HR
England

Dear Sirs,

Please purchase and ship on our account the undermentioned goods, or as many of them as possible:
Delivery: CIF Jakarta
Payment: Draw at 60 d/s D/A through Bank of Indonesia
Ship: By first available steamer
Mark: GACO Jakarta 100-upwards

Yours faithfully,
GANDASURIA & CO

J. K. Chan

No. or Quantity	Description	Manufacturer	Price or Quality	Remarks
	Ajax 26-in. Light-Weight Special Tracking Bicycles, 21-speed gear, chrome-plated headlights and warning bell, rear light / reflector	Ajax Co. Ltd, Manchester		
50	Men's models, red, with white and gold-colour trim		£... ex works	Transfer on frame: GANDASURIA & CO.
50	Women's models, blue with white and gold-colour trim		£... ex works	Transfer as above
	Bicycle accessories:			
100	Bicycle pumps		Good quality	
30	Saddle bags		Medium quality	

3.3 Terms and Phrases

3.3.1 Openings

Thank you for your quotation of … We would be pleased if you would supply us with …	*Wir danken Ihnen für Ihr Angebot vom … und wären Ihnen für die Lieferung von … dankbar.*
We agree to your terms and would like to place the following order with you:	*Wir sind mit Ihren Bedingungen einverstanden und möchten Ihnen folgenden Auftrag erteilen:*
Please book the following order for immediate delivery: …	*Bitte buchen Sie folgende Bestellung zur sofortigen Lieferung: …*
We enclose / We are enclosing order / indent no …	*Wir fügen den (laufenden) Auftrag Nr. … bei.*
Please send me the following articles and debit my account with the costs …	*Bitte schicken Sie mir folgende Artikel und belasten Sie mein Konto mit den Kosten …*

3.3.2 Buyer's instructions and conditions

Please acknowledge this order promptly by fax or e-mail, giving the earliest delivery date.	*Wir bitten um prompte Bestätigung dieses Auftrags per Fax oder E-Mail und Angabe des frühesten Liefertermins.*
Please ensure that the goods are shipped / airfreighted as soon as possible.	*Bitte veranlassen Sie, dass die Waren so bald wie möglich verschifft / per Luftfracht versandt werden.*
The delivery dates in our order must be strictly adhered to / observed.	*Die in unserer Bestellung genannten Liefertermine müssen genau eingehalten werden.*
We reserve the right to cancel the order if the goods are not delivered by …	*Wir behalten uns das Recht vor, die Bestellung zu stornieren, wenn die Lieferung nicht bis … erfolgt.*
We must hold you liable / responsible for any loss arising as a result of a delay in delivery.	*Für alle Verluste, die uns bei einer Lieferverzögerung entstehen, müssen wir Sie haftbar / verantwortlich machen.*
The goods must be up to / in accordance with the sample / … must correspond to / match the sample.	*Die Waren müssen dem Muster entsprechen.*
If you cannot match our sample, please send us the nearest substitute you have in stock.	*Falls Sie keine unserem Muster entsprechende Ware liefern können, senden Sie uns bitte die dem Muster am nächsten kommende Qualität, die Sie vorrätig haben.*

If the articles delivered deviate from the description given on your home page, we reserve the right to send them back immediately at your expense.	*Wenn die Artikel von der Beschreibung auf Ihrer Homepage abweichen, behalten wir uns das Recht vor, sie sofort auf Ihre Kosten zurückzuschicken.*
This order is subject to our General Terms and Conditions.	*Diese Bestellung unterliegt unseren Allgemeinen Geschäftsbedingungen / wird auf Grund unserer Allgemeinen Geschäftsbedingungen erteilt.*
We reserve the right to inspect the goods before delivery.	*Wir behalten uns das Recht vor, die Ware vor Versand zu besichtigen.*
The right is reserved to reject any goods not in accordance with this order and to cancel this order if these General Conditions are not complied with, or if delivery is not effected within the stipulated time.	*Wir behalten uns das Recht vor, die Annahme von Waren zu verweigern, die nicht dieser Bestellung entsprechen, und die Bestellung zu stornieren, wenn diese Allgemeinen Geschäftsbedingungen nicht eingehalten werden oder die Lieferung nicht innerhalb der festgesetzten Zeit erfolgt.*
Goods of inferior quality will be returned at supplier's risk and expense.	*Waren minderer Qualität werden auf Kosten und Gefahr des Lieferanten zurückgesandt.*
Packing and marking must correspond to the latest EU regulations.	*Verpackung und Markierung müssen den jüngsten EU-Vorschriften entsprechen.*
Packing must be seaworthy and strong enough to ensure the goods' adequate protection.	*Die Verpackung muss seemäßig und so fest sein, dass sie ausreichenden Schutz für die Waren bietet.*
When packing, please take into consideration that the crates are likely to receive rough handling at this end and that they must be able to withstand transport over very poor roads.	*Bitte berücksichtigen Sie bei der Verpackung, dass die Lattenverschläge hier voraussichtlich einer rauhen Behandlung ausgesetzt sein werden und den Transport auf sehr schlechten Straßen aushalten müssen.*
Detailed instructions regarding packing and shipping will follow.	*Genaue Anweisungen bezüglich Verpackung und Versand / Verschiffung werden nachgeschickt.*
Advice notes and invoices bearing our order no. are to be sent to us with each delivery.	*Versandanzeigen und Rechnungen, die unsere Auftrags-Nr. aufweisen, sind uns mit jeder Lieferung zuzusenden.*
Insurance will be taken out by us.	*Wir werden die Versicherung abschließen.*
Insurance is to be effected from warehouse to warehouse, covering the invoice value plus 10%.	*Die Versicherung ist von Haus zu Haus über den Rechnungswert plus 10% abzuschließen.*

3.3.3 Endings

We trust that you will give this order your usual prompt attention and care.	*Wir hoffen, dass Sie diesen Auftrag mit der gewohnten Pünktlichkeit und Sorgfalt erledigen werden.*
Your careful attention to our instructions will be appreciated.	*Für die genaue Beachtung unserer Anweisungen sind wir Ihnen dankbar.*
As our stocks of these articles are running low, we would appreciate your early delivery.	*Da unsere Lagerbestände an diesen Artikeln zur Neige gehen, wären wir für baldige Lieferung dankbar.*

3.3.4 Cancellation of orders

We are sorry to have to / We regret being compelled to / We regret having to cancel our order of …	*Wir bedauern, unsere Bestellung vom … stornieren zu müssen.*
As our customer has just informed us by phone / fax / e-mail that the device is no longer needed, we have no alternative but to cancel our order.	*Da unser Kunde uns soeben telefonisch / per Fax / per E-Mail mitgeteilt hat, dass das Gerät nicht mehr benötigt wird, bleibt uns nichts anderes übrig, als unsere Bestellung zu stornieren.*
We have just learned that the firm which had ordered this new software package / for which this new software package was intended has gone bankrupt.	*Wir haben soeben erfahren, dass die Firma, die dieses neue Software-Paket bestellt hatte / für die dieses neue Software-Paket bestimmt war, in Konkurs gegangen ist.*
You may be / rest assured, however, that we will let you have our instructions for any further requirements.	*Sie können jedoch sicher sein, dass wir bei weiterem Bedarf auf Sie zurückkommen werden.*
We hope that we will soon be able to make up for the inconvenience caused by placing another order.	*Wir hoffen, Sie bald durch Erteilung eines anderen Auftrags für die Ihnen entstandenen Unannehmlichkeiten entschädigen zu können.*

3.3.5 Refusal of offers; counter-offers

We regret that we are unable to make use of your offer at present.	*Leider können wir zur Zeit von Ihrem Angebot keinen Gebrauch machen.*
As your prices are too high / not competitive, we cannot take your offer into consideration.	*Da Ihre Preise zu hoch / nicht konkurrenzfähig sind, können wir Ihr Angebot nicht in Betracht ziehen.*

We cannot expect satisfactory sales unless you reduce your prices by at least ... per cent.	*Wir können nur dann mit einem zufriedenstellenden Absatz rechnen, wenn Sie Ihre Preise um mindestens ... Prozent reduzieren.*
This article is not suitable for our market.	*Dieser Artikel ist für unseren Markt nicht geeignet.*
We have only recently replenished our stock.	*Wir haben erst kürzlich unser Lager aufgefüllt.*
We feel that this software program is likely to become obsolete in the very near future, and have therefore decided not to place an order.	*Wir glauben, dass dieses Software-Programm in naher Zukunft wahrscheinlich veraltet sein wird, und haben uns daher entschlossen, es nicht anzuschaffen.*
If you are able to accommodate us with regard to the price, we may be interested in placing an order.	*Wenn Sie uns bezüglich des Preises entgegenkommen können, sind wir möglicherweise daran interessiert, einen Auftrag zu erteilen.*
The increasing tendency towards placing orders exclusively on a just-in-time basis makes it impossible for us to accept such long delivery times. If you wish to do regular business with us, you will have to deliver in accordance with our schedule.	*Die aufkommende Tendenz, Aufträge nur noch auf einer just-in-time-Basis zu erteilen, macht es uns unmöglich, so lange Lieferzeiten zu akzeptieren. Wenn Sie regelmäßig mit uns Geschäfte machen wollen, müssen Sie gemäß unseres Zeitplans liefern.*

3.4 Exercises

Please translate:

3.4.1 E-Mail von Telamel GmbH, Nürnberg (compu.telamel@aol.de) an Miller plc, Sheffield (millerplc@ac.uk)

Wir danken für Ihr E-Mail-Angebot vom 13. 04. und bestellen hiermit wie folgt: 2.000 Toner mit Tintenpatronen (*ink cartridges*), für alle Drucker verwendbar, recyclebar, zum Einheitspreis von 15 Euros, Gesamtpreis 30.000 Euros netto. Lieferzeit: Bis spätestens 30. 06., Lieferung frei unseren Geschäftsräumen in Nürnberg. Zahlung: 1/3 bei Lieferung, 1/3 30 Tage, 1/3 60 Tage nach Lieferung per Banküberweisung auf Ihr Konto bei der Midland Bank in Sheffield.

Da die Bestellung eilt, erfolgt sie per E-Mail vorab. Wir werden Ihnen in den nächsten Tagen eine Kopie dieses Auftrages per Post nachreichen.

Bitte bestätigen Sie diesen Auftrag umgehend per E-Mail.

3.4.2 Fax von Paul Schürer Digital KG, München (Fax-Nr.: 089-2873901) an SK Consulting Services Ltd, UK (Fax-Nr.: +44-1481-340986)

Vielen Dank für Ihr Angebot, für uns eine umfassende Analyse zur Erfassung kundenbezogener Daten durchzuführen.

Hiermit erteilen wir Ihnen vorab den Auftrag, eine solche Analyse durchzuführen.

Sie soll die Identifikation von Kunden und eine entsprechende Nutzung der Zielgruppeninformationen ermöglichen. Wir wollen auf Grund dieser Informationen eine Software in Auftrag geben, die die vorgenannten Verfahren in elektronischer Form abbildet.

Laut Ihrem Angebot ist eine solche Analyse innerhalb von 4 Wochen möglich, sie müsste also am 31.07.20.. vorliegen. Festpreis: £5.500,00. In diesem Preis sind alle wichtigen Informationen, die wir für die Erstellung der Software benötigen, enthalten.

Im Übrigen beziehen wir uns auf das uns vorliegende Angebot Ihrer Gesellschaft.

Wir bitten um schriftliche Bestätigung des Auftrags.

3.4.3 Der deutsche Nutzfahrzeughersteller Melchior & Braun AG, Göppingen erteilt der Compugraph Corporation in Boston, Mass. (USA) den folgenden Auftrag:

Bestellung Nr. 30 9587 XC 3045

Unter Bezugnahme auf unser Gespräch mit Mr. Chambers vom 26.05.20.. bestellen wir:

- 1 CAD-System für die Nutzfahrzeug-Konstruktion
- in Umfang und Ausführung entsprechend der in Ihrem Angebot vom 06.03.20.. enthaltenen technischen Beschreibung.

Gesamtfestpreis, einschließlich kompletter Montage, Elektro-Installation, Inbetriebnahme und Einweisung unseres Bedienungspersonals: US$75.400,00

Liefertermin: Betriebsfertige Übergabe 01.10.20.. in unserem Werk.

Die Betriebs- und Bedienungsanleitungen müssen in deutscher Sprache auf CD-ROM erstellt werden. Die Typenschilder sind in deutscher Sprache und mit internationalen Symbolen zu beschriften. Das Gleiche gilt auch für alle übrigen technischen Unterlagen wie Zeichnungen usw. Alle Maßangaben müssen dem metrischen System entsprechen.

Mit der Durchführung des Transports wurde die Spedition Kühne & Nagel Inc., One World Trade Center, Suite 2451, New York, N.Y, 10048, USA, beauftragt.

Bitte übermitteln Sie dieser spätestens 2 Wochen vor Versandbereitschaft per E-Mail oder Fax die für die Verladung und den Transport benötigten Daten. Wir behalten uns vor, alle Kosten, die sich durch Nichtbeachtung unserer Anweisungen ergeben, dem Lieferanten zu berechnen.

Zahlung: Per unwiderruflichem, bestätigten Akkreditiv zu Ihren Gunsten, zu eröffnen bei der Deutschen Bank, Göppingen.

Die Garantiezeit beträgt 3 Jahre.

Wir bitten um kurze Bestätigung des Auftrags und der Anerkennung unserer umseitigen Allgemeinen Geschäftsbedingungen.

Please draft letters, faxes or e-mails from the following particulars:

3.4.4 **Geschäftsfall:**

Ihre Firma, Matthias Lagerhaus GmbH, Postfach 23 11 98, 73734 Esslingen, Fax-Nr.: +49 (7 11) 48 73 90, E-Mail-Adresse: matt.lagerhaus@aol.de, hatte am 24. 08. von der britischen Gesellschaft Leon Richardson & Co. Ltd, P.O. Box 30 40, Gibraltar, Fax-Nr.: +3 50 (76) 39 10, E-Mail-Adresse: l.richardson@aol.com ein Angebot auf Badarmaturen (*bathroom fittings*) erhalten.

Aufgabe: Schreiben Sie im Auftrag Ihres Chefs, des Exportleiters Hans-Jürgen Aalmann, eine Bestellung unter Berücksichtigung der folgenden Punkte:

- Bestätigung des Erhalts des Angebots und der beigefügten Preisliste und Prospekte
- Sie bestellen: 100 Armaturen „De Luxe 2500", Einzelpreis: 150,– Euro, Gesamtpreis: 15.000,– Euro; 200 Armaturen „Sylvester 980", Einzelpreis 100,– Euro, Gesamtpreis: 20.000,– Euro; 50 Armaturen „Super Luxury 80", Einzelpreis 250,– Euro, Gesamtpreis: 12.500,– Euro.
- Wie versprochen erhalten Sie auf die Gesamtsumme einen Großhändlerrabatt von 15 %
- Lieferung: Ab Werk Gibraltar
- Lieferzeit: 4 Wochen nach Auftragserhalt
- Zahlung: Durch 90-Tage-Wechsel nach Sicht.
- Garantie auf die Armaturen: 1 Jahr nach Lieferung
- Bitte um sofortige Auftragsbestätigung per Fax oder E-Mail.

3.4.5 **Geschäftsfall:**

Sie arbeiten für die Chemische Fabrik Dr. Köhler GmbH, Wilhelm-Hale-Str. 11, 80639 München, Fax-Nr.: +49 (89) 29 30 97 84, E-Mail-Adresse: köhler.gmbh@reck.de, und haben von der Garfield Precision Instruments Ltd, 196 Queen Victoria Street, London EC4V 4DU, Fax-Nr.: +44 (17 09) 39 68, ein Angebot über elektronische Analysenwaagen (*analytical scales*) erhalten.

Aufgabe: Erteilen Sie den folgenden Auftrag:

- Sie bestellen sofort drei Analysenwaagen vom Typ PB zum Preis von £ 450,50 das Stück ab Werk;
- Lieferung innerhalb von 2 Wochen per Luftfracht, frachtfrei und versichert bis München;
- Bitten Sie Garfield, der Spedition Hofmeister & Ulrich, Postfach 11 90 38, 47118 Duisburg, Fax-Nr.: +49 (2 03) 8 03 49 57, die AWB (*Airway Bill*) Nummer und Flugdaten mitzuteilen, damit diese die Sendung in München abholen lassen kann;

- Bitten Sie Garfield, die üblichen Begleitpapiere beizufügen;
  Zahlung: Per Banküberweisung sofort nach Eingang und Prüfung der Waagen.

3.4.6 **Geschäftsfall:**

Ihre Firma, die Hüppe Lebensmittel GmbH, Humboldtstr. 114, 40237 Düsseldorf, Fax-Nr.: +49-2 11-66 56 39, E-Mail-Adresse: hueppe.gmbh@com.de, hatte auf der Homepage www.panhome.com der Firma Panhome Laptop plc, P.O. Box 30 609 84, London WC1H OXG, UK, E-Mail-Adresse: panhome.plc@bizlink.co.uk, eine Anzeige für den neuen Laptop „Digital Age" gesehen. Sie hatten daraufhin die Firma angemailt, Ihnen ein Angebot zu schicken. Dieses ist heute per E-Mail eingetroffen.

- Schicken Sie der Panhome Laptop plc einen Probeauftrag auf 5 Laptops „Digital Age" zum Vorzugspreis von £ 1.200 das Stück.
- Lieferung: sofort frei Haus, wie angeboten
- Zahlung: 1/3 als Vorauszahlung bereits überwiesen; Rest per Banküberweisung nach Erhalt der Ware
- Garantiezeit: 1 Jahr
- Bei Eignung Aussicht auf größere Bestellung.

3.4.7 **Geschäftsfall:**

Sie arbeiten für die Westbau AG, Frohnhardter Str. 24, 53639 Königswinter, Fax-Nr.: +49 (22) 44 30 95, E-Mail-Adresse: westbau.anl@pam.de, und haben für die Errichtung einer Versuchsanlage zur Erzeugung von Solarenergie den Zuschlag der Firma Africa Conferences Pty., P.O. Box 34 09 83, Pretoria, South Africa, Fax-Nr.: +27 (11) 8 03 07 16, E-Mail-Adresse: Conference@southafr.com.za erhalten. Die Sonnenkollektoren (*sun collectors*) sollten von der britischen Firma Energy Engineering Ltd, P.O. Box 34 08 79, 24 Kingsway, London WC 2B 6YE, London, U.K., Fax-Nr.: +44 (20) 75 46 68 93, E-Mail-Adresse: energy.eng@com.uk, geliefert werden.

Aufgabe: Richten Sie:

a. ein Fax oder eine E-Mail an Energy Engineering Ltd mit folgendem Inhalt:
   - Der Eigentümer des Grundes, auf dem die Anlage errichtet werden sollte, hat überraschenderweise die Bauarbeiten gestoppt;
   - Bitte, die Lieferung der Kollektoren zurückzustellen;
   - Dies ist laut Auskunft der Africa Conferences Pty. keine Auftragsannullierung;
   - Stilllegung der Baustelle erfolgte trotz offizieller Freigabe vor 4 Wochen;
   - Angeblicher Grund: Ungeklärte Grundstücksrechte;
   - Sie werden sofort nach Klärung der strittigen Fragen erneut Kontakt aufnehmen.

b. ein energisches Schreiben an die Africa Conferences Pty. unter Berücksichtigung folgender Punkte:
   - Bezugnahme auf Auftrag Nr. 34 09 XLZ vom … und Ihre Auftragsbestätigung vom …
   - Beifügung einer Kopie des Faxes oder der E-Mail an Energy Engineering;
   - Sie erwarten dringend Nachricht über Stand der Dinge
   - Falls unvorhergesehene Kosten entstehen, machen Sie die südafrikanische Firma jetzt schon haftbar
   - Haftung der südafrikanischen Firma ebenfalls für den Fall, dass Energy Engineering Ltd im Falle des Nichteinhaltens des Vertrages Schadensersatzansprüche stellt.

4. Acknowledgements

Letters in response to orders; acknowledgements; sales agreements

4.1 Introduction

Letters / Faxes / E-mails in response to orders. When an order is received by fax or e-mail, it is customary to send the buyer an acknowledgement to show that it has been received and accepted. In foreign trade, it is also customary to confirm orders of a certain value by letter. In domestic trade, it is not always necessary to confirm an order in writing if the goods can be delivered immediately. However, in all cases where doubts could arise or where it is necessary to make quite clear that orders placed by fax or e-mail are legally valid, a written acknowledgement is a safe way to make sure that the contract has been concluded.

Should the order be incomplete or not clear, the seller has to ask the customer for the missing details or the necessary clarification. If the buyer asked for a concession, or if the customer's order was not preceded by an offer or constitutes a counter-offer, the seller has to decide whether or not to grant the concession or accept the order.

The seller may find it impossible to accept the order, eg because the articles ordered are not available or the customer's terms cannot be accepted. In such cases, however, the seller will – whenever this is possible – not refuse the order outright, but offer substitutes or propose his/her own terms. It is then for the buyer to decide whether or not to accept the seller's counter-offer. Should the goods be only temporarily out of stock, the seller may place the order on file and inform the customer that it will be executed as soon as a new supply is received. Manufacturers selling through agents or dealers have to refer customers placing direct orders to the middleman in whose territory the customer is located. (The middleman is, of course, informed at the same time.)

Acknowledgements. The acknowledgement may or may not have legal significance. Where the order was placed on the basis of a firm offer, in good time and without any qualifications, there already exists a contract between seller and buyer, and the acknowledgement is merely sent to thank the customer for the order. In all other cases[1], the acknowledgement constitutes the seller's formal acceptance of the buyer's order, which brings about the existence of the contract. If delivery can be effected immediately or the order is delivered

[1] If a firm offer is accepted too late, or an order is placed in response to an offer without engagement; if the buyer's order is a qualified acceptance of the seller's offer (ie a counter-offer); if the order was not preceded by an offer.

"just-in-time", the acknowledgement can be combined with an advice of dispatch or a short message by e-mail or fax with the same effect.

Sales agreements. When a transaction has been concluded, a formal document (*sales agreement, sales contract, contract of purchase*) may be drawn up and signed by both parties. This is frequently done in the case of large contracts or those involving numerous or complex details.

4.2 Model correspondence

4.2.1 Publisher acknowledges subscription order

McGraw-Hill Publications Company

P.O. Box 576, Hightstown, New Jersey 08520 U.S.A.

Dear Subscriber:

Thank you for your recent subscription order. Your interest in our publication is appreciated. We know you will find our articles topical and informative.

Our invoice for the full amount of your subscription is enclosed. Please check your name and address carefully to be sure your copies are delivered promptly.

Please remember to indicate your customer number when filling in your payment form which is also enclosed or, alternatively, return your payment with the top portion of the invoice so we can credit your account correctly. A reply envelope is included for your convenience.

Again, thank you for your subscription order. We look forward to the pleasure of serving you.

Sincerely,

W.C. Bryan

W.C. Bryan
Circulation Credit

Encs: Invoice
Payment form
Reply envelope

4.2.2 British textile mill acknowledges order for shirting

e-mail

Mail from: johnsons.howard@aol.com.uk
to: Hallweither.gmbh@atex.de cc:
Subject: Your order no. th 360 of 14 June 20..

Dear Hallweither GmbH

Thank you very much for the order you gave the German representative, Gallmeister & Co, Düsseldorf. We have entered it as follows:
20,000 yards of shirting (composition: 50 % polyester, 50 % cotton)
of 65/67 g/sq m

Width:	35/36 inches			
Design:	No 245: 10,000 yards			
	No 300: 10,000 yards			
Colours:	each design assorted in four colours, ie			
	white 2,500 yards		rose beige	2,500 yards
	beige 2,500 yards		sky blue	2,500 yards
Price:	Design No 245: ...	per yard × 10,000 =	...	
	Design No 300: ...	per yard × 10,000 =	...	
	Packing and delivery to Bielefeld by road			
Delivery:	15 August / 30 September 20..			

This order is subject to our Conditions of Sale, of which we enclose a copy.

Regards
Johnsons & Howard Plc
Roger Tickmoor
Purchasing Manager

Conditions of Sale

Force Majeure: The Company accepts no liability for any delay in the execution of orders arising from wars, strikes, lockouts, fire, flood, unavailability of raw materials and other circumstances beyond its control. Carriage paid to Port of Shipment only or to Packing House in Great Britain.

Payment: Settlement of accounts is to be made in Sterling. 2½ % discount for payment within 60 days, or 120 days net.

The above terms also apply when payment is made by Bills of Exchange, and all charges and expenses thereon will be payable by the customers.

4.2.3 Tyre company acknowledges order replacing previous one

FAO: Mr Harry Dagobert
Halverstein KG, Berlin

Fax No.: ++49 (30) 53 56 88 17

From: Diane L. Perkins
Rubber Products Ltd, Isle of Man

Date: 26 July 20..

Subject: Your letter of 18 July 20..

fax

Dear Harry:

I refer to your a.m. letter and Order No. 28 91 plh, which replaces your previous Order No. 28 88 plf.

We have accordingly cancelled Order No. 28 88 plf and booked Order No. 28 91 plh as follows:

500 car tyres at £... each, total price: £...,
FOB U. K. Port.

The consignment will be ready for shipment in approximately 10 days' time.

Yours sincerely,

Diana L. Perkins
Export Department

4.2.4 Exporter offers substitutes

Dear Sirs,

We were pleased to receive your order of 15th May, but our suppliers have just informed us that they have discontinued production of Quality No. 2369 AA and 2369, which are their latest products.

We are enclosing our price list for these two qualities and also sample cuttings for your inspection. Will you please let us know as soon as possible which quality you prefer us to substitute, so that we can inform our suppliers accordingly.

Yours faithfully,

Encs

4.2.5 Letter of Intent and Purchase Order

INDIAN CONSTRUCTION COMPANY LTD
P.O. Box 34 90 New Delhi – 110 048 India

Confidential

Our Ref. Ramesh/04/00396

February 15, 20..

ANESTA AG
Buschhauser Str. 124
47167 Duisburg
Germany

Attn. Mr Caspar Rügenwalder

Dear Sir

Subject: Supply of construction material for the MUMBAI building site

Reference is made to our Invitation to Bid dated July 2, 20.., your proposal ref.: R/HL24/61 dated October 26, 20.. and all subsequent correspondence / clarifications as listed in Attachment 1.

We are pleased to confirm our intention to award a Purchase Order to Vendor for the supply of construction material for the Mumbai building site as stipulated in Attachment 2, to be made effective upon the issuance of the formal Purchase Order.

Pending issuance of the formal Purchase Order and finalization of the Bills of Materials, we authorize Vendor to proceed with the necessary action to fulfil its obligations that shall be contained in the Purchase Order.

Details of the award and the governing terms and conditions are outlined herein:

A. Scope of Supply
Vendor shall supply the construction material ("goods") in compliance to the requirements of the Indian Construction Company Ltd. Scope of Supply requirements as specified in the documents subject to the variations and amendments recorded in subsequent correspondence / clarifications between the Indian Construction Company and Vendor as listed in Attachment 1.

B. Terms of Payment
The Indian Construction Company Ltd will make payment to Vendor within forty-five (45) days from the date that a fully supported invoice is received by the Indian Construction Company Ltd, in accordance with Article 5.

C. Delivery Schedule
Vendor shall deliver the goods within fifteen (15) weeks FOB Port of Export upon receipt of the Purchase Order.

D. Delivery Terms
The delivery terms for the Purchase Order is FOB Port of Export. The Indian Construction Company reserves the right to change the delivery terms to CFR Bombay or DDU nominated fabrication yard using the price quoted by Vendor in the proposal.

E. Cancellation Charges
The applicable cancellation charges for the Purchase Order are stated in Attachment 3.

F. Inspection
The goods supplied under the Purchase Order are subject to inspection by the Indian Construction Company Ltd or their authorized representative as stipulated in Article 23. Other details shall be advised by the Indian Construction Company Ltd at a later date.

H. Purchase Order
The Purchase Order, when issued, shall contain the terms and conditions of purchase as per the documents, detailed Bills of Materials and Prices.

Notwithstanding the foregoing, the Indian Construction Company Ltd reserves the right, at their sole discretion, to terminate the effect of this Letter of Intent at any time until the issuance of the Purchase Order. In such an event, no compensation shall be paid to Vendor.

You are hereby requested to acknowledge receipt and acceptance of this Letter of Intent by affixing your signature in the space provided below and returning a copy of this letter to the undersigned.

With best regards
The Indian Construction Company Ltd

Sudarshi Maini

General Manager
Engineering & Construction

Vendor: ANESTA AG
Signature:
Name:
Designation:
Date:

Encs: 3 Attachments

Purchase Order

CONFIDENTIAL

PURCHASE ORDER No. 34 910/04/00396

DATE			
VENDOR	ANESTA AG	**ATTENTION**	Mr. Caspar Rügenwalder
ADDRESS	Buschhauser Str. 124 47167 Duisburg Germany	**TELEPHONE:**	+44 (2 03) 27 14 63
		FAX:	+44 (2 03) 27 14 64

Design, manufacture, inspection, testing, painting and preparation for shipment, and delivery of construction material as listed in Attachment 1.

The following documents previously provided in the Invitation to Bid Document and incorporated by reference herein:

1. Scope of Supply (Section C, Part I)
2. Administration Procedures (Section C, Part III)
3. Expediting & Inspection Instructions (Section B, Exhibit B – 7)
4. Bank Performance Guarantee (Section B, Exhibit B – 3)
5. Performance Guarantee (Section B, Exhibit B – 4)
6. Packing, Marking & Shipping Instructions and Documentations (Section B, Exhibit B – 10)

The following documents attached hereto and made an integral part of this PURCHASE ORDER.

1. Bill of Materials and Prices (Attachment 1)
2. Terms and Conditions of Purchase (Attachment 2)
3. List of Correspondences between INDIAN CONSTRUCTION COMPANY LTD and VENDOR (Attachment 3)
4. Technical Requisition Package (Attachment 4)

DELIVERY TERMS:	FOB PORT OF SHIPMENT	DELIVERY DATE (FOB):	
TERMS OF PAYMENT:	45 DAYS	CURRENCY:	USD

Total Purchase Order Value: **USD** 1,425,350.00
One Million Four Hundred Twenty-Five Thousand Three Hundred and Fifty
(Total Purchase Order Value in Words)

Vendor shall confirm their ACCEPTANCE of this PURCHASE ORDER by signing in the space below and returning to within seven (7) days after receipt of this PURCHASE ORDER.

FOR AND ON BEHALF OF INDIAN CONSTRUCTION COMPANY LTD	VENDOR
SIGNATURE: [signature] DATE: Febr. 15, 20..	SIGNATURE: DATE:
NAME: Sudarshi Maini	NAME:
DESIGNATION: **GENERAL MANAGER** **ENGINEERING & CONSTRUCTION**	DESIGNATION:

DISTRIBUTIONS:

a) Complete Set (Priced)

1. Original: Vendor
2. Copy 1: Procurement File
3. Copy 2: Buyer

b) Complete Set (Unpriced)

4. Copy 3: Project Engineer
5. Copy 4: Site Representative
6. Copy 5: Inspection Coordinator
7. Copy 6: Expeditor

c) PO (Cover) + Attachment 1 * Attachment 2 (Priced)

8. Copy 7: Accounting
9. Copy 8: Shipping Coordinator

PURCHASE ORDER No. 34.910/04/00396

4.3 Terms and phrases

4.3.1 Acknowledging orders

Thank you for your order, which we acknowledge as follows: …	*Besten Dank für Ihren Auftrag, den wir wie folgt bestätigen: …*
We were very pleased / delighted to receive your order.	*Wir haben uns sehr gefreut, Ihren Auftrag zu erhalten.*
Your order is being attended to.	*Ihr Auftrag wird bereits bearbeitet.*
Your order has been put in hand, and we will do our best / utmost to have the goods ready for dispatch by …	*Wir haben bereits mit der Ausführung Ihres Auftrages begonnen und werden uns bemühen, die Waren bis … zum Versand bereitzustellen.*
We will do everything possible to expedite the completion of your order.	*Wir werden alles uns Mögliche tun, um die Fertigstellung Ihres Auftrages zu beschleunigen.*
We are pleased to advise you that the goods ordered by you by letter / fax / e-mail on … have been shipped / sent / delivered today as requested.	*Wir freuen uns Ihnen mitzuteilen, dass die von Ihnen per Brief / Fax / E-Mail am … bestellten Waren heute wie gewünscht versandt / verschifft / geliefert wurden.*
Your order of / dated … has been received, and the urgently required goods will be delivered to you by courier immediately.	*Wir haben Ihren Auftrag vom … erhalten, und die dringend benötigten Waren werden Ihnen sofort per Kurier zugestellt.*
We will inform / notify you as soon as the consignment is ready for collection.	*Wir werden Sie benachrichtigen, sobald die Sendung abholbereit ist.*
We assure you that your instructions will be carefully observed / adhered to.	*Wir versichern Ihnen, dass Ihre Anweisungen genau beachtet werden.*
Special care will be devoted to the execution of your order.	*Wir werden Ihren Auftrag mit besonderer Sorgfalt ausführen.*
We hope that this first order will lead to further business.	*Wir hoffen, dass dieser Erstauftrag zu weiteren Geschäftsabschlüssen führen wird.*
… represents the first step in the establishment of / marks the commencement of / beginning of / a long and mutually satisfactory business relationship.	*… den ersten Schritt zu / den Beginn einer dauerhaften und für beide Teile zufrieden stellenden Geschäftsverbindung darstellt.*
We hope that the goods will arrive in good condition and look forward to the pleasure of serving you again.	*Wir hoffen, dass die Waren wohlbehalten ankommen, und würden uns freuen, weitere Aufträge von Ihnen zu erhalten.*
We hope that in the event of further requirements you will make use of our services again.	*Wir hoffen, dass Sie bei weiterem Bedarf auf uns zurückkommen werden.*

4.3.2 Refusal and modification of orders

Thank you for your order of …, but we regret to have to disappoint you.	*Wir danken Ihnen für Ihren Auftrag vom …, müssen Sie aber leider enttäuschen.*
We regret that we are unable to supply the goods ordered.	*Wir sind leider nicht in der Lage, die bestellten Waren zu liefern.*
We are sorry that we cannot accept your order.	*Leider können wir Ihren Auftrag nicht annehmen.*
It is not possible for us to execute your order at the prices stipulated / within the delivery period requested by you.	*Es ist uns nicht möglich, Ihren Auftrag zu den festgesetzten Preisen / innerhalb des von Ihnen gewünschten Lieferzeitraums auszuführen.*
As we do not supply these machines direct from the factory, we refer you to …, our authorized dealers in your area.	*Da wir diese Maschinen nicht direkt ab Werk liefern, verweisen wir Sie an den für Ihr Gebiet zuständigen Vertragshändler, die Firma …*
We have passed your order on to our agents.	*Wir haben Ihren Auftrag an unsere Vertretung weitergeleitet.*
The software ordered is in short supply at the moment and we would ask you to contact us again in another 3 weeks, if this is possible.	*Die bestellte Software ist im Augenblick schwer lieferbar und wir bitten Sie, sich wenn möglich in 3 Wochen nochmals mit uns in Verbindung zu setzen.*
We regret having to inform you that this article is out of stock / the production of this article has been discontinued due to lack of demand.	*Wir bedauern, Ihnen mitteilen zu müssen, dass dieser Artikel nicht auf Lager ist / die Produktion dieses Artikels wegen Nachfragemangels eingestellt worden ist.*
Article … is no longer available.	*Artikel … ist nicht mehr erhältlich.*
We are out of stock / have run out of stock / no longer stock this item.	*Wir führen diese Position nicht mehr.*
Our stocks have been sold out / have been cleared / are depleted.	*Unser Lager ist geräumt / geleert.*
A new supply will not be available until …	*Eine neue Lieferung wird nicht vor … erhältlich sein.*

4.3.3 Counter-offers and substitutes

Unless you instruct us otherwise, the goods ordered will be shipped / dispatched on receipt of new supplies.	*Wenn Sie keine anderen Anweisungen erteilen, erfolgt der Versand / die Verschiffung der bestellten Waren, sobald wir eine neue Lieferung erhalten.*
For article No. 223 we could substitute article No. 226, which is very similar to the quality ordered.	*An Stelle von Artikel Nr. 223 könnten wir Artikel Nr. 226 liefern, der der bestellten Qualität sehr ähnlich ist.*

If you increase your order to ..., we will be glad to supply the material at the price suggested in your counter-proposal.	*Wenn Sie Ihre Bestellung auf ... erhöhen, liefern wir Ihnen das Material gern zu dem in Ihrem Gegenangebot vorgeschlagenen Preis.*
The prices stated in your order have been taken from our price list of ..., which has in the meantime been superseded by a new one.	*Die in Ihrer Bestellung genannten Preise wurden unserer Preisliste vom ... entnommen, die inzwischen durch eine neue ersetzt worden ist.*
We suggest you purchase our new model ... instead of the old model ...	*Wir schlagen vor, Sie kaufen das neue Modell ... statt des alten Modells ...*
We have replaced article No. ... by a completely new version, which is more economical in use and much cheaper.	*Wir haben Artikel Nr. ... durch eine vollständig neue Version ersetzt, die wirtschaftlicher im Gebrauch und viel preisgünstiger ist.*

4.4 Exercises

Please translate:

4.4.1 E-Mail von schwarzenbeck.ag@aol.com.de an amaya.corp@co.th

Wir haben uns sehr gefreut, dass Ihr Executive Vice President, Herr M. Chahonyo, unseren Stand auf der Frankfurter Messe besucht hat, und danken Ihnen für den uns erteilten Auftrag.

Als Attachment erhalten Sie unsere Proforma-Rechnung. Wir möchten Sie bitten, das Akkreditiv so bald wie möglich eröffnen zu lassen, damit wir mit der Bearbeitung Ihres Auftrages beginnen können. Das Akkreditiv soll bis 30.06. gültig sein, da Sie die Verschiffung der Ware bis 20.06. wünschen.

Bitte bestätigen Sie unsere E-Mail und den Erhalt der Proforma-Rechnung und sichern Sie uns zu, dass die Gültigkeit des Akkreditivs bis 30.06. durch die Bank gewährleistet wird.

Besten Dank.

Mit freundlichen Grüßen

Attachment

4.4.2 Fax der Primus Werke AG, Erlangen (Fax-Nr.: +49-9131-37 09 84) an Gillott Corporation, Los Angeles, California, U.S.A. (Fax-Nr.: +1-213-24 09 86 74)

Wir danken Ihnen für Ihren Auftrag, den wir zusammen mit Ihrem Schreiben vom 8. Mai erhielten.

Mit getrennter Post haben wir Ihnen heute den von uns unterzeichneten Liefervertrag in doppelter Ausfertigung zugesandt. Wir bitten Sie, ein Exemplar mit Ihrer Unterschrift zu versehen und an uns zurückzusenden. Ihre Anweisungen bezüglich Verpackung und Versand werden wir genau befolgen.

Obwohl wir zur Zeit mit Aufträgen überhäuft sind, werden wir unser Möglichstes tun, um die Waren bis Anfang September zur Verschiffung bereitzustellen.

4.4.3 **Bürogeräte AG, Hannover, an Office Supplies Limited, London**

Wir danken Ihnen für Ihren Auftrag vom 16. Mai über 50 Taschendiktiergeräte TD-525. Dieses Gerät ist leider nicht mehr lieferbar, da es inzwischen durch eine verbesserte Version, das TD-535, ersetzt worden ist. Das neue Gerät ist noch kleiner, etwas flacher und noch handlicher als das Vorgänger-Modell. Es ist in der Lage, praktisch alle Funktionen eines großen Bürodiktiergerätes zu übernehmen. Das TD-535 ist sogar mit einer Markierungstaste zum sofortigen Auffinden der gewünschten Textstelle und einem Diktat / Konferenz-Schalter zum Aufzeichnen von Konferenzen ausgestattet. Zu Ihrer Information legen wir einen englischen Prospekt bei.

Trotz der wesentlichen Verbesserungen ist das TD-535 nur geringfügig teurer als das alte Modell. Der Preis ab Werk beträgt € ...

Wenn wir von Ihnen innerhalb der nächsten 14 Tage nichts Gegenteiliges hören, senden wir Ihnen anstelle der bestellten 50 Taschendiktiergeräte TD-525 die gleiche Menge des neuen Modells TD-535. Der Versand erfolgt, wie üblich, per Luftpost.

Wir sind sicher, dass unsere neuen Geräte von Ihren Kunden sehr positiv aufgenommen werden.

Anlage

4.4.4 **Joisten & Biedermann KG, München an Gibson Ltd, Glasgow, U.K.**

Sehr geehrter Herr McGregor,

vielen Dank für Ihre E-Mail von heute.

Leider ist es uns nicht möglich, Ihre Bestellung für 1.500 zusammenklappbare Servierwagen (*collapsible trolleys*) des Designs „Gartenwunder" anzunehmen, da dieses Modell von uns nicht mehr hergestellt wird.

Als Alternative empfehlen wir Ihnen unser neues Modell „Sommertraum", das in der Ausführung sehr ähnlich ist. Es ist mit einer besonders stoßfesten Kunststoffbeschichtung (*shock-resistant plastic coating*) ausgestattet. Seine Tragfähigkeit (*load capacity*) beträgt 30 kg, also 5 kg mehr als das alte Modell. Die Höhe beträgt ca. 72 cm, dies entspricht dem alten Servierwagen.

Der Preis beträgt € 35, also € 5 mehr als das Modell „Gartenwunder", doch sind wir bereit, Ihnen für die Menge von 1.500 Stück einen einmaligen Mengenrabatt von 15 % zu geben, also 5 % mehr als für das nicht mehr verfügbare Modell. Alle anderen Bedingungen bleiben unverändert.

Wir hoffen, dass Ihnen dieses Angebot zusagt, und stehen Ihnen für jede weitere Auskunft gern zur Verfügung. Wir fügen einen Prospekt über das neue Modell bei, aus dem alle näheren Einzelheiten, die Sie noch interessieren könnten, hervorgehen.

Unser Internet-Service www.jobi.de steht Ihnen Tag und Nacht zur Verfügung.

Mit freundlichen Grüßen

Anlage

Please draft letters, faxes or e-mails from the following particulars:

4.4.5 **Geschäftsfall:**

Sie arbeiten für die Firma Schreiner GmbH & Co. KG, Plaußiger Str. 11, 04318 Leipzig, Fax-Nr.: +49-341-807647, E-Mail-Adresse: schreiner.leipzig@gmx.de, und hatten der kanadischen Gesellschaft Briscoe Inc., 3028 Laird Blvd., Suite 408, Mount Royal, Quebec, Canada HrP 2TI, Fax-Nr.: +01 (541) 739 11 24, E-Mail-Adresse: briscoe.inc@visa.com.ca, ein Angebot auf Fahrrad-Sturzhelme (*crash helmets for cyclists*) unterbreitet. Die kanadische Firma schreibt Ihnen, dass Sie von dem Artikel sehr angetan ist, den Preis aber zu hoch findet.

Aufgabe: Beantworten Sie dieses Schreiben unter Berücksichtigung folgender Punkte:

- Dank für Lob Ihres Produkts
- Bedauerlicherweise können Sie keine Preiskonzession machen
- Geben Sie Gründe an: Sehr hohe Qualität, TÜV-Zulassung, bereits schärfste Preiskalkulation erfolgt, bei CIF-Lieferung müssen wegen der geringen Menge hohe Transportkosten usw. einkalkuliert werden
- Einzige Möglichkeit: Erhöhung der Bestellmenge auf 2.000 statt 1.000 Stück
- In diesem Fall wird Mengenrabatt von 8 auf 12 % erhöht
- Bitte um Verständnis und Hoffnung auf baldigen Auftrag.

4.4.6 **Geschäftsfall:**

Sie arbeiten bei dem Glas- und Porzellanhersteller Seidenstecker GmbH, Lübecker Str. 36, 20457 Hamburg, Fax-Nr.: +49 (40) 139307, E-Mail-Adresse: seidenstecker@aol.com, und haben von Stewards & Sons, P.O. Box 30611, Reading RG6 6BA, UK, E-Mail-Adresse: stewards.sons@ac.uk, einen Auftrag per E-Mail erhalten.

Aufgabe: Schicken Sie eine Auftragsbestätigung unter Berücksichtigung folgender Einzelheiten:

- Dank für Auftrag
- Bestätigung der Positionen wie folgt:
  300 Kaffeeservice „Flora", Gesamtpreis 4.500 Euros
  20 Esservice „Candlelight Dinner", Gesamtpreis 8.350 Euros
  12 × 12 Sektgläser „Rosemarie", Gesamtpreis 836 Euros
- Lieferung frei Haus
- Zahlungsbedingung: Vorauszahlung mit 3 % Skonto, 8 Tage nach Erhalt der Ware mit 2 % Skonto oder 30 Tage netto
- Zusicherung angemessener Verpackung, wie gewünscht
- Hoffnung auf gute Zusammenarbeit und weitere Aufträge.

4.4.7 Geschäftsfall:

Friedrich Decker AG, München, Fax-Nr.: +49-89-2403951
an Decker Limited, Stratford-upon-Avon, Fax-Nr.: +44-1789-30640
Bestätigen Sie als Exportsachbearbeiter(in) der Decker AG in München den Auftrag ihrer englischen Tochtergesellschaft wie folgt:

- Kommissions-Nr. 403011936
- 1 Bohrmaschine (*drilling machine*) Marke 415 V, Artikel Nr. 2540803
- 2 Werkzeugmaschinen (*machine tools*) Marke 390 TV, Artikel Nr. 3890620
- 1 Satz Bedienungsanleitung FP4A mit Bildschirm-Steuerung (*display-screen control*)

– *Preis:*	€ 33.024,– plus Verpackung € 600,–
– *Versandort:*	München
– *Spediteur:*	IPEC GmbH, München
– *Übernahmespediteur:*	IPEC UK, Northampton
– *Preise:*	ab Werk ausschließlich Verpackung, gesondert € 600,–
– *Preisgültigkeit:*	Festpreise bei Abnahme bis zum bestätigten Liefertermin
– *Zahlung:*	Gesamtbetrag zahlbar ohne Abzug innerhalb von 30 Tagen nach Rechnungsdatum, spätestens zum Ablauf des Folgemonats, durch Scheck oder Überweisung auf eines der Bankkonten der Friedrich Decker AG
– *Lieferzeit:*	3–4 Monate
– *Versicherung und Gefahrenübergang:*	Die Transportversicherung von Haus zu Haus und die Aufstellungsversicherung wird durch Decker Ltd gedeckt. Der Gefahrenübergang beginnt nach abgeschlossener Verladung ab Werk.
– *Lieferung:*	An die Spedition IPEC UK, Northampton
– *Dokumentation:*	*Packzettel englisch:* Je 3 Exemplare sind der Maschinenkiste beigepackt, ein Exemplar begleitet die Rechnung *Rechnung englisch:* 4 Exemplare werden Decker Ltd nach Versand der Maschine zugesandt, 4 Exemplare werden dem Spediteur ausgehändigt *Betriebsanleitung englisch:* Ein Exemplar wird der Maschinenkiste beigepackt.
– *Verpackung:*	Für den Landtransport
– *Kistenmarkierung:*	Decker Ltd 3191 403011936 Stratford-upon-Avon Gross Weight: ... Dimensions: ... Bedienungsschilder: In englischer Sprache

- *Garantie:* 12 Monate
- *Kunde/Endabnehmer:* Ist der Friedrich Deckel AG mit der Umsatz-Identifikations-Nr. noch bekanntzugeben.

4.4.8 Geschäftsfall:

Firma Lynderbaum & Schrader GmbH, Rhedaer Str. 234, 33397 Rietberg, Fax-Nr.: +49-52-44 36 11, E-Mail-Adresse: lynder.schra@call.de, an Thesaurus Inc., P.O. Box 3120, San Diego, California 92166, USA, Fax-Nr.: +01-6 19-2 24 90 57, E-Mail-Adresse: thesaurus.inc@compuserve.com

Richten Sie an Thesaurus Inc. ein höfliches Schreiben unter Berücksichtigung folgender Punkte:
- Dank für erhaltenen Auftrag
- Sie können diesen leider nicht annehmen
- Produktion wurde wegen Nachfragemangels eingestellt
- Sie fügen neues Herstellungsprogramm bei
- Bitte um Spezifizierung detaillierter Wünsche
- Sie sind jederzeit zu weiteren Auskünften bereit.

5. Credit Letters

5.1 Introduction

When a customer asks for credit, the supplier must first find out whether the customer is creditworthy. This can be done by making use of the various sources of information which are freely accessible (eg court judgements, company reports and profit and loss accounts, general information made available on the internet etc) or by obtaining information from other sources, of which the most important are:

- The customer himself (he may be asked to provide information, eg by filling in a credit application form or by submitting a copy of his latest balance sheet)
- The customer's bank references (the banks named by the customer, since banks are only authorized to give detailed references with the explicit permission of the customer, otherwise they provide only general information)
- The supplier's own bank
- Other firms known to have done business with the customer
- Credit enquiry (or credit reference) agencies, in America also called commercial agencies or credit bureaus. These institutions charge a fee for the service rendered.

When sending enquiries to the customer's trade references or to other firms, enquirers should be aware of the fact that they are asking a free-of-charge favour. They may therefore explicitly offer to reciprocate favours, although the willingness to do so can be taken for granted. Enquirers must assure the firm they are writing to that it will not be held responsible for the information given and that the information will be treated confidentially. Many letters of enquiry do not mention the name of the person or firm about whom the enquiry is being made; instead, a separate slip of paper with the name on it is attached to the letter. Letters requesting credit information, and the envelopes in which they are sent, are marked *Confidential, Strictly Confidential* or *Private and Confidential.*

Credit information. Business firms are under no obligation whatsoever to answer credit enquiries. Usually, however, they are quite willing to cooperate, knowing that they, too, have to ask such favours from time to time.

In replies to credit enquiries, the name of the person or firm about whom information is being given is frequently omitted; instead, reference is made to *the firm in question, the firm mentioned in your letter, the firm about which you enquire*, etc. Favourable reports should not be "over-enthusiastic". If they are "too good to be true", they are likely to arouse suspicion. When unfavourable reports have to be given, this should be done in a cautious and impersonal manner. In common law countries there are strict laws protecting individuals as well as business firms against oral defamation (*slander*) and written defamation (*libel*). An unfavourable credit report may, under certain circumstances, give rise to an action for libel. Business firms in these countries are therefore extremely careful when giving unfavourable information by letter. An unfavourable opinion is couched in rather general terms, and frequent use is made of such phrases as *it seems, we believe, we have learned from reliable sources*, etc. Instead of giving an unfavourable report, the firm asked to give information may also refuse to express an opinion. Many refusals to provide credit information are tantamount to an unfavourable report.

Business firms, banks and enquiry agencies giving credit information always point out in their letters that the information is given in confidence and that they assume no liability. Both the letter and the envelope are marked *Confidential, Strictly Confidential*, etc.

Since in today's business world most transactions are made on credit terms, many commercial institutions and organisations have started to develop their own information services. They help each other to bring them up to date and very often also make this information available to credit agencies.

Another modern scheme of evaluation is credit rating by banks and specialized institutions which are regularly published in the world's leading financial papers.

5.2 Model correspondence

5.2.1 Credit enquiry

May 16, 20..

Information Services GmbH
Austrian Division
Europaplatz 611
A-8970 Schladming

Dear Sirs

Private and Confidential

We have been referred to you by the firm mentioned on the enclosed slip and should be glad if you would give us as detailed information as possible regarding their financial status and business reputation. In particular, we should like to know whether, in your opinion, a credit to the extent of approx. £20,000 could be safely granted.

We thank you for your courtesy and assure you that your information will be treated confidentially.

Yours faithfully

Enc.

5.2.2 Credit enquiry

Orpington Corporation
220 Washington Avenue
Stamford, Connecticut 06904

February 5, 20..

Fuchs & Kolbe AG
Wolfratshauser Straße 76
D-81379 München

Information on Strohmeier KG, Kathi-Kobus-Str. 23, 80797 Munich

Gentlemen:

We understand that you are familiar with the affairs of the above company, from which we have just received an order to the value of US$85,000.00 (requested credit terms: 90 days).

Would you kindly give us your opinion of the company's financial responsibility, credit standing and general management. Do you think that they are good for the above-mentioned credit terms?

Your reply will be appreciated, and we assure you that any information you may give us will be held in strict confidence. Should the occasion present itself, we will be very glad to reciprocate the favor.

Sincerely yours,

C. F. Cummings
Credit Department

5.2.3 Enquiry from credit enquiry agency

fax

FAO: Mr Hans-Ulrich Meyer
Credit Controller
Moden Meyer KG
Boschetsrieder Str. 8 a
81379 München

Fax No.: +49 (89) 493 89 170

From: Mary Johnson
Collin Credit Information Agency
15 St James's Street
London SW1A 1HG

Date: 24 February 20..

Subject: Elegance Ltd, Liberty Square, London

Dear Mr Meyer

Ms McAllistair of the above company gave us your name as a trade reference. We would be obliged if you would answer the following questions on their account:

1. Age of account
2. Average monthly volume of business / credit limit
3. Terms of payment
4. Comments (eg manner of payment)

To facilitate the handling of this information, please use the attached neutral enquiry form.

I assure you that we will treat your information as strictly private and confidential. A speedy reply would be much appreciated, as this report is urgently required. Thank you for your time and cooperation.

Regards

Mary Johnson
Credit Information Department

Enc.: Enquiry form

5.2.4 Favourable information

Confidential

Dear Madam / Sir

In reply to your enquiry of 8 June, we are pleased to say that the firm in question enjoys a good reputation. The proprietors are reported to have considerable capital at their disposal. They have always met their obligations punctually. We would therefore have no hesitation in granting them credit to the extent you mention.

This information is given without responsibility on our part and on the understanding that you will treat it as confidential.

Yours faithfully

5.2.5 Unfavourable information

Private and Confidential

Gentlemen:

We regret to state, in response to your letter of May 28, that our experience with the firm in question has not been satisfactory.

During the ten months they have had an account with us, we have repeatedly had difficulties in collecting bills. It seems that their financial position is not very strong.

Under these circumstances we would advise you to proceed with caution and, if possible, to do business on cash terms only.

This information is given without any obligation on our part, and we trust that it will be held strictly confidential.

Sincerely yours,

5.2.6 Credit report from American bank

NATIONAL BANK AND TRUST COMPANY
Broadway
New York, N.Y. 10018

Handels- und Industriebank AG
Postfach 10 40 37
D-81379 München
Germany

July 10, 20..

Gentlemen:

We are pleased to reply to your enquiry of June 16 regarding Goldstein & Grey Inc., New York, New York.

Subject was chartered under New York Laws on May 15, 19.. and operates as importers of antiques and works of art. Principles include Samuel E. Goldstein, Chairman, Michael D. Grey, President and Treasurer, and A. L. Cosgrave, Vice President and Secretary.

Subject has maintained an account with us since August, 19.. and balances average in satisfactory proportions. We currently hold at subject's disposal a medium six figure line of credit, with a low five figure aggregate currently outstanding. Our facilities are actively and properly utilized.

Financial information is submitted to us in confidence. However, we can disclose that the latest statement in our possession dated 6 / 30 / .. shows a substantial net worth, with profitable operations sustained for the year then ended.

From our experience with Goldstein & Grey Inc., we believe that the company should prove responsible for its normal business commitments.

We hope the information will prove useful.

Cordially,

National Bank and Trust Company
R L Miles
Credit Department

RLM:kds

5.2.7 Refusal to give information

Private and Confidential

Dear Sirs

With reference to your enquiry of 30th June, we regret to say that we are unable to express an opinion on the financial standing of the firm in question.

Yours faithfully

5.2.8 Agency report

April 20, 20..

Nelson-Towers Trading Company
(Subsidiary of Nelson & Towers, Inc.)

288 Broad Street
New York, NY 10005

OFFICERS: John D. Nelson, President
Donald A. Towers, Vice-President
George L. Smathers, Secretary-Treasurer
DIRECTORS: The officers
RATING: NQ[1]

HISTORY

Incorporated under New York laws August 7, 19.., authorized capital $...

John D. Nelson, 60, single, native-born. Operated a partnership business with Donald A. Towers, which was succeeded by Nelson & Towers, Inc. in 19.. .

Donald A. Towers, 58, married, born in Canada. Partner of John D. Nelson before partnership was incorporated.

George L. Smathers, 41, married, native-born. Nine years employed by National City Bank of New York. 19.. joined Peel & Co., Inc., export merchants in this city, later managed finance department of that corporation, from which position he resigned on August 1, 19.. .

1 *Not Quoted* (in the rating book)

OPERATION–LOCATION

Wholly-owned subsidiary of Nelson & Towers, Inc., which operates as importers of general merchandise. Twelve persons are currently employed.

The company maintains a suite of offices on the 12th floor of a 35-story office building.

FINANCIAL INFORMATION

On April 18, 20.., A. J. Muller, office manager, reported that John D. Nelson was abroad on a business trip and that the other officers were out of town.

Mr. Muller stated that the subject company had been acting mainly as import agent. However, he stated that recently the company had placed orders with several domestic suppliers for merchandise to be exported overseas. He stated that the company had ample capital for these commitments and had at its own option included 60 % deposits with orders to ensure prompt delivery. Mr. Muller declined to submit balance sheet, stating he was not authorized to give full financial information on the company.

The parent company, Nelson & Towers, Inc., on December 31, 20.., showed net worth of $... and a good financial condition, with current assets over twice current liabilities, and a liquid condition maintained.

PAYMENTS

A. J. Muller stated that principal purchases so far had been made on a letter of credit or sight draft basis.

Accounts are maintained at two depositories in this city, which have in three instances made an advance to the subject company on a secured basis.

5.3 Terms and phrases

5.3.1 Openings

Your name has been given to us as a reference.	*Sie wurden uns von … als Referenz genannt.*
We have been told / We have been given your address by …	*Uns wurde von … gesagt / Wir erhielten Ihre Adresse von …*
The firm whose name appears / The firm mentioned on the enclosed slip has placed a first order to the value of …	*Die auf dem beiliegenden Blatt genannte Firma hat uns einen Erstauftrag in Höhe von … erteilt.*

As this firm is unknown to us, …	*Da uns diese Firma nicht bekannt ist, …*
As we have not done business with this firm so far … / As we have not had any previous dealings with this firm, …	*Da wir mit dieser Firma bisher nicht in Geschäftsverbindung standen, …*

5.3.2 Information requested

We would appreciate / be grateful for any information you can give us about the firm in question.	*Für jede Auskunft, die Sie uns über die betreffende Firma geben können, wären wir Ihnen dankbar.*
We would be glad / grateful if you could give us details / particulars regarding / concerning …	*Wir wären Ihnen dankbar, wenn Sie uns Näheres über … mitteilen könnten.*
financial standing / financial status	*finanzielle Lage / Vermögenslage*
credit standing / credit status / creditworthiness / financial responsibility	*Kreditwürdigkeit*
solvency / liquidity / ability to meet financial obligations	*Solvenz / Liquidität / Zahlungsfähigkeit*
turnover / sales (revenue) (AE)	*Umsatz*
sales / unit sales, unit volume (AE)	*Absatz*
business conduct	*Geschäftsgebaren*
business methods	*Geschäftsmethoden*
company performance	*Unternehmensleistung*
reliability	*Zuverlässigkeit*
profitability	*Rentabilität*
payment habits	*Zahlungsgewohnheiten*
Do you think it would be reasonable / justifiable / in order to allow them credit to a limit of …?	*Ist ein Kredit bis zu einer Höhe von … Ihrer Ansicht nach vertretbar?*
To what figure do you think we could safely go?	*Bis zu welchem Betrag könnten wir Ihrer Meinung nach ohne Risiko gehen?*
Does the company pay / settle its debts promptly / on time?	*Zahlt die Firma ihre Schulden prompt / pünktlich?*
How quickly does the company in question meet its financial obligations?	*Wie schnell kommt die in Frage stehende Firma ihren finanziellen Verpflichtungen nach?*
Any other / additional information you could give / provide / furnish / supply would be (much) appreciated.	*Für jede weitere Auskunft, die Sie uns geben könnten, wären wir Ihnen (äußerst) dankbar.*

5.3.3 Promising confidential treatment and offering reciprocate favours

Your reply will be treated as strictly confidential / in strict confidence / in absolute confidence.	*Ihre Auskunft wird streng vertraulich behandelt.*
We assure you that any information given will remain confidential.	*Wir versichern Ihnen, dass jede erteilte Auskunft vertraulich bleiben wird.*
You can rely on our treating your information with the utmost discretion.	*Sie können sich darauf verlassen, dass wir Ihre Auskunft mit größter Verschwiegenheit behandeln werden.*
If we can be of assistance to you in a similar case / If we can render you a similar service, please let us know.	*Wenn wir Ihnen einen ähnlichen Dienst erweisen können, so teilen Sie uns dies bitte mit.*

5.3.4 Favourable information

The firm about which you enquire / The firm mentioned in your enquiry / on the attached slip has an excellent reputation.	*Die von Ihnen / in Ihrer Anfrage / auf dem beigefügten Zettel genannte Firma genießt einen ausgezeichneten Ruf.*
They are old-established dealers who enjoy a good reputation / unlimited confidence.	*Es handelt sich um alteingesessene Händler, die einen guten Ruf / uneingeschränktes Vertrauen genießen.*
We are informed that the firm is sound / reliable / financially secure / well-known / well-respected.	*Uns wurde mitgeteilt, dass die Firma gesund / zuverlässig / finanziell sicher / bekannt / gut gelitten ist.*
They have considerable resources / considerable funds / a considerable amount of capital at their disposal.	*Die Firma verfügt über beträchtliche finanzielle Mittel / beträchtliches Kapital.*
They have always met their obligations promptly. / They have always been punctual in paying their bills. / They have always settled their accounts on time.	*Die Firma ist ihren Zahlungsverpflichtungen stets pünktlich nachgekommen.*
They usually take advantage of cash discounts.	*Die Firma zahlt meist unter Ausnutzung von Skonti.*
They have been regular customers of ours for the past five years.	*Seit fünf Jahren zählt die Firma zu unseren regulären Kunden.*
We think / believe that you will not be taking / running any risk in granting them credit up to …	*Unseres Erachtens können Sie der Firma risikolos einen Kredit bis zu … gewähren.*

5.3.5 Unfavourable information

In reply to your letter / fax / e-mail of …, we regret to inform you that we do not consider it advisable to grant any credit to the firm in question.	*In Beantwortung Ihres Briefes / Faxes / Ihrer E-Mail vom … müssen wir Ihnen leider mitteilen, dass es uns nicht ratsam erscheint, der betreffenden Firma Kredit zu gewähren.*
We have come to the conclusion that the company in question is financially unsound / in poor shape / insecure / badly run.	*Wir sind zu dem Schluss gekommen, dass die in Frage stehende Firma finanziell ungesund / in schlechtem Zustand / unsicher / schlecht geführt ist.*
We have gained the impression / learned from reliable sources that they are in financial difficulties.	*Wir haben den Eindruck gewonnen / aus zuverlässiger Quelle erfahren, dass die Firma mit finanziellen Schwierigkeiten zu kämpfen hat.*
It seems / It appears that the firm is undercapitalized / has insufficient capital / is running the risk of going bankrupt / has incurred heavy losses.	*Allem Anschein nach verfügt die Firma nicht über genügend Kapital / läuft die Firma Gefahr, in Konkurs zu gehen / hat die Firma schwere Verluste erlitten.*
In the past six months payments have been coming in slowly / there have been repeated delays in payment.	*Seit einem halben Jahr gehen die Zahlungen schleppend ein.*

5.3.6 Requesting confidential treatment

Please treat the above-mentioned details in strict confidence / strictly confidentially.	*Bitte behandeln Sie die obigen Einzelheiten streng vertraulich.*
This information is for your own use only and given without responsibility.	*Diese Auskunft ist nur für Sie bestimmt und wird ohne jede Haftung erteilt.*
Please note that any opinion expressed by us is based upon our own personal experience and must therefore be treated as strictly private and confidential.	*Bitte nehmen Sie zur Kenntnis, dass jede von uns geäußerte Meinung auf unserer persönlichen Erfahrung basiert und deshalb streng privat und vertraulich behandelt werden muss.*
May we point out that the information provided is given without any responsibility on our part / that we assume no obligation or liability for the views expressed.	*Dürfen wir darauf hinweisen, dass die gegebenen Informationen für uns unverbindlich sind / dass wir keine Verpflichtung oder Haftung für die geäußerten Ansichten übernehmen.*

5.4 Exercises

Please translate:

5.4.1 E-Mail der Schwarz KG, Leipzig (schwarz.ag@t-online.de) an Michael Davidson, Denver, Colorado (mick.davidson@com.us)

Die Firma Clinton & Baxter Inc. hat sich um unsere Vertretung in den USA beworben und Sie dabei als Referenz genannt. Bei Abschluss eines Vertretervertrages würden wir dieser Firma Konsignationswaren im Werte von ca. US$ 50.000,– zur Verfügung stellen.

Wir wären Ihnen deshalb für eine möglichst genaue Auskunft über die Vermögenslage dieser Firma und den Umfang ihrer Geschäfte dankbar. Vor allem würde uns interessieren zu erfahren, ob sie Ihrer Ansicht nach in der Lage ist, den amerikanischen Markt intensiv zu bearbeiten. Verfügt die Firma über gute Geschäftsverbindungen in ihrer Branche?

Wir versichern Ihnen, dass wir Ihre Auskunft als streng vertraulich behandeln werden und wären Ihnen äußerst dankbar, wenn wir Ihre E-Mail-Antwort bis zum ... erhalten könnten.

5.4.2 Fax von Theuringer AG, Ratingen (Fax-Nr.: +49-2102-201679) an Credit Enquiry Agency Paul Anderson, London (Fax-Nr.: +44-2076-35910)

Wir benötigen dringend eine Auskunft über die britische Gesellschaft Dynamic Ltd, 24–26 Slaidburg Crescent, Southport, Merseyside, PR9 9YF, UK. Uns interessieren besonders folgende Punkte:

- Ist die Firma für einen Warenwert von £ 50.000,00 bei einem Zahlungsziel von 90 Tagen gut?
- Entwicklung der Firma in den letzten 10 Jahren
- Was können Sie über die Vermögenslage der persönlich haftenden Gesellschafter und ihren Ruf sagen?

Wir bitten um schnellstmögliche Bearbeitung unserer Anfrage.

5.4.3 Fries & Co., Bremen, an Brown-Jefferson Plc, Sheffield

Die in Ihrem Schreiben vom 8. August erwähnte Firma ist uns seit längerer Zeit bekannt. Es handelt sich um ein gut fundiertes Außenhandelsunternehmen, das für eigene Rechnung und als Vertreter für einige namhafte ausländische Firmen tätig ist.

Die Inhaber sind tüchtige und zuverlässige Kaufleute, die über ausgedehnte Geschäftsverbindungen verfügen. Soweit uns bekannt ist, sind sie ihren Verbindlichkeiten stets prompt nachgekommen. Wir glauben daher, dass Sie den gewünschten Kredit ohne Bedenken gewähren können.

Wir bitten um vertrauliche Behandlung dieser Auskunft, für die wir keine Haftung übernehmen.

5.4.4 Bankauskunft

Ihre Anfrage vom: 1.04.20..
Wir erteilen Ihnen hiermit die gewünschte Auskunft, müssen jedoch ausdrücklich darauf hinweisen, dass diese streng vertraulich und ohne Verbindlichkeit für uns gegeben wird. Darüber hinaus müssen wir jede Haftpflicht für die aus der Verwertung unserer Angaben etwa entstehenden Folgen ablehnen.

Falls uns nachträglich Veränderungen in den Verhältnissen der betreffenden Firma bekannt werden sollten, können wir nur aufgrund einer neuen Anfrage darüber Auskunft geben.

Betrifft: Mirzner & Co. KG, München
Eintragung im HR: Nr. 38 298 Amtsgericht München
Gesellschafter: Georg Mirzner und Dipl.-Ing. Hans Buchberger (Komplementäre), 3 Kommanditisten
Geschäftsgegenstand: Herstellung von Formen für die Kunststoffindustrie

Die Geschäftsführung liegt in den Händen von Herrn Georg Mirzner (kaufmännischer Leiter) und Dipl.-Ing. Hans Buchberger (technischer Leiter). Herrn Mirzner haben wir als umsichtigen Kaufmann kennen gelernt. Herr Dipl.-Ing. Buchberger gilt als erstklassiger Fachmann auf seinem Gebiet. Wir stehen der Firma mit teilweise gesicherten mittleren Kontokorrent- und Diskontkrediten zur Verfügung, welche sehr beweglich in Anspruch genommen werden. Herr Mirzner verfügt über Grundbesitz in München, der normal belastet ist.

Nachteiliges ist uns in keiner Weise bekannt geworden. Die über uns gelaufenen Verbindlichkeiten wurden stets prompt erfüllt.

5.4.5 Hermann Koerner oHG, Bayreuth, an Lambert Engineering Company Ltd, Birmingham

Die in Ihrem Schreiben vom 20. Juni genannte Firma wurde erst vor 2 Jahren gegründet. Seit etwa 6 Monaten gehen die Zahlungen schleppend ein. Wir haben den Eindruck, dass die Firma mit großen Absatzschwierigkeiten zu kämpfen hat. Wie wir aus sicherer Quelle erfahren haben, hat die Firma jetzt eine Hypothek auf ihr Grundstück aufgenommen.

Unter diesen Umständen müssen wir Ihnen zur Vorsicht raten.

Wir bedauern, dass wir Ihnen keine bessere Auskunft erteilen können, und bitten um Verschwiegenheit.

Please draft letters, faxes or e-mails from the following particulars:

5.4.6 Geschäftsfall:

Sie arbeiten bei der Firma Breese & Co., Inselkammerstraße 82, 82008 Unterhaching, Fax-Nr.: +49 (89) 27 63 598, E-Mail-Adresse: breese.partner@hausbau.de, und erhalten von der Knight Incorporated, 2043 Airport Parkway, Cheyenne, WY 82001, USA, Fax-Nr.: +1 (307) 5 34 15 50, E-Mail-Adresse: knight.inc@preston.us, eine Bitte um Auskunft über die deutsche Gesellschaft Brockmann & Clasen in München, die Sie als Referenz angegeben hatte.

Aufgabe: Beantworten Sie diese Anfrage unter Berücksichtigung folgender Punkte:

- Brockmann & Clasen sind ein gut eingeführtes Export- und Import-Unternehmen
- Sie stehen seit ca. 5 Jahren mit dieser Firma in Geschäftsverbindung
- In dieser Zeit hat die Firma Ihnen regelmäßig Aufträge erteilt
- Zahlung erfolgte stets pünktlich
- Ihres Wissens ist die finanzielle Lage des Unternehmens in jeder Hinsicht zufriedenstellend
- Kreditrahmen in Höhe von US$ 35.000 Ihrer Meinung nach kein Problem
- Hinweis darauf, dass für diese Auskunft keine Haftung übernommen wird.

5.4.7 **Geschäftsfall:**

Die Handelsauskunftei Müngerer & Wasmer, Linienstraße 30, 10115 Berlin, Fax-Nr.: +49 (30) 3 47 98 51, E-Mail-Adresse: info@müngerer.wasmer.de, erhält von der Cranston Commercial Company Inc., 600 Ala Moana Blvd, 7-400 Honolulu, HI 95814, Fax-Nr.: +1 (8 08) 5 99 38 94, E-Mail-Adresse: cranston.inc@honululu.us, eine Anfrage über das deutsche Unternehmen Robel & Co. GmbH, Berlin.

Aufgabe: Beantworten Sie diese Anfrage wie folgt:

- Die Robel & Co. GmbH wurde 1990 als oHG gegründet und 5 Jahre später in eine GmbH umgewandelt
- 1997 übernahm der Gründer; Caspar Robel, sämtliche GmbH-Anteile
- Bis zu seinem Tode im Jahre 2001 hatte das Unternehmen einen ausgezeichneten Ruf
- Geschäftsführung ging dann auf seinen Sohn über, Oswald Robel
- Verhältnisse haben sich seitdem spürbar verschlechtert
- Dringend erforderliche Neuinvestitionen können wegen des Mangels an liquiden Mitteln nicht vorgenommen werden
- Lieferanten klagen über schleppenden Zahlungseingang
- Bei Aufträgen im fünfstelligen Bereich Vorsicht geboten.

6. Delivery

Execution of orders; invoices, statements, debit and credit notes

6.1 Introduction

Execution of orders. The seller executes the buyer's order by delivering the goods according to the terms of the contract (in the case of export orders see Incoterms under 2.3.3).

Before delivery can be made, the goods have to be carefully packed. Adequate packing is of particular importance in the case of overseas shipments. To make sure that the shipment is properly routed, the packages are provided with distinctive marks. Caution marks are usually added. Both the buyer's packing and marking instructions and the regulations of the importing country have to be strictly complied with. Very often environmental protection issues are also involved so that official rules and regulations may have to be adhered to.

Unless it has been agreed that the buyer is to collect the goods, the seller has to make arrangements for transport. For this purpose, use is made of the services of forwarding agents or carriers. Small packages are sent by parcel post. To protect the goods from the risk of loss or damage in transit, insurance is effected by the seller and/or the buyer.

After despatch (dispatch) of the goods, the seller sends the buyer or forwarding agents an advice note (*despatch advice, shipping advice*) or informs them orally. Depending on the terms of payment, the invoice and the other documents (bill of lading, certificate of origin, insurance policy or certificate, customs declaration, etc) are sent straight to the buyer or lodged with the exporter's bank for collection; they may also have to be presented to the bank which has advised or confirmed a documentary letter of credit opened by the importer's bank.

Buyers may request sellers to notify them when the goods are ready for despatch or to send them *progress reports* from time to time, informing them of the progress made in executing their orders.

Invoices. Invoices (*or:* bills[1]) are usually prepared on special invoice forms (*AE* billheads). An export invoice should contain the following details:

- Buyer's name and address
- Date and number of invoice
- Date and number of order

[1] The words *invoice* and *bill* are often interchangeable. *Bill* is the broader term; it is defined as "an itemized account that states the separate costs of goods sold, services rendered, or work done" (*Webster's Third New International Dictionary*). The term *invoice* is applied mainly to accounts relating to goods.

- Quantity and description of the goods; number of packages, weight, shipping marks
- Unit price and extension; deductions and additional charges (if any); total invoice amount
- Miscellaneous details, such as the method of transport, terms of payment, etc.

In this connection, the *pro forma invoice* should also be mentioned. A pro forma invoice may serve as a quotation or a request for payment in advance; it is also used when goods are sent on approval or consigned to an agent for sale. Free samples sent to a foreign customer may have to be accompanied by a pro forma invoice, and the foreign customer may need a pro forma invoice for presentation to the import control authorities when applying for an import licence.

Statements of account. A supplier who maintains an account for a customer will send the customer monthly or quarterly statements of account. The statement is, in effect, a copy of the customer's account since it was last balanced. It shows the balance at the beginning of the period, all invoices rendered and payments received during the period (including debit and credit notes, if any), and the balance at the end of the period. Statements also enable buyers to check their seller's entries against their own records; they also serve as a reminder that money is still owing.

Debit and credit notes. Debit and credit notes (AE debit and credit memoranda, debit and credit memos) are exchanged between two firms when, for example, faulty goods are returned by the customer, or an error or omission in an invoice or statement has to be corrected. When a debit note has been received and found correct, it is acknowledged by a credit note, and vice versa.

6.2 Model correspondence

6.2.1 Manufacturer advises exporter of completion of order

e-mail

Mail from: morgan.shuttle@nwu.uk

to: schreiter.export@com.de **cc:**

Subject: Your order for engraving machine EX 15

Attachment:

Dear Schreiter Export,

This is to advise you that the a. m. machine you ordered on 12 May for an overseas customer will be ready in about a fortnight.

We would therefore be glad to receive your packing and marking instructions. Please also inform us whether measurements, gross weights and net weights are to be stencilled on the cases.

We will let you have the exact date of completion within the next 7 days and would ask you to collect the consignment at our works within one week of this date, as we are short of storage space.

Regards,
Peter Richardson
Sales Department

6.2.2 Despatch advice

FAO: Herrn Jakob Reichert
Schreiber & Söhne GmbH
Lyoner Str. 50
69528 Frankfurt am Main

Fax No.: +49 (69) 45 36 095

From: Jenny Kellogg
Barings & Tangler plc
5 Ashburn Gardens
South Kensington
London SW7 4DG

Number of Pages: 2

Date: 23 October 20..

Subject: Your order No 247 KLB

Dear Jakob

This is to inform you that the above order has today been handed over to our forwarding agents, Williams & Sons (Forwarding) Ltd, for carriage to Frankfurt by road.

As attachment we enclose a copy of the commercial invoice. The original has been sent to you under separate cover. The necessary documents will accompany the consignment.

We still need your turnover tax identification number. Please advise us by fax or e-mail.

We trust the goods will reach you in good condition.

Kind regards

Jenny Kellogg

Attachment: commercial invoice

6.2.3 Despatch advice

Dear Sir or Madam

We are pleased to inform you that the optical instruments have today been picked up by our forwarding agents, CargoTrans Ltd, and will be sent to you CIP Munich Airport on British Airways Flight No. BA 5311 on 23 February. The instruments have been packed according to your instructions.

The required documents (airway bill, commercial invoice, packing list, insurance certificate) accompany the goods.

Please confirm the receipt of the goods.

Yours faithfully

6.2.4 Shipping advice

Dear Sirs

Your order no 177, dated 17th October

This is to advise you that the above-mentioned order was shipped on board the vessel "Ubana" from London to Mombasa on 25th November.

We are pleased to hand you enclosed copy of commercial invoice amounting to ... as well as non-negotiable copy of the bill of lading.

The original shipping documents (commercial invoice in triplicate, full set of clean on-board bills of lading, certificate of insurance and clean report of findings) have been presented to our bankers for collection through Barclays Bank International, Nairobi, Kenya, on a sight draft basis.

We will be glad to hear that the goods have arrived safely and in good order.

Yours faithfully

Encs(2)

6.2.5 Despatch advice – bill of exchange drawn

Dear Sirs

We are pleased to inform you that your order of 10th February has today been despatched by rail.

As agreed, we have drawn on you for the amount of our invoice at one month.
We enclose the draft, which please furnish with your acceptance and return to us.

Yours faithfully

Enc

6.2.6 Covering letter for sending statement of account

Dear Madam / Sir

We enclose Statement of Account for the first quarter of 20.., which shows a balance of £2,444.47 in our favour.

Will you please let us have your cheque for this amount after verification.

Yours faithfully

Enc

6.2.7 Apology for sending erroneous debit note

Dear Madam / Sir

We have received your letter rejecting the debit note for the amount of €240.50 which we sent you by mistake.

We have cancelled the corresponding entry in our books.

Please accept our apologies.

Yours faithfully

6.2.8 Invoice

MACMILLAN
Macmillan Distribution Ltd

Order & Payments To:
MACMILLAN DISTRIBUTION LIMITED
HOUNDMILLS, BASINGSTOKE,
HANTS, RG21 6XS, ENGLAND
Giro No. – 206 4057
Cables – PUBLISH BASINGSTOKE
Telex – 858493

Telephone – (01256) 329242
Fax (Home) – (01256) 812521/812558
Fax (Export) – (01256) 842084
Bank – NATIONAL WESTMINSTER
Code – 60-02-49
Account No. – 47301759
E-mail:-mdl@macmillan.co.uk

INVOICE
Inside Copy Swansea

NUMBER	56738080
DATE & TAX POINT	16-10-..
PICK LIST	69992/001 – ISX
PAGE NO.	2

021

PLEASE REMIT TO THE ABOVE ADDRESS

CHARGE TO
MAX HUEBER VERLAG
(MHELT STERLING A/C)
MAX HUEBER STRASSE 4
ISMANING BEI
MUNICH, D-85737
GERMANY D-85737, MU
Vat Number – DE1327004 7

ALWAYS QUOTE INVOICE No. AND RAISE QUERIES IMMEDIATELY

DESPATCHED TO
MAX HUEBER VERLAG
(MHELT STERLING A/C)
MAX HUEBER STRASSE 4
ISMANING BEI
MUNICH, D-85737
GERMANY D-85737, MU

Publisher Codes:

BL	Bloomsbury
FA	Faber and Faber
FR	W H Freeman
GU	Guiness World Records Ltd
KCH	Kingfisher, Chambers, Harrap
PM	Pan Macmillan
MH	Macmillan Heinemann ELT
MR	Macmillan Reference
PA	Palgrave
TS	Salamander Ltd
WF	W. Foulsham & Co Ltd
WLK	Walker Books
OTH	Others

CUSTOMER INFORMATION:-

ACCOUNT NO.	751160008
CONTACT NAME	MARGARET BURN
DIRECT TEL.NO. (DDI)	+44 01256 302814
PREFERRED DAY	Not Applicable
CARRIER/ROUTE	05 01
DESCRIPTION	ACTI. GERMAN
VAT NO.	GB 199 4406 21

SEE REVERSE FOR TERMS & CONDITIONS OF SUPPLY AND FOR NET BOOK AGREEMENT

PRINTED BOOKS UNLESS OTHERWISE STATED

INTERNAL USE ONLY	ORDER REF.	QTY	ISBN	ED	PUB	TITLE	AUTHOR	TYP	NET	PRICE DISC %	TRADE	VALUE	VAT	SOU
7C2732 * 40	2533.00	200	0435272500	01	MH	Oliver Twist HGR Int	Tarner M	P		–	–	–	1	
7C2775* 20	2534.00	800	0435272373	01	MH	Pearl The HGR Int 2nd Edn	STEINBECK JOHN	P		–	–	–	1	
7D1512* 40	2536.00	200	0435272411	01	MH	Sign Of Four HGR Int 2nd Edn	Collins A	P		–	–	–	1	
7C2633* 70	2540.00	150	0435272454	01	MH	Woman Who Disappear HGR Int 2nd Edn	Prowse P	P		–	–	–	1	
7C2641*	2543.00	200	0435272624	01	MH	Creative Impulse HGR Upp 2nd Edn	Milne J	P		–	–	–	1	
7D1122* 5	2592.00	80	043526401X	01	MH	English Sketches 1 Cass Pack	Doug Case Ken Wilson	S		–	–	–		
		** The above pack consists of the following compone component values are provided for information.**												
		1 x	0435263943	01	MH	English Sketches 1							1	
		1 x	0435263951	01	MH	English Sketches 1 Cassette							2	
7C2722*	2593.00	80	0435264036	01	MH	English Sketches 2 Cass Pack	Doug Case Ken Wilson	S		–	–	–		
		** The above pack consists of the following compone component values are provided for information.**								–	–	–		
		1 x	0435263978	01	MH	English Sketches 2							1	
		1 x	0435263986	01	MH	English Sketches 2 Cassette							2	
7A0312 27	2596.02	27	0435244884	01	MH	Pract Tests For First Cert Cass	Linton Stone			–	–	–	2	
8B1592*	2602.02		0435288393	01	MH	Hein Toefl Prep Course Pack 2nd Ed	DuffyMahnke Flamm	S		–	–	–		
	The above pack consists of the following compone component values are provided for information.**													
7D1164		1 x	0435288407	01	MH	Hein Toefl Prep Course +key 2nd Ed				–	–	–	1	
7A0271		1 x	0435288415	01	MH	Hein Toefl Prep Course Cass 2nd (x3				–	–	–	2	

BOOKS	
LINES	
WEIGHT	
CARTONS	
INV. DISTR.	402000

KEYED	MWB
BATCH	21506/001
BRICK	0330
TYPE	A INV
SPOOL FILE NAME	

From 1st September Palgrave will be the new name of Macmillan Press and St Martin's Press, Scholarly and Reference
www. palgrave.com

Items Zero Rated Unless Otherwise Stated

TOTAL	–
SUNDRIES	–
VAT	–
INVOICE TOTAL	–

http://www.macmillan-mdl.co.uk

Palgrave – Macmillan's global academic publishing

6.2.9 Statement of account

MACMILLAN
Macmillan Distribution Ltd

STATEMENT

MACMILLAN DISTRIBUTION LTD.
BRUNEL ROAD, BASINGSTOKE
HAMPSHIRE, RG21 6XS ENGLAND

BANKERS
NATIONAL WESTMINSTER PLC
NEW TOWN CENTRE BRANCH
BASINGSTOKE HANTS
CODE 60-02-49
ACCOUNT 47301759
GIRO No. 206 4057

ON BEHALF OF:
Chambers
Children's Books
Macmillan Direct Ltd
Harrap Publishers Ltd
Kibworth Books
Kingfisher
Larousse
Macmillan London
Palgrave
Pan Macmillan
Sidgworth & Jackson
Sunburst Books
W. Foulsham

Attn. DR. KURT BANGERT
MAX HUEBER VERLAG
(MHELT STERLING A/C)
MAX HUEBER STRASSE 4
ISMANING BEI
MUNICH; D-85737
GERMANY D-85737, MU

PAGE No.	1
MONTH ENDING	30-APR- ..
AGREED LEVEL OF RETURNS AS %	Not Applicable
CURRENT % MOVING ANNUAL TURNOVER	Not Applicable

CONTACT NAME.	Ross McLaughlan
DIRECT TEL NO (DDI)	01256 302950

DATE	TRANSACTION	OUR REF.	YOUR REF(if known)	PRE REF.	DEBIT	CREDIT
21-DEC-..	CREDIT	412211452	21097	3840482		---
06-OCT-..	INVOICE	4788261			---	
06-JAN-..	CREDIT	50216352	16099	46552669		---
23-FEB-..	INVOICE	51245316	02.2567		---	
03-JAN-..	INVOICE	5833756X		58012087	---	
25-JAN-..	INVOICE	58746352			---	
01-FEB-..	INVOICE	589764531			---	
07-FEB-..	CREDIT	59078057	00.2856	58958505		---
16-FEB-..	INVOICE	593336472			---	
20-FEB-..	CREDIT	59376453	012501-5	5833756X		---
20-FEB-..	CREDIT	5397764X				---

TOTAL BALANCE

PLEASE QUOTE ACCOUNT No.
ON ALL CORRESPONDENCE

TEL:BASINGSTOKE (01256) 329242
FAX: (01256) 363223 (HOME ACCOUNTS)
FAX: +44 1256 363223 (EXPORT ACCOUNTS)
CABLES: -PUBLISH BASINGSTOKE
TELEX:-858493

REMITTANCE ADVICE

MACMILLAN DISTRIBUTION LTD.
BRUNEL ROAD, BASINGSTOKE
HAMPSHIRE, RG21 6XS ENGLAND

MAX HUEBER VERLAG
Payable 3 Months

30-April-..
PLEASE RETURN
THIS ADVICE
WITH PAYMENT

ACCOUNT No.	SECTION	PAGE No.
75118097	W5	1

APPLY TO	OUR REF.	AMOUNT	
DEC	412211452	STG	--- ---
OCT.. 4788261		STG	--- --- ---
JAN.. 50216352		STRG	--- ---
FEB.. 58976453		STG	--- ---
JAN.. 5833756X	---	STG	--- ---
JAN .. 58746352	---	STG	--- --- ---
FEB-..	589764531		---
FEB-..	59078057		---
FEB-..	593336472		---
FEB-..	59376453		---
FEB-..	5397764X		---

DUE THIS MONTH

PLEASE REMIT >>

HEREWITH REMITTANCE FOR

6.2.10 Credit note

MACMILLAN
Macmillan Distribution Ltd

Order & Payments To:
MACMILLAN DISTRIBUTION LIMITED
HOUNDMILLS, BASINGSTOKE,
HANTS, RG21 6XS, ENGLAND
Giro No. – 206 4057
Cables – PUBLISH BASINGSTOKE
Telex – 858493

Telephone – (01256) 329242
Fax (Home) – (01256) 812521/812558
Fax (Export) – (01256) 842084
Bank – NATIONAL WESTMINSTER
Code – 60-02-49
Account No. – 47301759
E-mail:-mdl@macmillan.co.uk

CREDIT NOTE

Post Swansea

NUMBER	59377720
DATE & TAX POINT	02-02-..
PICK LIST	00000/001 – CSX
PAGE NO.	1

PLEASE REMIT TO THE ABOVE ADDRESS

ALWAYS QUOTE INVOICE No. AND RAISE QUERIES IMMEDIATELY

001

CHARGE TO
MAX HUEBER VERLAG
(MHELT STERLING A/C)
MAX HUEBER STRASSE 4
ISMANING BEI
MUNICH, D-85737
GERMANY D-85737, MU
Vat Number – DE1327004 7

DESPATCHED TO
MAX HUEBER VERLAG
(MHELT STERLING A/C)
MAX HUEBER STRASSE 4
ISMANING BEI
MUNICH, D-85737
GERMANY D-85737, MU

Publisher Codes:

BL	Bloomsbury
FA	Faber and Faber
FR	W H Freeman
GU	Guiness World Records Ltc
KCH	Kingfisher, Chambers, Harrap
PM	Pan Macmillan
MH	Macmillan Heinemann ELT
MC	Macmillan Caribbean
MI	Macmillan Education
MP	Other Macmillan
PA	Palgrave
TS	Salamander/Robson
WF	W. Foulsham & Co Ltd
WLK	Walker Books
OTH	Others

CUSTOMER INFORMATION:-

ACCOUNT NO.	751160008
CONTACT NAME	MARGARET BURN
DIRECT TEL.NO. (DDI)	+44 01256 302814
PREFERRED DAY	Not Applicable
CARRIER/ROUTE	
DESCRIPTION	
VAT NO.	GB 199 4406 21

SEE REVERSE FOR TERMS & CONDITIONS OF SUPPLY AND FOR NET BOOK AGREEMENT

PRINTED BOOKS UNLESS OTHERWISE STATED

INTERNAL USE ONLY	ORDER REF.	QTY	ISBN	ED	PUB	TITLE	AUTHOR	TYP	NET	PRICE DISC %	TRADE	VALUE	VAT	SOU
						Miscellaneous Credit								
						Damaged in transit Invoice 57697256	02-JAN-..			–	–	–	–	
7D2674* 10	00.2709	25	0435245201	01	MH	Proficiency Passkey SB	Nick Kenny	P						
						Supplied in error Invoice 57697256	02-JAN-..							
						WRONG BOOKS PACKED								
7C2832 23	01.2709	23	0333755081	01	MH	Proficiency Passkey WB With Key	Kenny Nick	P		–	–	–	–	
						PRICE ANALYSIS								
						23@.. 25@..								

BOOKS	48	**KEYED**	MWB
LINES	2	**BATCH**	99780/001
WEIGHT	22.285	**BRICK**	0330
CARTONS		**TYPE**	A CRRW
INV. DISTR.	402000	**SPOOL FILE NAME**	XCCCXA0000BI

From 1st September Palgrave will be the new name of Macmillan Press and St Martin's Press, Scholarly and Reference

www. palgrave.com

Items Zero Rated Unless Otherwise Stated

TOTAL	–
SUNDRIES	–
VAT	–
INVOICE TOTAL	–

http://www.macmillan-mdl.co.uk

Palgrave – Macmillan's global academic publishing

6.2.11 Debit note

MACMILLAN
Macmillan Distribution Ltd

Order & Payments To:
MACMILLAN DISTRIBUTION LIMITED
HOUNDMILLS, BASINGSTOKE,
HANTS, RG21 6XS, ENGLAND
Giro No. – 206 4057
Cables – PUBLISH BASINGSTOKE
Telex – 858493

Telephone – (01256) 329242
Fax (Home) – (01256) 812521/812558
Fax (Export) – (01256) 842084
Bank – NATIONAL WESTMINSTER
Code – 60-02-49
Account No. – 47301759
E-mail:-mdl@macmillan.co.uk

DEBIT NOTE

NUMBER	59377720
DATE & TAX POINT	02-02-..
PICK LIST	00000/001 – CSX
PAGE NO.	1

PLEASE REMIT TO THE ABOVE ADDRESS

ALWAYS QUOTE INVOICE No. AND RAISE QUERIES IMMEDIATELY

001

CHARGE TO
MAX HUEBER VERLAG
(MHELT STERLING A/C)
MAX HUEBER STRASSE 4
ISMANING BEI
MUNICH, D-85737
GERMANY D-85737, MU
Vat Number – DE1327004 7

DESPATCHED TO
MAX HUEBER VERLAG
(MHELT STERLING A/C)
MAX HUEBER STRASSE 4
ISMANING BEI
MUNICH, D-85737
GERMANY D-85737, MU

Publisher Codes:

BL	Bloomsbury
FA	Faber and Faber
FR	W H Freeman
GU	Guiness World Records Ltd
KCH	Kingfisher, Chambers, Harrap
PM	Pan Macmillan
MH	Macmillan Heinemann ELT
MC	Macmillan Caribbean
MI	Macmillan Education
MP	Other Macmillan
PA	Palgrave
TS	Salamander/Robson
WF	W. Foulsham & Co Ltd
WLK	Walker Books
OTH	Others

CUSTOMER INFORMATION:-

ACCOUNT NO.	751160008
CONTACT NAME	MARGARET BURN
DIRECT TEL.NO. (DDI)	+44 01256 302814
PREFERRED DAY	Not Applicable
CARRIER/ROUTE	
DESCRIPTION	
VAT NO.	GB 199 4406 21

SEE REVERSE FOR TERMS & CONDITIONS OF SUPPLY AND FOR NET BOOK AGREEMENT

PRINTED BOOKS UNLESS OTHERWISE STATED

INTERNAL USE ONLY	ORDER REF.	QTY	ISBN	ED	PUB	TITLE	AUTHOR	TYP	NET	PRICE DISC %	TRADE	VALUE	VAT	SOU
–	–	–	–			–	–			–	–	–		–
–	–	–	–			–	–			–	–	–		–

BOOKS	
LINES	
WEIGHT	
CARTONS	
INV. DISTR.	

KEYED	
BATCH	
BRICK	
TYPE	
SPOOL FILE NAME	

From 1st September Palgrave will be the new name of Macmillan Press and St Martin's Press, Scholarly and Reference

www. palgrave.com

Items Zero Rated Unless Otherwise Stated

TOTAL	
SUNDRIES	–
VAT	
INVOICE TOTAL	–

http://www.macmillan-mdl.co.uk

Palgrave – Macmillan's global academic publishing

6.3 Terms and phrases

6.3.1 Advising despatch

We are pleased to advise you that your order of ... has been despatched by rail / road / sea / air this morning.	*Wir freuen uns, Ihnen mitzuteilen, dass die Waren laut Ihrem Auftrag vom ... heute Morgen per Schiene / Straße / auf dem See- / Luftweg versandt wurden.*
This is to advise / inform you that the goods are now ready for collection at our warehouse / plant / premises in ...	*Hiermit teilen wir Ihnen mit, dass die Waren jetzt in unserem Lager / Werk / in unseren Geschäftsräumen in ... abholbereit sind.*
The goods are now ready for despatch. Please let us have your forwarding instructions.	*Die Waren sind nun versandbereit. Bitte geben Sie uns Ihre Versandanweisungen bekannt.*
S. S. "Eastern Trader" is scheduled / due to arrive in Singapore on ...	*Der Dampfer „Eastern Trader" soll am ... in Singapur eintreffen.*
The goods have been sent by train / lorry / ship / plane and we hope the consignment will arrive safely / reach you in good condition.	*Die Waren sind per Eisenbahn / Lkw / Schiff / Flugzeug versandt worden und wir hoffen, dass die Sendung wohlbehalten / in gutem Zustand bei Ihnen eintrifft.*
The goods have been loaded on board MV "Mary Ann" which is due to set sail for Rio de Janeiro on ...	*Die Waren wurden an Bord der MV „Mary Ann" verladen, die am ... nach Rio de Janeiro ausläuft.*

6.3.2 Sending invoice; requesting payment

We enclose invoice in duplicate / triplicate / 2-fold / 3-fold.	*Wir legen die Rechnung in 2-facher / 3-facher Ausfertigung bei.*
You will find enclosed our pro forma invoice, on settlement of which your order will be despatched without delay.	*Anbei finden Sie unsere Proforma-Rechnung. Der Versand der Waren erfolgt unverzüglich nach Eingang der Zahlung.*
As soon as we have received your cheque / remittance for ..., the goods will be sent to you immediately.	*Sobald wir Ihren Scheck / Ihre Überweisung für ... erhalten haben, werden Ihnen die Waren zugesandt.*
The consignment will be shipped as soon as the documentary letter of credit in our favour has been opened.	*Sobald das Dokumentenakkreditiv zu unseren Gunsten eröffnet worden ist, wird die Sendung verschifft / versandt.*
A copy of our invoice is enclosed; the original will be released / surrendered to you by the Mercantile Bank together with the other documents on payment of our draft for ...	*Rechnungskopie liegt bei. Das Original wird Ihnen zusammen mit den anderen Dokumenten von der Mercantile Bank bei Zahlung unserer Tratte über ... ausgehändigt.*

Please remit the invoice amount by bank draft, as arranged.	*Wir bitten um Zahlung des Rechnungsbetrages durch Bankscheck, wie vereinbart.*
Please transfer the invoice amount to our account with either of the following banks: ...	*Bitte überweisen Sie den Rechnungsbetrag auf unser Konto bei einer der beiden nachstehend aufgeführten Banken: ...*
We have drawn on you for the invoice amount at 60/90 d/s (days' sight) and enclose our draft for your acceptance.	*Wir haben einen 60/90-Tage Sichtwechsel auf Sie gezogen, den wir zum Akzept beifügen.*

6.3.3 Notations and declarations on invoices; reference to other documents

Please advise us if the goods are not delivered within 14 days from date of despatch, as otherwise the carrier may refuse payment for loss.	*Bitte benachrichtigen Sie uns, wenn die Auslieferung der Waren nicht innerhalb von 14 Tagen nach Versanddatum erfolgt, da der Frachtführer sonst bei Verlust die Schadenersatzleistung verweigern könnte.*
All unearned discounts will be charged back.	*Bei unberechtigtem Skontoabzug erfolgt Rückbelastung.*
Cardboard boxes are not returnable.	*Pappkartons können nicht zurückgegeben werden.*
Please return empties, carriage forward, to our factory.	*Bitte senden Sie das Leergut unfrei an unsere Fabrik zurück.*
Packing containers, if returned in good condition and carriage paid, will be credited to your account in full.	*Bei frachtfreier Rücksendung der Versandbehälter in gutem Zustand wird der volle dafür in Rechnung gestellte Betrag Ihrem Konto gutgeschrieben.*
Complaints will be considered only if made within 7 days from receipt of goods.	*Reklamationen können nur berücksichtigt werden, wenn sie innerhalb von 7 Tagen nach Erhalt der Waren erfolgen.*
In accordance with the conditions of our documentary letter of credit the following documents are enclosed:	*In Übereinstimmung mit den Bedingungen unseres Dokumentenakkreditivs sind folgende Dokumente beigefügt:*
complete set of clean, on-board bills of lading in triplicate	*voller Satz reiner Bordkonnossemente in dreifacher Ausfertigung*
2 originals of the commercial invoice	*2 Originale der Handelsfaktura*
customs declaration 3-fold	*Zollerklärung in dreifacher Ausfertigung*
certificate of origin	*Ursprungszeugnis*
The documents mentioned above have been sent to you by separate mail.	*Die oben genannten Dokumente sind mit separater Post an Sie abgegangen.*

6.3.4 Packaging

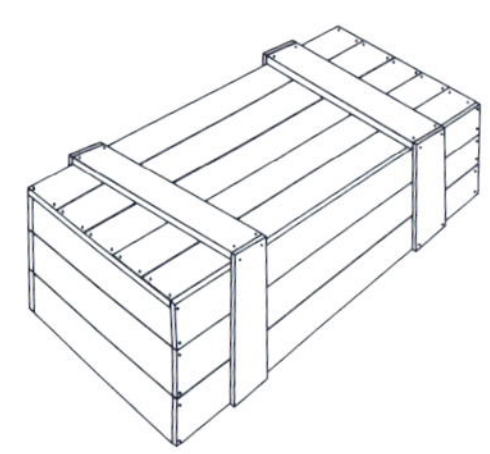

Wooden case, wooden box | *Holzkiste*

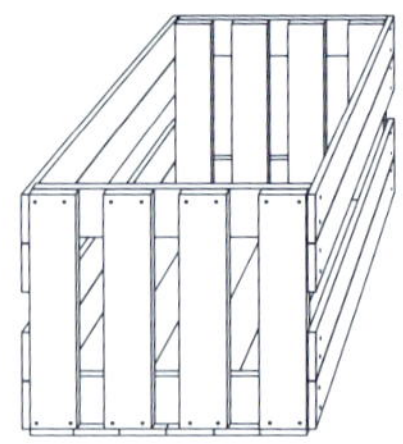

Crate | *Lattenkiste*

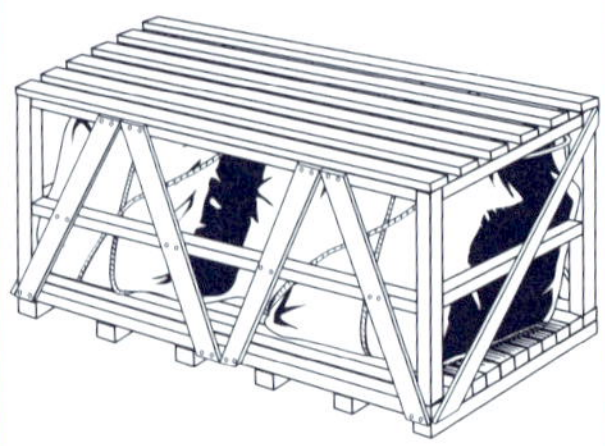

Crate | *Holzverschlag, Lattenverschlag*

Chest | *Teekiste*

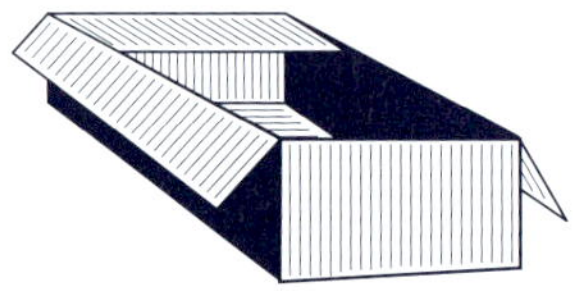

Cardboard box | *Pappkarton*

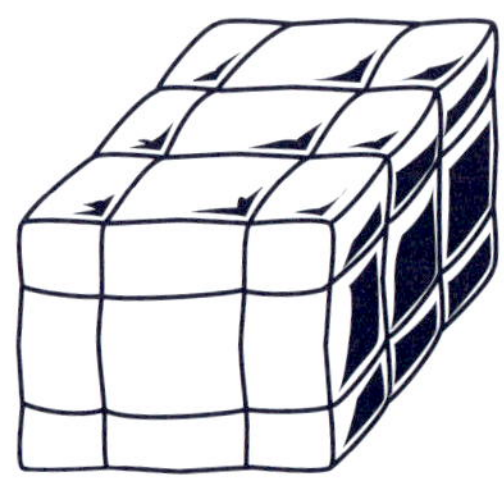

Bale | *Ballen*

Bag, sack | *Sack*

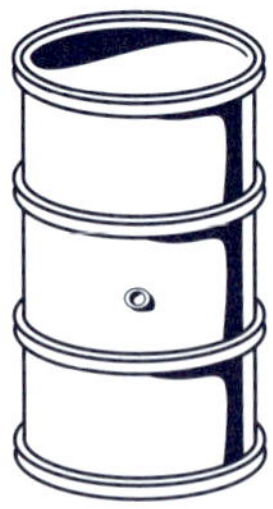

Drum | *Trommel*

Barrel | *Fass*

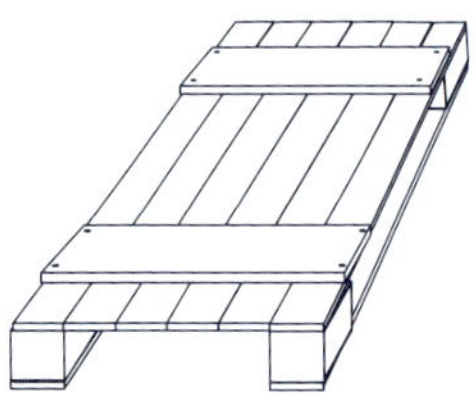

Pallet | *Palette*

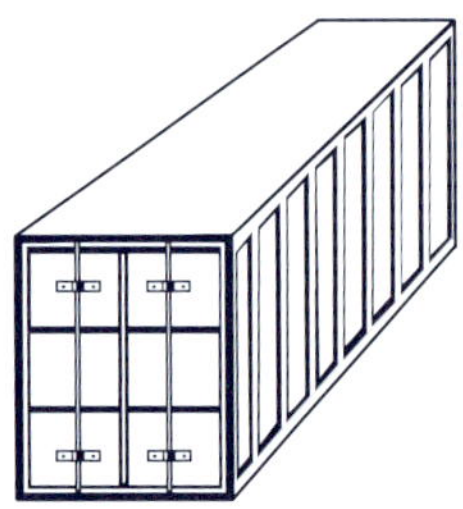

Container

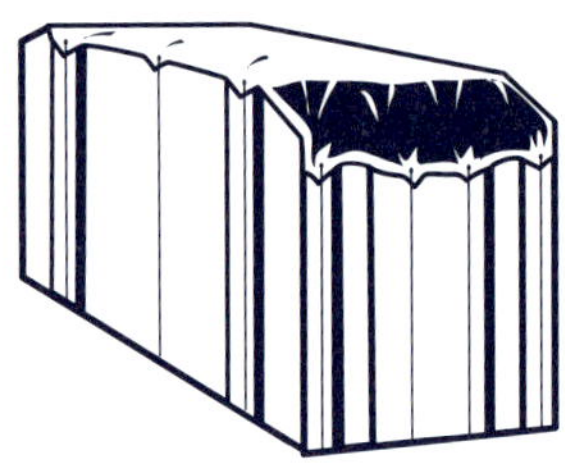

Igloo | *Iglu*

fibreboard (fiberboard) case	*Hartpappekiste, Panzerkarton*
carton	*Pappschachtel*
folding carton	*Faltschachtel*
paperboard, cardboard	*Pappe*
corrugated cardboard	*Wellpappe*
jute bag	*Jutesack*
5-ply paper bag	*fünffacher Papiersack*
carboy, demijohn	*Korbflasche*
metal band, steel band	*Metallband, Stahlband*
plastic band	*Kunststoffband*
steel strapping	*Stahlbandumreifung*
case with steel strapping, steel-strapped case, case bound with steel bands	*Kiste mit Stahlbandumreifung*
wrapping paper, kraft paper	*Packpapier*
waxed paper	*Wachspapier*
plastic film, plastic foil	*Kunststoff-Folie*
metal foil	*Metallfolie*
polystyrene (styrofoam) mo(u)ldings	*Styropor-Formteile*
cushioning material	*Füllmaterial*
desiccant	*Trockenmittel*
water-proof / water-resistant material	*wasserdichtes / wasserfestes Material*
recyclable / non-recyclable plastic	*recyclebarer / nicht recyclebarer Kunststoff*
environment-friendly (non-polluting) material	*umweltfreundliches Material*
bio-degradable packing	*biologisch abbaubare Verpackung*
disposable bag	*Wegwerftasche*

6.3.5 Marking

Shipping marks:

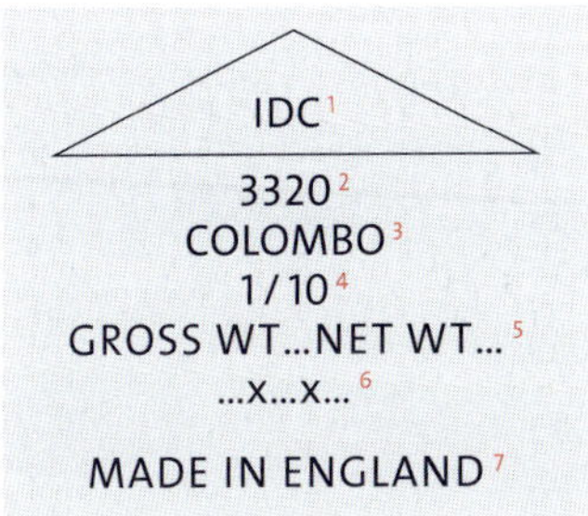

1	Consignee's mark	*Kennmarke des Empfängers*
2	Order number	*Auftragsnummer*
3	Port of destination	*Bestimmungshafen*
4	Number of package and total number of packages	*Nummer des Kollos und Gesamtzahl der Kolli*
5	Weight	*Gewicht*
6	Dimensions	*Abmessungen*
7	Mark of origin	*Ursprungsbezeichnung*

Caution marks:

Poison | *Gift*

Inflammable liquid | *Entzündbare Flüssigkeit*

Radioactive | *Radioaktive Substanz*

Glass – fragile | *Vorsicht Glas – zerbrechlich*

Keep dry | *Vor Nässe schützen*

This side up | *Oben*

Store away from heat | *Vor Hitze schützen*

Keep in cool place | *Kühl aufbewahren*

Use no hooks | *Nicht haken*

6.4 Exercises

Please translate:

6.4.1 E-Mail der Porzellanmanufaktur Gosser, Selb (Oberpfalz) (gosser.selb@t-online.de) an Bultman Whittaker Inc., 655 Clairmont Avenue, Providence, RI 02907, USA (bultman.whittaker@city.ac.us)

Wie wir Ihnen bereits gemailt haben, haben wir inzwischen zwei weitere Container von Selb an Ihre Adresse geschickt. Die entsprechenden Rechnungen vom 20. und 23. Juni sind mit separater Post an Sie unterwegs. Außerdem erhalten Sie als Attachment unsere Lastschriftanzeige über €654,33 für die im Zusammenhang mit Container Nr. USLU 625 745-5 angefallenen besonderen Verpackungskosten.

Bitte geben Sie uns Nachricht, sobald die Container eintreffen. Wir wünschen guten Empfang.

6.4.2 Fax der Martin Katzensteiner GmbH, Salzburg (Fax-Nr.: +43-662-620428) an Asian Development Inc., Manila (Fax-Nr.: +63-2-6363540)

Wir beziehen uns auf Ihren Auftrag Nr. 7789 vom 07.04. und teilen Ihnen mit, dass die bestellten Geräte mit M.S. „Barbara" verladen worden sind, das morgen aus Hamburg ausläuft.

Über Ihre Bank erhalten Sie unsere Handelsrechnung, über deren Betrag wir auf Sie per 90 Tage Sicht gezogen haben, sowie den Wechsel und die weiteren Versanddokumente (Konsulatsrechnung, Ursprungszeugnis, voller Satz reiner Bordkonnossemente, Versicherungspolice). Wir haben diese Unterlagen unserer Bank, der Salzburger Volksbank in Salzburg, übergeben.

Wir hoffen, dass die Maschine gut auf den Philippinen ankommt, und würden uns freuen, weitere Aufträge von Ihnen zu erhalten.

6.4.3 Vinespa GmbH, Mönchengladbach an Phillipp's Department Stores plc, Birmingham

Betr: Ihre Weinbestellung vom 17.11.20..

Vielen Dank für Ihre Bestellung für 110 Kartons à 12 Flaschen unseres Grauburgunders (*pinot gris*), Jahrgang (*vintage*) 20..

Wie Sie aus unserem Angebot ersehen, gelten unsere Exportpreise für die palettenweise Abnahme (*order by pallet*) mit je 50 Kartons pro Palette.

Da die von Ihnen bestellte Menge mehr als zwei, aber weniger als drei Paletten ergibt, schlagen wir vor, die Bestellmenge auf 150 Kartons zu erhöhen, und zwar mit einem Sonderrabatt von 3% bezogen auf die gesamte Menge.

Bei unseren Paletten handelt es sich um Euro-Paletten (*euro-pallets*), die entweder getauscht oder mit 8 Euros pro Stück in Rechnung gestellt werden. Falls getauscht werden soll, liefert Ihr Spediteur bei Abholung die entsprechende Menge an Leerpaletten bei uns ab.

Wir würden uns freuen, wenn Sie unser Angebot auf Erhöhung der Paletten annehmen würden, und sehen Ihrer Antwort mit Interesse entgegen.

Please draft letters, faxes or e-mails from the following particulars:

6.4.4 Geschäftsfall:

Sie arbeiten bei der Johann Hauser AG, Jessenstraße 23, 22767 Hamburg, Fax-Nr.: +49 (40) 38 97 34, E-Mail-Adresse: hauser.ag@mail.tele.de, und hatten von der Black & Sons Ltd, 35 Regent Street, London SW1Y 4LR, UK, Fax-Nr.: +44 (20) 845 43 72, E-Mail-Adresse: black.sons@worldwide.uk, einen Auftrag auf 500 Autositze der Marke „Thunderbird" erhalten.

Aufgabe: Senden Sie der englischen Firma eine Versandanzeige unter Berücksichtigung der folgenden Punkte:

- Dank für erhaltenen Auftrag
- Die Sendung wurde bereits heute der Bahn übergeben
- Beigefügt erhält der Kunde die Rechnung in Höhe von € 45.000,–
- Eine 3-Monats-Sichttratte über diesen Betrag ist ebenfalls beigefügt
- Bitte, diese zu akzeptieren und zurückzugeben
- Geeigneter Schlusssatz

6.4.5 Geschäftsfall:

Die Klimaanlagen-Herstellerfirma Ottmar Heisig GmbH, Rüsselsheimer Straße 75, 60326 Frankfurt/M, Fax-Nr.: +49 (69) 7 39 80 04, E-Mail-Adresse: klima.heisig@online.de, hatte von der indischen Firma Electrical Services Plc, 304 Ghandi Memorial Street, Bangalore 43 00 56, India, Fax-Nr.: +91 (80) 39 76 41, E-Mail-Adresse: electrical.plc@asiaweb.com, einen Auftrag für Klimaanlagen der Marke XZW.24 zum Preis von US$ 350.000,– erhalten.

Aufgabe: Schicken Sie eine Versandanzeige folgenden Inhalts:

- Die Klimaanlagen sind fertiggestellt und wurden gemäß Anweisung des Kunden verpackt
- Absendung per Luftfracht ab Flughafen Frankfurt bis Bangalore
- Voraussichtliches Abflugdatum: 3. Oktober 20..
- Lieferung: FCA Frankfurt
- Preis: US$ 350.000,– zahlbar mit unwiderruflichem, bestätigten Dokumentenakkreditiv
- Lieferung FCA Frankfurt
- Importlizenz Nr. 90 24 67 830
- Dokumente (Luftfrachtbrief, Handelsfaktura, Ursprungszeugnis) wurden der Bank bereits übergeben.

6.4.6 Geschäftsfall:

Die Firma Avus International AG, Zum Eisenhammer 5, 46049 Oberhausen, Fax-Nr.: +49 (2 08) 80 60 24, E-Mail-Adresse: info@avus-international.de, hatte der Sunrise Beverages Limited, P.O. Box 34 09 873, Glasgow G1 1XQ, UK, Fax-Nr.: +44 (1 41) 4 95 41 33, E-Mail-Adresse: sunrise@beverages.cfo.uk, telefonisch einen Auftrag auf 18.000 Flaschen Mineralwasser Marke „Mountain Well" à 0,5 l erteilt.

Aufgabe: Bestätigen Sie diesen Auftrag schriftlich und geben Sie folgende Anweisungen hinsichtlich der Verpackung und Versendung:

- Das Mineralwasser ist in blauen 0,5 Literflaschen gemäß beiliegendem Zeichnungsmuster abzufüllen
- Etiketten (*labels*) müssen in Deutsch und Englisch beschriftet und mit dem EAN-Code (*European Article Number*) versehen sein
- Sie müssen den „grünen Punkt" (*green dot*) aufweisen
- Kartons erhalten gesonderten EAN-Code gemäß beiliegender Vorlage und müssen ebenfalls den grünen Punkt tragen
- Die Lizenzgebühr für den grünen Punkt wird in Deutschland entrichtet
- Transport im Container.

7. Payment

7.1 Introduction

Acknowledging receipt of goods and making payment. Receipt of goods delivered is usually acknowledged by buyers only if they have been requested by sellers to do so. If payment is due immediately after receipt, the acknowledgement may at the same time serve as advice of payment. Before acknowledging receipt, however, buyers will examine their goods carefully; if they are not satisfied with them, they will send the sellers a complaint (*see Chapter 9*).

Before effecting payment, buyers carefully check sellers' invoices or statements of accounts and compare them with their own records. Should they discover any error or discrepancy, they will notify their sellers immediately. The matter is then investigated by the latter and, if it is found that the buyers are right, a correction is made.

A sum of money sent in any form to a person or firm at another place is called a *remittance*. (The word is also applied to the act of sending the money). Details regarding the invoice or statement being paid are given in a letter or on a printed form (*remittance advice*).

Companies which supply customers on a regular basis usually keep accounts for these customers. Payment is then effected by bank transfer, ie the supplier's and the customer's accounts are simply credited or debited and the corresponding credit and debit notes are exchanged.

Payment in foreign trade is usually effected by cheque (*AE* check), bank transfer (generally by *SWIFT* – the Society for Worldwide Interbank Financial Tele-Communication), bank draft, by bills of exchange (either documentary bills with documents attached or clean bills without documents), by international postal giro, international money order or by documentary letter of credit (the latter being the safest means of payment in export trade).

With the ever-increasing volume of financial transactions a new form of payment has become indispensable: *electronic banking*. Both retail and corporate customers can get a special programme installed on their computers which makes it possible for them to send order data direct to their bank by electronic data transfer. In this way they can obtain up-to-date information on their account balances and payment operations. They can also maintain accounts with different banks in different places, eg payment orders can be sent to banks online for further processing etc.

Export and import transactions involve the exchange of one currency for another. Instruments of payment (transfers, cheques, bank drafts, bills of exchange and travellers' cheques) denominated in foreign currencies are collectively known as *foreign exchange*. Foreign exchange (as well as foreign bank notes and coins) is bought and sold by banks. When one currency is converted into another, the current rate of exchange is applied.

Here again electronic banking can be useful. Special computer programmes keep customers informed on up-to-date exchange rates for many currencies.

Acknowledging receipt of payment. It is not necessary for the seller to acknowledge the buyer's remittance, unless the buyer has asked for a receipt. For many firms, however, such an acknowledgement is a welcome opportunity to promote goodwill and to solicit further business.

Errors, misunderstandings and other difficulties in connection with remittances have to be called to buyers' attention. For example, a buyer may have made an error in remitting, may have misunderstood the terms of payment, or may have forgotten to mention the invoice or invoices covered by the remittance. Sometimes customers take unearned discounts, ie discounts to which they are not entitled. Taking unearned discounts purposely ("discount piracy") is, of course, incompatible with sound business principles.

7.2 Model correspondence

7.2.1 Advising a supplier of the opening of a new account for making payments

e-mail

Mail from: banner.leitner@netcross.de
to: norton.jewels@jewels.co.uk **cc:**
Subject: Your invoice CBQR 934 of 2 Oct. 20.. for £12,500.00
Attachment:

Dear Norton Jewels Ltd

We are pleased to inform you that we have just opened a £-Sterling account with Midland Bank in London through which we will channel all payments to our UK suppliers in the future.

You will benefit from this arrangement by receiving your payments earlier and without the high charges for overseas transactions.

We are sure you will appreciate this improvement in our business relations.

Regards

Dr Wolfgang Brenner
Managing Director

7.2.2 Asking customer for bank account details

FAO: Ms Jeannette Grabenwirt
Oracle Software KG
Concorde Business Park 92
A-2320 Schwechat / Wien

Fax No.: +43 (810) 2 00 27 14

From: Julia A. Norwich
Taylor & Richardson Ltd
56 Queen Victoria Street
London EC4V 4JA

Date: 25 March 20..

Dear Jeannette

Delivery of software according to our order PLW-LN 250

Payment of your invoice No. 3590 of 20 March is due in a fortnight's time.

We used to pay our invoices by cheque, but have changed to paying by bank transfer, which is safer, quicker and less expensive for both of us.

I would be grateful if you could give me your bank account details as they are not printed on the invoice. Please do not forget to include the SWIFT address of your bank.

I hope you are well.

Kind regards

Julia.

7.2.3 Acknowledging receipt of goods – payment by cheque

Dear Ms Johnson

Today we have received the consignment of which you advised us on 7 January. We have examined the goods and have found them to be in order.

In payment of your invoice we enclose a crossed cheque for £… drawn on the District Bank Ltd in Manchester. Please send us your official receipt.

Yours sincerely

Enc

7.2.4 Advising settlement by bank transfer

Dear Sir or Madam

We are pleased to inform you that we have today instructed our bankers, Lloyds Bank in London, to transfer to your account with Dresdner Bank, Frankfurt, the sum of

€ 5,650.00

in settlement of your invoice No. 1348 JT of 7 July.

Please briefly acknowledge receipt by fax or e-mail.

Yours faithfully

7.2.5 Buyer acknowledges receipt of goods – returns draft with his / her acceptance

Thank you for your letter of 12 September, and for the prompt delivery of the 100 bags of Santos Coffee which arrived here yesterday in good condition.

Your draft for £…, which is due on 12 December, is being returned to you enclosed with our acceptance. We will not fail to honour this bill when it is presented for payment.

Yours sincerely

Enc

7.2.6 Buyer advises supplier of the opening of an L/C

Dear Sirs

Order No. LKF/311 PS

We have asked our bank to open an irrevocable documentary letter of credit in your favour for the a. m. order to the value of

US$35,480.00

redeemable by your drafts on us at 60 days' sight.

The following documents will be required:

Signed export invoices in duplicate, marine and war risk insurance certificate in compliance with the Institute Cargo Clause A, for 10 % above the CIF value of the goods; complete set of three clean shipped-on-board bills of lading made out to order of the shippers.

Further details are included in the L/C, which will be valid until …

We will send you an advance copy of the L/C by fax.

Yours faithfully

7.2.7 Error in invoice

Gentlemen:

We have just received your invoice No. 28801 of March 15 for $… and have to point out that you have made an error in your total. We calculate the correct figure at €2,240.80, not €2,340.80 as given by you.

Our cheque for the former amount is enclosed, and we ask you to amend the invoice or send us the necessary credit note.

Sincerely yours,

7.2.8 Discrepancies in statement

Dear Sirs

We have received your quarterly statement showing a balance of £2,416.20 in your favour.

When checking your figures against our own records, we noted the following discrepancies:

1. Invoice No. 4677 for £180.50 was charged twice. As you will see, you debited us with this amount on 16 September and again on 26 September.
2. Credit Note 10063 of 7 October for £75.80 is not included in your statement.

We are deducting £256.30 from the amount of your statement and will instruct our bank to transfer the balance of £2,159.90 to your account.

Yours faithfully

7.2.9 Disagreement on merchandise sent and charged

Dear Mrs Sing

<u>Our indent No. 241189, your invoice No. 2413 of 25 July 20..</u>

Thank you for promptly sending us the items under the a. m. order No. 241189 which have been checked in the meantime. We regret to inform you that there is a discrepancy between these goods and the amount invoiced.

Item No. 10 of our indent called for 200 ladies' sweaters size M, and we noted that your packing list showed 220 ladies' sweaters of this size. In fact we only received 200, but were invoiced for 220 items.

Please look into the matter and let us have a new invoice for the correct amount.

Yours sincerely

7.2.10 Supplier calls customer's attention to unearned discount taken

> Gentlemen:
>
> Thank you for your remittance in the amount of US$4,800.00 in payment of our invoice of Feb. 16 for US$4,680.00, on which you have taken a 2½ % cash discount.
>
> As our prices are cash prices, we cannot grant you any cash discount, and would therefore appreciate your sending us, at your convenience, a check for US$120.00, the amount of the discount in question.
>
> Sincerely yours,

7.3 Terms and phrases

7.3.1 Receipt of goods, invoices, etc

We acknowledge receipt of the goods ordered and thank you for the prompt delivery.	*Wir bestätigen den Eingang der bestellten Waren und danken Ihnen für die prompte Lieferung.*
The goods covered by your invoice of … arrived on M. S. "Hamburg" yesterday.	*Die Waren laut Ihrer Rechnung vom … kamen gestern mit M.S. „Hamburg" an.*
The shipment / consignment reached us safely and has turned out to our complete satisfaction.	*Die Sendung ist wohlbehalten bei uns eingetroffen und zu unserer vollen Zufriedenheit ausgefallen.*
Your statement for the last quarter has been received and found correct.	*Wir haben Ihren Kontoauszug für das letzte Quartal erhalten und finden ihn korrekt.*

7.3.2 Arranging payment

For Terms of Payment see Chapter 2.3.5

We enclose a cheque for £… Please credit this amount to our account / Please credit our account with this amount.	*Wir legen einen Scheck über £ … bei. Bitte schreiben Sie diesen Betrag unserem Konto gut.*
Enclosed please find a bank draft for US$ …, covering your invoice less / after deduction of 2 % cash discount.	*Beigefügt erhalten Sie einen Bankscheck über US$ … zum Ausgleich Ihrer Rechnung abzüglich 2 % Skonto.*

We have instructed our bank to transfer / remit the amount of £... to your account with Barclays Bank, Bedford.	*Wir haben unsere Bank angewiesen, den Betrag von £ ... auf Ihr Konto bei der Barclays Bank, Bedford, zu überweisen.*
We have accepted your draft and will honour it promptly at maturity.	*Wir haben Ihre Tratte akzeptiert und werden sie bei Fälligkeit prompt einlösen.*
We have checked your invoice against our records and are pleased to inform you that we have settled it by banker's transfer / international bank draft / international money order.	*Wir haben Ihre Rechnung an Hand unserer Unterlagen geprüft und freuen uns Ihnen mitzuteilen, dass wir sie per Banküberweisung / internationalem Bankscheck / internationaler Postüberweisung bezahlt haben.*
Please draw on us at 90 d/s in settlement of the invoice amount and send us your draft for acceptance.	*Bitte ziehen Sie in Begleichung der Rechnung auf uns einen 90-Tage-Sichtwechsel und schicken Sie uns Ihre Tratte zum Akzept.*

7.3.3 Errors in invoices and statements, discrepancies

When checking your invoice, we noted the following error: ...	*Bei Prüfung Ihrer Rechnung stellten wir folgenden Fehler fest: ...*
There is a discrepancy between the goods delivered and your statement of account.	*Die gelieferten Waren stimmen mit Ihrem Kontoauszug nicht überein.*
We would like to draw your attention to two credit items which have been omitted in your statement.	*Wir möchten Sie auf zwei Gutschriften aufmerksam machen, die in Ihrem Auszug nicht aufgeführt sind.*
May we draw your attention to the fact that we have been overcharged / undercharged by EUR ...	*Dürfen wir Sie darauf aufmerksam machen, dass Sie uns EUR ... zu viel / zu wenig berechnet haben.*
Please correct the statement. / Please issue a corrected statement.	*Wir bitten um Berichtigung des Kontoauszugs.*
Please pass the difference to our credit / debit.	*Bitte schreiben Sie uns den Differenzbetrag gut. / Bitte belasten Sie uns mit dem Differenzbetrag.*
Your monthly / quarterly statement shows a credit / debit balance which is not correct.	*Ihr monatlicher / vierteljährlicher Kontoauszug zeigt einen Guthaben-/Sollsaldo, der nicht stimmt.*

7.3.4 Errors in payment, etc

We are returning your cheque because it is postdated / because words and figures differ.	*Wir lassen Ihren Scheck an Sie zurückgehen, da er rückdatiert ist / da der Betrag in Ziffern nicht mit dem Betrag in Worten übereinstimmt.*
We regret to note that you have forgotten to sign / accept the draft.	*Leider stellen wir fest, dass Sie vergessen haben, die Tratte zu unterschreiben / akzeptieren.*
Please send us a credit / debit note for the difference.	*Bitte schicken Sie uns eine Gutschrift / Lastschrift für den Differenzbetrag.*
Since payment was made after expiry of the discount period, we cannot agree to your deducting a 2 % discount.	*Da die Zahlung nach Ablauf der Barzahlungsfrist erfolgte, können wir uns mit dem Abzug von 2 % Skonto nicht einverstanden erklären.*
You have taken a discount of … to which you were not entitled.	*Sie haben einen …%igen Nachlass in Anspruch genommen, zu dem Sie nicht berechtigt waren.*

7.4 Exercises
Please translate:

7.4.1 E-Mail von Schrader Maschinenbau GmbH, Dresden (schrader.gmbh@maschinen.htl.de) an Carriers Ltd, Brighton (carriers@t-co.uk)

Unser Transportauftrag 2648 LZW vom 28. 10. 20..

Unser Kunde, die Car Technologies plc in Manchester, hat uns mitgeteilt, dass die Maschine gut in Manchester angekommen ist.

Zum Ausgleich Ihrer Rechnung CC94 vom 3. 11. 20.. haben wir heute den Betrag von £ 1.495,30 auf das von Ihnen angegebene Konto der Bank of Scotland überwiesen.

Wir bitten um kurze Bestätigung des Eingangs der Zahlung.

7.4.2 Fax von Heide Schmieder, Berger & Hubermeyer oHG, Memmingen, Fax-Nr. +49-8331-937490, an John P. Eltville, Chamberlain Furniture Ltd, Perth, Australia, Fax-Nr.: +61-9-3497004

Ihr Kontoauszug vom 19. Januar 20..

Lieber John

vielen Dank für den o. a. Kontoauszug als Abrechnung für das vergangene Halbjahr, der einen Saldo zu Ihren Gunsten von EUR … aufweist.

Wie wir nachträglich feststellten, wurden folgende zwei Posten nicht berücksichtigt:

1) Gutschrift Nr. 25 vom 24.11. in Höhe von EUR 22.240,80, die wir für vom Kunden zurückgesandte Waren erhielten.
2) Rechnung Nr 5964 über EUR 12.530,00 steht noch aus.

Wir schlagen vor, diese beiden Posten in der nächsten Abrechnung gegeneinander aufzurechnen. Über den in Ihrem Kontoauszug ausgewiesenen Betrag erhalten Sie wie üblich per Einschreiben einen Verrechnungsscheck mit getrennter Post.

Weiterhin viel Erfolg!

Mit freundlichem Gruß

Please draft letters, faxes or e-mails from the following particulars

7.4.3 **Geschäftsfall:**

Ihre Firma, die Georg Mehlen KG, Bettinaplatz 110, 60325 Frankfurt/M, Fax-Nr.: +49 (69) 23 56 97, E-Mail-Adresse: mehlen.kg@t-online.de, hatte vorigen Monat bei der Baker & Co. Ltd, P.O. Box 340 693, St. Albans, Herts. SA3 5AD, UK, Fax-Nr.: +44 (17 27) 47 69 83, E-Mail-Adresse: baker.co.@complink.uk, mit Auftrags-Nr. 24 PH 350S 4.000 CDs bestellt, die 4 Wochen später geliefert werden sollten.

Aufgabe: Schreiben Sie an den Verkaufsleiter John S. Peterson eine Mitteilung unter Berücksichtigung folgender Punkte:

- Bezugnahme auf o. a. Auftrag
- Sendung ist eingetroffen
- Sie haben die CDs geprüft, Klang und Qualität stellen Sie sehr zufrieden
- Rechnungsbetrag in Höhe von £ 3.450,00 wurde heute auf das Konto von Baker & Co. Ltd bei der Midland Bank überwiesen
- Da Sie häufiger CDs bestellen wollen, fragen Sie an, ob bei regelmäßigen Aufträgen Mengenrabatte und Zahlungsziele gewährt werden.

7.4.4 **Geschäftsfall:**

Sie sind der/die deutsche Vertreter/in für die niederländische Gesellschaft Nederland Textiles, P.O. Box 1409, 6201 BE Maastricht, Niederlande, Fax-Nr.: +31 (43) 2 96 01 84 90, E-Mail-Adresse: nederland.textiles@nedtex.com. Das Büro Ihrer Firma Nedtex Textilimport GmbH befindet sich auf dem Platz der Vereinten Nationen, 10115 Berlin, Fax-Nr.: +49 (30) 29 87 54 30, E-Mail-Adresse: textilimport@nedtex.com.

Sie schicken Ihrem Prinzipal, der Nederland Textiles, die Abrechnung für die im 1. Quartal dieses Jahres verkauften Waren. Ihre Korrespondenzsprache ist Englisch.

Aufgabe: Berücksichtigen Sie hierbei die folgenden Punkte:

- Bezugnahme auf Quartalsabrechnung
- Die einzelnen Aufträge (*indents*) sind der beigefügten Liste zu entnehmen
- Gesamtsumme des Umsatzes beläuft sich auf € 25.320,00. Ihre Provision: 5 % = € 1.266,00
- Bitte um Überweisung

– Ein neuer Kunde stellt eine Bestellung über ca. € 20.000,00 in Aussicht. Bedingung: Zahlung mit 90-Tage-Wechsel
– Sie empfehlen, dieser Bitte nachzukommen.

7.4.5 **Geschäftsfall:**

Ihre Firma, die Hagen & Bauerfeind AG, Hegestraße 84, 45327 Essen, Fax-Nr.: +49 (201) 43 89 70, E-Mail-Adresse: hagen.bauerfeind@t-online.de, hatte bei der Hong Kong Silk Corporation Ltd, P.O. Box 34 09 853, Hong Kong, China, Fax-Nr.: +852 (25 39) 04 45, E-Mail-Adresse: hongkong.corp@silk.com, Waren im Wert von 45.500,00 US$ bestellt. Zahlung sollte per unwiderruflichem und bestätigtem Akkreditiv, zu eröffnen bei einer deutschen Bank, erfolgen. Die Firma schickt Ihnen heute eine E-Mail mit der Mitteilung, dass die Ware erst in 14 Tagen in Hong Kong verschifft werden kann. Die Firma bittet Sie daher, die Laufzeit des Akkreditivs um 4 Wochen zu verlängern.

Aufgabe: Schreiben Sie an die chinesische Firma unter Berücksichtigung folgender Punkte:

– Sie haben Ihre Bank gebeten, die Laufzeit des Akkreditivs um 4 Wochen zu verlängern
– Weisen Sie darauf hin, dass alle zusätzlichen Kosten zu Lasten des Lieferanten gehen
– Sie brauchen die Waren dringend, da darüber schon disponiert worden ist
– Daher ist eine weitere Akkreditivverlängerung ausgeschlossen
– Bitten Sie den Lieferanten, in Zukunft möglichst Lieferzeiten einzuhalten, da Sie selbst sonst gegenüber Ihren Kunden in Lieferschwierigkeiten geraten.

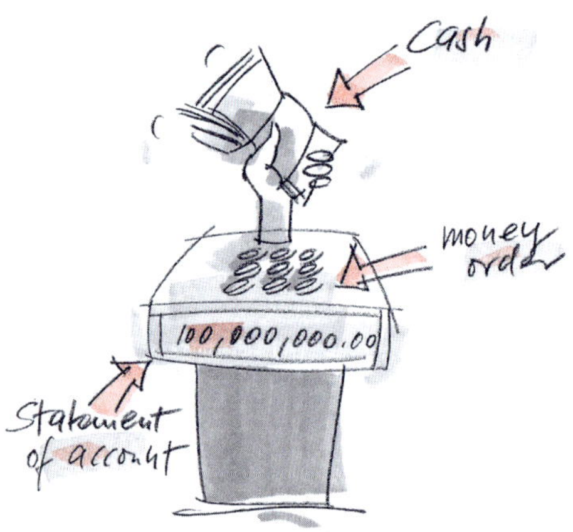

8. Delays in Delivery

Delays in delivery and non-delivery; reminders; sellers' response; missing consignments

8.1 Introduction

Delays in delivery and non-delivery. Delays in delivery and non-delivery constitute a breach of contract by the seller, unless they are due to force majeure or acts of God (floods, earthquakes, hurricanes) or other circumstances beyond the seller's control. If there are no such unusual circumstances, the buyer has the right to demand compensation from the seller – if necessary, by bringing action for damages – for the losses sustained as a result of the seller's failure to fulfil the contract. Sometimes the parties themselves, when concluding the contract, fix the amount of damages payable in the event of delayed performance or non-performance by the seller or contractor (penalty for non-fulfilment, liquidated damages).

Reminders. If the seller fails to deliver the goods on time, the buyer will send a reminder or warn the seller that the order will be cancelled unless the goods are delivered within a certain period of time or by a certain date. (One or several reminders may be sent before a final deadline for delivery is fixed.)

Reminders and the allowance of additional time can, of course, be dispensed with if the buyer has reserved the right to cancel the order in the case of any delay in delivery, or if it is obvious that the seller is not able or not willing to fulfil the contract.

Seller's response. In their reply to a letter from a customer complaining of a delay in delivery, a supplier will apologize and explain the situation. However, if difficulties arise with regard to delivery, suppliers should not wait until they receive a reminder from their customer, but they should inform the customer of these difficulties as soon as they arise.

In any case, suppliers should, if possible, tell their customers when they can expect to receive the goods. They may send part of the goods and promise to deliver the balance later. In order to induce customers to accept the goods

when they are delivered at a later date, sellers may offer a price reduction or a similar concession. If sellers find that they are unable to deliver the goods, they should ask the buyer to release them from the contract. It is better to seek a release than to commit a breach of contract and face the possibility of legal action.

Missing consignments. Sometimes a customer complains of a delay in delivery, although the goods have been despatched and should already have arrived at their destination. In such cases, investigations have to be made. These investigations may reveal that the consignment has been delayed, misdirected or lost in transit. Occasionally it is also discovered that the receiving department merely failed to notify the purchasing department of the arrival of the consignment or that some other error has been made (eg failure of the scanning system, wrong entry in the in-house stock control system etc).

8.2 Model correspondence

8.2.1 Reminder of delivery of photographic equipment

e-mail

Mail from: ramsey.ltd@photo.com

to: spiller@t-online.de **cc:**

Subject: Delay in delivery – Our order of 2 March 20..

Attachment:

Dear Spiller Digitalfoto

We are still waiting for the delivery of the 2,000 digital cameras as specified in our order of 2 March 20.., which you acknowledged on 10 March.

We urgently need these cameras some of which have already been sold to our own customers.

Please let us know immediately when we can expect the delivery.

Please reply without delay.

Yours faithfully

8.2.2 Outstanding order

FAO: Merz & Heinrichs GmbH
Gewerbestraße 10
D-83404 Ainring

Fax No.: +49 (86 54) 39 10 48

From: Facility Engineering Ltd
P.O. Box 49 08 32
London W1P 8AC,
UK

Date: 24 June 20..

Dear Sir or Madam

Our order VB 340916 of 30 May 20..

Delivery of this order was due in the second week of June, but we are still waiting for the instruments which you said you could send from stock.

We spoke to your Mr Schmidt by telephone on 22 June. He promised to let us have the exact delivery date on the same day, but we have not received any reply.

Should you not deliver the instruments by 30 June 20.., we will be forced to cancel this order and buy the material from a stockist at higher cost. The extra charges will have to be borne by you.

We are sending you a copy of this fax by separate mail.

Yours faithfully

Jeremy F. Boulster
Purchasing Manager

8.2.3 British representative of German company complains of repeated delays in delivery

Dear Sirs

The long delays in the execution of our orders are causing us great concern. We are tired of contacting you constantly by phone and fax in order to enquire about the delivery status of our various orders. In most cases we were given imprecise indications of the time of delivery and even these promises were broken.

From our various conversations you know that your unreliable deliveries have caused us serious problems with many of our customers. You will appreciate that things cannot go on like this. Both your company and ours will suffer serious damage if you are unable to improve your delivery record.

The latest cancellation is by Sheldon, Birmingham, a company which bought over £50,000.00 worth of equipment last year. The date of their order is 10 March, and when you acknowledged it on 23 March you promised to send the machines "within a few weeks".

While we are on the subject of delivery dates, we also have to remind you of the spare parts we ordered on 5 May. As these parts have not yet arrived, we have had to postpone several urgent repairs, a fact which has added to our customers' annoyance.

You will understand that we are very unhappy about this unsatisfactory state of affairs, and we only hope you will realise that this loss of confidence on the part of our customers will have very serious consequences for your company as well as ours.

We suggest arranging a meeting either in the UK or in Germany to discuss solutions to the problem.

Yours faithfully
NEWMAN & CO LTD

A. D. Black
Director

8.2.4 Shipment overdue

Dear Peter,

We are concerned about shipment of our order PXY 340 which is already overdue. If you cannot deliver before the end of this month, we will need quantities by air to maintain serviceability.

Please let us know your decision by return.

Regards,

8.2.5 Buyer gives warning of cancellation

Dear Sir or Madam

On 20th March we placed an order with you for 500yds of Harris Tweed, pointing out at the time that prompt delivery was essential. In the meantime, almost three weeks have passed, and we are still without the material.

As the tweed is urgently required for an export shipment, we shall be compelled to cancel our order if the consignment is not received here by 15th April.

Yours faithfully

8.2.6 Enquiry about status of orders

Telephone: +44 (2 07) 45 40
+44 (2 07) 55 43

A. H. LUDWIG & CO. (CHRYSTAL) **LTD**

Importers of Hand Cut Leadchrystal & Glassware

DIRECTORS:
R. E. WOODAGE
E. A. WOODAGE
M. ROLLINGS

6, VIGO STREET,
REEGENT STREET
LONDON W1X 1AH

10th August 20..
ludwig.co@glass.com

REW/PB

F. X. Nachtmann
Bleikristallwerke GmbH
Mr Alkhofer
D-92660 Neustadt a. d. Waldnaab

Dear Mr Alkhofer

Halebrook Deliveries

When the expected invoices for the above deliveries failed to arrive in London last week, I began to fear that this large consignment had not, in fact, left the factory. This fear was confirmed by a letter from Halebrook today, who had heard from Kühne & Nagel that his orders were not ready for shipment prior to the holiday closure. You will know that in recent letters and telephone conversations, the last of which was the day before the holiday shutdown, the subject of the Halebrook deliveries was raised, and there has never been the slightest hint that these consignments might not be ready for shipment by the end of July.

It may well be that you read this letter prior to the office re-opening on Monday, 23rd August, but, in any event, I will be telephoning earlier that day to ascertain the status of this customer's orders and also that of the sample Wine Carafes and Candleholder mentioned in my letter of 4th August. It would therefore be appreciated if you had answers ready to these queries and, particularly, the reasons for the failure to ship the Halebrook goods as expected, so that Mr Halebrook can be given an acceptable response to his very aggrieved letter.

With kind regards,

Yours sincerely,

R. E. Woodage

Director

REGISTERED IN LONDON NO. 601414 – REGISTERED ADDRESS: 24–30 Holborn EC1N 2HS

8.2.7 Status of orders – confirmation of telephone conversation (further letter by A. H. Ludwig (Crystal) Ltd to F. X. Nachtmann)

Dear Mr Alkhofer,

This is a brief confirmation of our telephone conversation this morning. I was relieved to have your assurance that the entire consignment for Mr Halebrook was leaving for Bremen today, and I am still waiting for information concerning the delayed delivery of ATHENS decanters, for which invoice 2423 has been received. Our forwarding agents have no news of the whereabouts of this shipment and therefore assume that the 15 cartons are still awaiting collection at Neustadt.

I hope that you can locate or quickly make repeat samples of the Handled and Unhandled Decanter and a Candleholder, identical to the pieces sent to London against your unnumbered invoice of 29th July, for direct Parcel Post shipment to Mr Halebrook.

When I mentioned the exhibition to be staged at Fortnum & Mason in London, you said that you would send us a selection of articles for display, so as to enable us to draw the visitor's attention to your products.

Finally, we would ask you to let us have a copy of your new price list as soon as it is available.

With kind regards

Yours sincerely,

R. E. Woodage
Director

8.2.8 Supplier apologizes for delay in delivery

Dear Sir / Dear Madam

We have received your letter of 13 March and offer our apologies for the delay in the execution of your order.

Unfortunately this order was overlooked in the pressure of business, but we are pleased to say that the goods are now ready for despatch. Shipment will be effected by M.V. "Norfolk" on 29 April, and the consignment should reach you about 12 May.

We hope this delay has not caused you any serious inconvenience and assure you that every effort will be made in future to ensure prompt delivery of your orders.

Yours faithfully

8.2.9 Delay in departure of vessel

Dear Sirs

We regret having to inform you that the departure of the vessel by which we have arranged shipment of your recent order, and which had originally been scheduled to sail o/a* 15th December, was delayed owing to bad weather. This vessel (S. S. "Martha") is now reported to sail from Southampton o/a* 29th December.

We regret this delay very much, on which, however, we have no influence.

Yours faithfully

8.2.10 Supplier asks to be released from contract

Gentlemen:

We are very sorry that we will not be able to supply the heavy-duty compressors you ordered on September 10.

Last week a fire broke out in our plant which destroyed several buildings, including our warehouse. We have cleared away the debris, but it will probably

* *on or about*

be several months before we can resume production. Under these circumstances we are compelled to ask you to release us from the contract.

We are sure you will understand the difficulty of our situation, which is due to circumstances beyond our control. You will hear from us as soon as we are in a position to serve you again.

Cordially,

8.2.11 Missing parcel

Dear Madam / Dear Sir

We are very much surprised to learn from your letter of 15th October that the parts you ordered on 10th September have not yet arrived. These parts werde despatched by parcel post on 27th September and should have reached you long ago.

We cannot understand this delay and would suggest that you ask the postal authorities to make investigations concerning the missing parcel.

Yours faithfully

8.3 Terms and phrases

8.3.1 Reminders and complaints concerning delays in delivery

The goods we ordered on … are … days / weeks overdue / behind schedule.	*Die am … bestellten Waren sind … Tage / Wochen überfällig.*
Despite your assurance that the work would be completed / performed / carried out by … we have to inform you that this is not the case.	*Trotz Ihrer Zusicherung, dass die Arbeiten bis … fertig gestellt / ausgeführt sein würden, müssen wir Ihnen mitteilen, dass dies nicht der Fall ist.*
We expressly stated in our order that the goods must reach us no later than …	*In unserer Bestellung haben wir ausdrücklich darauf hingewiesen, dass die Waren bis spätestens … hier eintreffen müssen.*

8.3.2 Seller's reply and explanations for the delay

We are sorry for the delay and will do our utmost to have the goods ready for shipment by ...	*Die Verzögerung tut uns Leid und wir werden unser Möglichstes tun, die Waren bis zum ... zum Versand bereitzustellen.*
We are sorry to note / We note with regret that the goods are late and will do everything possible to dispatch them by ...	*Wir stellen mit Bedauern fest, dass der Versand der Waren verzögert ist und tun unser Möglichstes, um Sie bis zum ... auf den Weg zu bringen.*
The acute shortage of qualified labour / A strike in our factory / An error on the part of ... is making it difficult for us to keep pace with the rush of incoming orders.	*Der akute Mangel an qualifizierten Arbeitskräften / Ein Streik in unserer Fabrik / Ein Fehler seitens ... bereitet uns Schwierigkeiten, mit der großen Anzahl der eingehenden Aufträge Schritt zu halten.*
On receipt of your letter we immediately contacted / got in touch with the shipping company, which informed us that M. S. "Marthe" had been held up due to engine trouble.	*Nach Eingang Ihres Schreibens setzten wir uns sofort mit der Reederei in Verbindung, die uns mitteilte, dass M. S. „Marthe" wegen eines Maschinendefekts nicht auslaufen konnte.*
The delay is due to / has been caused by the exceptionally strong demand during the past few months.	*Die Verzögerung ist auf die außergewöhnlich lebhafte Nachfrage während der letzten Monate zurückzuführen.*
Our forwarding agent was unable to book the necessary shipping space at an earlier date.	*Unser Spediteur konnte den benötigten Schiffsraum nicht zu einem früheren Zeitpunkt buchen.*
We have now contacted / got in touch with / obtained an explanation from ... and will let you know the new date of delivery as soon as possible.	*Wir haben jetzt mit ... Verbindung aufgenommen / von ... eine Erklärung erhalten und werden Ihnen so bald wie möglich das neue Lieferdatum mitteilen.*
Owing to a delay in the delivery of raw materials, we will probably be unable to carry out your order before the end of May.	*Wegen einer Verzögerung bei der Lieferung von Rohstoffen wird es uns voraussichtlich nicht möglich sein, Ihren Auftrag vor Ende Mai auszuführen.*
Unfortunately, equipment failure has upset our production schedule, but we are working overtime / to capacity to catch up on the production lost during downtime.	*Betriebsstörungen haben leider unseren Produktionsplan durcheinander gebracht, aber wir machen zur Zeit Überstunden / wir arbeiten zur Zeit mit voller Auslastung, um die während der Ausfallzeit eingetretenen Produktionsausfälle auszugleichen.*

Your delay in delivery places us in a difficult / embarrassing position.	*Ihr Lieferverzug bringt uns in eine schwierige / unangenehme Lage.*
Please look into the matter and advise us when the goods can be shipped.	*Wir bitten Sie, der Sache nachzugehen und uns mitzuteilen, wann die Waren verschifft werden können.*
We must have your definite promise that the goods will be despatched by the end of next week.	*Wir erwarten Ihre definitive Zusage, dass der Versand der Waren bis Ende der nächsten Woche erfolgt.*
We must insist on your informing us by fax / e-mail of the earliest possible delivery date.	*Wir müssen darauf bestehen, dass Sie uns per Fax / E-Mail das frühest mögliche Lieferdatum mitteilen.*
We must ask you to give top priority to all our outstanding orders.	*Wir müssen Sie bitten, alle unsere Bestellungen, bei denen die Lieferung noch aussteht, als vorrangig zu behandeln.*
... to expedite / hasten delivery, as our import licence will expire on ...	*... die Lieferung schnellstens auf den Weg zu bringen, da unsere Importlizenz am ... ausläuft.*
Should you fail to deliver the goods by ..., we will be forced / compelled to cancel the order.	*Falls Sie die Waren nicht bis zum ... liefern, sehen wir uns gezwungen, die Bestellung zu stornieren.*
... to obtain the goods elsewhere / from another supplier.	*... die Waren anderweitig / von einem anderen Lieferanten zu beschaffen.*
... to hold you liable for any losses incurred.	*... Sie für alle uns entstehenden Verluste haftbar zu machen.*
... to cancel this and all outstanding orders.	*... diesen und alle ausstehenden Aufträge zu stornieren.*
... to discontinue our business relations.	*... unsere Geschäftsbeziehungen zu beenden.*

8.3.3 Seller's apology and reassurance

We apologize sincerely for the delay which was unfortunately due to circumstances beyond our control.	*Wir entschuldigen uns aufrichtig für die Verspätung, die leider auf Umstände zurückzuführen ist, die außerhalb unserer Kontrolle liegen.*
We offer our apologies for the inconvenience caused and hope you will give us an opportunity to regain your confidence.	*Wir bitten Sie, die Ihnen entstandenen Unannehmlichkeiten zu entschuldigen, und hoffen, dass Sie uns Gelegenheit geben werden, Ihr Vertrauen wiederzugewinnen.*
... to renew our cordial relations.	*... unsere freundschaftlichen Geschäftsbeziehungen zu erneuern.*
As mentioned at the beginning of this letter, we very much regret the delay and will ensure that there will be no recurrence in the future.	*Wie bereits gesagt / am Anfang des Briefes erwähnt, bedauern wir die Verspätung sehr und werden sicherstellen, dass sich dies in Zukunft nicht wiederholt.*
We guarantee that all repair work will be carried out punctually in future.	*Wir garantieren, dass alle Reparaturarbeiten in Zukunft pünktlich ausgeführt werden.*
You may rest assured that there will be no such delays in future.	*Sie können sicher sein, dass solche Verzögerungen sich in Zukunft nicht wiederholen werden.*

8.4 Exercises

Please translate:

8.4.1 E-Mail der Walter Neubert oHG, Erfurt (neubert.ohg@t-online.de) an Blakeley & Co., Knitting Mills, Leeds (blakeley@knitting.tel.uk)

Vorige Woche (15. Juli) bestellten wir laut Order-Schein Nr. A-23/280 400 Herren-Wollpullover Design „Young man fashion 300" und 200 Damen-T-Shirts „Lady Twen 208" als Last-Minute-Order per E-Mail.

Sie schickten uns am 16. Juli eine E-Mail, mit der Sie den Last-Minute-Auftrag bestätigten und zusagten, dass uns die Ware spätestens gestern, also am 21. Juli, ab Ihrem Lager in Leipzig zugestellt würde. Wir haben aber bis jetzt weder die Ware noch eine Nachricht Ihrer Lagerleitung bekommen, warum die Sendung möglicherweise verspätet ist.

Wir benötigen die Sendung dringend für unsere nächste Woche beginnende Herbstmodenschau. Ihre Pullover und T-Shirts gehören zu mehreren Ensembles, die unsere Models vorführen sollen.

Wir bitten Sie daher dringend um Zusendung der Ware. Sollte eine Verspätung unvermeidlich sein, bitten wir um Mitteilung, damit wir kurzfristig Ersatz beschaffen können. Etwaige Kosten müssten wir dann aber Ihnen in Rechnung stellen.

8.4.2 Fax der Maurer Consulting GmbH, München (Fax-Nr.: +49-89-243712) an Johnson & Partners plc, Birmingham (Fax-Nr.: +44-121-769345), z. H. Herrn Jonathan Howard

Ihr Auftrag für die Erstellung einer Studie über den bayrischen Markt für Geschäftsimmobilien (*commercial properties*) vom 25.08.20..

Wir nehmen Bezug auf Ihren Auftrag, der bis zum 3. November dieses Jahres fertig gestellt werden sollte. Leider müssen wir Ihnen mitteilen, dass wir diesen Termin voraussichtlich nicht werden einhalten können. Dies ist weniger auf eigenes Verschulden zurückzuführen, sondern darauf, dass mehrere an Behörden und öffentliche Institutionen gerichtete Anfragen trotz mehrmaliger Erinnerung bisher noch nicht beantwortet wurden. Ohne gewisse behördliche Auskünfte ist aber eine sorgfältige Ausarbeitung der Studie nicht möglich.

Wir bitten Sie vorsorglich, uns den Liefertermin für die Marktstudie um einen Monat zu verlängern.

Bitte schicken Sie Ihre Nachricht an Frau Gabriele Pecher.

Wir danken im Voraus für Ihr Verständnis und sichern Ihnen die sorgfältige Ausführung Ihres Auftrags zu.

8.4.3 Maschinenfabrik Müller, GmbH, Ingolstadt, an Torrington Company Ltd, London

Vor ca. 3 Wochen sandten Sie uns die anlässlich der letzten Hannover-Messe bei Ihnen bestellte Bohrmaschine (*drilling machine*). Leider haben Sie jedoch den zum Antrieb erforderlichen Elektromotor nicht mitgeliefert.

Obwohl wir die Maschine für unseren Betrieb dringend benötigen, steht sie jetzt unbenutzt in unserem Lager, da wir auf die Lieferung des von Ihnen vorgesehenen Spezialmotors angewiesen sind.

Bei unserem Besuch auf der Messe haben wir Ihren Verkaufsleiter, Mr. Hardie, ausdrücklich darauf hingewiesen, dass unsere Bestellung nur unter der Voraussetzung pünktlicher Lieferung erteilt wird. Mr. Hardie sagte uns die Lieferung der kompletten Maschine innerhalb von 4 Wochen verbindlich zu. Mehrmalige Anrufe bei Mr. Hardie führten leider auch zu keinem Ergebnis. Sie werden unseren Unmut darüber verstehen, dass die Maschine jetzt mehr als 2 Monate nach Auftragserteilung immer noch nicht einsatzbereit ist.

Wir setzen Ihnen nunmehr eine Nachfrist bis zum 31. dieses Monats. Sollten wir bis dahin nicht im Besitze des Motors sein, lehnen wir die Annahme ab und senden Ihnen die bereits gelieferte Maschine zu Ihren Lasten zurück. Die geleistete Anzahlung in Höhe von ... bitten wir Sie in diesem Fall auf unser Konto bei der Dresdner Bank in Ingolstadt zu überweisen.

Please draft letters, faxes or e-mails from the following particulars:

8.4.4 Geschäftsfall:

Das Einrichtungshaus Gartmann & Heller GmbH, Am Schlosspark 84, D-82131 Gauting, Fax-Nr.: +49 (89) 82 45 97, E-Mail-Adresse: gartmann.heller@design.t-online.de, hatte bei der britischen Gesellschaft Peel Bros. Ltd, P.O. Box 4930, Reading RG6 7BA, UK, Fax-Nr.: +44 (118) 9 37 50 71, E-Mail Adresse: peel.bros.ltd@cbs.uk, am 23. 04. 20.. einen größeren Posten Teppichfliesen (*carpet tiles*) bestellt (Auftrags-Nr. 390 433). Herr Campbell von Peel Bros. Ltd hatte die Lieferung innerhalb von 4 Wochen zugesichert. Außerdem bestehen noch Lieferrückstände für die Aufträge Nr. 388 822 und 389 943. Nach Ablauf von 6 Wochen haben Gartmann & Heller trotz mehrmaliger Anrufe immer noch keine Versandanzeige für die Teppichfliesen erhalten. Auch die Lieferrückstände für die beiden anderen Aufträge bestehen weiterhin.

Aufgabe: Richten Sie ein Schreiben an die Peel Bros. Ltd, zu Händen von Herrn Campbell, und berücksichtigen Sie dabei folgende Punkte:

- Schildern Sie den o. a. Sachverhalt
- Sie haben Probleme mit mehreren Kundenaufträgen, die Sie nicht ausführen können
- Ihnen entsteht dadurch ein Gewinnausfall, abgesehen von den Unannehmlichkeiten mit der Kundschaft
- Setzen Sie für Auftrag Nr. 390 433 eine letzte Nachfrist von 14 Tagen
- Die Mengen für die Lieferrückstände der Aufträge Nr. 388 822 und 389 943 können Sie nur noch mit 20 % Preisermäßigung akzeptieren.

8.4.5 Geschäftsfall:

Beziehen Sie sich auf den Geschäftsfall 8.2.2, wonach der Einkaufsleiter Jeremy F. Boulster der Firma Facility Engineering Ltd, P.O. Box 490 832, London W1P 8AC, UK (Fax-Nr.: +44-20-1 83 1 74 93, E-Mail-Adresse: facilityltd@engineering.uk), Ihrer Firma, der Merz & Heinrichs GmbH, Gewerbestr. 10, D-83404 Ainring, (Fax-Nr.: +49-86 54-39 10 48, E-Mail-Adresse: merz.heinrich@gmx.de) am 24. 06. 20.. ein Fax schickte.

Aufgabe: Beantworten Sie dieses Fax mit Datum vom 25. 06. 20.. per Fax oder E-Mail unter Berücksichtigung der folgenden Punkte:

- Beziehen Sie sich auf den o. a. Fall (Auftrags-Nr. VB 340916 vom 30. Mai 20..) Bestätigen Sie den Eingang des Faxes und den Anruf von Herrn Boulster bei Herrn Schmidt am 22. 06.
- Herr Schmidt hatte in der Tat die Mitteilung der genauen Lieferzeit am gleichen Tag versprochen, konnte aber den Konstruktionsleiter nicht mehr erreichen
- Am folgenden Tag wurde er unterrichtet, die Instrumente seien versandbereit, doch müssten noch einige Formalitäten geklärt werden
- Die Instrumente sind heute abgesandt worden, so dass sie mit Sicherheit bis 30. 06. 20.. beim Kunden eintreffen werden

- Bedauern Sie das Versehen und die Verzögerung, die nicht wieder vorkommen wird
- Sichern Sie dem Kunden in Zukunft pünktliche Lieferung zu
- Sie hoffen auf weitere gute Geschäftsbeziehungen.

8.4.6 Geschäftsfall:

Die venezolanische Gesellschaft Telefónica de Venezuela S. A., Torre Financiera, Avenida Urdaneta, Esquina de Carmelitas, Caracas 1010, Venezuela, Fax-Nr.: +5 82 (7 09) 2 41 30, E-Mail-Adresse: telefonica.sa@org.ve, hatte bei der deutschen Firma Globaltechnik AG, Schwanallee 43, 35037 Marburg, Fax-Nr.: +49 (64 21) 39 87 50, E-Mail-Adresse: globaltechnik@online.de, eine Maschine vom Typ 985 PH im Wert von 450.500,00 US$ bestellt. Lieferzeit: Ende März 20.. Die Korrespondenzsprache ist Englisch.

Aufgabe: Schreiben Sie als Exportsachbearbeiter(in) an die venezolanische Gesellschaft und teilen Sie ihr Folgendes mit:

- Die Maschine ist versandbereit und sollte am 24. Februar mit der MS „Pearl Bay" in Hamburg verladen werden
- Ihr Spediteur, die Fa. Cargo Shipping GmbH, Gießen, informiert Sie heute, dass aus stautechnischen Gründen (*for technical reasons relating to stowage*) die Maschine wieder entladen werden musste
- Das nächste Schiff, die MS „Santa Maria", wird voraussichtlich erst Anfang März aus Hamburg in Richtung Venezuela auslaufen
- Ankunftszeit daher nicht vor Mitte April, da die Reise durch verschiedene Anlegestopps mit Sicherheit nicht unter 6 Wochen dauern wird
- Bitten Sie den Kunden um Verständnis, da Sie auf diese Verspätung leider keinen Einfluss nehmen konnten.

9. Complaints and Adjustments

Complaints concerning goods delivered or services rendered and adjustment of complaints

9.1 Introduction

Complaints concerning goods delivered or services rendered. If buyers are not satisfied with the goods delivered, they make a complaint. The wrong goods may have been received; the goods may have deficiencies; they may not correspond to the order as far as quality or quantity are concerned; or they may have arrived in a damaged condition.

The seller's failure to supply goods of the kind and quality ordered gives a buyer the right to rescind the contract. The faulty goods are placed at the seller's disposal, and, if any payments have already been made, the seller has to refund them. Should there still be interest in the proper goods, buyers will also place the faulty goods at the seller's disposal, but – instead of cancelling the contract – will demand replacements or substitutes. In the case of minor deficiencies, they will probably agree to keep the goods, but claim a reduction in price (*allowance*). In many instances, defects can be remedied by repair, or by the replacement of parts.

The same may happen with services rendered. They may be incomplete or faulty, there may be misinterpretations or other deficiencies.

It is common practice, particularly in the field of technical products, for manufacturers to give customers a written *guarantee* (or *warranty*). Under the terms of their guarantee, a manufacturer undertakes to replace or repair, free of charge, any article which may prove defective during the guarantee period, provided the defect is due to faulty material or workmanship.

Adjustment of complaints. When complaints are received from customers, the seller investigates the matter. If a decision cannot be made promptly, the seller should send the customer a brief acknowledgement, informing him that his letter is receiving attention.

Depending on the circumstances, the seller may accept the buyer's claim, reject it, or offer a compromise. Sellers who find themselves at fault should frankly admit this, offer apologies, and make a prompt adjustment. Should it be apparent that the buyer is to blame, the seller will, as a rule, reject the buyer's claims. However, if the seller is interested in accommodating a good customer who (erroneously) believes a claim to be justified, the claim may be accepted nevertheless (or at least a compromise may be reached). Unfounded complaints made by buyers who are obviously trying to take advantage of a seller are, of course, always rejected.

Provided the goods are properly packed by the seller, damage or loss in transit occurs only in unusual circumstances. Such damage or loss has to be taken up with the carrier or the insurance company. It should be noted, in this connection, that the liability of carriers for goods transported by them is always limited. Insurance companies pay compensation for damage or loss according to the terms of the policy, even if the damage or loss was due to negligence of the carrier or any other third party, but the insured have to transfer their rights against third parties to the insurers (*subrogation*).

Sometimes a customer's complaint gives rise to a dispute. This is the case, for example, if the buyer claims that the quality of the goods is not in accordance with the contract and the seller maintains that it is. Should the parties be unable to settle the dispute themselves (or through the good offices of a third party), the matter has to be referred to a court of law or a court of arbitration. Generally speaking, businesspeople prefer arbitration to litigation, which is both costly and time-consuming.

If deficiencies of goods supplied or services rendered result in unfavourable consequences or loss for the buyer, the seller may be liable to pay compensation under the conditions of contract or the law of the country agreed upon in the contract of purchase or sale.

9.2 Model correspondence

9.2.1 Complaint concerning drive belts

e-mail

Mail from: newton.howard@inc.compuserve.com
to: siehl.co@firmnetz.de   cc:
Subject: Our order of January 24
Attachment:

Dear Newton & Howard Inc.:

In execution of our order of January 24 you sent us ten industrial sewing machines for our factory.

We were very surprised to find that the drive belts for these machines, which are made of some sort of plastic material, tend to disintegrate within a short time. This has rendered the machines completely useless to us and has caused considerable loss of production.

It is indispensable that you airfreight replacement belts of the proper kind within the next three days in order to keep our losses to a tolerable minimum. We are holding the defective belts at your disposal, should you wish to have them examined.

Please let us know immediately when we can expect the replacement delivery.

Sincerely,

Peter Howard
Newton & Howard Incorporated

9.2.2 Complaint concerning newly delivered software

FAO: Hubernagel GmbH
Badstr. 9
D-91575 Windsbach

Fax No.: +49 (98 71) 60 91 48

From: Richard Jeremy Ashford
Simpson Ltd
P.O. Box 8301
Manchester PG7 2HG

Date: 26 February 20..

fax

Dear Madam / Sir

This is to inform you that we are were disappointed about the services you rendered to our company as per our order of 1st February 20..

You were invited to install software LWO 350 on all the computers in our company. You promised to begin to install this software on 18 February and to have this work finished by 22 February at the latest to ensure the continuation of our usual business. We had to interrupt our computer-based work for 4 days, which is the maximum period of time we can afford to have our routine work lie idle.

Nevertheless, and in spite of your promises, you did not finish this work as guaranteed on 22 February, and your personnel was on the premises for a further 2 days. This meant that we could not start operating our computers before 24 February.

We would have accepted this delay if further problems had not arisen in the meantime. Our staff complain that some of the computers do not operate under the new system as they should. They are unable to process the orders received.

It is absolutely essential that one of your service staff come to Manchester immediately to look at the system again. This will have to be entirely at your cost and expense.

Your contract provides for a guarantee for the first year of operation of the new software. We therefore hold you liable for all costs arising from the faulty installation if you cannot find the fault within the next 24 hours.

Yours faithfully

Richard J. Ashford

Richard J. Ashford
Purchasing Manager

9.2.3 Complaint concerning copying machine

JONES&WILLIAMS LIMITED
787 Turner Street Swansea SA1 6DB

PGD/JDE

20 October 20..

Marquardt (UK) Limited
250 Berkeley Street
LONDON
W1X 4DD

For the attention of the Managing Director

Dear Madam / Sir

MACO 671 COPYING MACHINE

My staff have brought to my attention the totally unsatisfactory situation concerning the MACO 671 Copying Machine that was ordered by us on 26 February (Our Order No 29601) and delivered by your Installation Engineer, Mr Elwood, four months later on 24 June.

When Mr Elwood put the copier into operation, he found that it produced poor copies and – upon closer examination – discovered scratches on the selenium-coated aluminium cylinder. Mr Elwood then disconnected the machine and stated his intention to return with a new cylinder. My staff naturally expected him to make this essential repair within a short period and became concerned when after three weeks he had not returned, leaving our newly purchased MACO 671 absolutely useless.

Enquiries to your company on 19 July resulted in promises that repair of our machine would be treated as a matter of urgency.

On 6 August Mr Williams arrived at our Swansea office to inspect the machine and informed us that Mr Elwood was no longer employed by your company. Of course, Mr Williams's inspection resulted in the same findings as those of Mr Elwood of 24 June, ie that the cylinder was scratched and in need of replacement.

Two weeks later, Mr Williams called Mr Steward, our Purchasing Manager, and told him that the machine would be repaired only if we agreed to pay the repair costs, since it was his opinion that the damage to the cylinder was due to staples or paper clips having been passed through the machine, which was careless use and therefore our responsibility. Mr Steward pointed out that the cylinder had already been scratched when Mr Elwood first delivered the MACO 671 on 24 June and demanded that it be put into perfect operating condition at your expense at the earliest possible date. Mr Williams said that he would have to take up the matter with the head of the repair department, and that was the last we heard of him.

Our patience is now exhausted. It is a completely unacceptable situation that today, almost four months after delivery, the copying machine is still not operational. We must therefore insist that the machine is either replaced or repaired to "as new" condition and put into operation within two weeks from this date and at no cost to us. Failing that action on your part, we shall be compelled to place the matter in the hands of our solicitors. A copy of this letter is being sent to your German parent company, Marquardt Kopiertechnik AG, Esslingen.

Yours faithfully
JONES & WILLIAMS LIMITED

P G Davenport

P G Davenport
Managing Director

9.2.4 Adjustment: claim granted

Dear Sirs

Thank you for your letter of 12th April, in which you included a cutting of the cloth you received from us some days ago.

You are quite right. The cloth is not of the quality you ordered; we sent you a thinner material by mistake. As requested, we are sending you Credit Note No 8773 to adjust the difference in price.

We offer our sincere apologies for this oversight and hope that the matter has now been settled to your complete satisfaction.

Yours faithfully

Enc

9.2.5 Suggestion of compromise

Dear Dr Bolz

Thank you for your letter of 5 October informing us of the mistakes on the title page of "Modern English Grammar – Englische Grammatik fuer Gymnasien": Englishe instead of Englische, Hans Wielhoff instead of Hans Wiethoff.

We have corrected the errors and are ready for a complete re-run of the 5,000 title pages for the first edition.

In looking over our records, however, we find that the proof of the title page was approved by your Herr Sackmann, who apparently also overlooked the errors. Since the mistake was thus only partly ours, my suggestion is that we share the expenses of printing the extra number. I believe that this would be a fair compromise. If you agree, please let me know as soon as possible, preferably by e-mail or fax, so that we can get started with the re-run.

Yours sincerely
Brown & Sons Ltd

Jim Masters
Managing Director

9.2.6 Adjustment: claim partly granted

Macdonald & Evans
Estover, Plymouth PL6 7PZ
Telephone: Plymouth (07 52) 70 52 51
Fax: (07 52) 70 53 52

BH/CG

21 February 20..

The Manager
The World Bookshop
PO Box 320
Kuwait

Dear Sir

Thank you for your letter of 13 February regarding shortages and damaged copies which you received against our invoice No 08906.

I have checked with our Despatch Department, who confirm that – according to their records – the quantities were picked out, separately checked, and then packed in pallets for despatch. Since you apparently received the pallets unopened, it is surprising that any copies should be missing.

I therefore wonder if the missing titles might not have been overlooked or incorrectly stored in your warehouse, and I would ask you to check once more to make sure that this has not happened.

We are, of course, crediting you for the damaged copies. A credit note for the amount in question will be sent to you shortly.

Yours faithfully

Brian Hulme
Export Sales Manager

9.2.7 Claim refused

Dear Sirs

PHFS Printers

Reference is made to your e-mail of 26 January and the visit of our Service Engineer, Mr Steward, to your factory last week.

Mr Steward reports that the unsatisfactory performance of the printers is due to the fact that your are not using paper supplied by one of our approved paper manufacturers. Our printers may work well with paper bought from other companies, but this cannot be guaranteed.

You will understand that, in these circumstances, we cannot assume any responsibility for the malfunction of the printers. If you use the right kind of paper, our printers will give you many years of satisfactory service.

Yours faithfully
COSGRAVE PRINTERS LIMITED

M L Goodwin
Chief Engineer

9.2.8 Damage in transit

Dear Sirs

We are sorry to hear that 558 jars of our most recent shipment of McMuir Marmalade were broken when they arrived in Hamburg. Your order was properly packed and shipped in good condition, as evidenced by the clean bill of lading issued by the shipping company. The damage must therefore have occurred in transit.

We are sending you replacements for the broken jars. Please let us have the survey report made out by Lloyd's Agent in Hamburg, so that we can report the damage to the insurance company.

We hope that the new consignment will arrive safely and in good time.

Yours faithfully

9.2.9 Seller appoints arbitrator

Theodor Ellentine Inc
Philadelphia
USA

Gentlemen:

We are having some difficulty with the company P L Dumbridge, Philadelphia, concerning a consignment of silk textiles which we shipped to them last March. They dispute the quality of the silk and refuse to pay the invoice until there has been an investigation of the material. We would be grateful if you could act as arbitrator for us in this matter. You will find details in the enclosed statement.

Our main contention is that a comparison between samples and consignment does not show any variation in quality outside the permitted limits. We have presented the material to a well-known manufacturer who confirms our contention.

Our contract with the customer foresees that he must inform our own arbitrator of the name of his arbitrator within a period of 10 days, and that his arbitrator must be a member of the Philadelphia Chamber of Commerce.

We hope you will be able and prepared to act on our behalf in this matter and that it will be possible for you to reach an agreement with our customer's arbitrator. This would make it unnecessary to refer to an umpire.

We thank you in advance for your cooperation and look forward to your early reply.

Sincerely yours

Encl

9.2.10 Warranty clause offered by supplier

Warranty

The Company warrants each machine for a period of six months from the date of delivery. Should any parts prove defective within this period, they should be returned to the Company's Works at ..., carriage paid. The Company will examine such parts carefully and, if satisfied that the defect is due to faulty material or workmanship, will repair the defective parts or supply new ones, free of charge.

9.2.11 Warranty clause requested by buyer (as part of Letter of Intent and Purchase Order under 4.2.5)

INDIAN CONSTRUCTION COMPANY LTD

Vendor warrants that it has the experience and capability, including sufficient and competent supervisors and other employees, to efficiently and expeditiously perform the works required in supplying the goods.

Vendor shall obtain available warranties and guarantees from the manufacturers or vendors of materials or goods for incorporation into the goods. Vendor shall extend such warranties and guarantees to buyer. The vendor shall ensure that all sub-orders have appropriate provisions giving effect to the foregoing.

Vendor warrants that the goods shall be free from any defects and are of merchantable quality for which such goods are specified and are free and clear of all liens, encumbrances, taxes and claims.

Buyer's remedy for breach of the warranties set forth in this item of the contract shall be as follows:

If any defect originating from the design, material, workmanship or operating characteristics of any goods arises within 24 months after delivery ex-works of the goods or 12 months after offshore commissioning whichever occurs earlier in accordance with the purchase order, buyer shall promptly notify vendor of the defect. Thereafter, supplier may, at its option, repair or replace the defective goods or direct vendor to repair or replace same within the time period specified by buyer. In the event buyer exercises the option to repair or replace the defective goods or part thereof, vendor shall reimburse buyer all costs and expenses incurred by buyer, whether direct or incidental, in carrying out the repair or replacement work. All costs of repair or replacement of the defective goods or part thereof whether undertaken by vendor or buyer, including, without limitation, costs of removal, transportation and reinstallation and customs duties shall be borne by vendor. All further claims, especially claims for consequential damages are excluded. Without prejudice to the foregoing, buyer reserves the right to accept the defective goods with a non-performance adjustment in the purchase price.

Where the goods have been repaired or replaced in whole or in part pursuant to this contract clause, then all the warranties stated in this clause shall continue to apply to the repaired or the replaced goods for a period of one year from the date of successful repair or replacement or until the expiration of the warranty period specified, whichever period expires later.

Buyer's inspection, testing, witness of tests, final release, certification or payment of invoices shall not relieve vendor from its warranty obligations as set forth in this contract clause.

Vendor's warranties under this contract clause do not extend to cover failures due to faulty operations by supplier or due to conditions or services more severe than stated in the specifications.

9.2.12 Special contract clause for rejection, repair and replacement of goods stipulated by the buyer (as part of Letter of Intent and Purchase Order under 4.2.5)

INDIAN CONSTRUCTION COMPANY LTD

The receipt of goods by buyer shall not prejudice buyer's right to reject and return the goods if the goods are not in accordance with the specifications. At buyer's request, vendor shall repair or replace goods not complying with the specifications or supply any shortfall in the event of shortfall in delivery, or buyer may at its option repair or replace such goods or supply any shortfall in the event of shortfall in delivery. Vendor shall bear all costs and expenses incurred by either vendor or buyer as a result of the rejection, repair or replacement of the goods or supply of shortfall in delivery including but not limited to the costs of transportation, labor and customs duties.

9.2.13 Special contract clause for arbitration (as part of Letter of Intent and Purchase Order under 4.2.5)

INDIAN CONSTRUCTION COMPANY LTD

All disputes, controversies or claims arising or in connection with the purchase order or the breach, termination or invalidity thereof unless settled by mutual agreement, shall be finally settled by arbitration in accordance with the United Nations Commission on International Trade Law (UNCITRAL) Arbitration Rules under the auspices of the Regional Centre for Arbitration, New Delhi.

9.3 Terms and phrases

9.3.1 Making complaints

We have just taken delivery of / We have just received …	*Wir haben soeben die Lieferung von … entgegengenommen / erhalten.*
We are sorry / We regret to inform you that your last consignment has not turned out to our satisfaction.	*Wir müssen Ihnen leider mitteilen, dass Ihre letzte Sendung nicht zu unserer Zufriedenheit ausgefallen ist.*
On / Upon / When opening the case, which showed no signs of damage from the outside, we discovered that 25 plates were broken.	*Beim Öffnen der Kiste, die äußerlich keine Anzeichen von Beschädigung aufwies, entdeckten wir, dass 25 Teller zerbrochen waren.*
When our Goods Inwards Department opened the boxes, they discovered that some of the articles were missing.	*Als unsere Warenannahme die Kisten öffnete, stellte man fest, dass einige der Artikel fehlten.*
After running the machine for a short time, we noticed that it does not meet our expectations / requirements / standards.	*Als wir die Maschine kurze Zeit laufen ließen, stellten wir fest, dass sie unsere Erwartungen nicht erfüllt / unseren Ansprüchen / unserem Standard nicht genügt.*
We have noticed a shortage in weight of …	*Wir haben ein Fehlgewicht von … festgestellt.*
Part of the goods were damaged in transit / during transport.	*Ein Teil der Waren ist auf dem Transport beschädigt worden.*
The damage seems to have been due to / have been caused by inadequate packing.	*Der Schaden ist anscheinend auf ungenügende Verpackung zurückzuführen.*
The samples taken from each of the three bags will show you that my claim is justified.	*Die Proben, die jedem der drei Säcke entnommen wurden, werden Sie von der Berechtigung meiner Beschwerde überzeugen.*
We have no use for the poor quality you sent us.	*Wir haben keine Verwendung für die schlechte Qualität, die Sie uns sandten.*
We are placing the faulty goods at your disposal.	*Wir stellen Ihnen die mangelhaften Waren zur Verfügung.*
We are holding the shipment for / pending your instructions.	*Wir halten die Sendung zu Ihrer Verfügung und erwarten Ihre Anweisungen.*
We have included a sample / copy of the document authenticating the damage to substantiate our claim.	*Wir haben ein Muster / eine Kopie des den Schaden aufzeigenden Dokuments beigefügt, um unsere Forderung darzulegen.*
You will be receiving a photograph as proof / by way of evidence.	*Als Beweis erhalten Sie ein Foto.*

Please let us have your comments / an explanation regarding this matter.	*Bitte geben Sie uns eine Stellungnahme / Erklärung bezüglich dieser Angelegenheit.*
Please let us know what you intend to do in this matter.	*Bitte teilen Sie uns mit, was Sie in dieser Angelegenheit zu tun gedenken.*
This has been a matter of great annoyance to me.	*Diese Angelegenheit hat mir viel Ärger eingebracht.*
You will appreciate that this has caused us considerable inconvenience / a lot of trouble / a considerable financial loss.	*Sie werden verstehen, dass uns dies große Unannehmlichkeiten / viel Ärger / einen erheblichen finanziellen Verlust eingebracht hat.*
We are prepared to keep the goods if you reduce the price by 20 % / if you grant a reduction of 20 %.	*Wir sind bereit, die Waren zu behalten, wenn Sie uns eine Preisermäßigung von 20 % gewähren.*
Please send us replacements for the damaged goods as soon as possible.	*Bitte senden Sie uns so bald wie möglich Ersatz für die beschädigten Waren.*
We have no choice / alternative but to ask you for an immediate replacement delivery.	*Wir haben keine andere Wahl als Sie um eine sofortige Ersatzlieferung zu bitten.*
We will unfortunately be obliged to cancel our order / take legal action.	*Wir sind leider genötigt, unseren Auftrag zu stornieren / gerichtliche Schritte zu unternehmen.*
Since the goods are unsaleable, we are returning them to you at your expense / carriage forward.	*Da die Waren unverkäuflich sind, senden wir sie Ihnen auf Ihre Kosten / unfrei zurück.*
Please devote more care to the execution of our orders in future.	*Bitte führen Sie in Zukunft unsere Aufträge sorgfältiger aus.*
We must point out that any further business will depend on how you settle this matter.	*Wir müssen darauf hinweisen, dass weitere Geschäfte davon abhängen, wie Sie diese Angelegenheit bereinigen.*
We can only place further orders if you devote more care to their execution in future.	*Wir können Ihnen nur weitere Aufträge erteilen, wenn Sie ihrer Ausführung in Zukunft mehr Aufmerksamkeit widmen.*

9.3.2 Granting claims

We have just received your e-mail / fax / telephone call in connection with …	*Wir haben soeben Ihre E-Mail / Ihr Fax / Ihren Telefonanruf im Zusammenhang mit … erhalten.*
Thank you for bringing this error / oversight / deficiency / fault to our attention.	*Vielen Dank, dass Sie uns auf dieses Versehen / diesen Fehler aufmerksam gemacht haben.*
We are sorry / we regret to hear that …	*Es tut uns Leid / Wir bedauern zu hören, dass …*

Your complaint is being processed / receiving attention.	*Ihre Beschwerde wird bearbeitet.*
As it will take some time to discover the reason for the damage, we ask you to let us have a few days to look into the matter.	*Da es einige Zeit dauern wird, die Ursache für den Schaden herauszufinden, bitten wir Sie um einige Tage Geduld, damit wir die Sache untersuchen können.*
The faulty goods / articles / items will be exchanged for faultless ones.	*Die mangelhaften Waren / Artikel / Positionen werden gegen einwandfreie umgetauscht.*
We are sending you ... to replace the goods mentioned in your letter / fax / e-mail of ...	*Wir senden Ihnen ... als Ersatz für die in Ihrem Schreiben / Fax / Ihrer E-Mail vom ... erwähnten Waren.*
A new consignment / shipment is being rushed to you today.	*Eine neue Sendung geht Ihnen heute auf dem schnellsten Wege zu.*
Please return the goods at our expense for credit.	*Bitte senden Sie die Waren auf unsere Kosten gegen Gutschrift zurück.*
Enclosed you will find our cheque for ..., representing a refund on the goods you recently returned to us.	*Anbei erhalten Sie einen Scheck über ... als Rückerstattung für die kürzlich an uns zurückgesandten Waren.*
We will file / enter a claim with the railway / airline / shipping line so that you will not be troubled further.	*Um Ihnen weitere Mühe zu ersparen, werden wir den Schaden der Eisenbahn / Luftgesellschaft / Reederei melden.*
We are anxious to settle the matter to your entire satisfaction.	*Es liegt uns sehr viel daran, die Angelegenheit zu Ihrer vollen Zufriedenheit zu regeln.*
We trust that you will agree to the arrangement suggested.	*Wir hoffen, dass Sie mit der vorgeschlagenen Regelung einverstanden sind.*
Please accept our apologies for the inconvenience caused by this error / oversight / fault.	*Bitte entschuldigen Sie die Unannehmlichkeiten, die Ihnen durch diesen Fehler / dieses Versehen entstanden sind.*
We will take all possible steps to ensure that such a mistake does not occur again.	*Wir werden alles tun, damit sich ein solcher Fehler nicht wiederholt.*

9.3.3 Refusing claims; ex gratia adjustments

Since the inspection did not reveal any fault in material or workmanship, we regret we are unable to make the adjustment you suggest.	*Da die Prüfung keinen Material- oder Verarbeitungsfehler ergab, ist es uns leider nicht möglich, diese Angelegenheit Ihrem Vorschlag entsprechend zu regeln.*

Our enquiries have shown that we are in no way at fault so that we are unable to accept your claim.	*Unsere Nachforschungen haben ergeben, dass uns absolut keine Schuld trifft, so dass wir nicht in der Lage sind, Ihre Forderung zu akzeptieren.*
We regret that in this case we cannot accept the return of the goods.	*Wir bedauern, dass wir in diesem Fall die Waren nicht zurücknehmen können.*
You will agree that under these circumstances we cannot be made / held responsible for the loss.	*Sie werden zugeben müssen, dass wir unter diesen Umständen für den Verlust nicht verantwortlich gemacht werden können.*
We cannot assume any liability in this case.	*Wir können in diesem Fall keine Haftung übernehmen.*
We suggest that you report the damage to the insurance company / forwarding agency.	*Wir schlagen vor, dass Sie den Schaden der Versicherungsgesellschaft / Spedition melden.*
We are confident that the machine will give satisfactory service if you follow our operating instructions.	*Wir sind sicher, dass Sie mit der Leistung der Maschine zufrieden sein werden, wenn Sie unsere Betriebsanleitung beachten.*
Although the guarantee period has already expired, we are willing to accommodate you and make the necessary repairs free of charge.	*Obwohl die Garantiezeit bereits abgelaufen ist, sind wir bereit, Ihnen entgegenzukommen und die notwendigen Reparaturen kostenlos durchzuführen.*
The equipment will be checked / serviced / repaired / overhauled at our expense as a gesture of our goodwill.	*Die Ausrüstung wird als Zeichen unseres Entgegenkommens auf unsere Kosten geprüft / gewartet / repariert / überholt.*
As a special free-of-charge service we offer our customer hotline available to you 24 hours a day, 7 days a week.	*Als kostenlosen Service bieten wir unsere Kundendienst-Hotline an, die Ihnen 24 Stunden 7 Tage in der Woche zur Verfügung steht.*

9.3.4 Arbitration

The contract calls for settlement of disputes by arbitration.	*Dem Vertrag entsprechend sind Streitigkeiten durch ein Schiedsverfahren beizulegen.*
The consignee has claimed arbitration against the consignment.	*Der Empfänger hat für die Sendung Arbitrage beantragt.*
We are prepared to submit to arbitration.	*Wir sind bereit, uns einem Schiedsverfahren zu unterwerfen.*
We will inform you of the arbitration award as soon as possible.	*Wir werden Sie so bald wie möglich über den Schiedsspruch informieren.*

9.4 Exercises

Please translate:

9.4.1 E-Mail von Siehl & Co. KG, Karlsruhe (siehl.co@firmnetz.de) an Newton & Howard Inc. Philadelphia (newton.howard@inc.compuserve.com) (in Beantwortung der E-Mail 9.2.1)

Sehr geehrter Herr Howard,

danke für Ihre E-Mail. Wir bedauern außerordentlich, dass die Antriebsriemen defekt waren und haben Ihnen bereits heute 12 Ersatz-Antriebsriemen per Luftfracht (Flug LH 3971, Airway Bill No. 309481) geschickt.

Wir bedauern diesen Vorfall sehr. Unser Zulieferant hatte bei einer Sendung versehentlich ein falsches Material eingesetzt. Die Ersatz-Antriebsriemen wurden vor Versand von uns geprüft und entsprechen den Anforderungen.

Die fehlerhaften Antriebsriemen werden nicht mehr benötigt.

Wir hoffen, dass nunmehr die Industrie-Nähmaschinen einwandfrei arbeiten und bitten nochmals, unser Versehen zu entschuldigen.

Mit freundlichen Grüßen
Günther Hallig
Exportleiter
Siehl & Co. KG

9.4.2 Fax der Mauerberger GmbH, Stuttgart (Fax-Nr.: +49-711-587890) an Jefferson Ltd, Beckenham, Kent, UK (Fax-Nr.: +44-181-3057009)

Die am 30.8. bestellte Sendung Porzellanwaren kam gestern endlich mit M.S. „Cynthia" an.

Es stellte sich jedoch heraus, dass statt der auf der Rechnung aufgeführten 15 Kisten nur 13 geliefert wurden. Nach einem Vermerk auf dem Konnossement sind die Kisten Nr. 8 und 11 nicht zur Verladung gekommen. Außerdem wurde beim Auspacken der Sendung festgestellt, dass ein Teil des Inhalts der Kisten 6, 7 und 9 während des Transports beschädigt wurde, da das Porzellan nicht sorgfältig genug verpackt war. Wir müssen Sie darauf aufmerksam machen, dass wir mit der Ausführung unseres Auftrags äußerst unzufrieden sind. Erstens wurde die in Ihrer Auftragsbestätigung genannte Lieferzeit von 4 Wochen nicht eingehalten, so dass wir zweimal mahnen mussten, und zweitens ist die gelieferte Sendung unvollständig und teilweise beschädigt.

Wir bitten Sie daher dringend, uns die beiden fehlenden Kisten sowie Ersatz für die beschädigten Waren, über die wir eine Aufstellung beilegen, umgehend zu liefern. Eine Fortsetzung unserer Geschäftsbeziehungen müssen wir von der prompten Erledigung unserer Beschwerde abhängig machen.

Anlage

Please draft letters, faxes or e-mails from the following particulars:

9.4.3 **Geschäftsfall:**

Sie arbeiten für die Firma Riess & Co., Modewarenimport, Colonia-Allee 12–14, 51067 Köln, Fax-Nr.: +49 (2 21) 38 97 40, E-Mail-Adresse: riess.moden@colonia.de, und beziehen regelmäßig thailändische Seidenstoffe von der Khwang Limited, 304 Ratchadaphisek Road, Bangkok 10310, Fax-Nr.: +6 62 (6 94) 30 96, E-Mail-Adresse: khwang.silk@tat.or.th. Die letzte Sendung aus Thailand gab zu Beanstandungen Anlass.

Aufgabe: Schreiben Sie an den thailändischen Lieferanten eine Beschwerde und berücksichtigen Sie dabei folgende Punkte:

- Die Sendung ist pünktlich angekommen
- Leider sind 22 der 150 Seidenballen nicht in Ordnung
- Beanstandung: Die Seide ist an manchen Stellen zu lose gewebt und verzieht sich dadurch
- Daher können diese 22 Ballen nicht zu hochwertigen Damenkleidern verarbeitet werden
- Mit getrennter Post schicken Sie ein Muster der fehlerhaften Seide an Khwang
- Bitten Sie um umgehende kostenlose Nachsendung der Ballen frei Haus
- Wenn die gleiche Farbe und Qualität (Nr. 3812 AH) nicht geliefert werden kann, bitten Sie um ein möglichst ähnliches Material
- Da die Seide für die bevorstehende Sommerkollektion bestimmt ist, ist eine Nachlieferung per Luftfracht bis ... erforderlich.

9.4.4 **Beantwortung des Faxes unter 9.2.2**

Geschäftsfall:

Ihre Firma, die Hubernagel GmbH, Badstr. 9, D-91575 Windsbach, Fax-Nr.: +49 (98 71) 60 91 48, hatte von Herrn Richard Jeremy Ashford der Firma Simpson Ltd, P.O. Box 8301, Manchester PG7 2HG, UK, Fax-Nr.: +44 (1 61) 37 06 45 per Fax eine Beschwerde über unzulängliche Service-Leistungen erhalten.

Aufgabe: Beantworten Sie dieses Fax als Kundendienstleiter (*Head of After-Sales Service*) unter Berücksichtigung der folgenden Punkte:

- Sie bestätigen den Eingang des Faxes vom 26.02.
- Sie bedauern, dass der Einbau der Software LWO 350 statt vier sechs Tage in Anspruch genommen hat
- Grund: Es wurde mehr Speicherkapazität (*storage capacity*) benötigt als ursprünglich angenommen
- Daraufhin wurde von Ihnen kostenlos eine Speichererweiterung vorgenommen
- Sie sind erstaunt, dass das System trotzdem noch nicht einwandfrei arbeitet
- Bevor Sie erneut einen Fachmann nach England schicken, brauchen Sie genaue Angaben, an wie vielen Computern welche Fehler aufgetreten sind

- Sie schlagen zunächst eine online-Diagnose vor
- Sollte diese zu keinem Ergebnis führen, werden Sie selbstverständlich einen Experten nach Großbritannien senden.

9.4.5 **Geschäftsfall:**

Sie arbeiten bei der Produktimport Schneider KG, Frankfurter Straße 211, 63263 Neu-Isenburg, Fax-Nr.: +49 (61 02) 5 43 83 11, E-Mail-Adresse: produktimport@schneider.com. Ihre Firma hatte von der Peanuts Incorporated, Dakota Dunes, South Dakota SD 23010, Fax-Nr.: +01 (6 05) 2 32 84 37, E-Mail-Adresse: peanuts.inc@distance.com, eine Sendung Erdnüsse gekauft. Der Vertrag sah im Falle von Streitigkeiten ein Schiedsverfahren nach den Regeln der „Hamburger freundschaftlichen Arbitrage" vor. Nach Ankunft der Ware stellt Ihre Wareneingangsstelle fest, dass ein Teil der Säcke ranzige Ware (*rancid merchandise*) enthält, die offensichtlich aus früheren Ernten stammt. Daher hatten Sie bei der Peanuts Inc. einen Minderwert von 20 % geltend gemacht. Sie erhalten daraufhin eine E-Mail der Peanuts Inc., in welcher diese sich weigert, eine entsprechende Minderung des Kaufpreises vorzunehmen.

Aufgabe: Beantworten Sie diese E-Mail der Peanuts Incorporated unter Berücksichtigung folgender Punkte:

- Beziehen Sie sich auf den oben beschriebenen Sachverhalt
- Weisen Sie auf die Schiedsklausel (*arbitration clause*) in Ihrem Kaufvertrag hin
- Sie haben infolgedessen Herrn Georg Tiedemann, Hamburg, zu ihrem Schiedsrichter bestellt
- Fordern Sie Peanuts Inc. auf, innerhalb einer Woche ihrerseits einen Schiedsrichter zu benennen
- Der Schiedsrichter muss im Gebiet der Bundesrepublik Deutschland seinen Wohnsitz und Aufenthaltsort haben.

10. Delays in Payment

Delays in payment and non-payment; reminders and collection letters; debtor's response

10.1 Introduction

Delays in payment and non-payment. Delays in payment occur if an invoice is overlooked by the customer, if the customer fails to pay within the credit period granted by the supplier, or if temporary financial difficulties arise. Non-payment may be due to the buyer's insolvency, the buyer's failure to take up the documents or to honour a draft, or to political events or government action preventing the buyer from meeting his obligations. If the buyer fails to perform the contract for reasons within the buyer's control, and the seller is unable to obtain payment through any other means, legal action is the last resort. Because of the difficulties involved in a lawsuit, particularly if it is brought against a foreign firm, such a step is considered only if the amount in question is large and there is a reasonable chance of success. A default summons in Britain, like the German "Mahnbescheid", is a legal instrument which – unless an objection is lodged by the debtor – enables the creditor, after it has been declared enforceable by execution, to levy execution on the debtor's property without a formal court hearing.

The risks of buyer's insolvency or failure to pay (*commercial risks* or *buyer risks*) can be shifted to an agent willing to assume the del credere or to a factoring company; they can also be insured with an insurance company handling credit insurance. *Political risks* (war, revolution, imposition of new import restrictions, etc) are more difficult to place. Del credere agents do not assume them (and factors only to a limited extent), nor can they be insured in the commercial insurance market. The only protection available against these risks is that provided by government institutions. In Britain, for example, there is the *Export Credits Guarantee Department*, which insures both commercial and political risks.

Reminders and collection letters. When an account becomes overdue, the initial assumption is that it has been overlooked by the customer. It is therefore brought to the customer's attention by means of a telephone call, a copy of the invoice or statement, a printed notice, letter, etc. These are called reminders. A reminder may also be included in an offer or sales letter sent to a customer (*hidden reminder*). If the reminder does not produce any results, it is followed by two (or more) collection letters (*dunning letters*). In these letters, various arguments and appeals are used to obtain payment or at least an explanation from the customer. The request for payment becomes increasingly insistent and urgent. In the final collection letter a period or date is fixed, and the creditor warns the debtor that certain steps will be taken unless payment is made within the period, or by the date, fixed. Such steps may be, for example, to suspend deliveries; to withdraw credit privileges; to report the matter to a diplomatic or consular mission, a chamber of commerce, a trade association or a similar body; to draw a sight draft for collection through the debtor's bank; or to turn the account over to a collection agency or a lawyer. (*Note:* The terms *collection letter and dunning letter* should not be used in correspondence with the customer.)

Debtor's response. The customer's reply to a request for payment is either a letter of apology notifying the creditor that the amount is being paid or a request for an extension. However, a debtor experiencing temporary financial difficulties should not wait until a reminder from the creditor is received, but should ask for an extension as early as possible. To show his good will, the debtor may make a part payment (*payment on account*) and ask the creditor to grant an extension for the balance. Sometimes the debtor offers to accept a bill of exchange for the amount owing, so as to give the creditor the assurance that the amount will be paid. On the other hand, a customer who was supplied on a draft basis may be unable to honour this draft at maturity and may thus be compelled to ask the drawer for a prolongation. (When an extension or prolongation is granted, the creditor is entitled to charge interest on the debt for the additional time allowed.)

10.2 Model correspondence

10.2.1 First reminder

e-mail

Mail from: houston.barter@ust.uk
to: breitensteiger@umwelt.com cc:
Subject: Attn: accounts department
Attachment:

May we draw your attention to our statement of account for June, which shows a balance of £6,550.70 in our favour. Our terms are 30 days net, and we therefore ask you to let us have your remittance soon.

Regards
John L. Barter
Houston & Barter Ltd

10.2.2 Hidden reminder

Dear Sirs

We have pleasure in sending you enclosed our latest brochure and price list. As you will note, we have rounded off our successful SE Series by adding a semiautomatic model, the SE 1021. We have also introduced improved versions of some of our other machines.

May we take this opportunity to remind you that our invoice of 26 January for £15,610.35 is still unpaid. We look forward to receiving your remittance soon.

Yours faithfully

Enc

10.2.3 Second reminder

fax

FAO: Ms Gudrun Wolf
Schröder & Müller GmbH
Alte Poststr. 48
D-47877 Willich

Fax No.: +49 (21 54) 16 93 06

From: David O. Graham
Andrews Limited
P.O. Box 31119
Melbourne, Victoria
Australia

Date: 11 April 20..

Dear Ms Wolf

We wrote to you on 25 March, asking for payment of the overdue balance of A$15,610.35, but have not received any reply from you so far.

If there is an error or any other problem, please let us know, and we will look into the matter at once. Otherwise we must ask you to remit the outstanding amount without further delay.

Yours sincerely

David O. Graham

David O. Graham
Accounts Department

10.2.4 Third reminder

Dear Sirs

Although two previous requests have been made to you for settlement of the overdue balance of £15,610.35 on your account, no remittance has yet been received.

Unless the balance is cleared within the next two weeks, we shall have no alternative but to place the matter in the hands of our solicitor.

Yours faithfully

10.2.5 Lawyer makes last request for payment

Dear Sirs

My clients, Smithson & Co Ltd, have informed me that their repeated requests for payment of your long overdue account for £15,610.35 have been ignored by you.

This is the final demand for settlement on an amicable basis. Unless payment of the above amount is made immediately, I shall be compelled to institute legal proceedings against you without further notice.

Yours faithfully

10.2.6 Supplier informs customer that claim will be passed on to collection agency

Dear Sirs

Despite our repeated reminders of ... and of ... your account still remains unpaid. We herewith grant you a last respite of 10 days to settle your debt.

Should we not receive a remittance covering all balances due within this period of time, we shall have no alternative but to pass our claim on to our collection agency.

All further costs arising in this matter will be charged to you.

Yours faithfully

10.2.7 Collection series

Reference

R. D. BAXTER COMPANY
1212 Pasadena Avenue
LOS ANGELES, CA 90001

Account Number

Date ______ 20___

If your remittance has already been sent, please disregard this notice. If not, we shall appreciate your prompt attention, and a remittance covering your past due account.

COURTESY NOTICE

AMOUNT DUE $______________
PLEASE ENCLOSE THIS NOTICE
WITH YOUR REMITTANCE.

Reference

R. D. BAXTER COMPANY
1212 Pasadena Avenue
LOS ANGELES, CA 90001

Account Number

Date ______ 20___

Just to remind you of your overdue account, which has doubtless been overlooked. Now that we have again reminded you, won't you please send us a remittance promptly? The amount due is $______________, and settlement will be confidently expected within the next week.

PAST DUE NOTICE

ENCLOSE THIS NOTICE WITH
YOUR REMITTANCE.

Reference

R. D. BAXTER COMPANY
1212 Pasadena Avenue
LOS ANGELES, CA 90001

Account Number

Date ______ 20___

Repeated requests for settlement of your past due account have, apparently, been ignored. Unless payment is received within ten days, immediate action will be taken. Your past due balance amounts to $______________.

FINAL NOTICE

THIS NOTICE IS TO BE ENCLOSED WITH YOUR REMITTANCE.

10.2.8 Customer apologizes for delay in payment

Dear Sirs

With reference to your letter of 28 December, we have today instructed our bank to transfer the amount of £840.50 to your account.

We are sorry that the due date of your invoice was overlooked in the pressure of business. Please accept our apologies for the delay.

Yours faithfully

10.2.9 Customer makes payment on account – asks for extension for the balance

Dear Madam / Sir

We have received your letter of 10 August and are sorry about the delay in settling our account.

Owing to the slackness of trade during the past few months, we have not yet been able to dispose of your last consignment. In addition, many of our customers have been slow in meeting their obligations.

We are sending you a cheque for £1,000 on account and would be grateful if you could grant us an extension for the balance until 30 September. You can rely on receiving a remittance in full settlement by that date.

Thank you in advance for your understanding.

Yours faithfully

Enc

10.2.10 Request for prolongation of draft

Dear Sirs

We regret to inform you that we will not be able to meet our acceptance for £3,450 on 1 October.

The prolonged strike in our area has resulted in a general decline in business activity, leaving us temporarily short of ready cash. However, our financial position is sound and, as a settlement of the strike has just been negotiated, the business situation is expected to improve very soon.

Under these circumstances we would be grateful if you could renew the bill, on which we will pay interest at 6 per cent, until 1 November. This would give us time to meet our obligations without increasing our loan from the bank.

We hope that in view of our long and pleasant business relations you will accommodate us in this matter and grant us this favour.

Yours faithfully

10.3 Terms and phrases

10.3.1 Reminders

We wish to call / draw your attention to our invoice of ..., which is now ... days overdue.	*Wir möchten Sie auf unsere Rechnung vom ... aufmerksam machen, die bereits vor ... Tagen fällig war.*
Our statement of account of ... has obviously been overlooked.	*Anscheinend haben Sie unseren Kontoauszug vom ... übersehen.*
We are sorry to note / It may have escaped your notice that our invoice of ... has not yet been settled / paid.	*Leider müssen wir feststellen, / Ihnen ist anscheinend entgangen, dass unsere Rechnung vom ... noch nicht beglichen ist.*
Looking through / Going over our books we find / note that there is an outstanding balance of ... on your account.	*Bei Durchsicht unserer Bücher stellen wir fest, dass auf Ihrem Konto noch ein Saldo von ... offensteht.*
We regret that no advice of payment has yet been received from our bankers for our shipment of ...	*Für unsere Lieferung vom ... haben wir bisher leider noch keine Zahlungsanzeige von unserer Bank erhalten.*
This is to inform you that our invoice for the amount of ... is still overdue.	*Hiermit teilen wir Ihnen mit, dass unsere Rechnung für den Betrag von ... noch überfällig ist.*
We refer to our previous letter(s) dated ... with regard to our invoice / statement of ... showing an outstanding balance of ... in our favour.	*Wir beziehen uns auf unsere(n) vorhergehenden Brief(e) vom ... bezüglich unserer Rechnung / unseres Kontoauszugs vom ..., die / der einen ausstehenden Saldo von ... zu unseren Gunsten ausweist.*
Our invoice / statement of ... is now ... weeks / months overdue.	*Unsere Rechnung / Unser Kontoauszug vom ... ist jetzt ... Wochen / Monate überfällig.*

10.3.2 Request for payment

We would appreciate an early settlement of our invoice / statement.	*Für baldigen Ausgleich unserer Rechnung / unseres Kontoauszugs wären wir dankbar.*
As payment has usually been made on time, we have not contacted you before.	*Da die Zahlung normalerweise pünktlich erfolgt ist, haben wir Sie bis jetzt noch nicht angesprochen.*
Please give us an explanation as to why payment has not yet been effected.	*Bitte geben Sie uns eine Erklärung, warum die Zahlung noch nicht erfolgt ist.*
Please remit the amount due within the next few days.	*Bitte überweisen Sie den fälligen Betrag innerhalb der nächsten Tage.*

Although we have several times urgently requested payment of your long overdue account, we have not yet had a response from you.	*Obwohl wir mehrmals die Zahlung Ihrer längst fälligen Rechnung anmahnten, haben wir immer noch nichts von Ihnen gehört.*
If you do not settle our invoice / statement by ..., we will reconsider our terms of business with you.	*Wenn Sie Ihre Rechnung / Ihren Kontoauszug nicht bis ... begleichen, werden wir unsere Geschäftsbedingungen mit Ihnen überdenken.*
... it may be necessary for us to change our open account terms of business to CWO (*cash with order*).	*... ist es möglicherweise nötig, dass wir unsere Geschäftsbedingungen eines offenen Zahlungsziels in Barzahlung bei Auftragserteilung ändern.*
You are evidently not interested in settling this matter amicably / out of court, since you have ignored our previous letters.	*Sie sind offensichtlich nicht daran interessiert, diese Angelegenheit gütlich / ohne Einschaltung des Gerichts zu regeln, da Sie unsere bisherigen Schreiben ignoriert haben.*
We regret to inform you that we have no alternative but to withhold all further deliveries until your account has been balanced.	*Wir müssen Ihnen leider mitteilen, dass wir keine andere Wahl haben, als alle weiteren Lieferungen an Sie einzustellen, bis Ihr Konto ausgeglichen ist.*
As we are still without reply to our various reminders / requests for payment, we will collect the overdue amount, plus interest and charges, by sight draft through the ... Bank.	*Da unsere verschiedenen Mahnungen / Zahlungsaufforderungen unbeantwortet geblieben sind, lassen wir den fälligen Betrag zuzüglich Zinsen und Kosten per Sichttratte durch die ... Bank einziehen.*
Unless payment is received by ..., we will reluctantly be compelled to take immediate (legal) steps to recover the amount due.	*Falls die Zahlung nicht bis zum ... eingeht, sehen wir uns zu unserem Bedauern gezwungen, unverzüglich (gerichtliche) Schritte zur Einziehung des fälligen Betrages zu unternehmen.*
... we will have the amount collected through a collection agency.	*... werden wir den Betrag durch ein Inkassoinstitut eintreiben lassen.*
... we will be forced to institute legal proceedings / to go to court / to recover the debt at law / to place the matter in the hands of our solicitors.	*... sind wir gezwungen, gerichtliche Schritte zu unternehmen / das Gericht einzuschalten / die Schuld gerichtlich einzutreiben / die Sache unseren Anwälten zu übergeben.*
Unless we receive your cheque within 7 days, we will file an action / take legal action against you.	*Falls wir Ihren Scheck nicht innerhalb von 7 Tagen erhalten, werden wir eine Klage gegen Sie anstrengen.*
Should the amount have been paid in the meantime, please disregard this letter.	*Sollte der Betrag inzwischen bezahlt worden sein, betrachten Sie dieses Schreiben bitte als gegenstandslos.*

10.3.3 Debtor's reply; request for extension

This is to inform you that your invoice / statement of … was in fact paid on …	*Hierdurch teilen wir Ihnen mit, dass unsere Rechnung / unser Kontoauszug vom … tatsächlich am … beglichen wurde.*
We have discovered that your invoice was misplaced. Please accept our apologies for the delay.	*Wir haben festgestellt, dass Ihre Rechnung verlegt wurde. Bitte entschuldigen Sie die Verzögerung.*
Business has been slow / slack during the past few months.	*In den letzten Monaten war das Geschäft schleppend.*
The seasonal lull has caused us temporary financial difficulties.	*Die jahreszeitlich bedingte Flaute hat uns vorübergehend in finanzielle Schwierigkeiten gebracht.*
We are in arrears of payment because of …	*Wir sind in Zahlungsverzug wegen …*
… a fire in our works.	*… eines Feuers in unserer Fabrik.*
… a strike / industrial action in the steel trade.	*… eines Streiks / Arbeitsunruhen im Stahlhandel.*
… a breakdown in our computer system.	*… eines Versagens in unserer Computeranlage.*
… an unexpected rise in raw materials / wage costs.	*… eines unerwarteten Anstiegs der Rohstoffe / der Lohnkosten.*
… a cashflow problem in our company.	*… eines Cashflow-Problems in unserem Unternehmen.*
… difficulties in collecting our outstanding accounts.	*… Schwierigkeiten, unsere ausstehenden Zahlungen einzutreiben.*
The unexpected failure / bankruptcy of one of our customers has caused us considerable losses.	*Der unerwartete Konkurs eines unserer Kunden hat uns erhebliche Verluste verursacht.*
In view of these difficulties we hope you will agree to a prolongation of the draft by 30 days.	*Angesichts dieser Schwierigkeiten hoffen wir, dass Sie sich mit einer Prolongation des Wechsels um 30 Tage einverstanden erklären.*
Owing to circumstances beyond our control we regret to inform you that we will not be able to balance our account within the time stipulated.	*Aus Gründen außerhalb unserer Kontrolle bedauern wir, Ihnen mitteilen zu müssen, dass wir unser Konto nicht innerhalb der festgesetzten Zeit ausgleichen können.*
We ask you to allow us … weeks to settle your invoice / statement of …	*Wir bitten Sie, uns … Wochen zur Zahlung Ihrer Rechnung / Ihres Kontoauszugs vom … zu gewähren.*
In view of our good payment record in the past, we would very much appreciate it if you could extend the deadline for payment by …	*Angesichts unserer bisherigen guten Zahlungsmoral wären wir Ihnen sehr dankbar, wenn Sie die Zahlungsfrist um … verlängern könnten.*

10.3.4 Granting or refusing extension

As you have always paid your bills / invoices promptly, we are prepared to grant you the extension requested.	*Da Sie Ihre Rechnungen stets prompt bezahlt haben, sind wir bereit, Ihnen den gewünschten Zahlungsaufschub zu gewähren.*
If you send us a cheque for half the amount of your invoice, we will draw on you at 60 d/s (*days' sight*) for the balance.	*Wenn Sie uns einen Scheck über die Hälfte des Rechnungsbetrages schicken, ziehen wir auf Sie für den Restbetrag einen Wechsel per 60 Tage Sicht.*
After careful consideration of the matter, we are prepared to prolong the bill by one month.	*Nach eingehender Prüfung der Angelegenheit sind wir bereit, den Wechsel um einen Monat zu verlängern.*
Under these circumstances we are exceptionally prepared to grant you a respite of ...	*Unter diesen Umständen sind wir ausnahmsweise bereit, Ihnen einen Aufschub von ... zu gewähren.*
As we will have to meet considerable commitments shortly, we are unfortunately unable to comply with your request for a prolongation of payment.	*Da wir in Kürze erheblichen Zahlungsverpflichtungen nachkommen müssen, ist es uns leider unmöglich, Ihrer Bitte um Zahlungsaufschub nachzukommen.*
Since we have already been waiting ... weeks for payment, we cannot accept your request for a final deadline.	*Da wir bereits ... Wochen auf Zahlung warten, können wir Ihre Bitte um einen endgültigen Termin nicht annehmen.*
Although we understand / appreciate your difficulties, we cannot allow you to postpone payment of this account any longer.	*Obwohl wir für Ihre schwierige Lage Verständnis haben, können wir Ihnen nicht gestatten, die Zahlung dieser Rechnung noch länger hinauszuschieben.*
We regret that we cannot see our way to accommodating you any further.	*Wir sehen leider keine Möglichkeit, Ihnen in dieser Angelegenheit noch weiter entgegenzukommen.*

10.4 Exercises

Please translate:

10.4.1 E-Mail von Becker & Sohn KG, Nürnberg (becker.sohn@spielwaren.gmx.de) an Peter Ward Ltd, Glasgow (ward.limited@toys.com)

Lieber Peter,

wir freuen uns, Ihnen mitzuteilen, dass unser neuer Katalog für mechanische Spielwaren rechtzeitig herauskommt, damit unsere Kunden sich schon jetzt für das Weihnachtsgeschäft eindecken können. Wir haben Ihnen daher Ihr Exemplar bereits mit separater Post zugehen lassen. Da mit einer großen Nachfrage nach unseren Neuheiten zu rechnen ist, können wir unseren Kunden rechtzeitige Lieferung nur dann zusichern, wenn sie ihre Bestellungen frühzeitig aufgeben.

Bitte denken Sie auch daran, unsere Rechnung vom 08.07., die seit 4 Wochen überfällig ist, zu begleichen. Als Attachment erhalten Sie nochmals eine Kopie dieser Rechnung. Sollten Sie diese inzwischen beglichen haben, bitten wir, diese Erinnerung als gegenstandslos zu betrachten.

Mit bestem Gruß,

Hans-Jörg Becker Jr.

Attachment

10.4.2 Fax von Digital-Systeme GmbH, Josef-Mayburger Kai 98, A-5020 Salzburg, Österreich (Fax-Nr.: +43-662-458307) an Garrett Industries Inc., P.O. Box 457431, Nairobi, Kenya (Fax-Nr.: +254-2-524310)

Unsere Rechnung LSH 324 / wn vom 16.03.20.., fällig am 30.04.20..

Unsere 1. Mahnung vom 15.05.20..

Unsere 2. Mahnung vom 15.06.20..

Nachdem wir Ihnen 2 × ein Erinnerungsschreiben für die Begleichung unserer obigen Rechnung geschickt und keine Überweisung, aber auch keine Erklärung von Ihnen erhalten haben, warum die Zahlung nicht erfolgt, setzen wir Ihnen nunmehr eine letzte Frist zum 30.07.20..

Sollte bis zu diesem Zeitpunkt eine Zahlung nicht erfolgt sein, sehen wir uns leider genötigt, rechtliche Schritte gegen Sie einzuleiten.

Das Original dieses Schreibens erhalten Sie per Luftpost-Einschreiben.

Mit freundlichen Grüßen

Digital-Systeme GmbH

Konrad Merzenberger

Leiter der Rechnungsabteilung

10.4.3 Schultze & Co., Mannheim an Minerva Express Ltd, Chester, UK

Wir haben Ihr Schreiben vom 21.09.20.. erhalten und bedauern sehr, dass es uns bisher nicht möglich war, Ihre Rechnung zu begleichen.

Der unerwartete Konkurs eines unserer Kunden hat uns selbst vorübergehende Liquiditätsprobleme bereitet. Wir sind jedoch zuversichtlich, diese in absehbarer Zeit in den Griff zu bekommen.

Wir wären Ihnen aus diesem Grunde sehr dankbar, wenn Sie uns einen Zahlungsaufschub von 4 Wochen gewähren könnten. Für die Überziehungsperiode bieten wir Ihnen eine Zinszahlung von 7,5 % p.a. an.

Wir danken Ihnen im Voraus für Ihr Verständnis.

Mit freundlichen Grüßen

Please draft letters, faxes or e-mails from the following particulars:

10.4.4 **Geschäftsfall:**

Sie arbeiten bei der Marketing GmbH, Reinzstr. 17, D-89233 Neu-Ulm, Fax-Nr.: +49 (7 31) 46 09 33, E-Mail-Adresse: marketing.gmbh@t-online.de, und hatten für die Ferguson Ltd, Howbery Park, Wallingford, Oxon OX10 8BA, Fax-Nr.: +44 (14 91) 82 07 96, E-Mail-Adresse: ferguson.limited@engineering.com, eine Studie für den deutschen Markt erstellt. Am 18. 09. 20.. schickten Sie der Ferguson Ltd eine Rechnung in Höhe von insgesamt 25.340,00 Euro, zahlbar in 2 Raten, eine sofort und eine 4 Wochen nach Rechnungsdatum fällig, also am 18. 10. 20.. Die 1. Rate in Höhe von 12.715,00 Euro ging fristgemäß ein. Auf die 2. Rate warten Sie heute, am 1. 11. 20.., noch immer.

10.4.5 1. **Aufgabe:**

Schicken Sie ein erstes freundliches Erinnerungsschreiben an die Ferguson Ltd unter Berücksichtigung der folgenden Punkte:

- Bestätigen Sie dankend den Erhalt der 1. Rate
- Fügen Sie nochmals eine Kopie der Rechnung Nr. XH/593 bei
- Falls die Überweisung inzwischen erfolgt ist, bitten Sie, das Erinnerungsschreiben als gegenstandslos zu betrachten

10.4.6 2. **Aufgabe:**

Da Sie am 15. 11. 20.. keine Reaktion auf Ihre 1. Mahnung erhalten haben, schicken Sie eine 2. Mahnung an die Ferguson Ltd und berücksichtigen Sie dabei folgende Punkte:

- Bezugnahme auf Rechnung XH/593 vom 18. 09. 20..
- Erinnerung, dass die 2. Rate in Höhe von 12.715,00 Euro, zahlbar am 18. 10. 20.. immer noch aussteht
- Bitte um sofortige Begleichung
- Falls Zahlungsschwierigkeiten aufgetreten sind, bitte um Darlegung von Gründen

10.4.7 3. **Aufgabe:**

Nachdem wieder 3 Wochen verstrichen sind, ohne dass der Kunde eine Reaktion gezeigt hat, schicken Sie eine 3. und letzte Mahnung an die Ferguson Ltd, in der folgende Punkte zu berücksichtigen sind:

- Bezugnahme auf die beiden vorangegangenen Erinnerungsschreiben (Datum angeben!)
- Nennen Sie nochmals Nummer und Ausstellungsdatum der Rechnung sowie den noch fälligen Betrag
- Setzen Sie eine letzte Frist zum 31. Dezember 20..
- Sollte diese ungenutzt verstreichen, sehen Sie sich leider genötigt, rechtliche Schritte gegen den Kunden einzuleiten oder ein Inkassoinstitut mit der Eintreibung der Forderung zu beauftragen.

10.4.8 4. Aufgabe:

Die letzte Frist, der 31. 12. 20.., ist nun auch ergebnislos verstrichen. Richten Sie an die Ihnen bekannte Inkassoagentur Templeton Credit Agency, P.O. Box 25 30 69, Southport, Merseyside, PR9 9YF, Fax-Nr.: +44 (17 04) 33 83 05, E-Mail-Adresse: templeton@credit.enquiries.com, ein Schreiben folgenden Inhalts:

- Schildern Sie den obigen Fall
- Beziehen Sie sich auf Ihre drei erfolglosen Mahnungen
- Erteilen Sie der Inkassoagentur den Auftrag, das Geld notfalls gerichtlich einzutreiben
- Fügen Sie Kopie des Vertrages, der Rechnung und der drei Mahnungen bei.

10.4.9 Geschäftsfall:

Sie arbeiten für die Werkzeugfabrik Hagen & Co. GmbH, Bruckmannring 22, 85764 Oberschleißheim, Fax-Nr.: +49 (89) 3 15 79 84 16, E-Mail-Adresse: Hagen.co@werkzeuge.de, und hatten mit der African Tool Company in Abidjan, Elfenbeinküste (*Ivory Coast*), einen Vertrag über die Lieferung von Elektrowerkzeugen abgeschlossen. Auf Drängen Ihres dortigen Vertreters, der Firma African Development Agency, P.O. Box 1579, Abidjan, Ivory Coast, Fax-Nr.: +2 25 (20 83) 44 69, E-Mail-Adressse: afr.development@agency.com, erklären Sie sich bereit, auf der Basis „Kasse gegen Dokumente“ zu liefern, obwohl die African Tool Company ein neuer Kunde ist.

Kurze Zeit nach Versand erfahren Sie von Ihrer Bank, dass sich die African Tool Company geweigert hat, die Dokumente aufzunehmen. Nach der Auskunft, die die Bank aus Abidjan erhalten hat, befindet sich die Firma in Zahlungsschwierigkeiten.

Aufgabe: Richten Sie an Ihren Vertreter, die African Development Agency, ein Schreiben, in dem Sie folgende Punkte berücksichtigen:

- Hinweis darauf, dass Sie nur auf den ausdrücklichen Wunsch Ihres Vertreters dem Kunden die Zahlungsbedingung „Kasse gegen Dokumente“ eingeräumt haben
- Aufforderung, die Sache sofort zu regeln
- Vorschlag: Ihr Vertreter übernimmt die Dokumente gegen Zahlung des Gegenwerts und verkauft sie anschließend auf eigene Rechnung
- Sendung befindet sich im Moment im Zolllager
- Ihr Vertreter soll sich unverzüglich mit der Inkassostelle der Bank of Africa in Abidjan in Verbindung setzen, um die Dokumente auszulösen
- Kosten gehen auf Grund der Sachlage zu Lasten des Vertreters
- Lagerrisiko wird durch Versicherung gedeckt (bis max. 90 Tage nach Ankunft der Sendung im Bestimmungshafen).

11. Agencies and Distribution, Foreign Branches and Subsidiaries

11.1 Introduction

Foreign agents. Foreign agents are either commission agents or consignees.

A *commission agent* sells or buys goods for a principal on a commission basis. An exporter's selling agent in a foreign country solicits orders from customers or enters into contracts with them in the name of the principal. In addition, the agent assists the principal in advertising, supplies market and credit information, provides after-sales service, helps to settle disputes, etc. An importer's buying agent abroad buys goods for a principal on the basis of indents (see Chapter 3).

A *consignee* is an agent to whom the exporter (*consignor*) consigns goods for sale. The stock of goods placed at the consignee's disposal is known as a *consignment stock*. Consignees sell the consignment goods in their own name, but for the consignor's account, on a commission basis. From time to time the consignee has to render an account, the *account sales* (A/S), showing all sales effected during the period covered by the account and the total sales proceeds. From these proceeds the consignee deducts a commission before remitting the balance to the principal.

Foreign agents (*selling agents*) may assume the *del credere*, thus guaranteeing the solvency of the customers introduced by them to their principals. For undertaking this risk, they are entitled to an extra commission (*del credere commission*). An agent who has the exclusive right to represent a principal in a territory is known as a *sole* or *exclusive agent*. The rights and duties of the agent and the principal are laid down in the *agency agreement*. Agents sometimes also receive money from their principals to advertise products and to provide *after-sales service*.

Foreign distributors. They are importers doing business for their own account who are granted the exclusive right of sale for a certain territory. The contract between the exporters and their foreign distributors is called *distributorship agreement*.

Agents who have been doing good business for their principals may be offered a salary and become fully employed by them. They are then *representatives* or *delegates* of the company, but usually they also additionally receive a bonus or commission on the products they sell.

Companies who have been successful in selling their products abroad may think of establishing a *branch* or *subsidiary* in the foreign country. A foreign branch forms part of the domestic market structure and is headed by a branch manager appointed by the domestic (main) office. A foreign subsidiary, on the other hand, is a separate legal entity set up under the laws of the foreign country. The majority of its shares, or its entire capital, is in the hands of the parent company by which it was established or acquired.

The branch or subsidiary may be entrusted only with selling and related functions (advertising, after-sales service, etc), but it may also be engaged in assembling or manufacturing.

When manufacturers have their own production facilities, their products are, of course, not subject to tariffs and import restrictions in the foreign country. (Assembly offers a tariff advantage if the aggregate duty on the parts to be assembled is less than the duty on the finished product). The manufacturer can also make use of locational advantages offered by the host country (eg lower wages, tax benefits and financial assistance provided by the government). Besides, proximity to the market helps to facilitate business (closer contacts with customers, earlier delivery dates, savings in delivery costs). Many companies have also shifted or outsourced part of their production to low-wage countries to minimize costs.

On the other hand, setting up operations abroad entails considerable capital expenditure and also involves risks. To minimize these, countries conclude treaties and agreements on the promotion and protection of investments. Export-credit insurance covering the political risks attaching to direct investments in foreign countries is also available. Relief from double taxation on income earned abroad (in both the host country and the home country) is provided through the conclusion of double taxation agreements (*tax treaties*).

11.2 Model correspondence

11.2.1 British manufacturer looks for agent in Euro-area

e-mail

Mail from: jennifer.thomas@forklifts.group.com
to: straeter.consult@t-online.de cc:
Subject: Agency for our products in Continental Europe
Attachment: manufacturing.doc

Dear Straeter Consult,

We are manufacturers of weighing systems and wish to appoint an authorized dealer for the sale and service of our equipment in the Euro area. For your information we enclose an attachment on our manufacturing programme.

So far we have been selling mainly on the British market and in the United States. We are now making substantial efforts to extend our activities to the whole of Western Europe and later to Eastern Europe.

For this reason we wish to set up an agency, preferably in Germany. The firm we are looking for should have several years' experience in selling weighing systems or similar equipment. The firm should have adequate maintenance and repair facilities, too.

Please help us to get in touch with suitable firms and send us an offer for the additional services you provide.

Yours sincerely,

Jennifer Thomas
Forklifts Group Plc

11.2.2 Reply to application for agency in Western Europe

FAO: Ms Lydia Oberstein
International Distribution GmbH
Postfach 1730
77649 Offenburg

Fax No.: +49 (7 81) 6 43 70 52

From: Benny Phillips
Ashley Plc
38 Ennismore Gardens
London SW7 1AQ

Number of Pages: 1

Date: 2 November 20..

Subject: Your application for an agency in Western Europe

Dear Ms Oberstein

Thank you for your application of 25 October 20.. Before taking it into consideration, however, we would be grateful if you would answer the following questions:

- How long has your agency been established?
- What warehouse facilities do you have?
- Size of staff?
- What territory have you covered so far and which companies do you represent?
- Do you have any British principals?
- What backup services can you offer?
- Do you carry spares and replacement parts?
- Who are your bankers?
- Please name two trade references with their respective addresses.
- How are product ranges promoted and sold?

As soon as we have received your answers to these questions, we will be in a position to give your application our full consideration.

We look forward to your early reply.

Yours sincerely

Benny Phillips

Benny Phillips
Head of Export Division

11.2.3 American company looks for agent in Germany – writes to German trade association

Gentlemen:

The German Consulate General in New York has been so kind as to provide us with your address.

Our company is a well-known maker of first-class tennis balls and rackets, which we sell throughout the United States and export to many foreign countries. As we would also like to get a foothold in the German market, we are looking for a well-introduced and reliable German firm interested in acting as our agent.

We would therefore be grateful if you could bring our inquiry to the attention of reputable sporting goods dealers among your members.

Thank you for your kind assistance in this matter.

Yours sincerely,

Fairview Sporting Goods Company Inc.
Gordon Shafer
President

11.2.4 British company wishes to act as dealer or agent for German firms – writes to chamber of commerce in Germany

Dear Sirs

We are anxious to act as distributors (on our own account) or as commission agents in the United Kingdom for German firms whose products are in demand in this country.

We have offices in London and Halifax, from where we and our travellers cover the whole country. In addition to the products of one large German firm which we distribute in the United Kingdom, we are now looking for other lines.

Would you please insert our enquiry into your next publication and advise us by what other means we might get in touch with interested German manufacturers.

First-class British and German references can be furnished.

Thank you for your assistance in this matter.

Yours faithfully

11.2.5 Offer to act as buying agent

Dear Sir / Dear Madam

Our mutual business friend, Mr John Baker of Ronalds & Wagner Limited in Toronto, has informed us that you are looking for an agent to handle your purchases of British cutlery and tableware. We would like to take this opportunity to offer you our services.

We are well-known to manufacturers of first-class cutlery and tableware in this country and also know the requirements of the North American market, having acted as buying agents for Ronalds & Wagner Limited for over seven years. For references, please get in touch with this company and the companies mentioned on the attached sheet. They will confirm to you that we have considerable experience in the cutlery and tableware trade and can obtain for our principals the best products in the market at reasonable prices. Besides, our principals have the full benefit of the very favourable rates we have arranged with shipping and insurance companies.

The terms on which we normally do business are as follows:
1. All purchases are made in the name and on the account of our principals.
2. All accounts are passed to our principals for settlement direct with the suppliers.
3. Our commission, which amounts to ...% of the FOB value of each shipment, is payable quarterly.

We hope our offer will interest you and look forward to hearing from you soon.

Yours faithfully

Enc

11.2.6 Japanese company writes to German principal

Kimura Import Incorporated
Yamato-machi, Niigata 949-6306
Japan
Tel.: +81 (2 57) 64-11 80
Fax.: +81 (2 57) 64-37 43
E-Mail: kimura@import.inc.jp

Our ref.: PG/lo

Date: 1st March 20..

Dr. Patrick Neuss
Stürzelberg AG
Niederkasseler Kirchweg 25–27
D-40547 Düsseldorf

Dear Dr Neuss

This is to thank you very much for the kind welcome you gave me during my visit to Germany. I returned to Japan only a few days ago.

Enclosed please find your copy of the Representation Agreement duly signed by me.

I will do my best to develop the Japanese market for your range of products and look forward to a fruitful cooperation with your company.

Yours sincerely

Takeshi Kimura
Kimura Import Incorporated

Encl.

11.2.7 Agency agreement between German and Japanese company

Representation Agreement

This agreement, dated 24 February 20.., between:

Stürzelberg AG, a company duly organized and existing under the laws of Germany, having its registered office at Niederkasseler Kirchweg 25–27, 40547 Düsseldorf, Germany, (hereinafter called 'the Company');

and

Kimura Import Incorporated, a company duly organized and existing under the laws of Japan, having its registered office at Yamato-machi, Niigata 949-6306, Japan (hereinafter called 'the Representative').

The parties hereto hereby agree as follows:

Article 1
Appointment of Representative

1.1 The Company hereby appoints the Representative, who accepts, during the term of this Agreement and upon the terms and conditions herein set forth, to be its exclusive representative in Japan ('the Territory') for the customers and for all products manufactured by Stürzelberg AG ('the Products').

1.2 The Representative shall receive a commission on all sales of Products in the Territory as further specified.

1.3 Notwithstanding the foregoing, the Company reserves the right to sell products to its competitors without having to pay a commission to the Representative with respect to such direct sales, it being understood that competitors shall mean any company having as its principal activity the manufacture and sale of products competing with the products.

Article 2
Non-competition; confidentiality

2.1 In consideration of the exclusive representation granted hereby, neither the Representative nor any Affiliate thereof shall, without the prior written consent of the Company, during the term of this Agreement, directly or indirectly engage or have any interest in the business of manufacturing, promoting, purchasing, selling or otherwise distributing any product in the Territory which is similar to or competitive with any of the Products.

2.2 During the term of this Agreement and thereafter, neither the Representative nor any Affiliate thereof shall disclose or permit the disclosure to any third party of any document, promotional material, sample or other information furnished to it under this Agreement by the Company or any Affiliate thereof or relating to the Products without the express written consent of the Company.

Article 3
Expenses

Unless agreed otherwise on a case-by-case basis, the Representative shall bear all expenses in connection with the performance of his duties hereunder; the Company shall have no responsibility for any expense incurred by the Representative without the Company's prior written consent.

Article 4
Duties of the Representative

4.1 The Representative shall use his best efforts to find customers for the Products in the Territory and to promote and maximize sales of the Products in the Territory for the benefit of the Company. On the other side, the Company shall use its best efforts in supporting the Representative in the fulfilment of his duties and meeting customers' requirements.

4.2 The Representative shall transmit to the Company any orders or inquiries received for Products. The Representative shall have no express or implied authority to assume or create any obligation on behalf of or otherwise bind the Company in any manner. The Representative shall not misrepresent to any third party the scope of his authority under this Agreement. The Representative shall be an independent contractor hereunder and shall not be deemed the agent or legal representative of the Company.

4.3 The Representative shall assist the Company in connection with the negotiation and preparation of proposed Products orders, all of which shall be submitted to the Company for its approval.

Article 5
Sales conditions and orders

5.1 All sales of Products shall be subject to the general terms and conditions of sale specified from time to time by the Company and such terms and conditions shall be included in any offer to sell or quotation furnished by the Representative for any Products.

5.2 The Company shall have the sole right to determine the sales price and the terms and conditions of sales and payment for all Products.

Article 6
Remuneration of the Representative

6.1 The Company shall pay the Representative a commission on sales of Products to customers in the Territory equal to … per cent calculated and paid on the invoice price before tax of the Products in the currency of the order. Representative's claim to commission shall become effective only after delivery of contract and after receipt by the Company of all payments due without any reserve. All due commissions shall be paid on a monthly basis in euros.

6.2 In the event of cancellation of all or any portion, the Representative shall not be entitled to any commission of such order or cancelled portion thereof.

6.3 In the event of any termination or expiration of this Agreement, the Representative shall be entitled to commissions only in respect of orders received by the Company prior to the date of such termination or expiration.

6.4 The commissions payable hereunder shall constitute the Representative's entire compensation for the performance of his obligations hereunder, including any out-of-pocket expenses and other costs incurred by the Representative in connection therewith.

Article 7
Term

7.1 This Agreement shall become effective on the date first above written for an initial period of thirty-six (36) months unless earlier terminated in accordance with this article.

7.2 Thereafter this Agreement shall automatically be prolonged for a further twelve-month period, unless terminated by either party in writing with twelve (12) months' prior notice.

Article 8
Governing law; disputes

8.1 The parties shall make every effort to settle amicably any controversy or claim arising out of or in connection with or related to this Agreement, its interpretation or the breach thereof. Disputes or claims, if any, which cannot be settled amicably shall be finally settled by arbitration under the Rules of Arbitration of the International Chamber of Commerce by one or more arbitrators appointed in accordance with the said Rules. The place of arbitration shall be Paris, France. Arbitration proceedings shall be conducted in the English language. The decision of the arbitrators shall be final, binding and enforceable upon the parties and judgment upon any award rendered by the arbitrators may be entered in any court having jurisdiction thereof.

8.2 The arbitrators shall apply the provisions contained in this Agreement, the mandatory provisions of the respective EU legislation and the principles of law generally recognized in international trade as applicable to international agency contracts, with the exclusion of national laws.

Düsseldorf, 24 February 20..

Signed on behalf of:	Signed on behalf of:
STÜRZELBERG AG	KIMURA IMPORT INC.

11.2.8 British company complains to its German distributor about poor sales and unsatisfactory after-sales service

CRAMPTON & GALWORTH PLC
29–34 Hill Street • London NW7 5HL

RT/JM
7 November 20..

Mr Ernst Brueckner
Manager
Carl Leitmann GmbH
Landsberger Strasse 405
D-81241 München
Germany

Dear Ernst

Despite the economic recovery in Germany, your orders for compressors are still at a low level. This is highly disappointing for us, as we have been expecting a revival in sales. We realize that there may be a good reason why your sales have so far failed to respond to the business upswing, but, as you will certainly understand, we would like to have your views on this subject.

There is yet another matter that is causing us great concern. In the past few months we have received several complaints from customers in northern Germany concerning your company's maintenance and repair service. It seems that, in some cases, customers had been waiting for several weeks before a service engineer was sent from Munich to repair a defective compressor.

It is needless to say that considerable efforts on your side will be necessary to improve the situation. You will no doubt agree with me that in a recovery phase your sales should be substantially above the minimum annual turnover laid down in our contract. At this stage it seems, however, that, unless there is a major upsurge before the end of the year, they will be only marginally higher than the minimum figure.

I look forward to your comments with great interest.

With best regards

Yours sincerely

Roger

11.2.9 German company's consignee in New Zealand complains of difficulties

Dear Mr Mayer

We enclose Account Sales for May. Our sales for that month amounted to NZ$...; the amount of NZ$... remaining after deduction of our commission has been transferred to your account.

The May figure was, as we readily admit, highly disappointing. There are two reasons for the sharp decline in sales: the late arrival of your last consignment and increasing price competition.

As you will remember, you had promised to send us a new consignment by the end of February. Not having received the goods by the middle of March, we enquired by fax and learned that the goods had not yet been despatched.

This delay was most unfortunate, as it left our stock temporarily depleted. As a result, several of our customers turned to other suppliers, and we may have lost their custom for good. That is what is worrying us a lot more than the loss of business caused by the late delivery.

The other problem is that of prices. The prices of your products are – for the most part – higher than those of our competitors, notably the Japanese companies operating in New Zealand. This makes it rather difficult for us to achieve satisfactory sales.

On a long-term view, we cannot hope to maintain our position in the market unless you find a way to make your prices more competitive. But, above all, it will be necessary to prevent such hitches as the delay in delivery mentioned above, which practically put us out of action for several weeks.

Yours sincerely,

Enc

11.2.10 Asian company informs customers worldwide about opening of a subsidiary in Europe

Dear Sirs

Our direct exports to European countries have risen to such an extent that we have decided to open a subsidiary located in Germany. Our new address will be:

China Trading Company GmbH
Goetheplatz 16
D-28203 Bremen
Tel. No.: +49 (4 21) 27 13 98
Fax No.: +49 (4 21) 27 16 07
e-mail: china.trade@aol.com

We are pleased to enclose a leaflet on the product range of our new company which will, of course, remain in closest contact with us and make sure that you receive the best possible service, even faster and more efficient than in the past. We are now on the spot and can help you immediately if you wish to have information, advice, spare parts or accessories from stock. In addition, our multi-lingual after-sales service is available under the following direct telephone number 24 hours a day: +49 (4 21) 76 03 15.

In this company we employ highly qualified skilled personnel who perform the services you require. You are welcome to visit us at our new premises in Bremen where we have a showroom and new warehousing and servicing facilities.

We look forward to hearing from you in the near future.

Yours faithfully
China Trading Company GmbH

Encl.

11.3 Terms and phrases

11.3.1 Looking for agents: replies to applications for agency

We are seeking / looking for commission agents to handle the sale of our products to … manufacturers.	*Wir suchen Handelsvertreter für den Verkauf unserer Erzeugnisse an … Hersteller.*
As the demand for our products in … is steadily growing / increasing, we are considering appointing an agent there to look after our interests.	*Da die Nachfrage nach unseren Produkten in … ständig zunimmt, beabsichtigen wir, einen Vertreter einzusetzen, der unsere Interessen auf diesem Markt wahrnimmt.*
We are looking for a company which would be able to open up the German market for our products / services.	*Wir suchen eine Firma, die in der Lage ist, unseren Produkten / Dienstleistungen den deutschen Markt zu erschließen.*
We believe that there is enormous market potential waiting to be tapped / a promising market waiting to be developed.	*Unserer Ansicht nach besteht ein erhebliches Marktpotential, das nur darauf wartet, genutzt zu werden.*
The person / company we have in mind must have a sound knowledge of the local market / local business practices.	*Die Person / Firma, an die wir denken, muss über fundierte Kenntnisse des örtlichen Marktes / örtlicher Geschäftspraktiken verfügen.*
As our business has expanded beyond all our expectations, we are considering opening a branch / subsidiary in your area.	*Da unser Geschäft sich über unsere Erwartungen hinaus vergrößert hat, denken wir daran, eine Filiale / Tochtergesellschaft in Ihrem Gebiet zu eröffnen.*
Please let us know if you would be prepared to cooperate with us in these circumstances.	*Bitte teilen Sie uns mit, ob Sie bereit wären, unter diesen Umständen mit uns zusammenzuarbeiten.*

11.3.2 Looking for agency / branch / subsidiary: replies to agency offers

We would be interested in acting as your (sole) agents.	*Wir wären an der Übernahme Ihrer (Allein)Vertretung interessiert.*
We saw your advertisement in the … magazine / on the internet and wish to offer our services as agents for the sale of your products / as representatives of your company / as distributors with the exclusive right of sale in the … area.	*Wir haben Ihre Anzeige in der … Zeitschrift / im Internet gesehen und möchten Ihnen unsere Dienste als Vertreter für den Verkauf Ihrer Produkte / als Repräsentanten Ihrer Gesellschaft / als Vertragshändler mit dem Exklusivverkaufsrecht im … Gebiet anbieten.*

We have learned from ... that you are looking for an agent / a company to assist you in marketing your products in ...	*Wir haben von ... erfahren, dass Sie einen Vertreter / eine Firma suchen, der / die Sie beim Vertrieb Ihrer Produkte in ... unterstützt.*
We are well-known distributors in this country, with branches in all the principal cities.	*Wir sind in diesem Land als Vertriebsfirma bestens bekannt und unterhalten Filialen in allen größeren Städten.*
As leading importers in this line, we have an extensive sales organization and a thorough knowledge of the market.	*Als führende Importeure in dieser Branche besitzen wir eine weitverzweigte Verkaufsorganisation und gründliche Kenntnis des Marktes.*
We have spacious and well-equipped showrooms / a large warehouse in ... and an experienced team of sales representatives.	*Wir verfügen über geräumige und gut ausgestattete Ausstellungsräume / ein großes Lager in ... und einen Stab erfahrener Vertreter.*
We could do business with you either on a consignment basis or by placing firm orders.	*Die Abwicklung unserer Geschäfte mit Ihnen könnte auf Konsignationsbasis oder durch Erteilung fester Aufträge erfolgen.*
We will render you monthly accounts sales. Your drafts on us for the amount of these sales, less our commission, will be accepted promptly.	*Sie erhalten von uns monatliche Verkaufsabrechnungen. Ihre auf uns über den Betrag dieser Verkäufe abzüglich unserer Provision gezogenen Wechsel werden wir prompt akzeptieren.*
We are willing to take over the del credere on orders placed through us, for which we would charge an additional commission of ... %.	*Wir sind bereit, für die durch uns vermittelten Aufträge das Delkredere zu übernehmen. Dafür würden wir eine zusätzliche Provision von ... % berechnen.*
If you grant / entrust us with the agency, we will do everything to justify your confidence.	*Wenn Sie uns Ihre Vertretung übertragen, werden wir alles tun, um Ihr Vertrauen zu rechtfertigen.*
We are confident that our extensive experience and valuable connections will enable us to introduce your products / services successfully to our market.	*Wir sind davon überzeugt, dass unsere weitreichende Erfahrung und wertvollen Beziehungen uns in die Lage versetzen werden, Ihre Produkte / Dienstleistungen erfolgreich auf dem hiesigen Markt einzuführen.*
We are pleased to hear that you envisage opening a branch / subsidiary in this country. It will be a great challenge for us as your agents to help build it up. Please let us have further details in due course.	*Wir freuen uns zu erfahren, dass Sie vorhaben, eine Filiale / Niederlassung in unserem Land zu eröffnen. Es wird eine große Herausforderung für uns als Ihre Vertreter sein, Ihnen beim Aufbau behilflich zu sein. Bitte lassen Sie uns zu gegebener Zeit weitere Einzelheiten zukommen.*

11.3.3 Letters from agents

We are encountering / facing strong competition from local manufacturers.	*Wir sehen uns starkem Wettbewerb durch lokale Hersteller ausgesetzt.*
Our competitors have a strong position / are firmly established in this market.	*Unsere Konkurrenten haben hier eine starke Marktposition.*
Our sales are benefiting from the acceleration of the economic revival / from the abolition of foreign currency restrictions in this area.	*Unsere Verkaufszahlen profitieren von der Beschleunigung des Wirtschaftsaufschwungs / von der Abschaffung der Devisenschranken in diesem Gebiet.*
The slump in demand has been aggravated by the unsettled political situation / by the increasing volume of online sales in this product range.	*Der drastische Rückgang der Nachfrage ist durch die unsichere politische Lage / durch steigende Zahlen im Online-Verkauf bei dieser Art von Produkten noch verstärkt worden.*
The latest increase in customs duties has made our position extremely difficult.	*Die jüngste Zollerhöhung hat unsere Lage extrem erschwert.*
If your company wishes to hold its market position, a price reduction is advisable / unavoidable.	*Wenn Ihre Firma ihre Marktposition behalten will, ist eine Preissenkung ratsam / unerlässlich.*

11.3.4 Letters to agents

We regret to note that sales in your territory have fallen sharply in the past few months.	*Wir stellen mit Bedauern fest, dass der Absatz in Ihrem Verkaufsgebiet in den letzten Monaten stark gefallen ist.*
Since your sales figures are encouraging, we are willing to extend your contract by two years.	*Da Ihre Verkaufszahlen ermutigend sind, sind wir bereit, Ihren Vertrag um zwei Jahre zu verlängern.*
Please keep us regularly informed on the situation / further trends in your market.	*Bitte halten Sie uns über die Situation / weitere Tendenzen auf Ihrem Markt regelmäßig auf dem Laufenden.*
In view of the disappointing results in the past year, we must postpone any review of your commission rate.	*In Anbetracht der enttäuschenden Ergebnisse im letzten Jahr müssen wir eine Überprüfung Ihres Provisionssatzes zurückstellen.*
As sales have been disappointing for several years now, we have decided to close down our branch in your area for cost reasons.	*Da der Absatz seit Jahren enttäuschend ist, haben wir beschlossen, unsere Filiale in Ihrem Gebiet aus Kostengründen zu schließen.*

11.3.5 Correspondence relating to the establishment or relocation of branches or subsidiaries

Many advantages are available to your company when you relocate to …	*Viele Vorteile bieten sich Ihrer Firma, wenn Sie deren Sitz nach … verlegen.*
… has factories available for immediate occupation.	*In … stehen Fabriken zum sofortigen Bezug zur Verfügung.*
… offers serviced industrial sites for immediate development.	*… bietet erschlossene, baureife Grundstücke.*
… prime industrial and office development land at reasonable prices.	*… erstklassige gewerbliche Grundstücke und Büros zu günstigen Preisen.*
… an adequate supply of skilled labour / IT experts.	*… ein ausreichendes Angebot an Facharbeitern / IT-Experten.*
… good road / rail access to …	*… gute Straßen- / Schienenverbindung nach …*
… excellent leisure facilities, including extensive sailing waters and golf courses surrounded by delightful countryside.	*… erstklassige Freizeiteinrichtungen, darunter ausgedehnte Segelgewässer und Golfplätze in schöner Landschaft.*
The … Government provides incentives to encourage industrial development in the … area.	*Die … Regierung bietet Anreize, um eine Industrieansiedlung in dem … Gebiet zu fördern.*
There are EU subsidies for the establishment of companies in …	*Es gibt EU-Zuschüsse für die Gründung von Firmen in …*
Loans on preferential terms / low-interest loans / interest-free loans are available towards the cost of the investment.	*Zur Finanzierung der Investition werden Kredite zu Vorzugsbedingungen / Darlehen mit niedrigem Zinssatz / zinslose Darlehen gewährt.*
To qualify for assistance, the project must either create new employment or safeguard existing jobs.	*Förderungswürdig sind Projekte, durch die entweder neue Arbeitsplätze geschaffen oder bestehende Arbeitsplätze gesichert werden.*

11.4 Exercises

Please translate:

11.4.1 E-Mail der Sport Bauer KG in Bad Nauheim (sport.bauer@online.de) an Fairview Golf Equipment Inc., 80 John F. Kennedy Street, Cambridge, MA 02138, USA (fairview@golf.ac.us)

Sehr geehrte Fairview Golf Equipment Inc.,

vom Fachverband für Sportartikel in Frankfurt haben wir erfahren, dass Sie einen Vertreter für den Vertrieb Ihrer Golfausrüstungen im Gebiet der Europäischen Union suchen.

Wir sind sehr an dieser Vertretung interessiert. Unsere Firma existiert seit 20 Jahren und hat in dieser Zeit, vorwiegend in Deutschland und Westeuropa, eine leistungsfähige Verkaufsorganisation aufgebaut. Wir sind im Begriff, im Zuge der EU-Erweiterung nach Osten auch dort Fuß zu fassen. Wir verfügen über gute Beziehungen zum einschlägigen Großhandel sowie zu Waren- und Versandhäusern.

Unser Geschäftsführer und persönlich haftender Gesellschafter, Herr Jürgen Bauer, ist seit 5 Jahren Präsident des Golfclubs in Bad Nauheim. Außerdem ist er Ehrenmitglied mehrerer Clubs in anderen europäischen Städten und kennt daher viele prominente Amateurgolfer und Professionals persönlich.

Als Referenzen nennen wir Ihnen die im beiliegenden Attachment aufgeführten Firmen und Banken. Falls Sie daran interessiert sind, uns mit der Vertretung Ihrer Interessen zu beauftragen, sind wir gern bereit, mit Ihnen in den USA oder hier in Deutschland ein ausführliches Gespräch zu führen.

Ihrer Antwort sehen wir mit Interesse entgegen.

Mit freundlichen Grüßen

Sport Bauer KG

Attachment

11.4.2 Fax der Maschinenbau, Hamburg (Fax-Nr.: +49-40-96 53 20) an African Import Ltd, Abidjan, Ivory Coast (Fax-Nr.: +2-25-58-95 67 83)

Lieber Nuri,

vielen Dank für Ihre Monatsabrechnung für das 1. Quartal 20.. Wir freuen uns, dass Sie Ihren Umsatz um ca. 10 % erhöhen konnten. Die Ihnen zustehende Summe von $ 24.395,00 haben wir wie üblich an Sie überwiesen.

Die Probleme bei der Akkreditiveröffnung Ihres neuen Kunden Power Station Ltd konnten mit Hilfe unserer Bank kurzfristig gelöst werden. Bitte weisen Sie jedoch den Kunden darauf hin, dass beim nächsten Akkreditiv der vorgeschriebene Weg eingehalten werden muss, um unnötige Verzögerungen zu vermeiden.

Die Maschine VX 930 für die Firma African Trade Ltd wird Mitte nächster Woche verschifft. Wir hoffen, dass die aus technischen Gründen entstandene Verspätung von ca. 2 Wochen nicht tragisch ist, da die Lieferung noch innerhalb der Gültigkeit des Akkreditivs erfolgen wird.

Können Sie uns bitte die nächste Quartalsabrechnung bis 25. Juni zuschicken, damit wir sie in unserer internen halbjährlichen Abrechnung noch berücksichtigen können?

Vielen Dank im Voraus.

Mit freundlichen Grüßen

Harald Contzen

Verkaufsleiter Übersee

11.4.3 Hans Schmidt, Verkaufsleiter von Ebner & Co. GmbH in Fulda, an Olaf Jakobsen, Mitinhaber der Firma Jacobsen & Heggstad, Oslo

Sehr geehrter Herr Jakobsen,
besten Dank für Ihre Gastfreundschaft während meines Besuches in Norwegen. In der Anlage übersenden wir Ihnen den unterschriebenen Händlervertrag in zweifacher Ausfertigung und bitten Sie, uns ein Exemplar unterzeichnet zurückzusenden.

Wie vereinbart, werden Sie in Norwegen mindestens 5 Vertretungen mit Servicestationen einrichten, wobei die Belieferung mit unseren Produkten nur über Ihre Gesellschaft erfolgt.

Um eine erfolgreiche Zusammenarbeit sicherzustellen, werden wir Ihnen jede werbliche und technische Unterstützung bei der Erschließung Ihres Marktes für unsere Produkte geben. Wir hoffen, dass es Ihnen gelingen wird, in dem vereinbarten Zeitraum von 3 Jahren das Mindestumsatzvolumen von 2,5 Millionen Euro zu erreichen.

Das notwendige Werbematerial erhalten Sie von uns kostenlos in englischer Sprache. Für die Übersetzung in das Norwegische stellen wir Ihnen die Logos, Fotos und Filme zur Verfügung. Ihre Servicetechniker erhalten kostenfreie Schulung in unserem Hause. Der erste Lehrgang findet vom … bis … statt.

Wir haben unter Berücksichtigung der Konkurrenz in Ihrem Land unsere Preise einer nochmaligen genauen Kalkulation unterzogen und freuen uns, Ihnen mitteilen zu können, dass wir Ihnen bei Abnahme von mindestens 100 Einheiten pro Bestellung einen Rabatt in Höhe von 10 % geben können. Außerdem möchten wir Ihnen empfehlen, uns einen Rahmenauftrag über jeweils einen Jahresbedarf zu erteilen und die einzelnen Lieferungen zum Zeitpunkt des Bedarfs abzurufen. In diesem Fall könnten wir Ihnen noch einen weiteren Rabatt von 5% einräumen. Diese Zusage gilt bis auf Widerruf.

Um von Anfang an eine termingerechte Belieferung sicher zu stellen, bitten wir Sie, uns Ihre Verkaufsprognose für 20.. bis spätestens 30. November zuzusenden.

Wir hoffen auf eine angenehme und erfolgreiche Zusammenarbeit.

Mit freundlichen Grüßen

Anlage

Da die norwegische Firma englisch korrespondiert, ist der obige Brief ins Englische zu übertragen.

11.4.4 Memo an britische Filiale einer deutschen Supermarktkette über die Einführung eines neuen Warenwirtschaftssystems

Memo

An: Frau Malloon
Betr.: Einführung von KW 33

Da seit Beginn des letzten Quartals das neue Warenwirtschaftssystem KW 33 europaweit einwandfrei läuft, sind ab sofort die monatlichen Bestandsmeldungen am 7. Werktag nach Monatsende per Datenübertragung abzugeben.

Altbestände, die noch nicht mit den neuen EANs (*European Article Numbers*) scannerfähig ausgezeichnet sind, müssen bis 15. Werktag nach Monatsende eingereicht werden.

Bei organisatorischen Fragen wenden Sie sich bitte an Frau Müller (Nebenstelle 3805) und bei Problemen bei der Übertragung an Herrn Seiferth (Nebenstelle 9846).

Peter Steigenberger

Please draft letters, faxes or e-mails from the following particulars:

11.4.5 Geschäftsfall:

Sie arbeiten bei der Firma Achenbach & Co. GmbH, Postfach 273406 in 45289 Essen, Fax-Nr.: +49 (201) 337459, E-Mail-Adresse: achenbach.gmbh@t-online.de, und stellen Transport- und Fördergeräte her. Auf einer kürzlich in Südafrika stattgefundenen Messe, auf der Ihr neuer Gabelstapler „FL 2010" vorgestellt wurde, haben Sie Herrn Jonathan Riverside von der südafrikanischen Firma Pan African Trade Ltd, 246 Rivonia Boulevard, Rivonia, South Africa, Fax-Nr.: +27 (13) 16598, E-Mail-Adresse: panafrican.trade@ltd.za, kennen gelernt. Herr Riverside bekundete Interesse daran, die Vertretung Ihrer Produktpalette und insbesondere dieses neuen Gerätes für die Länder Zentralafrikas und Südafrika zu übernehmen.

Aufgabe: Schreiben Sie an Herrn Riverside einen Brief / Fax / eine E-Mail und berücksichtigen Sie dabei die folgenden Punkte:

- Bezugnahme auf das obige Gespräch
- Sie sind grundsätzlich bereit, der Pan African Trade Ltd für zunächst drei Jahre die Exklusivvertretung für das gewünschte Gebiet zu übertragen
- Danach wäre eine Verlängerung möglich
- Aufbau eines Händlernetzes Bedingung
- Wie stellt sich Herr Riverside eine Zusammenarbeit vor?
- Bitte um eine detaillierte Auflistung seiner Vertriebs- und Lagerhaltungsmöglichkeiten, usw.

- Bitte um fundierte Prognosen der Absatzmöglichkeiten in den Jahren 1, 2 und 3, gestaffelt nach Industriebranchen
- Weitere Einzelheiten (Provision, Lagerung, Unterstützung bei Messen und Werbekampagnen, Schulung der Mechaniker, usw.) müssten in einem persönlichen Gespräch in Ihrem Werk geklärt werden.

11.4.6 Geschäftsfall:

Sie arbeiten bei der Mähringer GmbH, Hochkreuzallee 56, 53175 Bonn, Fax-Nr.: +49 (2 28) 31 07 65, E-Mail-Adresse: maehringer@t-online.de, welche sich mit dem weltweiten Import von Camping- und Freizeitartikeln beschäftigt. Sie importieren seit Jahren als selbständiger Vertragshändler die Produkte der Firma Trackworld Inc., 1503 Teaneck Road, Teaneck, New Jersey, USA 07666, Fax-Nr.: +1 (2 01) 2 39 48 57, E-Mail-Adresse: trackworld.inc@newworld.com.

Aufgabe: Schicken Sie dem amerikanischen Prinzipal ihren 4. Quartalsbericht für das laufende Jahre mit folgenden Einzelheiten:

- Nach schlechtem Jahresbeginn steigende Umsatzzahlen wegen des guten Weihnachtsgeschäfts (siehe Anlage)
- Besonders gut liefen die Wanderstiefel „Lightwear“ und der neue Rucksack „Tracker's Delight“
- Für beide Produkte benötigen Sie dringend Nachschub. Bestellen Sie je 200 Paar Stiefel in allen gängigen Größen und 3.000 neue Rucksäcke
- Zahlung erfolgt wie gewohnt per Überweisung 90 Tage nach Lieferung in US$
- Bitten Sie Trackworld, Ihnen mit der nächsten Sendung weitere 10.000 neue Prospekte in deutscher Sprache zu schicken, da Ihr Vorrat so gut wie aufgebraucht ist.

11.4.7 Geschäftsfall:

Ihr Stammhaus, die Sailing & Motor Boats Ltd in 346 Whitfield Street, London W1P 5RT, UK, Fax-Nr.: +44 (20) 73 86 15 45, E-Mail-Adresse: boats.ltd@compuserve.com, hat in Portugal, Av. 5 de Outubro, 75–7°, P-1000 Lisboa, Portugal, Fax-Nr.: +351 (21) 77 93 65, E-Mail-Adresse: barcos.ltda@com.pt, eine Filiale mit dem Namen Barcos Limitada eröffnet. Die Geschäftssprache ist Englisch.

Aufgabe: Schreiben Sie als Filialleiter(in) Ihren Quartalsbericht für die Monate Juli bis September wie folgt:

- Der Boom bei Segel- und Motorbooten hat deutlich nachgelassen (nur 80 Neuverkäufe gegenüber 360 im 1. und 240 im 2. Quartal). Siehe beiliegende detaillierte Aufstellung.
- Angesichts der zu Ende gehenden Saison ist dies jedoch nicht beunruhigend
- Besonderer Beliebtheit erfreut sich das neue kleine Motorboot „Speed Cruiser“
- Sie empfehlen eine besondere Werbekampagne für dieses Boot, auch in anderen EU-Ländern, da Ihre Kunden vielfach ausländische Touristen sind

- Versicherung, dass Sie Ihre Verkaufsanstrengungen verstärken werden, die Marktlage jedoch nicht einfach ist
- Das Boot „Sailing Miracle A 300" ist Ihrer Meinung nach zu teuer für den kontinentaleuropäischen Markt, da die starke Konkurrenz aus den USA Ihnen hier zuvorkommt. Kann Preis ggf. gesenkt werden?
- Die Rezession in ganz Europa macht sich stark bemerkbar. Sie empfehlen daher Konzentration auf kleinere, sportliche Modelle.

11.4.8 **Geschäftsfall:**

Sie arbeiten bei der Netcom GmbH, Ruppenkampstr. 26, 49031 Osnabrück, Fax-Nr.: +49 (541) 60 13 52, E-Mail-Adresse: netcom@de, die kürzlich als Niederlassung der Netcom Incorporated, 6400 Uptown Boulevard, Suite 398 W, Albuquerque, NM 87110, USA, Fax.-Nr.: +1 (800) 340 66 93 47, E-Mail-Adresse: netcom.inc@compuserve.com, gegründet worden ist.

Aufgabe: Schreiben Sie an Ihr Mutterhaus, dass noch folgende Formalitäten zu erledigen sind:

- Für die Eintragung ins Handelsregister wird eine beglaubigte Übersetzung des Gesellschaftervertrages benötigt. Die Übersetzung sollte von einem in Osnabrück ansässigen, vereidigten Übersetzer angefertigt werden.
- Zur Einrichtung eines Zolllagers wird eine deutsche Kurzbeschreibung der Geräte zusammen mit den jeweiligen internationalen Zoll-Nummern (*nomenclature numbers*) benötigt. Eine von Ihnen gefertigte Liste wird zwecks Überprüfung beigefügt.
- Die neuen Geschäftsräume in der Ruppenkampstraße wurden bezogen. Die vereinbarte Kaution ist dem Vermieter in Form einer Bankgarantie auszuhändigen. Bitte um Rücksendung des beigefügten Antrags der Deutschen Handelsbank, Osnabrück mit Unterschrift.
- Liste mit einer Aufstellung der bisher aufgelaufenen Gründungskosten wird mit der Bitte um Erstattung beigefügt.

12. Cooperation; Joint Ventures; Licensing; Mergers and Acquisitions

12.1 Introduction

A company which is growing finds itself faced with many obstacles. On the one hand the company needs constant investment in plant and machinery, product and service development, and last but not least, people with the appropriate skills to export these products and services. On the other hand it can export know-how or intellectual property.

Cooperation. Cooperation between firms across national boundaries has become quite common in recent years. Some of the principal areas in which firms cooperate are research and development, production and marketing. By cooperating, firms can increase their potential and share expenditure with their partners.

Joint venture. A joint venture is a venture undertaken by two or more parties for the purpose of carrying out a joint operation. It may involve the establishment of a common subsidiary, either in the country of one of the joint-venture partners or in a third country.

The terms *cooperation* and *joint venture* are often used interchangeably; both may refer to licensing.

Licensing. Licensing (in international trade) is an arrangement by which a license holder, the *licensor*, allows another party, the *licensee*, to use, make or sell his know-how, products or services. The licensor enters into a *licence* (AE *license*) agreement with the licensee, under which the licensor places patents, trademarks, designs, registered designs, copyright and know-how at the licensee's disposal against payment of compensation, called *licence fee* or *royalty*. (The foreign licensee may be a subsidiary of the domestic licensor). The registration of trademarks and designs is dealt with by so-called *patent attorneys* who file applications at the Patent Office. The negotation of technology transfer is done by *licensing agents* or by the company lawyers themselves.

Payment for a licensing agreement may take the form of an annual payment, a percentage fee based on sales or profits, or a cross-licensing arrangement, by which a mutual exchange of know-how and/or patents is agreed upon.

Mergers and Acquisitions (M&A). At the turn of this century the world saw a marked increase in amicable or hostile take-overs, leveraged buyouts, management buy-ins and buy-outs, mergers with other companies or acquisitions of majority shareholdings. In some cases the reasons were a need for *diversification* (*horizontal or vertical integration of products or services*), in others a desire to spread risks by enlarging product and service ranges and crossing international borders, or – in many cases – the straightforward intention to increase *shareholder value*. The results have not always been successful. Although in some cases it has been possible to rationalize and streamline production facilities by coordinating manufacturing and sales strategies, cutting down on staff or outsourcing parts of the production, other disadvantages occurred, such as problems with lay-offs, negative effects on labour relations and a disregard of cultural and national features. M&As require staff and management to be absolutely flexible and to put their company's objectives before personal priorities.

Advantages may accrue from M&As in that prices for standardized products and services can be reduced. On the other hand, the dangers cannot be overlooked. Work may be transferred to low-wage countries and price wars among competing companies may result, not only endangering jobs but also the quality of the product or service itself.

12.2 Model correspondence

12.2.1 British manufacturer looks for joint venture partner in Germany

UE

UNIVERSAL ELECTRONICS LIMITED
20 Thornton Street • Leeds, LS3 8KL
Telephone: (05 32) 9 43 10 • Fax: (05 32) 9 43 81
e-mail address: universal.electronics@firmnet.co.uk

PB/CM

29 July 20..

Industrie- und Handelskammer Muenchen und Oberbayern
Max-Joseph-Strasse 2
D-80333 Muenchen
Germany

Dear Sirs

I am writing at the suggestion of the Leeds Chamber of Commerce to seek your assistance in locating a possible joint venture partner in Germany.

The joint venture might take the form of:

(1) A marketing arrangement, under which we sell our partner's products here in Britain

(2) A licensing arrangement, under which we manufacture and sell our partner's products here in Britain

(3) A reciprocal arrangement, under which we market or manufacture/market each other's products in our respective markets.

The third option would be preferred.

Products of interest to us are electronics-based products, mainly those concerned with process automation. Our preferred partner would be small to medium sized, but with a well-established reputation in their home market for product quality and service.

We currently manufacture and market, largely in Britain, the following electronic equipment:

(1) Stabilized power supplies, mainly for use in the telecommunications industry

(2) Electronic weighing systems which are sold to a wide range of manufacturing industries

(3) Microprocessor-based process monitoring and control systems

.../2

Directors: P.H. Cartwright (Chairman), H.N. Adams, P. Bolton, J. Graham
Registered Office: 20 Thornton Street, Leeds. Registered No. 566 736 London

Industrie- und Handelskammer Muenchen und Oberbayern
29 July 20..
Page 2

Our company was established in 1956 and now has 120 employees. We have a well-equipped development department, and our manufacturing facilities, including electronics assembly, sheet metal working and machining, are quality-approved to British Telecom and Ministry of Defence standards. Our sales force of technically qualified sales engineers is backed by similarly well-trained service engineers and a small marketing team. We offer any potential collaborator a highly professional batch manufacturing capability and a high-calibre marketing, sales and service team.

Any help you can give me in locating suitable partners would be very much appreciated. I would be quite happy for the contents of this note to be circulated to your members, but would ask that our identity should not be revealed without prior consultation. Perhaps interested parties could respond to us through yourselves equally anonymously and with a similar profile so that we may conduct a preliminary assessment of responses in confidence.

I do hope you may be able to assist us and look forward to hearing from you soon.

Yours faithfully

Dr P Bolton
Director

12.2.2 Enquiry concerning licensing arrangement

ELCRON RESEARCH ASSOCIATES INC P.O. Box 7540, San Diego, CA 92166 USA
Tel. +1(619)5307064, Fax +1(619)5307065, e-mail: elcron@compuserve.com

Intersil Datel GmbH
Bavariaring 8
D-80336 Muenchen
Germany

Gentlemen:

We have been referred to you by the German Consulate General in Chicago. A client of ours, an established U.S. company, is seeking to license complementary products and technology. It would initially be interested in a distribution arrangement for an interim period until the economics justify a full-scale license.

Our client has a strong position in the market. Its products, which include fire-alarm systems and accessories, signals, clocks and timers, security and communication equipment, enjoy an excellent reputation. The company's national sales organization is presently serving the commercial, institutional and light industrial sectors; annual sales are in the $25 million range. Apart from its flexible manufacturing capability, which enables it to handle both medium and large-volume series, it has an efficient national service organization.

Our client is interested in products which fit in with its present production and marketing capabilities. We understand that your company is manufacturing such products as electric and electronic clocks and timers, and we therefore believe that it might be in a position to offer attractive products and technology to a highly qualified prospective U.S. partner.

We look forward to hearing from you whether you would be interested in cooperating with our client and would appreciate receiving information describing your company's products and activities.

Sincerely yours,

John D. Turner
Research Associate

12.2.3 Indian company seeks cooperation with German manufacturer

FAO: Mr. Karlheinz Wegener
Burgunder Str. 30–32
D-79104 Freiburg

Fax No.: +49 (7 61) 33 10 54

From: Suren Karmalker
Karmalker Limited
Radj Mahal Villas 310
Bangalore, India

Date: 30 October 20..

Dear Mr Wegener

PROPOSAL FOR SETTING UP A PLANT IN INDIA

We thank you for the above proposal providing us with a range of alternatives for the manufacture of commercial vehicles in India.

As you know, it is our objective to set up at Bangalore a plant with a high degree of self-sufficiency in the long run, capable of producing commercial vehicles that are technically up-to-date, competitive in price and fuel efficiency and suitable for our roads and local conditions.

We are planning to manufacture at Bangalore all the principal aggregates of the vehicles, such as engines, the complete power train, axles, etc. Such items as are locally available in the requisite quality and specifications to fit into these aggregates will be bought from local sources. The automobile ancillary industry in this country could produce for us a number of components, such as forgings, castings, bearings, valves, pistons, etc. We are certain that many of these ancillary manufacturers could be persuaded to expand capacity to the extent necessary to supply the Bangalore plant on a regular basis.

For this project we are seeking a collaborator interested in a long-term relationship with us. As we need a number of additional details for our further planning, we would be grateful if you would complete the enclosed questionnaire and return it to us.

In your proposal you indicated various models of vehicles which may be suitable for our requirements. The information given in the questionnaire should relate to these models.

We appreciate your kindness in providing this information, which will help us to evaluate the financial viability of the project and to obtain the necessary industrial licence from the government.

Yours faithfully
Karmalker Limited

Suren Karmalker

Suren Karmalker
Managing Director
Enclosure: Questionnaire

12.2.4 Joint venture with Chinese company

ADM/LD
20 October 20..

Mr Chen Ho Fung
Director
CMT China Machine Tool Company
P.O. Box 43 08 517
Beijing
People's Republic of China

Dear Mr Chen

WUHAN FACTORY PROJECT

Reference is made to our recent meeting in London. I was delighted to make your acquaintance and have pleasure in summarising the results of our talks as follows:

CMT intends to set up shortly at its plant in Wuhan a line for the assembly, from CKD kits, of certain FLETCHER machine tools. Furthermore, components for these machines are to be manufactured in CMT's plant.

CMT wishes to procure the necessary CKD kits from FLETCHER and expects from FLETCHER delivery of the CKD kits as well as assistance during the start-up phase of assembly and in the manufacture of components.

Moreover, CMT contemplates the possibility of building further factories (or fitting out existing plants) for the manufacture of these machine tools in other parts of China.

CMT therefore wishes to acquire a licence to manufacture the machine tools in question and possibly also to build and operate a further factory in the form of a joint venture with FLETCHER. This joint venture is to comprise also the sectors marketing, sales, spare parts and after-sales service.

FLETCHER is prepared in principle to examine with CMT the mutual possibilities for the joint realisation of the new factory project in the form of a joint venture according to the currently valid Chinese legislation. At this stage, FLETCHER signifies its agreement to co-operate in preparing a feasibility study should CMT so desire. FLETCHER assumes that such a feasibility study would suitably and adequately take into account the legitimate interests of both parties.

FLETCHER does not rule out the possibility of capitalising at least part of the licence fee under such a joint venture.

I look forward to the conclusion of an agreement along these lines between our two companies in the near future.

With my best personal regards

Yours sincerely

A D Mortimer
Managing Director

12.2.5 British company informs an advertising agency about a takeover

e-mail

Mail from: netscap.ltd@compuserve.com
to: marketing.agentur@t-online.de **cc:** PaulHasselkamp.carOrder@gorex.de
Subject: Reorganization of marketing affairs
Attachment:

Dear Ms Antje Stürzelberg

We have recently acquired a majority of 52 % of the shares of the German company carOrder selling cars online by website.

As from 22 July 20.. our marketing department will take over the activities of the marketing department of carOrder. This means that we wish to renegotiate the terms for both companies, and of course also coordinate all publicity activities.

We would like to deal with this either on 10 or 14 August 20.. at the premises of carOrder in Munich. We hope that you and your colleague Mr Greifswald will be able to make it on one of these days. Please bring all your files to the meeting. Mr Paul Hasselkamp of carOrder and I myself will also be present.

Yours sincerely
Jennifer Bold
Head of Marketing

12.3 Terms and phrases

We are considering licensing a German firm to manufacture our products.	*Wir beabsichtigen, einer deutschen Firma die Lizenz zur Herstellung unserer Produkte zu erteilen.*
We understand that you are interested in manufacturing air conditioning equipment under licence.	*Wie wir erfahren haben, sind Sie daran interessiert, Klimageräte in Lizenz herzustellen.*
When I last visited you in Frankfurt, you indicated that your company might have an interest in securing a licence from us.	*Bei meinem letzten Besuch in Frankfurt deuteten Sie an, dass Ihre Firma eventuell daran interessiert wäre, von uns eine Lizenz zu bekommen.*
Our company seeks to exploit its patent for the hardening of the inner surface of steel pipes. We therefore ask for your help in finding a suitable joint-venture partner.	*Unsere Firma möchte ihr Patent für die Härtung der Innenfläche von Stahlrohren verwerten. Wir bitten Sie deshalb, uns bei der Suche eines geeigneten Joint-Venture-Partners zu helfen.*
Thank you for your detailed reply of ..., in which you specified your ideas for a joint venture.	*Vielen Dank für Ihre ausführliche Antwort vom ..., in der Sie Ihre Vorstellungen eines Joint Venture darlegten.*
As we have spare capacity, we are looking for products complementary to our present range which we might either manufacture under licence or sell as sole agents.	*Da wir freie Kapazität haben, suchen wir Produkte zur Ergänzung unserer jetzigen Produktpalette, die wir entweder unter Lizenz oder als Alleinvertreter vertreiben könnten.*
We have contacted B2B companies to find out if any of them is interested in joint activities with us.	*Wir haben mit B2B-Firmen Kontakt aufgenommen um herauszufinden, ob eine von ihnen an einer Zusammenarbeit mit uns interessiert ist.*
We are planning a tour of Southern Europe for the purpose of seeking out opportunities for cross-licensing, manufacturing under licence, joint research and development, and co-production.	*Wir planen eine Reise durch Südeuropa, um Möglichkeiten des Austausches von Lizenzen, der Lizenzherstellung, der gemeinsamen Forschung und Entwicklung sowie der Kooperation im Bereich der Produktion zu suchen.*
We are a mail-order company specialized in selling its products by catalogue and via the internet. We are looking for suitable partners with a complementary range who would like to cooperate with us.	*Wir sind ein Versandhaus, das sich darauf spezialisiert hat, seine Produkte per Katalog und über das Internet zu vertreiben. Wir suchen geeignete Partner mit einer ergänzenden Palette, die mit uns zusammenarbeiten möchten.*

We have specialized expertise / know-how in ... and the facilities necessary to manufacture a broad range of products.	*Wir verfügen über spezielles Fachwissen / Know-how in ... und über die nötigen Einrichtungen zur Herstellung einer breiten Palette von Produkten.*
For reasons of rationalisation / diversification we have decided to merge with ...	*Aus Gründen der Rationalisierung / Diversifizierung haben wir beschlossen, mit ... zu fusionieren.*
We would like to inform you that we have acquired / taken over ...% of the share capital of ...	*Wir möchten Ihnen mitteilen, dass wir ...% des Aktienkapitals der ... erworben / übernommen haben.*
Patent applications are pending in many countries.	*In vielen Ländern sind Patentanmeldungen anhängig.*
As soon as we have agreed on the principal details of such a cooperation, we will send you a draft licence agreement.	*Sobald wir uns über die wichtigsten Einzelheiten einer derartigen Kooperation geeinigt haben, senden wir Ihnen den Entwurf eines Lizenzvertrages.*

12.4 Exercises

Please translate:

12.4.1 E-Mail von marketing.agentur@t-online.de an netscap.ltd@compuserve.com als Antwort auf 12.2.5

Neuordnung Ihrer Marketing-Aktivitäten

Cc: Paul Hasselkamp, carOrder@gorex.de

Sehr geehrte Frau Jennifer Bold

Wir haben Ihre heutige E-Mail erhalten und zur Kenntnis genommen, dass Sie jetzt die Aktienmehrheit an carOrder halten.

Zwecks Neuordnung Ihrer Marketingabteilung sind wir gern bereit, Sie am 14.08.20.. in den Geschäftsräumen der carOrder in München zu treffen. Bitte nennen Sie uns die für Sie günstigste Zeit. Herr Greifswald und ich werden alle für das Gespräch erforderlichen Unterlagen mitbringen.

Alle weiteren Einzelheiten werden Sie sicher mit Herrn Hasselkamp besprechen.

Mit freundlichen Grüßen

Antje Stürzelberg

12.4.2 Antwort der Industrie- und Handelskammer für München und Oberbayern an Universal Electronics Limited (vgl. 12.2.1)

Sehr geehrter Herr Dr. Bolton,

wir danken Ihnen für Ihr Schreiben vom 29. Juli, dem wir entnehmen, dass Sie einen Kooperationspartner in Deutschland suchen. Wir sind gerne bereit, Sie bei Ihren Bemühungen zu unterstützen.

Nach unserer Erfahrung ist es um so leichter, potentielle Partner für Kooperationen zu finden, je mehr über die anfragende Firma und die gewünschte Art der Kooperation bekannt ist. Um Ihnen eine Vorstellung davon zu vermitteln, welche Fragen üblicherweise von unseren Mitgliedsfirmen bei Kooperationsangeboten aus dem Ausland gestellt werden, legen wir einen von uns ausgearbeiteten Fragebogen bei.

Sollten Sie eine Vermittlung durch die Kammer wünschen, dürfen wir Sie bitten, uns den ausgefüllten Fragebogen zusammen mit zusätzlichen Unterlagen, z. B. Prospekten, Jahresberichten usw., zuzusenden. Wir werden dann unsere Mitgliedsfirmen durch eine Anzeige in unseren „AWI – Außenwirtschaftsinformationen" ohne Nennung Ihres Namens auf Ihr Angebot aufmerksam machen. Die Firmen, die sich auf diese Anzeige hin bei uns melden, erhalten jedoch die uns von Ihnen zur Verfügung gestellten Informationen und werden gebeten, sich direkt mit Ihnen in Verbindung zu setzen.

Falls Sie mit diesem Verfahren nicht einverstanden sein sollten, können Sie sich auch direkt an die in Frage kommenden Firmen wenden. Zu diesem Zweck senden wir Ihnen als Anlage eine Liste der Hersteller sowie der Exporteure und Importeure von elektronischen Produkten in unserem Kammerbezirk.

Wir hoffen, Ihnen mit diesen Informationen gedient zu haben. Sollten Sie sich für das erste Verfahren entscheiden, so bitten wir um Ihre Mitteilung.

Mit freundlichen Grüßen
Industrie- und Handelskammer für München und Oberbayern
Außenwirtschaftsabteilung
(Unterschrift)
Anlagen

12.4.3 Wiedemann & Co. GmbH, Aschaffenburg, an Mr Cooper, Managing Director von Gardiner & Co. Ltd, London

Sehr geehrter Mr Cooper,

vielen Dank für Ihren Brief vom 22. 10. 20..

Sie suchen für Ihren Geschäftspartner in Indonesien eine deutsche Papierfabrik, die zuerst Papiere für die Filtration von Benzin und Öl liefert und anschließend mit ihrem Know-how beim Aufbau einer Papierfabrik sowie einer Impregnieranlage in Indonesien hilft. Dazu sind wir grundsätzlich bereit.

Bitte teilen Sie uns noch Einzelheiten über das benötigte Papier mit, z. B. Grammgewicht, Rollenbreite, Hülsendurchmesser, Luftdurchlässigkeit. Wir werden dann das passende Papier anbieten und wunschgemäß 20 Musterbögen DIN A4 sowie Spezifikationen an Sie senden. Sobald die Frage der Papierqualität geklärt ist, kann über den Aufbau der Papierfabrik gesprochen werden.

Mit dem Besuch einer indonesischen Delegation sind wir einverstanden. Bitte informieren Sie uns rechtzeitig über den geplanten Termin und die Anzahl der Besucher.

Ihrer Antwort sehen wir mit Interesse entgegen.

Mit freundlichen Grüßen

Please draft letters, faxes or e-mails from the following particulars:

12.4.4 **Geschäftsfall:**

Die Firma Rustikal-Möbel GmbH, Am Wasserturm 10, 40668 Meerbusch, Fax-Nr.: +49 (21 50) 9 15 41 88, E-Mail-Adresse: rustikal.gmbH@abit.de sucht in den USA einen Kooperationspartner für den Vertrieb ihrer rustikalen Bauernmöbel. Über die deutsch-amerikanische Handelskammer in New York hat sie die Anschrift der Continental Furniture Import Inc., 180 Park Avenue, New York, NY 10016, USA, Fax-Nr.: +1 (212) 6 82 13 44, E-Mail-Adresse: furniture.imports@inc.com erhalten. Mit einem ersten Fax hat die amerikanische Firma Interesse bekundet und bittet um weitere Einzelheiten.

Aufgabe: Richten Sie ein Schreiben an die Continental Furniture Import Inc. unter Berücksichtigung folgender Punkte:

- Freude über Interesse an Kooperation
- Sie würden die Möbel in zerlegtem und verpacktem Zustand liefern
- Die Möbel könnten von CFI in diesem Zustand an die Kunden weitergeliefert oder auch von CFI montiert geliefert werden
- Für eine begrenzte Zeit könnten Sie einen Schreinermeister nach New York senden, der die Einarbeitung der amerikanischen Schreiner übernimmt
- Die beiliegende Preisliste enthält ab-Werk-Preise. Zur Errechnung von FOB- und CIF-Preisen werden getrennte Angebote erstellt, sobald Liefermenge bekannt ist
- Günstigste Fracht bei Lieferung kompletter Container
- Vorgeschlagene Zahlungsbedingung: Bei Aufträgen über 10.000,– US$ unwiderrufliches Dokumentenakkreditiv, bei Aufträgen darunter „Kasse gegen Dokumente"
- Unterstützung bei anfänglicher Werbekampagne möglich (Poster und Aufkleber könnten zur Verfügung gestellt werden).

12.4.5 **Geschäftsfall:**

Die St. Gallen Solartechnik AG, Marktplatz 15, CH-9004 St. Gallen, Fax.-Nr.: +41 (71) 13 60 84, E-Mail-Adresse: st.gallen@solartechnik.com, hat ihre Erzeugnisse auf der Hannover-Messe ausgestellt und dort Mr. Huang von der vietnamesischen Firma Hanoi Technology Inc., 37 Phan Boi Chau, Hanoi, Viet Nam, Fax-Nr.: +84 (4) 7 35 62 01, E-Mail-Adresse: hanoi.technology@org.vn kennen gelernt, der Interesse an einer Lizenzfertigung der Anlagen zeigt. Nach dem Austausch einiger Informationen werden Sie gebeten, ein allgemeines Lizenz-Angebot zu erstellen.

Aufgabe: Richten Sie dieses an Mr. Huang der Firma Hanoi Technology Inc. und berücksichtigen Sie dabei folgende Punkte:

- Sie sind grundsätzlich bereit, der vietnamesischen Gesellschaft eine exklusive Lizenz für die Herstellung und den Vertrieb Ihrer Solaranlagen in Südostasien zu erteilen
- Sie würden als Lizenzgeber dem Lizenznehmer Ihre Patente und Ihr Know-how zur Verfügung stellen

- Die Mindestlizenzgebühr, die jährlich an die St. Gallen Solartechnik AG zu zahlen ist, beläuft sich auf 20.000,– Schweizer Franken. Dieser Betrag entspricht 4 % eines angenommenen Mindestumsatzes von 500.000,– Schweizer Franken
- Sollte dieser Umsatz überschritten werden, ist auf den Mehrbetrag ebenfalls eine Gebühr von 4 % zu zahlen
- Eine Erteilung von Unterlizenzen ist nicht gestattet
- Bei Nachfolgeerfindungen und Verbesserungen müsste die vom Lizenznehmer zusätzlich zu zahlende Gebühr in beiderseitigem Einvernehmen festgelegt werden
- Absolute Geheimhaltung aller Unterlagen erforderlich
- Vorgeschlagene Probezeit: 5 Jahre
- Im Falle von Streitigkeiten, die sich aus dem Vertrag ergeben sollten, schlagen Sie die Zuständigkeit des Schiedsgerichts der Internationalen Handelskammer Paris vor
- Bitte um baldige Stellungnahme, damit baldiger Vertragsabschluss möglich.

12.4.6 Geschäftsfall:

Die deutsche Firma Promotion GmbH, Birkweg 96, 24999 Wees, Fax-Nr.: +49 (46 31) 50 30 06, E-Mail-Adresse: promotion.gmbh@csgi.de kooperiert seit Jahren mit der britischen Gesellschaft Customer Care Ltd, Janus House, 58 St. Andrews Street, Cambridge CB2 3AH Fax-Nr.: +44 (12 83) 34 09 66, E-Mail-Adresse: customer.care@mailorder.com. Beide Unternehmen sind auf dem Gebiet des Versandhandels und Direktmarketings tätig. Aus Kosten- und Diversifizierungsgründen haben die beiden Firmen beschlossen zu fusionieren.

Aufgabe: Schreiben Sie als eine/r der beiden neuen Geschäftsführer/in(nen) per E-Mail ein Rundschreiben an Ihre Kunden mit folgendem Inhalt:

- Name der neuen Gesellschaft: Promotion Care Ltd, Hauptsitz in Cambridge (engl. Anschrift) mit selbständiger Niederlassung als Promotion Care GmbH in Wees (deutsche Anschrift)
- Die E-Mail-Adresse der englischen Firma ändert sich in: promotion.care@mailorder.com, die E-Mail-Adresse der deutschen Niederlassung lautet von jetzt an: promotion.care@mailorder.de
- Die Homepage für beide Firmen lautet: www.promotion.com
- Geschäftsführer der britischen Gesellschaft: Mr Peter Gordon Reading, Managing Director
- Geschäftsführer/in der deutschen Niederlassung: Ihr Name, Geschäftsführer(in)
- Schildern Sie auf positive Weise die Gründe der Fusion (größerer Kundenstamm, Internationalisierung, Rationalisierung des Vertriebs, gemeinsames, sich ergänzendes Know-how)
- Adressen bleiben unverändert, Geschäfte werden wie bisher weitergeführt
- Sie sind sicher, dass Ihre Kunden in Zukunft noch effizienter bedient werden können.

13. Banking

13.1 Introduction

Banks act as financial intermediaries, accepting and safeguarding money on deposit from customers, lending the surplus of money deposited with them to customers who wish to borrow, and making a profit, like any other commercial organisation, by rendering services to borrowers and depositors.

Banks assist their customers in a large variety of transactions such as:

- **Payment by cheque.** There are different kinds of cheques, ie bearer cheques, order cheques, open and crossed cheques. An open cheque can be cashed over the counter, while a crossed cheque can only be debited (or credited) to an account.

- **Payment by bank giro or credit transfer.** For this transaction customers need a giro or current account with their bank. Banks transfer money by SWIFT (Society for Worldwide Interbank Financial Tele-Communication). This is an interbanking computer system linking the banks of the major industrial and trading countries.

- **Payment by standing order or direct debiting:** In the first case customers ask their bank to transfer a certain amount of money on a certain day; in the second case they authorize a person, company or institution to withdraw money from their account.

- **Payment by cheque, debit or credit cards.** The banks issue such cards which can be presented by customers on purchase of goods or services. Sometimes they can only be used with teller machines or cash dispensers.

- **Payment by bill of exchange.** If bills of exchange have been issued by drawers at sight or at a certain date and have been accepted by the drawees for payment, these Bs/E may be domiciled with the bank for presentation on the day of maturity. Bs/E can also be endorsed and passed on by endorsers to endorsees.

- **Payment by letter of credit.** One of the safest means of payment in foreign trade is by L/C. Its purpose is to guarantee payment to the exporter and to provide a form of security to the importer. At least two banks are involved in an L/C transaction: The buyer's bank as the issuing bank guarantees the credit sum if the conditions of the L/C have been complied with, while the seller's bank as the advising bank looks after the interests of the seller and only guarantees payment of the amount if the L/C is a confirmed L/C. The most common type of L/C is the irrevocable documentary letter of credit, which is accompanied by documents that must be sent to the issuing bank before payment is made. These documents are checked by the banks and only released if they are found to be in order.

- **Payment by collection.** If the exporter does not wish to be paid by L/C, a fairly secure way to obtain payment is by asking a bank in the importer's country to collect the money from the customers either in cash (documents against payment; D/P) or by arranging for them to accept a bill of exchange (documents against acceptance; D/A).

Other services by banks include the granting of overdrafts, personal or corporate loans, and mortgages on real estate.

They also provide references or credit information on companies, give advice on investments to retail and corporate customers (Stock Exchange dealing for stocks and shares, bonds and debentures; futures trading in foreign exchange; leasing and factoring transactions). They are often involved in credit risk and credit insurance and deal with performance bonds and guarantees.

A completely new field of activity for banks is e-commerce, where banks provide traditional banking products electronically. Many basic functions such as checking balances, transferring funds, or the application for credit cards can easily be done via web sites on the internet. Some banks have established internet portals for financial and non-financial bank products. Billing and collection services can also be provided electronically. Banks are offering firms the technology for electronic business-to-business commerce by automating the entire information flow associated with the procurement and distribution of goods and services among businesses. This is a natural extension of the automated cash management services banks provide to large companies.

13.2 Model correspondence

13.2.1 American company asks German bank to open an account in euros

e-mail

Mail from: reagan.inc@compuserve.com
to: eurobank@online.de cc:
Subject:
Attachment:

Dear Eurobank:

We have been doing considerable business in Western Europe for a number of years, particularly in Germany. For the convenience of our customers we are now thinking of opening a euro account with your bank.

Please take the necessary steps to open such an account and inform us of your terms. If you require references, please let us know.

We would also like to know which e-commerce services you provide. Do you have an internet portal?

Regards,

Henry Reagan
Chief Executive Officer

13.2.2 British bank informs German bank that the amount covered by a B/E collection has not yet been received

FAO: Mr Heinrich Ritter
Frankfurter Bank AG
Straßburger Str. 24
D-60529 Frankfurt

Fax No.: +49 (69) 8 26 09 31

From: Jennifer A. Turner
Sealand Bank Plc
Ashridge
Berkhamsted
Hertfordshire HP4 1NS

Date: 2 July 20..

Export Order 45 09 PKH of Messrs Smith & Sons, Ashridge of 31 May 20..
for £34,100.00

Dear Mr Ritter

We cannot trace the equivalent of £34,100.00 in our account as of today.
Please inform us asap about the whereabouts of the sum in question.

If the sum has been paid by the German customer, please let us know which banks were involved in this transfer.

We await your reply urgently because the B/E was due on 30 June.
Thank you in advance.

Regards

Jennifer A. Turner

Jennifer A. Turner
Foreign Division

13.2.3 British company wants bank loan for setting up subsidiary in Germany

The Manager
Münchner Bank AG
Munich Branch
Promenadeplatz 15
D-80333 München

Dear Madam / Sir

We have now had a bank account with you for several years. This account has been used to receive payments in deutschmarks and recently also in euros from our German customers.

Since our business in Germany is rapidly expanding, we are planning to establish a subsidiary there, which will be domiciled in Munich. To avoid exchange risks, we intend to raise at least some of the funds for this project locally, and are therefore wondering if you would be prepared to grant us a loan to the amount of €300,000.

I will be in Munich from 6-12 June and would be pleased to discuss the matter with you in detail. Please let me know on what day and at what time it would be convenient for me to call and what documents you will require. I will, in any case, bring our Company's Annual Reports for the past few years.

Yours faithfully
ENTECH LIMITED

H L Andrews
Managing Director

13.2.4 British bank informs bank in Germany of increase in guarantee

Dear Sirs

We have been advised that you will increase the credit line to Martin-Brescoe PLC, Cambridge, Great Britain, to the amount of €120,000 by €80,000 to €200,000 against the irrevocable and unconditional increase of our Security Bond dated 21 May 20...

This being promised, we hereby increase irrevocably and unconditionally our Security Bond dated 21 May 20.., granted in your favour to the amount of €120,000, by €80,000 to

€200,000
(two hundred thousand euros),

inclusive of accrued interest and other credit costs. All other conditions of the Bond dated 21 May 20.. remain unchanged.

Yours faithfully

13.2.5 Canadian bank gives reference on its customer to German credit enquiry agency

Dear Ms Falkenstein:

Your request for information about Simpson Inc., P.O. Box 2709, Toronto

We have received your fax of 15 February 20.. and are pleased to give you the following information, to which our customer has given his consent.

This company has been doing business with our bank for many years and they have credit facilities with us for a limit of Can$100,000. The company's nominal share capital amounts to Can$500,000. They have always met their outstanding debts on time.

As far as the company's reputation and payment record are concerned, these can be judged as positive. The company is run by a Board of Directors whose Chairman, Mr Daniel A. Williams, is a man of impeccable standing who is involved locally in many commercial and charitable institutions.

We have been Simpson Inc.'s bankers for nearly 20 years and carry out all financial transactions with them to our mutual satisfaction.

Therefore we have no hesitation in warmly recommending this company.

This information is, of course, given without any obligation on our part.

Yours faithfully
BANK OF CANADA

13.2.6 Opening of an L/C

P.O. Box 2032, Nicosia 1598, Republic of Cyprus **Cyprus Popular Bank Limited**

22 April 20..

Rheinische Bank AG
Postfach 25 98 00
D-51148 Köln
Germany

Dear Sirs

This is to inform you that we have opened an irrevocable documentary letter of credit in the name of Christakis Georgiadu Ltd, 12, Mesokeleos Street, 1042-Nicosia, Cyprus in favour of Naval Construction GmbH, German Office, Brabanther Str. 49, D-51447 Köln. This L/C was sent to you by SWIFT Message on 21 April 20..

The value of the L/C amounts to €178,830.00 and will be payable against documents and beneficiary's draft at 60 days after the transport document date.

Please confirm receipt and send us the documents required in the L/C in due course.

Yours faithfully
CYPRUS POPULAR BANK LIMITED

P. Theodorakis
Division Manager

13.2.7 Letter of Credit as a SWIFT message

ISSUE OF A DOCUMENTARY CREDIT

ISSUING BANK		:	CYPRUS POPULAR BANK LIMITED 302002 P.O. Box 2032 001 NICOSIA 1598 ZYPERN, REPUBLIK
USER HEADER	SERVICE CODE 103	:	
	BANK. PRIORITY 113	:	
	MSG USER REF. 108	:	181DC00042101137
	INFO. FROM CI 115	:	
SEQUENCE OF TOTAL	*27	:	1 / 1
FORM OF DOC. CREDIT	*40 A	:	IRREVOCABLE
DOC. CREDIT NUMBER	*20	:	305/00/10554
DATE OF ISSUE	31 C	:	..0421
EXPIRY	*31 D	:	DATE ..1015 PLACE GERMANY
APPLICANT	*50	:	CHRISTAKIS GEORGIADU LTD 12, MESOKELEOS STREET 1042-NICOSIA CYPRUS
BENEFICIARY	*59	:	NAVAL CONSTRUCTION GMBH BRABANTHER STR. 49 51147 KÖLN GERMANY
AMOUNT	*32 B	:	CURRENCY / AMOUNT EUR 178.830,00
AVAILABLE WITH/BY	*41 D	:	RHEINISCHE BANK AG IN GERMANY BY NEGOTIATION
DRAFTS AT ...	42 C	:	AGAINST DOCUMENTS AND BENEFICIARY'S DRAFTS AT 60 DAYS AFTER TRANSPORT DOCUMENT DATE.
DRAWEE	42 D	:	ISSUING BANK
PARTIAL SHIPMENTS	43 P	:	ALLOWED
TRANSSHIPMENT	43 T	:	NOT ALLOWED

LOADING ON BOARD/DISPATCH/TAKING IN CHARGE AT/FROM ... 44 A :
ANY GERMAN PORT

FOR TRANSPORT TO ... 44 B :
LIMASSOL PORT

SHIPMENT PERIOD 44 D :
1ST SHIPMENT (2/6 UNITS) MUST BE EFFECTED AT THE END OF JUNE

DESCRIPTION OF GOODS AND/OR SERVICES 45 A :
6 UNITS INFLATABLE BOATS MODEL BOLERO 740 P
EXW BENEFICIARY'S WAREHOUSE, INCOTERMS 2000

DOCUMENTS REQUIRED 46 A :
01. COMMERCIAL INVOICES IN QUADRUPLICATE, ALL DULY STAMPED AND ORIGINALLY SIGNED BY THE BENEFICIARY, CERTIFYING THAT GOODS ARE OF GERMAN ORIGIN.

02. FULL SET CLEAN ON BOARD BILL OF LADING ISSUED OR ENDORSED TO THE ORDER OF THE CYPRUS POPULAR BANK LTD MARKED FREIGHT PAYABLE AT DESTINATION, NOTIFYING APPLICANT (FULL NAME AND ADDRESS) AND THE CYPRUS POPULAR BANK LTD, TRADE FINANCE UNIT (305), P.O. BOX 2032, NICOSIA.
03. PACKING LIST IN TRIPLICATE.
04. PHOTOCOPY OF THE ORIGINAL EUR1 MOVEMENT CERTIFICATE EVIDENCING THAT IT HAS BEEN DULY STAMPED AND SIGNED BY THE CUSTOMS AUTHORITIES OF THE EXPORTING COUNTRY. EUR1 CERTIFICATE MUST EITHER BE TYPEWRITTEN OR HANDWRITTEN IN INK AND CAPITAL LETTERS.
05. CERTIFICATE DULY STAMPED AND SIGNED BY BENEFICIARY CONFIRMING THAT THE ORIGINAL EUR1 AND COPIES OF THE COMMERCIAL INVOICE AND PACKING LIST HAVE BEEN HANDED TO THE MASTER OF THE VESSEL FOR ONWARD DELIVERY TO APPLICANT.

ADDITIONAL COND. 47 A :

01. TRANSPORT DOCUMENTS MUST BEAR THE FOLLOWING CLAUSE: 'VESSEL IS NOT SCHEDULED TO CALL ON ITS CURRENT VOYAGE AT THE PORTS OF FAMAGUSTA OR KYRENIA OR KARAVOSTASSI, CYPRUS'.
02. INVOICES TO CERTIFY THAT GOODS SHIPPED ARE IN ACCORDANCE WITH BENEFICIARY'S PROFORMA INVOICE DATED 03.04.20.. AND THAT EACH PACKING UNIT BEARS AN INDELIBLE MARK INDICATING THE COUNTRY OF ORIGIN OF THE GOODS.
03. ALL DOCUMENTS MUST BE ISSUED IN THE ENGLISH LANGUAGE, EXCEPT FOR THE EUR1 CERTIFICATE WHICH MAY BE ISSUED IN THE LANGUAGE OF THE EXPORTING COUNTRY.
04. SHIPPING MARKS SHOULD ALSO INCLUDE OUR D/C NO. AND TRANSPORT DOCUMENTS MUST SO EVIDENCE.
05. ALL BANK CHARGES OUTSIDE CYPRUS ARE FOR BENEFICIARY'S ACCOUNT. A EUR 45,00 DISCREPANCY FEE PLUS ALL RELATIVE TELETRANSMISSION CHARGES WILL BE DEDUCTED FROM THE REIMBURSEMENT CLAIM FOR EACH PRESENTATION OF DISCREPANT DOCUMENTS UNDER THIS DOCUMENTARY CREDIT. NOTWITHSTANDING ANY INSTRUCTIONS TO THE CONTRARY, THESE CHARGES SHALL BE FOR THE ACCOUNT OF THE BENEFICIARY.
06. WE ARE INFORMED THAT INSURANCE IS BEING ARRANGED BY APPLICANT. TRANSPORT DOCUMENTS BEARING A DATE PRIOR TO THE L/C DATE ARE NOT ACCEPTABLE.
07. SEPARATE SET OF DOCUMENTS AND SEPARATE PRESENTATIONS MUST BE MADE FOR EACH SHIPMENT OF GOODS.
08. CHARGES FROM EXW TO FOB ANY GERMAN PORT ARE PAYABLE AT DESTINATION BY APPLICANT OUTSIDE THE CREDIT TERMS.

PRESENTATION PERIOD 48 : DOCUMENTS MUST BE PRESENTED WITHIN 10 DAYS AFTER THE DATE OF ISSUANCE OF THE TRANSPORT DOCUMENTS BUT WITHIN THE VALIDITY OF THE CREDIT:
CONFIRMATION *49 : WITHOUT
REIMBURSING BANK 53 D : RHEINISCHE BANK AG
POSTFACH 25 98 00
51148 KÖLN
GERMANY, FEDERAL REPUBLIC OF
INSTRUCTIONS 78 :
CLAIM BY AUTHENTICATED MESSAGE FROM THE ISSUING BANK'S H/O EUR ACCOUNT NO. 375 8039 00 WITH RHBKDEKN AT MATURITY. REIMBURSEMENT IS SUBJECT TO ICC URR525. A COMPLETE SET OF DOCUMENTS (INCLUDING AT LEAST THREE INVOICES) MUST BE FORWARDED TO THE CYPRUS POPULAR BANK TRADE SERVICES (181), P.O. BOX 2032, NICOSIA CY-1598 BY COURIER/REGISTERED AIRMAIL AND THE REMAINING DOCUMENTS BY SUBSEQUENT REGISTERED AIRMAIL.
SEND. TO REC. INFO. 72 : PLEASE ACKNOWLEDGE RECEIPT. PLEASE ADVISE THE ISSUING BANK BY AIRMAIL IN CASE OF NON UTILIZATION OF THIS CREDIT. THIS CREDIT IS SUBJECT TO ICC DECISION IN RESPECT OF THE EURO.
TRAILER ORDER IS <MAC:> <PAC:> <ENC:> <CHK:>
<TNG:> <PDE:>
MAC/********
CHK:493095811C6E

13.2.8 First and second Bills of Exchange as first part payment for the Letter of Credit amount under 13.2.7

Drawn against Credit No. 305/00/10554, dated April 21.20..
of the Cyprus Popular Bank Limited, Nicosia
Köln, July 12.20.. For **€59.600,00**
At 60 days after transportdocument ie ..0919 pay this FIRST Bill of Exchange
(Second unpaid) to the order of ourselves
the sum of
Euros fiftyninethousandsixhundred (00/100) only
value which place to account as advised by
To Cyprus Popular Bank Limited
Nicosia 1598, Zypern Republik
No. **231/2869-1**

Bestell-Nr. 115 Wilhelm Köhler Verlag · Minden · Frankfurt · Hamburg · Bonn

Naval Construction GmbH
Brabanther Straße 49
D-51447 Köln

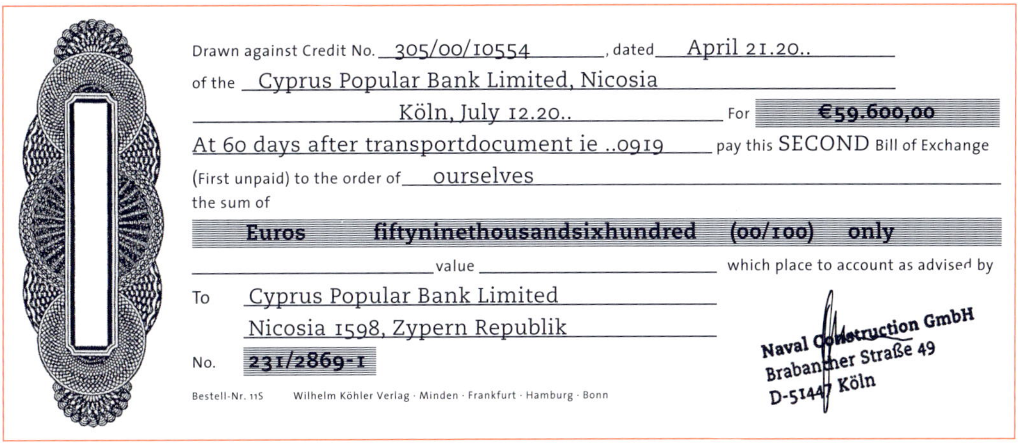

Drawn against Credit No. 305/00/10554, dated April 21.20..
of the Cyprus Popular Bank Limited, Nicosia
Köln, July 12.20.. For €59.600,00
At 60 days after transportdocument ie ..0919 pay this SECOND Bill of Exchange
(First unpaid) to the order of ourselves
the sum of
Euros fiftyninethousandsixhundred (00/100) only
value which place to account as advised by
To Cyprus Popular Bank Limited
Nicosia 1598, Zypern Republik
No. 231/2869-1
Bestell-Nr. 11S Wilhelm Köhler Verlag · Minden · Frankfurt · Hamburg · Bonn

Naval Construction GmbH
Brabanther Straße 49
D-51447 Köln

13.3 Terms and phrases

13.3.1 Accounts, statements, cheques

We wish to open a current / giro account with your bank and ask you to inform us about the formalities which have to be complied with.	*Wir möchten ein laufendes / Girokonto bei Ihrer Bank eröffnen und bitten Sie uns mitzuteilen, welchen Formalitäten wir entsprechen müssen.*
We would be grateful if you could let us have the details required to open an account.	*Wir wären Ihnen dankbar, wenn Sie uns die für die Eröffnung eines Kontos erforderlichen Einzelheiten mitteilen würden.*
The signatories authorized to sign cheques on our behalf are: …	*Die Zeichnungsberechtigten für unsere Schecks sind: …*
We enclose a cheque for … as a first deposit.	*Als erste Einlage erhalten Sie einen Scheck über …*
Please address all correspondence or the statements of account to: …	*Bitte schicken Sie die gesamte Korrespondenz oder die Kontoauszüge an: …*
Please transfer the monthly credit balance of our giro account to our deposit account no. …	*Bitte überweisen Sie den monatlichen Guthabensaldo unseres Girokontos auf unser Sparkonto Nr. …*
After examining the statement of account you sent us we confirm that the entry dated … has not been credited and ask you to excuse this omission.	*Nachdem wir den von Ihnen gesandten Kontoauszug geprüft haben, bestätigen wir, dass die Eingangsbuchung vom … nicht gutgeschrieben worden ist. Wir bitten, dieses Versehen zu entschuldigen.*
Please credit us / debit us with the sum in question.	*Bitte belasten Sie uns mit der infrage stehenden Summe / Bitte schreiben Sie uns die infrage stehende Summe gut.*
The credit / debit balance on your account is …	*Der Guthaben- / Schuldensaldo auf Ihrem Konto ist …*

The sum of ... has been paid into / withdrawn from your account no. ...	*Die Summe von ... ist auf Ihr Konto Nr. ... eingezahlt worden / von Ihrem Konto Nr. ... abgehoben worden.*
We have credited your account with the amount of ... resulting from your crossed cheque no. ...	*Wir haben Ihrem Konto die Summe von ... aus Ihrem Verrechnungsscheck Nr. ... gutgeschrieben.*

13.3.2 Credit applications, loans and overdrafts

We would like to ask you to open / issue an irrevocable documentary letter of credit for us.	*Wir bitten Sie, für uns ein unwiderrufliches Dokumentenakkreditiv zu eröffnen.*
Please let us know your conditions for the opening of a letter of credit / for granting us an overdraft facility / for granting us an unsecured credit (unsecured credit facilities, an unsecured loan).	*Bitte teilen Sie uns Ihre Bedingungen für die Eröffnung eines Akkreditivs / die Gewährung eines Überziehungskredits / die Einräumung eines Blankokredits mit.*
We intend to import considerable quantities of ... in the near future and would therefore need to know the terms on which you would grant us a short-term / medium-term / long-term loan / grant us credit facilities.	*Wir beabsichtigen, in naher Zukunft erhebliche Mengen von ... zu importieren und müssten daher die Bedingungen wissen, zu denen Sie uns einen kurzfristigen / mittelfristigen / langfristigen Kredit einräumen würden.*
We are prepared to offer you the assignment of all our accounts receivables as security / collateral.	*Als Sicherheit sind wir bereit, Ihnen die Abtretung aller unserer Außenstände anzubieten.*
Should you require any additional security, please let us know.	*Sollten Sie zusätzliche Sicherheiten benötigen, teilen Sie uns dies bitte mit.*
Please inform us about your conditions for the granting of a loan to the amount of ...	*Bitte teilen Sie uns Ihre Bedingungen für die Gewährung eines Darlehens in Höhe von ... mit.*

13.3.3 The forwarding of documents, payment

We have advised the ... bank that an irrevocable documentary L/C has been opened in favour of ...	*Wir haben der ... Bank mitgeteilt, dass ein unwiderrufliches Dokumentenakkreditiv zugunsten von ... eröffnet worden ist.*
Please instruct your correspondent bank to release the documents on payment of our draft.	*Bitte weisen Sie Ihre Korrespondenzbank an, die Dokumente gegen Zahlung unseres Wechsels auszuhändigen.*
In accordance with the terms stipulated in our letter of credit we are sending you enclosed the required documents.We ask you to present the 60-day sight draft, forwarded to you last week, to the drawee for acceptance.	*In Übereinstimmung mit den in unserem Akkreditiv festgesetzten Bedingungen übersenden wir Ihnen beiliegend die geforderten Dokumente.Wir bitten Sie, den Ihnen vorige Woche zugesandten 60-Tage Sichtwechsel dem Bezogenen zum Akzept vorzulegen.*
As soon as the L/C amount has been paid, we ask you to credit the sum to our account no. ... at ... Bank.	*Sobald der L/C-Betrag gezahlt worden ist, bitten wir Sie, die Summe unserem Konto Nr. ... bei der ... Bank gutzuschreiben.*
Please directly debit our account no. ... with the costs of these proceedings.	*Bitte buchen Sie die Kosten dieses Verfahrens direkt von unserem Konto Nr. ... ab.*
We have settled your transfer by SWIFT and you will be informed as soon as our foreign branch confirms that the sum has been debited.	*Wir haben Ihre Überweisung per SWIFT erledigt. Sie werden informiert, sobald unsere Auslandsfiliale bestätigt, dass die Summe abgebucht worden ist.*
As from now you will be able to place all banking orders with us online via our internet portal.	*Durch unser Internet-Portal können Sie ab jetzt alle Bankaufträge mit uns online erledigen.*
Your debit/credit card enables you to make non-cash payments at all times.	*Unsere Geld-/Kreditkarte macht es Ihnen möglich, jederzeit bargeldlos zu zahlen.*
Encoded reference numbers will ensure maximum possible safety for our online customers.	*Verschlüsselte Kennzifferkodierungen garantieren die größtmögliche Sicherheit für unsere Online-Kunden.*

13.4 Exercises

Please translate:

13.4.1 As Naval Construction GmbH is a subsidiary of Naval Construction plc in Great Britain, the following letter of non-recourse financing has to be translated for the parent company in the UK.

STADTSPARKASSE KÖLN

AUSLANDS GESCHÄFT

Naval Construction GmbH
German Office
Brabanther Str. 49
51147 Köln

12. Juli 20..

Forfaitierung Nr. F 129
Akkreditiv Nr. 305/00/10554 der Cyprus Popular Bank Limited, P.O. Box 2032, Nicosia 1598, Zypern vom 21.04.20..
Über € 178.830,00
i. A. Christakis Georgiadu Ltd., 12, Mesokeleos Street, 1042 – Nicosia, Zypern

Sehr geehrte Damen und Herren,

Sie informierten uns, dass Sie mit der oben aufgeführten Firma einen Vertrag über die Lieferung von 6 UNITS INFLATABLE BOATS MODEL BOLERO 740 P gemäss oben aufgeführtem Akkreditiv im Wert von insgesamt € 178.830,00 abgeschlossen haben. Die Bezahlung des Kaufpreises erfolgt durch ein unwiderrufliches Akkreditiv Nr. 305/00/10554 der Cyprus Popular Bank Limited, Nicosia, Zypern vom 21.04.20...

Wir bestätigen Ihnen hiermit unsere mündliche Vereinbarung, die Forderung aus dem vorgenannten Liefergeschäft in Höhe max. € 178.830,00 zu nachfolgend genannten Bedingungen ohne Rückgriff auf Sie anzukaufen:

Zahlungsverpflichtete:	Cyprus Popular Bank Limited, Nicosia, Zypern
Ankaufsbetrag:	Gegenwert der uns unter Akkreditiv Nr. 305/00/10554 der Cyprus Popular Bank Limited, Nicosia, Zypern eingereichten Dokumente bis zu einem Höchstbetrag von € 178.830,00

Hahnenstraße 57
50667 Köln
Postfach 10 35 44
50475 Köln
Telefon: (02 21) 2 26-1
Telefax: (02 21) 2 26 34 08
Amtsgericht Köln
HRA 7961
T-ONLINE: * SK #
Telex: 8 881 760 klna d
SWIFT-Adresse: COLS DE 33
www.sk-koeln.de
kontakt@sk-koeln.de
Bankleitzahl: 370 501 98

Stadtsparkasse Köln
eine gute Empfehlung

-forfaitierungsvertrag

STADTSPARKASSE KÖLN

AUSLANDS
GESCHÄFT

- 2 -

Ankauf:	nach Vorlage akkreditivkonformer Dokumente in unserem Hause oder nach Vorlage der Bestätigung der Cyprus Popular Bank Limited, Nicosia, Zypern über die ordnungsgemäße Aufnahme von Dokumenten mit Angabe des Zahlungstermins.
Fälligkeit der Forderung:	60 Tage nach B/L-Datum
Zahlstelle:	Stadtsparkasse Köln
Diskontsatz:	nom. 9,75 % p. a.
Zinsfälligkeit:	Die Zinsen sind bei Auszahlung fällig.
Zinsmethode:	365/360 Tage (Eurozinsmethode)
Auszahlung:	Wir werden den Ankaufsbetrag abzüglich der angefallenen Bereitstellungsprovision und der anfallenden Zinsen Ihrem Konto 13012373 in unserem Hause gutschreiben.
Zinsen nach Fälligkeit:	Sollten fällige Zahlungen nicht fristgerecht bei uns eingehen, so berechnen wir Ihnen auf ausstehende Forderungen vom Zahlungstermin bis zum Zeitpunkt des Eingangs der Zahlungen der Cyprus Popular Bank Limited, Nicosia, Zypern bei uns Zinsen in Höhe von 9,75 % p. a.. Diese Nachzinsverpflichtung endet für Sie 30 Tage nach Eintritt der jeweiligen Fälligkeit.
Sonstige Provisionen:	Für unsere Ankaufszusage berechnen wir neben den zu Ihren Lasten gehenden Provisionen im Zusammenhang mit der Akkreditivabwicklung eine Bereitstellungsprovision i. H. v. 2,5 % p. a. ab dem 12. 07. 20.. bis zum Ankauf der Dokumente.

Hahnenstraße 57
50667 Köln
Postfach 10 35 44
50475 Köln
Telefon: (02 21) 2 26-1
Telefax: (02 21) 2 26 34 08
Amtsgericht Köln
HRA 7961
T-ONLINE: * SK #
Telex: 8 881 760 klna d
SWIFT-Adresse: COLS DE 33
www.sk-koeln.de
kontakt@sk-koeln.de
Bankleitzahl: 370 501 98

Stadtsparkasse Köln
eine gute Empfehlung

-forfaitierungsvertrag

STADTSPARKASSE KÖLN

AUSLANDS
GESCHÄFT

- 3 -

Voraussetzungen:

- Vorlage einer durch die Rheinische Bank AG avisierten Akkreditivänderung, die besagt, dass die Stadtsparkasse Köln die Zahlstellenfunktion in o. a. Akkreditiv übernimmt.
- Schriftliche Annahme unseres Angebotes.
- Abtretung der Rechte und Ansprüche aus dem Liefergeschäft sowie der Auszahlungsansprüche aus dem Akkreditiv gemäß beiliegender Abtretungserklärung.
- Vorlage akkreditivgerechter Dokumente bei uns
  oder
  Bestätigung der Cyprus Popular Bank Limited, Nicosia, Zypern über die ordnungsgemäße Aufnahme von Dokumenten mit Angabe des Zahlungstermins.

Die Abtretung der Rechte und Pflichten aus dem Liefervertrag sowie der Auszahlungsansprüche werden wir der Christakis Georgiadu Ltd., 12, Mesokeleos Street, 1042 – Nicosia, Zypern und der Cyprus Popular Bank Limited, Nicosia, Zypern bis auf weiteres nicht offen legen.

Gemäß den Akkreditivbedingungen gehen alle außerhalb Zyperns entstehenden Bankgebühren sowie die Unstimmigkeitsprovision und alle Fax- und Reimbourskosten zu Ihren Lasten. Sollten derartige Gebühren anfallen und darüber hinaus Steuern, Abgaben, Gebühren und/oder sonstige Abzüge gleich welcher Art erfolgen, so werden Sie uns den Differenzbetrag zu dem vollen geschuldeten Betrag erstatten.

Hahnenstraße 57
50667 Köln
Postfach 10 35 44
50475 Köln
Telefon: (02 21) 2 26-1
Telefax: (02 21) 2 26 34 08
Amtsgericht Köln
HRA 7961
T-ONLINE: * SK #
Telex: 8 881 760 klna d
SWIFT-Adresse: COLS DE 33
www.sk-koeln.de
kontakt@sk-koeln.de
Bankleitzahl: 370 501 98

Stadtsparkasse Köln
eine gute Empfehlung

-forfaitierungsvertrag

STADTSPARKASSE KÖLN

AUSLANDS
GESCHÄFT

- 4 -

Änderungen des Akkreditivs bedürfen unserer ausdrücklichen Zustimmung.

Sie garantieren uns, dass

1. Sie ordnungsgemäß geliefert haben/liefern werden und alle Verpflichtungen, insbesondere auch Gewährleistungsverpflichtungen, aus dem Liefervertrag erfüllen.
2. die Ansprüche aus dem Liefergeschäft und dem Akkreditiv nicht anderweitig abgetreten sind.
3. die Forderung unter dem Akkreditiv frei von Einreden und Einwendungen entstanden ist.
4. die Christakis Georgiadu Ltd., 12, Mesokeleos Street, 1042 – Nicosia, Zypern nicht gegen die Forderung aufrechnet, sie keine Zurückbehaltungsrechte geltend macht und keine sonstigen Einwendungen erhebt.
5. die Abtretung aus dem oben genannten Akkreditiv nicht ausgeschlossen ist.
6. es sich bei der gelieferten Ware weder direkt noch indirekt um Rüstungsgüter handelt, auf ihnen kein verlängerter Eigentumsvorbehalt lastet und Ihnen für die Durchführung des Geschäftes alle erforderlichen und behördlichen Genehmigungen vorliegen.
7. die Zahlungen aus dem dem Liefervertrag zugrunde liegenden Akkreditiv nur an uns erfolgen. Erfolgen dennoch Zahlungen auf ein anderes Konto, werden Sie diese unverzüglich an uns weiterleiten. Alle im Zusammenhang mit dem genannten Liefergeschäft eingehenden Gelder gelten als an uns verpfändet.

Ferner verpflichten Sie sich,

1. uns jederzeit über alle im Zusammenhang mit den übertragenen Rechten stehenden Fragen Auskunft zu geben und uns auf Verlangen die zur Geltendmachung erforderlichen Unterlagen zur Verfügung zu stellen.
2. alle mit der Abtretung und ihrer Durchführung verbundenen Kosten zu tragen.

Hahnenstraße 57
50667 Köln
Postfach 10 35 44
50475 Köln
Telefon: (02 21) 2 26-1
Telefax: (02 21) 2 26 34 08
Amtsgericht Köln
HRA 7961
T-ONLINE: * SK #
Telex: 8 881 760 klna d
SWIFT-Adresse: COLS DE 33
www.sk-koeln.de
kontakt@sk-koeln.de
Bankleitzahl: 370 501 98

Stadtsparkasse Köln
eine gute Empfehlung

-forfaitierungsvertrag

STADTSPARKASSE KÖLN

AUSLANDS
GESCHÄFT

- 5 -

3. im Fall einer Nichtzahlung durch die Christakis Georgiadu Ltd., 12, Mesokeleos Street, 1042 – Nicosia, Zypern bzw. der Akkreditivbank in Abstimmung mit uns gemäß unseren Weisungen alle erforderlichen Schritte – gerichtlicher und außergerichtlicher Art – zur Durchsetzung unserer Ansprüche zu unternehmen. Die in diesem Zusammenhang entstehenden Kosten gehen zu unseren Lasten. Diese Verpflichtung gilt nur für den Fall, dass eine nachträgliche Abtretung/Offenlegung der Abtretung – gleich aus welchem Grund – nicht möglich ist.

Sollte die Inanspruchnahme und/oder Zahlung aus dem Akkreditiv durch Arrest, Pfändung, einstweilige Verfügung oder sonstige gerichtliche Entscheidungen und/oder Eilverfahren aus mit dem Grundgeschäft zusammenhängenden Gründen untersagt werden, sind wir berechtigt, die angekauften Forderungen zurückzuübertragen.

In diesem Falle werden Sie uns die von uns unter dieser Vereinbarung erhaltenen Beträge zuzüglich Zinsen zurückerstatten.

Bitte reichen Sie uns die Durchschrift dieses Schreibens wie vorgesehen rechtsverbindlich unterzeichnet zurück.

Mit freundlichen Grüßen

STADTSPARKASSE KÖLN
Auslandsgeschäft

Anlagen

Wir nehmen Ihr Angebot an und erklären uns mit dem Inhalt dieses Schreibens einverstanden.

Köln, den 21.8.20..

Naval Construction GmbH
Brahmsstraße 42
D-51447 Köln

Hahnenstraße 57
50667 Köln
Postfach 10 35 44
50475 Köln
Telefon: (02 21) 2 26-1
Telefax: (02 21) 2 26 34 08
Amtsgericht Köln
HRA 7961
T-ONLINE: * SK #
Telex: 8 881 760 klna d
SWIFT-Adresse: COLS DE 33
www.sk-koeln.de
kontakt@sk-koeln.de
Bankleitzahl: 370 501 98

Stadtsparkasse Köln
eine gute Empfehlung

-forfaitierungsvertrag

13.4.2 **The Declaration of Assignment of Naval Construction GmbH also has to be translated for the parent company.**

Naval Construction GmbH

German Office
Brabanther Straße 49, 51447 Köln,
Tel.Nr. ++49 (2 01) 45 09 31, Fax Nr.:++49 (2 01) 45 09 32,
E-Mail: naval.constructions@online.de

An
Stadtsparkasse Köln
Auslandsgeschäft
Hahnenstr. 57
50667 Köln

ABTRETUNGSERKLÄRUNG

Wir, die unterzeichnende Naval Construction GmbH, Brabanther Str. 49, 51447 Köln, haben mit der Christakis Georgiadu Ltd, 12, Mesokeleos Street, 1042-Nicosia, Zypern einen Vertrag über die Lieferung von 6 Schlauchbooten, Modell Bolero 740 P gemäß Akkreditiv Nr. 305/00/10554 der Cyprus Popular Bank Limited, Nicosia, Zypern im Wert von insgesamt EUR 178.830,00 abgeschlossen. Dieses Liefergeschäft ist durch ein Akkreditiv Nr. 305/00/10554 der Cyprus Popular Bank Limited, Nicosia, Zypern vom 21.04.20.. unterlegt.

Hiermit treten wir unsere gegenwärtigen und zukünftigen Forderungen aus dem genannten Liefervertrag sowie dem genannten Akkreditiv in voller Höhe von EUR 178.830,00 mit allen damit verbundenen Neben- und Vorzugsrechten unwiderruflich an die dies annehmende Stadtsparkasse Köln ab.

Im übrigen gelten die Regelungen Ihres Zusageschreibens vom 12. Juli 20.. und die in ihm enthaltenen Zusicherungen sowie ergänzend Ihre „Allgemeinen Geschäftsbedingungen“ und die „Einheitlichen Richtlinien und Gebräuche für Dokumenten-Akkreditive (Revision 1993) der Internationalen Handelskammer (Publikation Nr. 500)“.

Köln, den 21.08.20..

Naval Construction GmbH
German Office

Peter R. Howard

Peter R. Howard
Managing Director

Please draft letters, faxes or e-mails from the following particulars:

13.4.3 **Geschäftsfall:**

Sie arbeiten als Assistent(in) des Abteilungsleiters Ausland in der Münchner Bank AG, Promenadeplatz 15, D-80333 München, Fax-Nr.: +49 (89) 26 98 75, E-Mail-Adresse: deutschebank@online.de, und haben von Ihrem Chef die Anweisung erhalten, auf das unter 13.2.3 aufgeführte Schreiben der Entech Limited, Omega Park, Alton, Hampshire, GU34 2PG, Fax-Nr.: +44 (14 20) 27 35 11, E-Mail-Adresse: entech.ltd@org.uk, unter Berücksichtigung folgender Punkte zu antworten:

- Dank für erhaltenes Schreiben
- Sie sind gern bereit, Herrn Andrews zwischen dem 6. und 12. Juni in Ihrer Bank zu empfangen und über einen Kredit zu sprechen
- Sie können aber einen Kredit nur gewähren gegen
  a) eine harte Patronatserklärung (*hard letter of comfort*) des britischen Unternehmens und/oder
  b) Eintragung einer Grundschuld (*registration of a land charge*) auf möglicherweise zu erwerbenden Grundbesitz
- Bitten Sie Herrn Andrews, zu einem Treffen möglichst vollständige Unterlagen mitzubringen, z. B. Jahresberichte, Bilanzen, Gewinn- und Verlustrechnungen der letzten Jahre, Exportzahlen des Unternehmens.

13.4.4 **Geschäftsfall:**

Sie arbeiten bei der Hanseatischen Bank, Freihafenstr. 39, 20539 Hamburg, Fax-Nr.: +49 (40) 37 81 06, E-Mail-Adresse: hanse.bank@online.de, und haben ein Schreiben von Mr Roland Checkers, Lambswool Pty., P.O. Box 3096, Darwin, N.T. 0801, Australia, Fax-Nr.: +61 8 (89 42) 11 53, E-Mail-Adresse: lambswool.pty@org.com, erhalten, mit welchem er Ihnen mitteilt, dass er bei Ihrer Bank ein Kontokorrentkonto für seine Firma eröffnen will.

Aufgabe: Beantworten Sie dieses Schreiben unter Berücksichtigung folgender Punkte:

- Sie benötigen für die Eröffnung eines solchen Kontos, übersetzt und notariell beglaubigt:
- Die Gründungsurkunde und Satzung der australischen Gesellschaft;
- Die Registrierungsbestätigung (*Certificate of Incorporation*) der Gesellschaft in Darwin
- Einen schriftlichen Beschluss der Firmenleitung, aus welchem hervorgeht, welche Personen verfügungsberechtigt sein sollen
- Eine Liste der für die Gesellschaft Unterschriftsberechtigten mit Bankbestätigung
- Nach Prüfung dieser Unterlagen werden Sie das gewünschte Konto eröffnen.

13.4.5 **Geschäftsfall:**

Vertiefen Sie sich nochmals in den unter 13.2.6 beschriebenen Fall des Akkreditivs, das von der Cyprus Popular Bank Limited für die Georgiadu Ltd in Zypern zugunsten der Naval Construction GmbH eröffnet wurde.

Aufgabe: Schreiben Sie als Mitarbeiter(in) der Rheinischen Bank AG an die eröffnende Bank Cyprus Popular Bank Limited in Nicosia (Anschriften wie unter 13.2.6 und 13.2.7) und teilen Sie ihr mit, dass die im Akkreditiv aufgeführten Dokumente an die Cyprus Popular Bank Limited abgesandt worden sind. Diese Dokumente sind aus dem Akkreditiv ersichtlich unter „Documents Required 46 A“. Da das Akkreditiv von der Rheinischen Bank nicht bestätigt wurde, bitten Sie die Cyprus Popular Bank um Überweisung des Betrages an Sie.

14. Transport and Forwarding; Insurance

14.1. Introduction

Transport and forwarding. For the transport of goods, exporters and importers need the assistance of forwarding agents and carriers. *Forwarding agents* (also called *freight forwarders* or *forwarders*) act as intermediaries between those having to send or collect goods and those who arrange for transport, they may also transport goods themselves. Since forwarding agents handle goods for many different customers, they can obtain lower freight rates by combining several small consignments into a large one (*grouped consignment*; AE *consolidated shipment*). International forwarders have a network of foreign branch offices and/or correspondents for the transport of goods to and from all parts of the world. In addition to the forwarding of goods, forwarding agents render many important services to their customers, either directly or through their foreign branches or correspondents, such as collecting and transporting goods from and to the docks, paying shipping charges and freight, making arrangements with the shipping companies, obtaining the necessary shipping documents (eg bills of lading, consular invoices, certificates of origin, certificates of value and weight, insurance policies etc), attending to customs formalities, warehousing goods (eg in bonded warehouses) and handling collections.

Carriers are engaged in transporting goods (and/or passengers). There are road, rail, air, inland-water and ocean carriers. Goods sent by air are usually high quality, expensive or perishable. Rail transport is less expensive and not affected by peak hour traffic like *haulage* (transport by road). This kind of transport makes door-to-door delivery possible, but implies certain risks, especially when dangerous goods are to be carried. Furthermore, heavy price competition between hauliers worldwide has led to a strict rationalization of costs. Computerized just-in-time delivery has led to over-congested roads and parking areas on certain international motorways or highways.

Containerisation has also revolutionized transport, making it possible to load and unload goods at special terminals in harbours, at airports or railway stations.

Transport by sea and inland waterways is the cheapest form for goods to be transported in bulk. There are many different types of ships available, eg liners, tramp ships, roll-on-roll-off ferries etc.

Three kinds of transport documents have to be distinguished: *consignment notes (waybills)* for road and rail transport, *airway bills* for air transport and *bills of lading* for sea transport. The latter are, in addition, documents of title. This is especially important when payment of goods has been arranged on an L/C basis.

Planes and ships can also be chartered. In ocean shipping, the contract concluded between the owner and the charterer is known as a *charter party*; it is either a contract of carriage covering the whole (or a large part) of the ship's carrying capacity for a certain voyage (*voyage charter*) or the hire of a ship for a certain period of time (*time charter*).

Multimodal transport, ie transport of unitized freight such as pallets and containers by a combination of two or more carriers, is growing in importance.

Insurance. Insurance comprises such a wide range of areas that in this context only the insurance relating to the transport of goods can be covered. Which particular contract of insurance is concluded depends on the type of transport chosen. Cargo policies refer to the movement of goods exported from or imported to a country. At some point the insurable interest will pass from the seller to the buyer, depending on the contract of sale. There are 13 different types of arrangement made between importers and exporters which affect the insurance policy required. They are defined in a set of internationally agreed commercial terms, the INCOTERMS (see 2.3.3. and Glossary).

Insurance is provided by insurance companies and Lloyd's underwriters. Under a contract of insurance, the insurer agrees, for a specified premium, to compensate the insured, up to a certain amount, for damage or loss caused to the insured property by any of the risks insured against. Insurance contracts are evidenced by *insurance policies* and *certificates*. There are different kinds of policies, eg *valued* and *unvalued policies*, *voyage* and *time policies*, the most important probably being the *floating policy*, which is issued for a large sum from which the individual insurance amounts are deducted (or written off) whenever insurance is taken out.

A large part of goods insurance is covered by marine insurance. Under a marine insurance contract the underwriter is relieved of certain risks under the so-called *Institute Cargo Clauses*. These are divided into three Clauses:

Clause C	(FPA – free of particular average) covers: general average & major perils, ie disasters (sinking, fire, collision)
Clause B	(WPA – with particular average) covers: FPA (Clause C) & minor perils of the seas (sea water), ship's sweat, wind, etc
Clause A	(AR – against all risks) covers: WPA (Clause B) & damage from other causes (theft, rough handling, burglary, etc)

14.2. Model correspondence

14.2.1 Irish company asks German forwarding agent for transport offer

e-mail

Mail from: howards.ltd@dublin.ie
to: hansen.spedition@firmennetz.de cc:
Subject:
Attachment:

Dear Hansen Spedition

We have bought 5 pallets of German wine, containing 50 cases each of 12 bottles respectively, to be collected at the vineyard Gut Traubenfels in Trier/Moselle next week.

Please send us your offer including all transport costs and the handling of documents to our premises in Dublin.

Regards
John Stevens
Purchasing Department

14.2.2 Freight offer from American forwarding agent to German company

fax

FAO: Ms Marion Jacobs
Shipping Department
Stuhldreher & Welters
Alte Bahnhofstr. 11
44892 Bochum

Fax No.: +49 (234) 98 73 60

From: Peter Dunningham
Special Shipping Services
Industrial Estate
New Jersey 07666
USA

Dear Marion:

Thank you for your freight enquiry of 5 September 20.. regarding the transport of 100 tonnes of special palletised construction equipment (steel). Our offer is as follows:

M.V. Cynthia at US$150 per metric
tonne or 10 cubic metres, at steamer's
option, with 6 lay days.

Enclosed please find the sailing card of the shipping line, whose vessel is currently located in New York and is due to dock in Rotterdam on 10 November 20... Loading will commence as from 12 November 20... An additional charge of US$300 will be payable for every day of demurrage.

If this offer meets your requirements, please send us the charter party in triplicate to enable us to issue the necessary instructions to the ship's captain, Mr Alfred Winters.

Always at your service.

Regards,
Peter

Enc

14.2.3 Forwarding agency offers its services

Dear Ms Walters:

This is in reference to the telephone conversation I had with you this morning. I enclose brochures explaining the services that DANZAS and its sister company, ALLTRANSPORT INC., provide, and a booklet enabling you to locate our offices all over the world.

We rank among the top international freight forwarding companies, maintaining a vast network of operations on five continents. Thanks to our worldwide presence as well as to our expertise and experience, we are in a position to offer the best possible service to our customers, including door-to-door delivery.

We handle general cargo, special and dangerous cargo, RO-RO, sea-land, rail-road combinations, etc. We can send urgent cargo directly by next available vessel or flight. We consolidate as practical, necessary, or desired.

We have two weekly airfreight consolidations from every major airport within Germany as well as ocean freight consolidations from Hamburg and Bremen.

We look forward to the pleasure of doing business with you. Should you need any further information or assistance, please do not hesitate to contact the undersigned.

Sincerely yours,

DANZAS Commercial Delegation Inc., New York

Encl.

14.2.4 Forwarding agent asks correspondent for quotation

Gentlemen:

A client of ours has received an order for an automatic lamp-bulb making plant, which is to be shipped to Bucharest. The plant will be ready for shipment in early October. It will be packed in five containers, total weight: ... Delivery will be made to Rotterdam, where the containers are to be taken over for conveyance by rail or road to their destination.

Please let us know whether you would be prepared to handle this shipment for us. If so, we would be glad if you could let us know the cost, including your charges, of transporting the containers from Rotterdam to Bucharest. Since you are familiar with rate structures in Europe, we are sure you will be able to suggest a mode of conveyance, or a combined mode, entailing the least costs. We would also like to know how long the transit from Rotterdam to Bucharest will probably take.

We look forward to receiving your quotation soon.

Sincerely yours,

14.2.5 Forwarding agent quotes freight rates and clearance charges

Dear Ted:

With reference to our recent telephone conversation, I am pleased to submit to you, as promised, the following rates:

Ocean freight to Baltimore:

One (1) 40' container	$0,000.00 all incld.

Customs clearance charges in Baltimore:

ID Entry	$000.00
Bond fee	$0.00 per $0,000.00 with a minimum of $00.00
Import duty	as per outlay
Special messenger	$00.00

Please note that there is a customs examination charge of $00.00 for every opening through U.S. Customs.

Trucking charges to Springfield, OH:

One (1) 40' container	$000.00

We hope that our rate proposal will meet with your approval and look forward to receiving an early reply.

Sincerely yours,

14.2.6 Liner company wants to charter vessel

Dear Sir or Madam

A customer of ours will have to supply fertiliser in bulk and in bags to Central America over the next six months, and we would therefore be glad if you could fix us a time charter for a suitable vessel.

The vessel should have a cargo capacity of some 1m cubic feet and should, fully loaded, be capable of steaming about 13–14 knots. We would also expect the vessel to be in the highest class at Lloyd's Register of Shipping or a similar classification society. The vessel will have to be available in the port of Liverpool by the end of June 20...

Please let us know if, and on what terms, you can arrange a time charter for us.

Yours faithfully

14.2.7 Announcing new container service

Dear Sirs

We are pleased to inform you that Ben Line, in co-operation with Geest North Sea Line BV, will be offering a regular, fast and competitive through container service between the UK and the Continent commencing in April this year. The service will make use of slots on the six sailings per week already operated by Geest between the ports of Ipswich and Hull to and from Rotterdam. It is anticipated that in due course the involvement of Ben Line will enable the two Lines to increase the number of vessels operating and eventually open up new routes.

The Ben Europe Container Service (BECS) will be marketed through Ben Line's existing agency network, working in parallel with Geest's existing selling organisation. The Joint Service will utilise equipment and inland transport arrangements available to both Lines from their involvement in this and other trades. In the UK, Killick Martin & Company Limited will act as Principal Agents for BECS, and cargo bookings for the new service will be handled by them and by other existing Ben agencies in England and Wales. In Scotland, Ben Line's Head Office in Edinburgh will be responsible for marketing.

On the Continent, the main agents for the BECS service will be CONVA in Rotterdam, who will perform a co-ordinating role and will work closely with Geest North Sea Line BV and the existing Ben Line agents in northern Europe.

We very much hope your company and its subsidiary in the UK will avail themselves of the Ben Europe Container Service. For further details please contact any of the agencies mentioned above.

Yours faithfully

14.2.8 Air carrier informs customer about airfreight delivery

e-mail

Mail from: airfreight.international@t-online.de
to: rauthenbacher.handel@firmenlink.de **cc:**
Subject: Request for leaflets and pricelists
Attachment: Waybill DUS-40051921.doc

Dear Mr Smith

Enclosed please find as an attachment copy of the Air Waybill DUS-4005 1921 covering airfreight of 30 kg of samples from Düsseldorf Airport to Beijing Airport, China.

Please inform consignee and see all further details in the Air Waybill.

Regards
Airfreight International GmbH

Attachment

Set your tabulator stops here

Fix the lines here

DUS-4005 1921

DUS-4005 1921

Shipper's Name and Address RAUTHENBACHER HANDEL AG HOEHERWEG 271A 40231 DUESSELDORF	Shipper's Account Number 143751-8
Not negotiable **Air Waybill*** Issued by Carrier:	180-8636 4876 AIRCARRIER INTERNATIONAL GMBH LANGER WEG 36 D-40441 DORTMUND/GERMANY

Copies 1, 2 and 3 of this Air Waybill are originals and have the same validity

Consignee's Name and Address RAUTHENBACHER BEIJING OFFICE ATTN. MR. HINZ / MRS. TRACY SMITH 24 A JIANGUOMENWAI AVENUE 100004 BEIJING	Consignee's Account Number HANDEL AG

It is agreed that the goods described herein are accepted in apparent good order and condition (except as noted) for carriage SUBJECT TO THE CONDITIONS OF CONTRACT ON THE REVERSE HEREOF. ALL GOODS MAY BE CARRIED BY ANY OTHER MEANS INCLUDING ROAD OR ANY OTHER CARRIER UNLESS SPECIFIC CONTRARY INSTRICTIONS ARE GIVEN HEREON BY THE SHIPPER, AND SHIPPER AGREES THAT THE SHIPMENT MAY BE CARRIED VIA INTERMEDIATE STOPPING PLACES WHICH THE CARRIER DEEMS APPROPRIATE. THE SHIPPER'S ATTENTION IS DRAWN TO THE NOTICE CONCERNING CARRIER'S LIMITATION OF LIABILITY. Shipper may increase such limitation of liability by declaring a higher value for carriage and paying a supplemental charge if required.

Issuing Carrier's Agent Name and City

Accounting Information
PROFORMA INVOICE

Agent's IATA Code | Accounting No.

Airport of Departure (Addr. of First Carrier) and Requested Routing
DUESSELDORF, GERMANY

Reference Number: P.O. NO.: E C D'S : P.19 AWV /

Optional Shipping Information

To	By First Carrier (Routing and Destination)	To	By	To	By	Currency	CHGS Code	WT/VAL PPD	WT/VAL COLL	Other PPD	Other COLL	Declared Value for Carriage	Declared Value for Customs
SEL	KE	BJS	KE			€		PP		PP		NVD	NCV

Airport of Destination	Requested Flight/Date		Amount of Insurance	
BEIJING	KE0506/23	KE 0851/25	XXX	INSURANCE – If Carrier offers insurance, and such insurance is requested in accordance with the conditions thereof, indicate amount to be insured in figures in box marked "Amount of Insurance"

Handling Information
MARKS: ADDRESS

SCI "C"

(For U.S.A. use only): These commodities, technology or software were exported from the United States in accordance with the Export Administration Regulations. Diversion contray to USA law prohibited.

No. of Pieces RCP	Gross Weight	kg lb	Rate Class	Commodity Item No.	Chargeable Weight	Rate / Charge	Total	Nature and Quantity of Goods (incl. Dimensions or Volume)
1	30. 0 "FREE HOUSE" (DDP)	K	A	MM	30. 0	...	...	SAMPLES FOR TESTING (TUBES,PLATES,RODS) VOL.WGHT.: 3.5 KG DIMS: 1/100x25x8 cm
1	30.	K					...	.020 cbm

Prepaid	Weight Charge	Collect
...		
	Valuation Charge	
	Tax	
	Total Other Charges Due Agent	
...	Total Other Charges Due Carrier	

Other Charges
FULL HAWB 6.00 C

Shipper certifies that the particulars on the face hereof are correct and that **insofar as any part of the consignment contains dangerous goods, such part is properly described by name and is in proper condition for carriage by air according to the applicable Dangerous Goods Regulations.**

AIRCARRIER
INTERNATIONAL GMBH
Ref. No. 2040064124 MARCO SANZ

Signature of Shipper or his Agent

Total Prepaid	Total Collect
...	
Currency Conversion Rates	CC Charges in Dest. Currency

AIRCARRIER
INTERNATIONAL GMBH
20. 10. .. DUESSELDORF GERMANY

Executed on (date) at (place) Signature of Issuing Carrier or its Agent

For Carrier's Use only at Destination	Charges at Destination	Total Collect Charges

DUS-4005 1921

Extra Copy

14.2.9 Original documents as requested in the L/C under 13.2.7 and 13.4.5 Bill of Lading

88660

BILL OF LADING B/L No. **CONT 002**

Shipper's Ref.

F/Agent's Ref.

BORCHARD LINES
LIMITED

DURRANT HOUSE, CHISWELL STREET, LONDON, EC1Y 4XY

Telephone: 0171-628 696 1/6
Telex: LONDON 88-69-00
Telegrams: BORLINES, LONDON, E.C.1

It is agreed that no responsibility shall attach to the Carrier or his Agents for fallure to notify the Consignee of the arrival of the goods.

Shipper
Naval Construction GmbH
German Office
Brabanther Straße 49
51147 Köln
GERMANY

Consignee (if ‚Order' state Notify Party and Address)
TO THE ORDER OF THE CYPRUS POPULAR BANK LTD

Notify Party and Adress (leave blank if stated above)
CHRISTAKIS GEORGIADU LTD
12, MESOKELEOS STREET
1042-NICOSIA
CYPRUS

Local vessel	from (Local Port of loading)
Ocean vessel RACHEL BORCHARD 367	Port of loading ANTWERP, BELGIUM PORT
Port of discharge LIMASSOL PORT	Final destination (if on carriage)

Marks and Nos; Container No:	Number and kind of packages: description of goods	Gross Weight	Measurement
L/C 305/00/10554 CAXU 425030 0 Seal: 176685	Said to contain 1 x 40' Dry 8' 6" container(s) STC 2 UNIT(S) INFLATABLE BOATS MODEL BOLERO 740 P EXW COLOGNE INCOTERMS 2000 IRREVOCABLE DOC. CREDIT NUMBER 305/00/10554 FREIGHT PAYABLE AT DESTINATION	5600 kg	

‚VESSEL IS NOT SCHEDULED TO CALL ON ITS CURRENT VOYAGE
AT THE PORTS OF FAMAGUSTA OR KYRENIA OR KARAVOSTASSI,
CYPRUS'.
***** SECOND NOTIFY *****
THE CYPRUS POPULAR BANK LTD.
TRADE FINANCE UNIT (305)
P.O. BOX 2032 NICOSIA
FREIGHT COLLECT
SHIPPERS LOAD STOW AND COUNT

SHIPPED ON BOARD
JOHN P. BEST & CO. N.V.
AS Agents
FOR BORCHARD LINE LTD:
21/07/..

Particulars of goods are those declared by Shippers **Shippers load, count and stowage.**

The terms, conditions and exceptions of this contract (upon which the rate of freight is based) and which are hereby mutually agreed upon, are as follows:-
Received by the Carrier from the Merchant in apparent good order and condition (unless otherwise noted herein) the total number or quantity of containers or other packages or units indicated, stated by the Merchant to comprise the goods specified above, for carriage subject to all the terms hereof (INCLUDING THE TERMS ON THE REVERSE HEREOF AND THE TERMS OF THE CARRIER'S APPLICABLE TARIFF) from the Place of Receipt or the Port of Delivery, whichever is applicable. In accepting this Bill of Lading, the Merchant expressly accepts and agrees to all its terms, conditions and exceptions whether printed, stamped or written or otherwise incorporated, notwithstanding any local privileges and customs and/or the nonsigning of this Bill of Lading by the Merchant.

ORIGINAL	Ocean Freight Payable at LIMASSOL	Place and date of issue **ANTWERP** 21/07/..
CRB(1)	Number of Original Bs/L 3/THREE	IN WITNESS whereof three (3) original Bills of Lading (unless otherwise stated herein) all of this tenor and date have been signed one of which being accomplished the other(s) to be void.
CONDITIONS CONTINUED OVERLEAF	Number of Packages (in words) ONE	by **JOHN P. BEST & Co. N.V. Antwerp-Belgium** (full legal title and country of incorporation of agent) as agent, for and on behalf of Borchard Lines Ltd. England as Carrier under the Bill of Lading

Commercial Invoice

Naval Construction GmbH
German Office
Brabanther Straße 49
51147 Köln
Tel. +49 (2 01) 45 09 31
Fax +49 (2 01) 45 09 32
E-Mail: naval.construction@online.de

CHRISTAKIS GEORGIADU LTD
12, MESOKELEOS STREET
1042-NICOSIA
CYPRUS

12 JULY 20..

COMMERCIAL INVOICE

1ST SHIPMENT (2/6 UNITS) OF

6 UNITS INFLATABLE BOATS
MODEL BOLERO 740 P

EXW COLOGNE, INCOTERMS 2000

SERIAL NOS.: DE-PIS R 007G000
DE-PIS R 008G000

PACKED IN ONE 40' CONTAINER
NETWEIGHT: 900 KG / UNIT

EXW COLOGNE €159.600,00

WE CERTIFY THAT THE GOODS ARE OF GERMAN ORIGIN AND THAT GOODS SHIPPED ARE IN ACCORDANCE WITH BENEFICIARY'S PROFORMA INVOICE DATED 03. 04. 20.. AND THAT EACH PACKING UNIT BEARS AN INDELIEBLE MARK INDICATING THE COUNTRY OF ORIGIN OF THE GOODS.

DRAWN UNDER LETTER OF CREDIT 305/00/10554
OF CYPRUS POPULAR BANK LIMITED, NICOSIA DD. 000421

Packing List

Naval Construction GmbH
German Office
Brabanther Straße 49
51147 Köln
Tel. +49 (2 01) 45 09 31
Fax +49 (2 01) 45 09 32
E-Mail: naval.construction@online.de

CHRISTAKIS GEORGIADU LTD
12, MESOKELEOS STREET
1042-NICOSIA
CYPRUS

12 JULY 20..

PACKING LIST

1ST SHIPMENT (2/6 UNITS) OF

6 UNITS INFLATABLE BOATS
MODEL BOLERO 740 P

EXW COLOGNE, INCOTERMS 2000

SERIAL NOS.: DE-PIS R 007G000
DE-PIS R 008G000

PACKED IN ONE 40' CONTAINER
NETWEIGHT: 900 KG / UNIT

SHIPPING MARKS: L/C 305/00/10554
CAXU 425030 0
SEAL: 176685

DRAWN UNDER LETTER OF CREDIT 305/00/10554
OF CYPRUS POPULAR BANK LIMITED, NICOSIA DD. ..0421

Certificate confirming that documents have been handed to the master of the vessel for onward delivery to applicant

Naval Construction GmbH
German Office
Brabanther Straße 49
51147 Köln
Tel. +49 (2 01) 45 09 31
Fax +49 (2 01) 45 09 32
E-Mail: naval.construction@online.de

CHRISTAKIS GEORGIADU LTD
12, MESOKELEOS STREET
1042-NICOSIA
CYPRUS

24 JUL 20..

CERTIFICATE

1ST SHIPMENT (2/6 UNITS) OF

6 UNITS INFLATABLE BOATS
MODEL BOLERO 740 P

EXW COLOGNE, INCOTERMS 2000

SERIAL NOS.: DE-PIS R 007G000
DE-PIS R 008G000

WE CONFIRM THAT THE ORIGINAL EUR1 AND COPIES OF THE COMMERCIAL INVOICE AND PACKING LIST HAVE BEEN HANDED TO THE MASTER OF THE VESSEL FOR ONWARD DELIVERY TO APPLICANT

DRAWN UNDER LETTER OF CREDIT 305/00/10554
OF CYPRUS POPULAR BANK LIMITED, NICOSIA DD. ..0421

14.2.10 Enquiry for insurance rates

MATHESON, MAYDELL AND PARTNERS
Consulting Engineers | 112 Compton Street | London EC1V 0EU

15 January 20..

Multimode-Transport Versicherungs-AG
International Insurance Company
Saebener Platz 29-31
D-81545 Muenchen

Dear Sirs

Under a contract with the Korean State Railways, which have commissioned us with the modernisation of their rolling stock and installations on the Seoul-Pusan line, we have ordered 5 locomotives from a company in Munich, electronic signalling equipment from a company in Wuerzburg, 20 freight wagons from a company in Paris, and 20,000 metric tons of steel rail from a supplier in Uddeholm, Sweden.

Delivery of the locomotives, freight wagons, rails and signalling equipment has been scheduled in such a way that they will arrive in Rotterdam at roughly the same time (in early May), where they will be combined into a shipload. For transporting the cargo, MS SEAGULL has been chartered, which is scheduled to leave port for Seoul on 15 May. The total value of the shipment is approx. US$ ... CIF Seoul.

The Korean State Railways want us to place the insurance in Germany, since the equipment supplied by German companies will make up the bulk of the total amount. Cover is to be provided on the following terms: Institute Cargo Clause A, including rust and oxidation, war, SR&CC, from warehouse to warehouse (remaining in effect until 60 days after discharge). The policy is to cover the CIF value plus 10 %.

Please inform us on which terms you are prepared to insure the shipment detailed above.

Yours faithfully

MATHESON, MAYDELL AND PARTNERS

14.2.11 Company informs insurer about an insurance claim after sea-damage

Dear Sirs

This is to inform you that the goods of which we have just taken delivery arrived here in partly damaged condition. 25 of the 100 bicycles show signs of rust, which has obviously been caused by sea water.

We enclose photos of the damaged bicycles together with a survey of the average adjuster.

We therefore place a claim with you for the damaged goods, the details of which are as follows:

Sea-damage 25 bicycles	£4,523.00
Additional expenses	£ 195.00
Total	£4,718.00

Please arrange for the transfer of this sum to our account with the Biron Bank in Cardiff.

Please also find enclosed the documentation related to this consignment:

1. Insurance certificate
2. Survey of the average adjuster
3. Freight forwarder's invoice
4. Copy of the B/L
5. Refusal of the ship broker to grant our claim.

We look forward to the early settlement of this matter.

Yours faithfully

Encs

14.2.12 Insurance company in Hong Kong sends copies of documents to British insurance company

Dear Madam / Sir

CUBICLES FOR COMMUNICATION EQUIPMENT EX M/S DARTMOOR

For your perusal we enclose copies of the following documents submitted by the insured:

1. Bill of Lading No 3829485
2. Claim Report
3. Survey Report

In the meantime, please arrange to remit your 75 % share of the survey fees of ... and also advise the details of insurance declaration for this consignment. Invoice and packing list can be obtained from the insured's head office in Bradford.

Yours faithfully

Encs

14.2.13 Claim Report

Claim Report No 48568
15 June 20..

Ref.: Cubicles for Communication Equipment ex M/S Dartmoor
B/L No 3829485
Contract No E134-7899

Delivery of four packages containing cubicles for communication equipment. Out of these four packages, two were found damaged on unpacking:

1. VDT Cubicle, Factory No 93345-A0088. One swing frame is bent. All modules will have to be tested when cubicle is commissioned. We reserve the right to claim for the cost of the tests after commissioning.

Repair: Replacement of swing frame; new frame to be sent from the UK.

2. VDT Cubicle, Factory No 93345-A5858. One swing frame slightly bent; one holding rack damaged.

Repair: Straightening of swing frame and holding rack. Repairs will be made locally.

We reserve the right to claim damages on all modules installed in the cubicles, as these can be tested only during commissioning.

Yours faithfully

14.2.14 Insurance company sends Certificate of Insurance

Dear Mr Howard

Enclosed please find the Certificate of Insurance for the partial delivery of goods under our Insurance Policy No. 45000.

We ask you to complete the blank parts, including the exact insurance amount, the description of the goods to be transported and the details of the sea voyage.

Please return a copy of the completed document for our files.

Yours sincerely
MARINA VERSICHERUNGS-AG
H. Löffler

Encl.

Certificate of Insurance

MARINA VERSICHERUNGS-AG
HAMBURG

Triplicate

Prämie bezahlt
premium paid
prime acquise
premio pagado

Versicherungs-Zertifikat (Police) No.

Certificate of Insurance (Policy) / Certificat d'Assurance (Police) / Certificado de Seguro (Póliza)

Ausfertigungen / Specimen / Exemplaires / Ejemplares:
Mit Zahlung gegen eine Ausfertigung werden die anderen ungültig.
By payment against one copy the other ones will become null and void.
Dès paiement contre un exemplaire les autres seront considérés sans effet.
Efectuado el pago contra un ejemplar perderá an su validez los otros.

ausgestellt zu Gunsten:
issued in favour of:
etabli pour le compte de:
emitido a favor de:

für Rechnung, wen es angeht, für die folgenden Güter:
for account of whom it may concern, for the following goods:
facture à compte de qui de droit pour la marchandise suivante:
factura para quien corresponda de las sigulentes mercaderlas:

gemäß Police No.: 45000
according to policy No.:
selon police No.: Howard & Johnson Ltd
según póliza No.: Richmond

per Transportmittel:
LKW, Eisenbahn, Flugzeug, Flußschiff, Seeschiff
by transport medium: truck, railway, aeroplane, riverboat, ocean vessel
par moyen de transport: camion, chemin de fer, avion, navire fluviale, navire
por medio de transporte: camion, ferrocarril, avion, barco fluvial, barco

versicherte Summe:
sum insured:
somme assure:
suma asegurada:

für die Reise von:
for the voyage from:
pour le voyage de:
para el viaje desde:

nach:
to:
a:
hasta:

Bedingungen:
Conditions:
Condiciones:

Risks Covered
This insurance covers all risks of loss of or damage to the subjectmatter insured except as provided in Clauses 4, 5, 6 and 7 as per Institute Cargo Clauses (c) 1/1/82 Cl. 254.
Including TPND-Clause, including damage due to ordinary breakage, bending, denting, twisting, embezzlement, sabotage, but excluding ordinary rust and/or oxydation.
The Institute Radioactive Contamination Exclusion Clause 1/10/90 Cl. 356 applies.

War and Strike
Including War Risks as per Institute War Clauses (Cargo) 1/1/82 Cl. 255;
including Strike as per Institute Strikes Clauses (Cargo) 1/1/82 Cl. 256.

Schäden sind festzustellen durch:
Claims to be ascertained by:
Pour la constatation d'un sinistre s'adresser a:
En caso de siniestro dirigirse a:

ohne dessen/deren Havarie-Zertifikat ein Schaden nicht anerkannt wird.

and no damage is recognized without his/their average-certificate.
Et sans le certificat d'avarie de celui-çi/ceux/çi aucun sinistre sera reconnu.
Sin el certificado de averia de éste/éstos, no se reconocer a ningún siniestro.

Hamburg, ______________________ 20..

H. Scheffler P. Friedrich

Bitte wenden, turn over please, tournez s'il vous plait, doblar por fabor

14.3 Terms and phrases

14.3.1 Transport and forwarding

Customer's enquiry

Please quote your lowest rates for regular shipments of goods to …	*Bitte geben Sie uns Ihre günstigsten Sätze für regelmäßige Warensendungen nach … an.*
The goods are to be insured against all risks / in accordance with Institute Cargo Clauses A (B or C).	*Die Waren sind gegen alle Risiken / in Übereinstimmung mit den Institute Cargo Clauses A (B oder C) zu versichern.*
We intend to charter a ship / plane and ask you to let us know what shipping / airline company you recommend.	*Wir haben vor, ein Schiff / Flugzeug zu chartern und bitten Sie uns mitzuteilen, welche Schifffahrt- / Luftfahrtgesellschaft Sie empfehlen.*
The shipment consists of … and is extremely valuable / fragile / perishable / highly dangerous.	*Die Sendung besteht aus … und ist äußerst wertvoll / zerbrechlich / verderblich / höchst gefährlich.*
The goods are to be collected from our factory in …	*Die Waren sind in unserer Fabrik in … abzuholen.*
Please collect the consignment at our … Works and arrange shipment to … by the first available steamer.	*Bitte holen Sie die Sendung in unserem Werk in … ab und veranlassen Sie die Verschiffung nach … mit dem ersten verfügbaren Dampfer.*
Please let us know the date on which the ship closes for cargo.	*Bitte teilen Sie uns das Datum des Ladeschlusses für das Schiff mit.*
As payment will be made by documentary credit we would ask you to provide the necessary documents / a full set of clean on-board Bs/L.	*Da die Zahlung per Dokumentenakkreditiv erfolgt, bitten wir Sie, die nötigen Dokumente / einen vollen Satz reiner an-Bord-Konnossemente zu beschaffen.*
Can you obtain the certificate of origin / the legalisation document? We would require you to clear the goods through customs.	*Können Sie das Ursprungszeugnis / Legalisierungsdokument beschaffen? Sie müssten die Zollabfertigung für die Waren durchführen.*
Please let us know the difference in cost between transport by train ferry via Dover / Dunkerque and roll-on / roll-off via Dover / Calais.	*Bitte nennen Sie uns die Kostendifferenz zwischen einer Verladung mit Eisenbahnfähre über Dover / Dünkirchen und einer Ro/Ro-Verladung über Dover / Calais.*
Would haulage transport through the Channel Tunnel be cheaper for these goods?	*Wäre ein Lkw-Transport durch den Kanaltunnel für diese Waren billiger?*

Freight forwarder's offer

We would charge … for the transport by road of … goods from … to …	*Wir würden … für den Straßentransport von … Waren von … nach … berechnen.*
The total charges for transport by rail including the collection from your premises and delivery free domicile in … would amount to …	*Die Gesamtgebühren für Schienentransport einschließlich Abholung von Ihren Geschäftsräumen und Lieferung frei Haus in … würden sich auf … belaufen.*
We can quote very favourable groupage rates / special rates for container space.	*Wir können sehr günstige Sammeltarife / spezielle Sätze für Container-Raum anbieten.*
We have our own freight office at the airport, which handles incoming and outgoing air shipments.	*Wir unterhalten im Flughafen ein eigenes Frachtbüro, das eingehende und ausgehende Luftfrachtsendungen abfertigt.*
M. S. … is receiving cargo from 12 January to 18 January inclusive and is expected to commence loading on 14 January.	*M. S. … nimmt vom 12. bis 18. Januar einschließlich Ladung an. Voraussichtlicher Ladebeginn ist am 14. Januar.*
M. S. … has just completed a charter and will be at Liverpool dock and ready to load by the end of next week.	*Die Charter für M. S. … ist soeben abgelaufen. Das Schiff liegt Ende nächster Woche ladebereit am Kai in Liverpool.*
ETA (*Estimated time of arrival*) of M. V. … is …	*Die voraussichtliche Ankunftszeit der … ist …*
We will make arrangements for the goods to be stored in a bonded warehouse / on pallets / in a refrigerated room.	*Wir werden dafür sorgen, dass die Waren in einem Warenzollverschluss-Lager / auf Paletten / in einem Kühlraum gelagert werden.*

14.3.2 Insurance

We would like to take out insurance for the transport of …	*Wir möchten gern eine Versicherung für den Transport von … abschließen.*
Please quote your lowest rate for an open policy covering the usual risks.	*Bitte nennen Sie uns Ihre niedrigsten Sätze für eine Generalpolice, die die üblichen Gefahren deckt.*
Please inform us on what terms you can undertake insurance of … against all risks, including breakage and pilferage.	*Bitte teilen Sie uns mit, zu welchen Bedingungen Sie die Versicherung von … gegen alle Gefahren, einschließlich Bruch und Beraubung, übernehmen können.*
The goods are to be insured with general average (WGA) / free of particular average(FPA) / with particular average (WPA).	*Die Waren sind mit allgemeiner Havarie / ohne besondere Havarie / mit besonderer Havarie zu versichern.*

Please arrange for the full insurance cover of these goods according to Institute Cargo Clause C.	*Bitte veranlassen Sie eine volle Versicherungsdeckung für diese Waren gemäß der Institute Cargo Clause C.*
We are sending you enclosed insurance certificate no. … for the goods you wish to insure during their transport from … to …	*Wir senden Ihnen anbei das Versicherungszertifikat Nr. … für die Waren, die Sie während des Transports von … nach … versichern wollen.*
Our time policy / open policy / floating policy no. … is running out on … Please inform us if you wish to renew it.	*Unsere Zeitpolice / Generalpolice / Abschreibepolice Nr. … läuft am … ab. Bitte teilen Sie uns mit, ob Sie sie erneuern möchten.*
As per Cover Note enclosed, we have insured your shipment against all risks. The policy is being prepared and will be sent to you within the next few days.	*Gemäß beiliegender Deckungszusage haben wir Ihre Sendung gegen alle Gefahren versichert. Die Police ist in Vorbereitung und geht Ihnen in den nächsten Tagen zu.*
M.S. … has sustained average and will land the greater part of her cargo in damaged condition.	*M.S. … hat Havarie erlitten und wird den größten Teil der Ladung in beschädigtem Zustand an Land bringen.*

14.4 Exercises
Please translate:

14.4.1 Petersen GmbH, Internationale Spedition, Hamburg, an Richardson & Brown PLC, Chelmsford (Essex)

Betr.: Nawab Industries, Karachi/London (NI)
Purchase Order No.: 3496-54

Sehr geehrte Damen und Herren,

wir sind beauftragt, die Koordination und Verladung der von NI von Ihnen gekauften Waren vorzunehmen. Entsprechende Instruktionen liegen sowohl Ihnen als auch uns vor.

Nach den vorliegenden Anweisungen unseres gemeinsamen Kunden informieren Sie das Londoner Büro von NI mindestens 14 Tage vor dem effektiven Lieferdatum. Geben Sie uns bitte gleichzeitig die entsprechende Fax- oder Briefkopie nach Hamburg zu Händen von Frau Christina Wagner.

Vor Verladung benötigen wir von Ihnen:

2 Kopien der Handelsrechnung
2 Kopien der Packliste
2 Kopien des Prüfzertifikats
2 Kopien des Ursprungszeugnisses
1 Kopie des Akkreditivs
1 Speditionsauftrag, ausgefüllt und ordnungsgemäß unterschrieben.

Nach Bestätigung des effektiven Lieferdatums erhalten Sie den verbindlichen Abruf für die Lieferung nach London, wo die Sendung von unserem dortigen Korrespondenten, Jones & Co. (Forwarding) Ltd, übernommen wird. Diese Firma ist jedoch gerne bereit, den Transport ab Werk durchzuführen.

Gemäß Kontrakt sind Sie als Lieferant für die Erstellung aller erforderlichen Papiere verantwortlich und tragen die entsprechenden Kosten. Falls wir Ihnen bei der Auftragsabwicklung in irgendeiner Weise behilflich sein können, teilen Sie uns dies bitte mit.

Mit freundlichen Grüßen

14.4.2 **Menzell & Co., Schiffsmakler in Hamburg, verfasst folgendes Rundschreiben:**

Sehr geehrte Damen und Herren,

nach Beendigung des Hapag Lloyd / Ben Ocean Gemeinschaftsdienstes nach Indonesien, worüber die Verlader bereits am 13. 8. informiert wurden, gibt Ben Ocean jetzt die Einführung eines neuen, direkten Container- und konventionellen Dienstes nach Indonesien bekannt.

In dem Bemühen, den Wünschen nach verschiedenen Verlademöglichkeiten seitens der Ablader Rechnung zu tragen, wird dieser Dienst eine größere Anzahl von Containerstellplätzen bieten, gleichzeitig aber weiterhin genügend Raum für konventionelle Ladung vorsehen.

In Europa werden folgende Ladehäfen bedient: Hull, Hamburg, Bremerhaven, Rotterdam, Antwerpen. In Indonesien werden Djakarta und Surabaya direkt angelaufen, während Semarang, Ujung Pandang und Balik Papan in Umladung via Surabaya bedient werden. Bei genügendem Ladungsangebot können diese Häfen ebenfalls direkt angelaufen werden.

Die erste Abfahrt im Rahmen dieses neuen Dienstes wird mit MS „PATROCLUS“ durchgeführt:

Hull	14. 9.
Hamburg	18. 9.
Rotterdam	22. 9.
Antwerpen	24. 9.

Danach werden monatliche Abfahrten mit den Schiffen „BENVORLICH“, „PHRONTIS“ und „BENGLOE“ angeboten.

Agenten:	UK	Killick Martin & Co. Ltd, London
	Hamburg / Bremen	Menzell & Co Schiffsmakler
	Amsterdam / Rotterdam	OCL Agencies BV
	Antwerpen	De Keyser Thornten S. A.
	Djakarta	Ben Ocean Representative

Zur Information der Verlader in Belgien, den Niederlanden und den skandinavischen Ländern soll dieses Rundschreiben ins Englische übersetzt werden.

14.4.3 **Fax von Summer GmbH, Freiburg an Fortune Insurance, Hull**

Meldung eines Seeversicherungsschadens

Unser Auftrag Nr. 89 07 564

Sehr geehrte Damen und Herren,

von unserem deutschen Kunden, der Fa. Steinhuber & Bögel in Duisburg, haben wir eine Schadensmeldung erhalten. Es handelt sich um eine Sendung mit 30 Kisten Elektrokabel für U.S.A, die Sie seinerzeit mit Police Nr. 3945 versicherten.

Laut Havariezertifikat ist die Sendung in stark beschädigtem Zustand in New York angekommen. Der Gutachter führt die Beschädigung darauf zurück, dass die Kisten unsachgemäß im Laderaum des Schiffes verstaut wurden.

Alle weiteren Einzelheiten entnehmen Sie bitte den beigefügten Attachments wie folgt:

Kopie des Konnossements
Rechnung der Befrachter
Havariezertifikat des Gutachters
Kopie unserer Versicherungspolice

Die Originale dieser Attachments werden Ihnen mit separater Post zugeleitet.

Wir bitten um baldige Schadensregulierung und Rückgabe der Originaldokumente.

Mit freundlichen Grüßen

Please draft letters, faxes or e-mails from the following particulars:

14.4.4 **Geschäftsfall:**

Die Speditionsfirma Gerwald & Hennings (G+H), Coburger Str. 34, 28219 Bremen, Fax-Nr.: +49 (4 21) 23 13 07, E-Mail-Adresse: gerwald.hennings@spedition.can.de, hat für einen Kunden eine Sendung von 100 Kisten chemischer Apparaturen übernommen, die für die Shulmann Chemical Corporation in Louisville, Kentucky, bestimmt ist. Der Absender ist die DEWA-Apparatebau AG in Hannover. Die Verladung soll am 18. März in Bremen mit M.S. „American Ambassador" erfolgen, das am 19. März nach Norfolk, Virginia, ausläuft. Voraussichtliches Ankunftsdatum: 28. April.

Aufgabe: Schreiben Sie als Sachbearbeiter(in) der G+H an Ihren Korrespondenten in Norfolk, McGee & Co. Inc., International Freight Forwarders, P.O. Box 12 09 48, Norfolk, Virginia 30 78 94, U.S.A., Fax-Nr.: +1 (8 04) 24 09 17, E-Mail-Adresse: international.freight@inc.com und teilen Sie ihm Folgendes mit:

- Bitte um Übernahme der Sendung
- Angabe der genauen Daten wie oben
- Angabe des Absenders wie oben
- Bitte um zollamtliche Abfertigung der Sendung und Weiterleitung nach Louisville

- Geben Sie an, dass die zur Verzollung notwendigen Dokumente sofort nach Versand per Luftpost an McGee & Co. abgehen werden
- Da vereinbarte Lieferbedingung DDP Louisville, Kentucky lautete, gehen Einfuhrzoll, Zollabfertigungsgebühren und Transportkosten bis Louisville zu Lasten der Lieferfirma
- Rechnung nach Abwicklung des Auftrags an Sie.

14.4.5 **Geschäftsfall:**

Beantworten Sie als Sachbearbeiter(in) der Hansen-Spedition die unter 14.2.1 erhaltene E-Mail unter Berücksichtigung der folgenden Punkte:

- Dank für erhaltene Anfrage
- Sie können den Transport der 5 Paletten zu einem Preis von 200,– Euros pro Palette durchführen
- Die folgenden Vorschriften müssen beachtet werden:
- Es muss sich um Europaletten handeln, die beladen nicht höher als 1,80 m sind und pro Stück nicht mehr als 800 kg wiegen
- Die Kartons müssen entweder durch Folie (*foil*) oder durch Bänder (*strapping*) gesichert sein
- Der Transport beinhaltet alle Kosten einschließlich Handhabung der Dokumente bis zum Lager des Empfängers in Dublin
- Alle weiteren Einzelheiten gemäß den umseitig aufgeführten Geschäftsbedingungen der Spedition.

14.4.6 **Geschäftsfall:**

Sie arbeiten für die Business Multimedia GmbH, Bultkamp 32, 33611 Bielefeld, Fax-Nr.: +49 (521) 84 36 95, E-Mail-Adresse: business.multimedia@aol.com,und wollen eine Sendung von 500 SnapScan e25-Scannern an Ihren Kunden, die Townsgate plc, 24 The Broadway, Amersham, Buckinghamshire HP7 0HP, schicken. Die Scanner müssen während des Transports versichert werden.

Aufgabe: Schicken Sie an die Bell & Howards Insurance Ltd, Palmer's Avenue, Manchester PG3 2LH, GB, Fax-Nr.: +44 (161) 39 05 44, E-Mail-Adresse: bellhoward@insurance.co.uk, eine Anfrage unter Berücksichtigung der folgenden Punkte:

- Bitte um Ausarbeitung einer Transportversicherung für die 500 Scanner, Rechnungswert: 8,– € pro Stück
- Sie benötigen eine Deckung aller Risiken vom Lager Bielefeld bis Lager des Kunden in Amersham
- Transport als Sammelladung im Container
- Die Sendung wird vom Spediteur in Ihrem Lager in Bielefeld übernommen und in Amersham ausgeliefert
- Gewünschte Versicherungsdeckung: Rechungswert der 500 Scanner plus 10 %.

15. Trade Fairs and Exhibitions; Hotel Accommodation

15.1 Introduction

Trade Fairs. Trade fairs are typically held at the same place at regular intervals. They are organized for the purpose of transacting business and therefore cater mainly for trade buyers and businesspeople, although the general public may be admitted on certain days. Some fairs are limited to the products of a particular industry, others comprise the products of various different industries.

Exhibitions. Exhibitions (or shows, eg the Motor Show, the Chelsea Flower Show) are mainly intended as a source of information for all those interested in the products displayed, both businesspeople and the general public. Like fairs, exhibitions may cover a narrow or wider range of products. International trade fairs and exhibitions give manufacturers an opportunity to introduce their products to trade buyers and visitors from all over the world. These events are therefore ideally suited for establishing business contacts.

Hotel Accommodation. In spite of the increasing use of modern telecommunications, conference facilities via satellite etc, worldwide travel has not decreased. In many cases a face-to-face discussion is still important in business negotiations. The hotel and catering trade therefore plays an important role in the GDP (gross domestic product) of many countries, not only in the tourist, but also in the business and convention sector. Many companies prefer to hold their conferences, seminars and conventions at hotels and centres located in their vicinity or in other attractive venues.

15.2 Model correspondence

15.2.1 Irish company asks for quotation for a hotel booking during a fair in Germany

e-mail

Mail from: Cheltenham.ltd@ucd.ie
to: schlosshotel@t-online.de **cc:**
Subject:
Attachment:

Dear Sir or Madam

Our company is taking part in the Cebit Fair in Düsseldorf and will have a stand there. The Fair takes place from 14 to 28 September 20..

From 13 to 29 September 20.. we will need 10 single rooms for non-smokers with bath or shower, including breakfast. The rooms must be equipped with a telephone which can be used day and night.

Please quote your best groupage rate for these rooms including all taxes and costs.

We look forward to your quotation.

Yours faithfully

Cheltenham Limited
Henry P. Shears
Advertising Department

15.2.2 American hotel offers rooms and conference facilities to German company

FAO: Mr Hans-Werner Fern
Sträther & Ullrich GmbH
Blumenstraße 40
44139 Dortmund

Fax No. +49 (231) 47 13 06

From: Jennifer L. Probert
The Bloomington Palace
Minneapolis, MN 330748
USA

fax

Dear Mr Fern:

Thank you for your enquiry about the reservation of rooms and the booking of conference facilities for your meeting in Minneapolis from 8 to 11 July.

We can offer you single rooms with bath and / or shower, WC, TV and minibar for 30 people at a special rate of US$60 per day, ie at a total price of US$7,200. This price includes breakfast.

A conference room for about 50 people can be placed at your disposal for this period free of charge, provided all meals are taken at the hotel. The conference room is equipped with a video recorder, overhead projector, a TV-set and a flip chart. A small office is also available which has internet and e-mail facilites, telephone and fax connections. Bilingual staff (German / English) can be hired locally.

Our conditions of payment would be: ⅓ in advance, ⅓ on arrival of the guests, ⅓ on departure of the guests.

We hope our offer meets with your approval. If so, we would ask you to book early since at this time of the year booking can be difficult.

Kind regards

Jennifer L. Probert

Jennifer L. Probert
Reservation Officer
The Bloomington Palace Hotel

15.2.3 Invitation to participate in a fair

BULLARD ASSOCIATES-Public Relations • Advertising • Marketing
P.O. Box 61567 • Sunnyvale, California 94086 U.S.A

BULLARD ASSOCIATES

October 26, 20..

Evans Real-Time GmbH
Burghausener Str. 23
D-80634 München
Germany

Gentlemen:

We are currently putting the finishing touches on plans for the United States pavilion at SYSTEMS 20.., October 17–21.

As participants – on behalf of your parent company in New Jersey – in last year's SYSTEMS, you are very much aware of the pre-eminent position this biennial trade fair holds in the European and worldwide computer and EDP community.

We will be happy to assist you at every step of your planning and participation. Bullard Associates has ten years' experience in putting together successful American pavilions at overseas exhibitions and has organized more than a dozen "Made in America" programs in Germany alone.

Full details on SYSTEMS 20.. are given in the enclosed brochure. Space is limited, so please act promptly. We look forward to working with you on behalf of your parent company at next year's SYSTEMS.

Sincerely yours
Bullard Associates

James D. Schroder

JDS: mm

Encl.

15.2.4 Exhibitor announces participation

Dear Madam / Sir

We are now commencing our preparations for the 20.. Ceramitec exhibition. This year we have decided in favour of a much bigger presence, having identified Ceramitec as the most significant ceramic industry exhibition in Europe.

We are writing to you early, hoping that we can be reserved prime space; we envisage taking 4, 6 or possibly more units.

Being a British company, we have the option to join the British delegation organised by the British Ceramic Plant and Machinery Manufacturers Federation and backed financially by the British Overseas Trade Board. However, we do no wish to do this if it should in any way prejudice our location within the exhibition hall.

Could you therefore send us a plan of the layout of stands, indicating blocks of 4 or 6 still available, together with rates and other relevant information.

We would also appreciate it if you could recommend any exhibition contractors based in Munich who would be capable of designing, building and erecting a stand for this event.

Yours faithfully
Colin Harrison & Sons Ltd

D I Ramsden
Executive Sales Director

15.2.5 Request for information on fair

Okunfe Exports Limited
125 Market Street · Accra, Ghana

CA/EW
10 February 20..

Ausstellungs-Messe-Kongress-GmbH
Messedamm 22
14055 Berlin
Germany

Dear Sirs

Dr Delius of the Trade Section of the German Embassy in Accra has referred us to you. We understand that you are the organisers of the Overseas Import Fair "Partners for Progress", which is specifically designed to assist exporters from the Third World wishing to introduce their products to the German market.

We are dealers in a wide range of products made by West African craftsmen (pottery, leatherwork, jewellery, wood sculptures), which we buy from local artisans and export to Europe and the United States. As it seems that there is considerable demand for genuine African handiwork in Germany, we should like to get in touch with German importers interested in the products handled by us.

According to Dr Delius, displaying our products at the Overseas Import Fair "Partners for Progress" would be a useful first step. He also told us that exhibitors from developing countries can obtain financial assistance from the German government. We should therefore be pleased to receive detailed information on this fair and the assistance available to foreign exhibitors.

Yours faithfully
Okunfe Exports Ltd

Charles Adama

15.3 Terms and phrases

15.3.1 Fairs and Exhibitions

We recently attended a specialized fair / specialized exhibition / specialist show in …	*Wir haben kürzlich eine Fachmesse / Fachausstellung in … besucht.*
We have seen your trade fair's home page on the internet and are interested in taking part in next year's spring event.	*Wir haben die Homepage Ihrer Fachmesse im Internet gesehen und sind daran interessiert, an der Frühjahrsveranstaltung nächsten Jahres teilzunehmen.*
Please send us an exact plan of the fair grounds to enable us to get an idea of the open-air site.	*Bitte schicken Sie uns einen genauen Plan des Messegeländes, damit wir einen Eindruck des Freigeländes bekommen können.*
We would like to book a stand with an exhibition area of …	*Wir möchten einen Stand mit einer Ausstellungsfläche von … buchen.*
Please quote us for the following:	*Bitte bieten Sie uns Folgendes an:*
conference facilities	*Konferenzeinrichtungen*
conference room	*Konferenzraum*
exhibition stand	*Ausstellungsstand*
office equipment	*Büroausrüstung*
lockable back / side room	*abschließbares Hinter- / Seitenzimmer*
seating area	*Sitzraumfläche*
shelves for our exhibits	*Regale für unsere Ausstellungsstücke*
bookshelves	*Bücherregale*
literature rack	*Prospektständer*
stage	*Bühne*
running hot and cold water	*fließendes heißes und kaltes Wasser*
electrical sockets	*Elektrosteckdosen*
fully equipped kitchen unit	*voll ausgerüstete Kücheneinheit*
halogen lighting	*Halogenbeleuchtung*
fluorescent tubes	*Leuchtröhren*
floodlights	*Flutlicht*
stage lighting	*Bühnenbeleuchtung*
carpet floor, fitted carpet	*Teppichboden*
carpet tiles	*Teppichfliesen*
parquet flooring	*Parkettboden*
upholstered armchair	*gepolsterter Sessel*
swivel chair	*Drehstuhl*
wooden conference table	*Konferenztisch aus Holz*
display case	*Schaukasten*
display panel	*Schautafel*
cassette recorder	*Kassettenrekorder*
video-recorder	*Videorekorder*

slide (overhead) projector	*Dia-(Overhead-)Projektor*
flipchart	*Flipchart*
projection device	*Projektionsvorrichtung*
photocopier	*Fotokopierer*
colour copier	*Farbkopierer*
fax machine	*Faxgerät*
internet link	*Internetanschluss*
mobile phone, AE cellphone	*Handy*
security camera	*Überwachungskamera*
security alarm	*Alarmanlage*
video surveillance	*Videoüberwachung*
digital video camera	*digitale Videokamera*

15.3.2 Hotel accommodation

We have seen an advertisement placed by your hotel in the ... magazine and would ask you to send us your hotel leaflet.	*Wir haben eine Anzeige Ihres Hotel in der ... Zeitschrift gesehen und bitten Sie um Zusendung Ihres Hotelprospekts.*
Your hotel was recommended to us by ...	*Ihr Hotel wurde uns von ... empfohlen.*
Before making a reservation please give us the following information:	*Bevor wir eine Buchung machen, geben Sie uns bitte folgende Informationen:*
Is the hotel within easy reach of the airport / railway station / exhibition centre / motorway (highway) / trade fair?	*Ist das Hotel vom Flughafen / Bahnhof / Ausstellungsgelände / von der Autobahn / Fachmesse aus leicht zu erreichen?*
Do you have single / double / twin rooms?	*Haben Sie Einzel- / Doppelzimmer?*
Does your hotel have a bar / restaurant / swimming pool / sauna / tennis court / parking facilities?	*Hat Ihr Hotel eine Bar / ein Restaurant / Schwimmbad / eine Sauna / einen Tennisplatz / Parkgelegenheiten?*
Do you serve vegetarian food?	*Servieren Sie vegetarische Kost?*
Do you offer corporate rates to business travellers?	*Bieten Sie Geschäftsreisenden Firmentarife an?*
As we frequently send our employees to this area, we would like to know whether you offer special rates.	*Da wir unsere Angestellten oft in dieses Gebiet schicken, möchten wir gern wissen, ob Sie Sondertarife anbieten.*
Can Ms / Mrs / Mr ... be collected / picked up at the airport by the hotel?	*Kann Frau / Herr ... vom Hotel am Flughafen abgeholt werden?*
Ms / Mrs / Mr ... will be arriving on flight ... landing at London Heathrow at ... hours.	*Frau / Herr ... wird mit Flug ... , der um ... Uhr in London Heathrow landet, ankommen.*

Our conference / convention will take place on ... Please let us know if it is possible to accommodate a party of 50 people in your hotel from ... to ...	*Unsere Konferenz / unsere Tagung wird am ... stattfinden. Bitte lassen Sie uns wissen, ob es möglich ist, eine Gesellschaft von 50 Personen vom ... bis ... in Ihrem Hotel aufzunehmen.*
A working / business lunch is to be served at 1 pm.	*Ein Arbeits- / Geschäftsmittagessen soll um 13 Uhr serviert werden.*
The presentation of our new device is scheduled to take place at 5 pm.	*Die Vorführung unseres neuen Geräts ist für 17 Uhr geplant.*
We would require a buffet dinner for ... people in your hotel garden restaurant at ... o'clock.	*Wir benötigen ein Büfett-Dinner für ... Personen um ... Uhr in Ihrem Hotel-Gartenrestaurant.*

15.4 Exercises

Please translate:

15.4.1 Antwort der Münchener Messe- und Auslandsgesellschaft mbH an Colin Harrison & Sons Ltd, Keele Road, Stoke-on-Trent, Staffordshire ST4 8oA, England, auf deren Schreiben unter 15.2.4

zu Händen von: Herrn D.I. Ramsden, Executive Sales Director

Sehr geehrter Herr Ramsden,

vielen Dank für Ihr Schreiben vom 31.05. Wir freuen uns, dass Sie die Ceramitec für die wichtigste europäische Veranstaltung der Keramikindustrie halten und vorhaben, sich mit einem größeren Stand an der Ceramitec 20.. zu beteiligen.

Aus dem Übersichtsplan im beiliegenden Prospekt können Sie ersehen, dass die Hallen 23–25 als Ausstellungshallen vorgesehen sind. Voraussichtlich werden wir jedoch auch die Halle 21 (EU) mitbelegen. Dort werden die leichteren Maschinen und der Bereich Rohstoffe, Farben (*dyes*), Glasuren (*glazes*) etc. untergebracht, die Schwermaschinen in den übrigen Hallen. Für die britische Beteiligung ist in beiden Bereichen je ein Stand vorreserviert.

Da wir Anfang nächsten Jahres mit der Planung beginnen, bitten wir Sie, das beiliegende Anmeldeformular auszufüllen und an uns zurückzusenden, damit wir Ihre Platzwünsche berücksichtigen können. Aus dem Übersichtsplan können Sie ersehen, wo die beiden britischen Beteiligungen untergebracht sein werden. Bitte teilen Sie uns mit, ob Sie als Einzelaussteller oder als Aussteller des britischen Gemeinschaftsstandes teilnehmen wollen.

Die Mietpreise für die Stände sind aus den anhängenden Teilnahmebedingungen ersichtlich. Außerdem legen wir diesem Schreiben einen Lieferantennachweis bei, in dem auch Standbaufirmen aufgeführt sind.

Wir freuen uns auf Ihre Antwort.

Mit freundlichen Grüßen
MÜNCHENER MESSE- UND AUSSTELLUNGSGESELLSCHAFT MBH
Projektleiter Ceramitec
Anlagen

15.4.2 Rundschreiben an Aussteller

Betr. INHORGENTA 20..

Sehr geehrte Damen und Herren,

nachdem sich Ihre Gesellschaft an der diesjährigen INHORGENTA als Aussteller beteiligt hat, dürfen wir Ihnen als Anlage die kompletten Messeunterlagen überreichen und Sie erneut zu einer Teilnahme einladen.

Bitte berücksichtigen Sie den Anmeldeschluss 1. August 20..

Dem beiliegenden Ausstellerprospekt können Sie entnehmen, dass wiederum die Hallen 18–25 zur Verfügung stehen und die diesjährige Brancheneinteilung im nächsten Jahr im Wesentlichen beibehalten wird.

Wir würden uns freuen, Sie im nächsten Jahr wieder als Aussteller auf der INHORGENTA begrüßen zu dürfen, und sehen Ihrer Anmeldung gern entgegen.

Mit freundlichen Grüßen
MÜNCHENER MESSE- UND AUSSTELLUNGSGESELLSCHAFT MBH
Projektleitung INHORGENTA
Anlagen

15.4.3 E-Mail des Hotels Kaiserhof, Frankfurt (kaiserhof@t-online.de) an Townson & Co.Ltd., Bristol (townson.co.ltd@aol.com)

Sehr geehrter Herr Smith,

vielen Dank für Ihre Eilanfrage. Wir können Ihnen vom 3. – 5. Mai 20.. die Luxussuite „Kaiserhof" zum Preis von 400.– Euro pro Nacht einschließlich Zimmerfrühstück anbieten. Diese Luxussuite enthält alles, was der moderne Luxusgast erwartet: 2 Marmorbäder mit Whirlpool-Badewanne, Farb-TV in allen Räumen, Louis XV-Möbelausstattung im Salon, Internet-und Fax-Anschluss im Arbeitsraum, dazu ein perfekter 24-Stunden-Service.

Bitte teilen Sie uns mit, ob wir die Suite für Sie belegen dürfen.

Wir freuen uns auf Ihren Besuch und holen Sie, wenn gewünscht, am Flughafen ab.

Mit freundlichen Grüßen
Die Geschäftsleitung
HOTEL KAISERHOF

Please draft letters, faxes or e-mails from the following particulars:

15.4.4 Geschäftsfall:

Beantworten Sie die E-Mail unter 15.2.1 an die irische Gesellschaft unter Berücksichtigung folgender Punkte:

- Sie bestätigen den Eingang der Zimmerbestellung vom 13. bis 29. September 20.. einschließlich
- Leider sind für den gesamten Zeitraum nur noch 8 Einzelzimmer mit Bad oder Dusche zu haben
- Sie können der Cheltenham Ltd aber noch 2 Doppelzimmer mit Bad oder Dusche reservieren, diese kosten etwas mehr
- Der Einzelzimmerpreis beträgt 110,– € pro Übernachtung, der Doppelzimmerpreis 140,– €
- Auf den Gesamtpreis für 17 Tage von 19.720,– € gewähren Sie einen Pauschal-Messe- und Kundenrabatt von 20 % bei Vorauszahlung
- Ihre Zimmerpreise schließen ein Büfettfrühstück ein
- Alle Räume sind Nichtraucherräume
- Alle Zimmer haben Telefonanschluss.

15.4.5 **Beantworten Sie als Hans-Werner Fern das Faxangebot 15.2.2 des amerikanischen Hotels nach folgenden Richtlinien:**

- Sie bestätigen den Erhalt des Angebots und bestellen für die Zeit vom 7. Juli (Ankunft abends) bis 12. Juli 20.. (Abfahrt morgens), also jeweils 5 Übernachtungen, 30 Einzelzimmer zu US$ 60,– pro Tag zu einem Gesamtpreis von US$ 7.200,– einschließlich Frühstück
- Sie bestellen den Konferenzraum vom 8. bis einschließlich 11. Juli 20.. mit allen im Angebot enthaltenen Einrichtungen
- Sie bestellen für die Dauer der Konferenz morgens und nachmittags Getränke im Konferenzraum, mittags ein leichtes Büfett, nachmittags Kaffee mit Kuchen
- Das Abendessen wird im Hotel eingenommen; entsprechende Sammelbestellungen werden am jeweiligen Tag mit dem Restaurant abgesprochen
- Zahlungsbedingungen 1/3 im Voraus, 1/3 bei Ankunft der Gäste, 1/3 bei Abreise werden bestätigt
- Sie erwarten für die Konferenz ca. 20 amerikanische Besucher aus Minneapolis. Der Konferenzraum sollte daher für ca. 50 Personen ausgestattet werden
- Könnte das Hotel die deutschen Besucher am Flughafen abholen und auch wieder dorthin zurückbringen?
- Bitte um schriftliche Bestätigung

15.4.6 **Geschäftsfall:**

Die Katja Puschner Modeagentur, Deichstr. 40, 20459 Hamburg, Fax-Nr.: +49 (40) 67 91 34, E-Mail-Adresse: puschner.moden@t-online.de, möchte für die Fashion Show, die vom 16. bis 23. September 20.. in London stattfinden wird, einen Stand bestellen. Sie hat bereits ein Angebot der Messefirma Jalton Ltd vorliegen.

Aufgabe: Schreiben Sie an die Jalton Ltd, zu Händen Mary Simpsons, 16 Lime Street, London EC3 7JE, Fax-Nr.: +44 (2 07) 4 59 08 83, E-Mail-Adresse: jalton.ltd@aol.com, unter Berücksichtigung folgender Punkte:

- Bestätigung des Erhalts des Angebots und des Messeplans
- Sie interessieren sich für einen Stand der Größe B2 in Halle 7 R
- Der Stand soll folgendermaßen ausgerüstet sein: kleine Bühne, die sich zur Vorführung von Modellen eignet; Flutlicht und Bühnenbeleuchtung; Teppichfliesen in dunkelrot; runder oder ovaler Tisch mit 6 gepolsterten Stühlen; kleine Küche mit fließendem warmen und kalten Wasser; genügend Steckdosen für Beleuchtung und Bürokommunikationsanschlüsse; 4 Prospektständer; Überwachungskamera auf dem Stand
- Können vor Ort ein CD-Player, ein Overheadprojektor, eine digitale Videokamera, ein Kopier- und ein Faxgerät gemietet werden?
- Gibt es in der Nähe des Standes einen Internetanschluss?
- Kann Frau Simpsons Ihnen eine Agentur nennen, die geeignetes Standpersonal zur Verfügung stellt?
- Übernimmt die Jalton Ltd die Standausrüstung selbst oder kann sie diesen Auftrag an eine geeignete Standbaufirma weitergeben?
- Bitte um genaue Preise, Lieferbedingungen und -termine.

16. Office Communication

16.1 Introduction

In every company in-house communication plays an important role. The work done in an office comprises many diverse activities such as receiving and dispatching mail; sorting and storing documents and information electronically; recording information in computerized systems; gathering statistical and non-statistical data; preparing correspondence, reports and visual material such as graphs; reproducing documents by duplicating or copying processes; telephone, fax and e-mail operating; extracting, collecting and analysing data and information.

All these services used to be carried out by secretaries. Times, however, have changed, and whereas formerly every junior manager used to have his or her own secretary, there is today one person generally in charge of the office duties of a whole department. Commercial clerks today are used to handling their own correspondence and to operating EDP-computer programs which enable them to send messages internally and externally themselves.

This does not mean, however, that office work is becoming redundant. There is a greater need than ever for office staff that is well-trained in order to monitor and control in-house activities in the field of finance, production, security, stock control etc.

The need for internationally trained personnel is also increasing. Foreign language correspondents, for example, are required to deal with the increasing number of foreign language communications. A further important job is that of a P. A. (Personal Assistant). Company executives need a person that is able and willing to assist them in their comprehensive duties and is responsible for the organization and writing of reports, invitations to business meetings and conferences, letters of appreciation, congratulation and sympathy or condolence.

To the extent that office communication takes place in written form, it includes all kinds of communications such as in-house memoranda, reports, invitations to meetings etc.

A network which is commonly used by companies for their in-house information cycle is the Intranet; it is confined to a single organization, but not necessarily to a single site. This system is often set up as a web site, but accessible only to organization members.

16.2 Model correspondence

16.2.1 Intranet Memorandum

To all members of staff:

We have carried out a survey of printing requirements in our head office in order to ensure that in-house printing is financially efficient and to reduce the time factor.

It has been decided that the number of documents printed in our various branches and subsidiaries can be reduced considerably by using letterheads that are stored in company notebooks and computers. We enclose a sample of a letterhead with the company's logo. The individual branches could fill in their own addresses, telephone and fax numbers and e-mail address.

Please let us have your comments on this letterhead design and suggest any changes or improvements you would like to make so that it can be used in all types of mail in our company worldwide.

Since forms such as invoices and other printed material have been printed in-house up to now, we are also considering developing a kind of letterhead suitable for use in all our branches and subsidiaries. This would mean that these forms could be easily developed by each branch or subsidiary locally and fed into the computer writing program without creating major problems.

The desirability of these changes is clear: we can cut costs and avoid the problems involved in storing printed forms.

Your comments on these changes would be very much appreciated.

Best regards,

Richard Jonathan Pierce
Company Secretary

Attachment

16.2.2 Daily report of agent to head office by Intranet

Today I have been able to finalise 6 new contracts to the total value of €7,420. You might say this was a very successful day!

I enclose my daily sales report with the 6 new orders.

I need 200 new leaflets on the KL 700 immediately. Could you please ensure that I get these in the course of this week? Thanks.

That's all for now.

Jeremy Masters

Attachment

16.2.3 British agent arranges appointment for joint meeting with managing director of German principal

Dear Sirs

We refer to our letter of 16 May concerning the proposed visit of Herr Seibert, Managing Director of Maschinenfabrik Neumann AG, to this country.

Herr Seibert will arrive in London on Wednesday, 19 June so that we could call on you for a brief discussion on Thursday, 20 June, or Friday, 21 June. Please let us know which of these days you would prefer and at what time our visit would be convenient.

Yours faithfully

Marilyn Miller
Personal Assistant to Mr Stone

16.2.4 Confirmation of appointment

Dear Ms Redding

With reference to your phone call today I hereby confirm that Herr Seibert and Mr Stone will call on Mr Wescott on Thursday, 20 June, at 11.00 am.

Yours sincerely

Marilyn Miller
Personal Assistant to Mr Stone

16.2.5 Invitation

Dear Ms Schwarz:

Thank you for your letter of September 4 in connection with your impending visit to the United States. I am very much looking forward to renewing our acquaintance after such a long time.

When do you plan to arrive? Do you want me to reserve a room for you in Washington, D. C.?

Do you think you could arrange to come to Philadelphia on October 4 to meet the other members of the Board and then spend the weekend as my guest at home? We could then fly to Washington together.

I do not know, of course, whether you have already made other arrangements. At any rate, it would be nice if you could look in on us, and I will do my best to adjust my schedule to fit in with yours.

Sincerely,

Jane D. Coleman
President

16.2.6 Formal invitation

Mr and Mrs John D. Taylor
request the pleasure of the company of
Mr and Mrs Steinhauer
at a reception Thursday, October eleventh, six to nine o'clock.

R.S.V.P. *23 Westmore Hill*

16.2.7 Formal acceptance

Mr and Mrs Steinhauer
accept with pleasure the kind invitation of
Mr and Mrs Taylor
to a reception Thursday, October eleventh,
six to nine o' clock,
23 Westmore Hill.

16.2.8 Formal refusal

Mr and Mrs Steinhauer
regret that, owing to a previous engagement,
they are unable to accept the kind invitation of
Mr and Mrs Taylor
to a reception Thursday, October eleventh.

16.2.9 Itinerary

e-mail

Mail from: peter.cunningham@miller.ltd.uk
to: Hansjoerg.Fulda@miller.com cc:
Subject:
Attachment:

Dear Hansjoerg

This is my time schedule for next week's visit to Germany:

Monday, 22 May
Arrival by flight LH 7210 10.15 am

12.00	Meeting Dr Strahl and Frau Junkermann of Ostdeutsche Import GmbH, for business lunch
16.30	Appointment with someone from Schnitzler & Grubenhauer, Leipzig

Overnight stay in Leipzig at Hotel Koenigshof

Tuesday, 23 May
Train journey to Cologne, arrival at 15.20

16.00	Meeting people from Friedrich Lauch KG, Cologne with presentation of our new device Chart 5000
20.00	Meeting our customer Dr Verena Koch from Juelicher Tageblatt in Cologne for dinner and discussion of further business

Overnight stay in Cologne at Hotel Rheinischer Hof

Wednesday, 24 May

8.30	Visit to new potential customers in the area of North Rhine-Westphalia by car together with you
18.00	Meeting Frau Hasseler and Herr Veith of Gladbacher Software GmbH, Moenchengladbach

Overnight stay in Cologne at Hotel Rheinischer Hof

Thursday, 25 May

All day — Visit to your agency office in Cologne and meeting all our staff there

Overnight stay in Cologne at Hotel Rheinischer Hof

Friday, 26 May

8.30 — Meeting bank manager Ulrich Schaefer of Rheinische Bank in Cologne to discuss credit line for us

11.30 — Visit to Steinkuehler AG in Huerth near Cologne

16.15 — Return flight to London with BA 5407

Could you please pick me up at 15.20 at Cologne railway station on Tuesday. I would like you to accompany me on all visits in Cologne and surroundings during my stay there. Please make sure the hotel booking in Cologne is OK.

Look forward to seeing you next week.

Regards

Peter

16.2.10 Fax Memo to Head Office from travelling staff member

fax

FAO: Mr Gary Simpsons
Simpsons & Brown Plc
Paradise Road 11
London E2 4 PB

Fax No.: +44 (208) 34 91 441

From: Harry Jackson
Hotel Buenaventura
Mexico-City
Mexico

Number of Pages: 1

Date: 15 July 20..

An overnight fax from Guadalajara says that the pump which is already on order and due for dispatch by sea on Friday is urgently needed. Can we air freight it out to Mexico-City today? Will you take steps to get it crated and I will look after the paper work and let you know flight times. Get in touch with me at once if there is any problem. Top priority on this please.

Thanks.
Harry

16.2.11 Letter of appreciation

Dear Mr and Mrs Lane

I have at last returned to London from my trip to the United States and wish to thank you for the gracious hospitality you showed to me during my stopover in Chicago.

My stay with you was the most enjoyable experience of my three-week tour, and I wish to express my sincere appreciation of all you did to make me feel welcome and comfortable. The recollection of Mrs Lance's delicious coq au vin, by the way, is stamped indelibly on my memory.

I do hope you will give me an opportunity to repay your kindness when you visit London next summer.

Yours sincerely

16.2.12 Congratulation on new appointment

Dear Dr Konrad

Herr Sommer told me during his recent visit to Leeds that you have been appointed to your company's Managing Board. I congratulate you most sincerely on this appointment and wish you every success in your new position.

With my best personal regards

Yours sincerely

16.2.13 Letter of condolence on the passing away of a business friend

Dear Wolfgang:

We are mourning with you for Harry Jost, who was a wonderful friend of ours for so many years.

My associates and I convey to you and your colleagues our heartfelt condolences at Harry's death. We have long and fond memories of Harry Jost. It was a great challenge to negotiate with this vigorous and far-sighted man and a great satisfaction to come to terms with him. Harry combined business acumen with great personal charm; a talk with him always gave food for thought, and his ready wit was delightful.

The loss of Harry Jost is equally hard for your company and ours. Our thoughts and best wishes are with you and Harry's family.

Sincerely,

16.3 Terms and phrases

16.3.1 Making appointments

I refer to our telephone conversation this morning and confirm the date of our appointment for Wednesday, June 2, at 3 pm.	*Ich beziehe mich auf unser Telefongespräch von heute Morgen und bestätige das Datum unseres Treffens für Mittwoch, den 2. Juni, um 15 Uhr.*
Please ring my secretary, Helen Waters, next week to arrange the date and time of our meeting.	*Bitte rufen Sie meine Sekretärin, Helen Waters, nächste Woche an und vereinbaren Sie mit ihr Tag und Zeit unseres Treffens.*
Please confirm as soon as possible that the date proposed for the conference is suitable so that we can finalise the arrangements accordingly.	*Bitte bestätigen Sie uns so bald wie möglich, dass Sie mit dem vorgeschlagenen Konferenztermin einverstanden sind, so dass wir die endgültigen Vorbereitungen treffen können.*
If you suggest a time, I will try to fit the appointment into my schedule.	*Wenn Sie eine Zeit vorschlagen, werde ich versuchen, den Termin in meinen Zeitplan einzubauen.*
Please tell us the exact date and time of your flight so that we can arrange for someone to meet you at the airport.	*Bitte teilen Sie uns genau Datum und Zeit Ihres Fluges mit, damit wir Sie am Flughafen abholen lassen können.*

16.3.2 Invitations; acceptance and refusal

During your stay in … I would very much like you to be my guest for lunch / to join me for lunch on any day that suits your schedule.	*An einem Tag, der in Ihren Zeitplan passt, würde ich Sie während Ihres Aufenthalts in … gerne zum Mittagessen einladen.*
Would it be convenient to meet me for an informal dinner at the … Hotel next Monday at about 8 pm?	*Wenn es Ihnen recht ist, würde ich Sie gerne am Montag gegen 20 Uhr zu einem zwanglosen Abendessen ins … Hotel einladen.*
I was very pleased to receive your kind invitation and will meet you, as suggested, in the lounge of the Hilton Hotel, on Tuesday, 7 April, at 1 pm.	*Ich war sehr erfreut, Ihre Einladung zu erhalten, und werde Sie wie vorgeschlagen am Dienstag, den 7. April, um 13 Uhr im Foyer des Hilton-Hotels treffen.*
Thank you very much for your invitation to the … conference in … on …, which I gladly accept.	*Vielen Dank für Ihre Einladung zur … Konferenz am … in …, die ich gern annehme.*

I sincerely regret that I cannot accept your kind invitation to ..., as I am leaving for Hong Kong tomorrow / as I have an important business meeting at the same time.	*Ich bedauere außerordentlich, dass ich Ihre nette Einladung für ... nicht annehmen kann, da ich morgen nach Hongkong abreise / da ich zur gleichen Zeit eine wichtige geschäftliche Besprechung habe.*
I would very much like to be with you on that occasion, but, unfortunately, business commitments will make it impossible for me to attend the reception.	*Ich würde gern bei diesem Anlass mit Ihnen zusammentreffen, aber wegen geschäftlicher Verpflichtungen ist mir eine Teilnahme am Empfang leider nicht möglich.*

16.3.3 Instructions for business travel

As you can see from the enclosed itinerary, I will arrive in New York on Monday morning, 7 July, at 6.30. Please arrange for someone to pick me up from the airport and take me to the hotel.	*Wie Sie aus dem beigefügten Reiseplan entnehmen können, werde ich am Montag, den 7. Juli, um 6.30 Uhr in New York ankommen. Bitte sorgen Sie dafür, dass mich jemand am Flughafen abholt und ins Hotel bringt.*
When I arrive at Rio de Janeiro, I would like to use a rental car to get to our branch office. Could you please make the necessary arrangements.	*Wenn ich in Rio de Janeiro ankomme, möchte ich einen Mietwagen benutzen, um zu unserer Filiale zu kommen. Bitte treffen Sie die nötigen Vorkehrungen.*
During my stay in Australia, I would very much like a member of our staff there to accompany me. Please work out a time schedule.	*Während meines Aufenthalts in Australien möchte ich, dass mich ein Mitglied unserer dortigen Belegschaft begleitet. Bitte arbeiten Sie einen Zeitplan aus.*
On arrival in ... I wish to meet Mr ... Please make the necessary arrangements.	*Bei Ankunft in ... möchte ich Herrn ... sehen. Bitte treffen Sie die notwendigen Vorkehrungen.*
Before I take the night train to Bilbao, I need to speak to the manager of our Spanish bank in Madrid. Could you please arrange a dinner with him in a restaurant near the railway station.	*Bevor ich den Nachtzug nach Bilbao nehme, muss ich den Manager unserer spanischen Bank in Madrid sprechen. Würden Sie bitte ein Abendessen mit ihm in einem Restaurant in Bahnhofsnähe vereinbaren.*

16.3.4 In-house arrangements

We would like to draw your attention to the fact that all our in-house information will be in English in the future.	*Wir möchten Sie darauf aufmerksam machen, dass alle innerbetrieblichen Informationen in Zukunft in Englisch erfolgen werden.*
In our recent memorandum we asked all members of our staff to comment on the introduction of … We still await your comments in this matter.	*In unserem kürzlichen verfassten Memorandum baten wir alle Mitglieder unserer Belegschaft um Ihre Meinung zur Einführung von … Wir erwarten diesbezüglich noch Ihre Stellungnahme.*
This is to inform you that my monthly report will be e-mailed to you in the course of this week. I cannot do this earlier, because I am still waiting for an order from Messrs … which has to be included in this report.	*Hiermit teile ich Ihnen mit, dass mein monatlicher Bericht im Laufe dieser Woche per E-Mail an Sie abgeht. Ich kann dies nicht früher tun, weil ich noch einen Auftrag der Firma … erwarte, der in diesen Bericht gehört.*
We would like to inform you that as from … our company will introduce flexitime. Our core working time will be from 9.00 am to 4.00 pm, but flexitime starts 2 hours earlier and finishes 3 hours later. The core working time is, however, compulsory.	*Wir möchten Ihnen mitteilen, dass unsere Firma ab … gleitende Arbeitszeit einführen wird. Unsere Kernarbeitszeit ist von 9.00 bis 16.00 Uhr, aber die gleitende Arbeitszeit beginnt 2 Stunden früher und endet 3 Stunden später. Die Kernarbeitszeit ist jedoch Pflicht.*

16.3.5 Letters of appreciation and congratulation

Whenever there is an opportunity for us to reciprocate, please do not hesitate to let us know.	*Sollten wir zu irgendeiner Zeit die Möglichkeit haben, Ihre Freundlichkeit zu erwidern, teilen Sie uns dies bitte mit.*
I hope that I may soon have an opportunity to return your kindness.	*Ich hoffe, dass sich bald eine Gelegenheit ergibt, Ihre Freundlichkeit zu erwidern.*
I am very grateful for your help and ask you to give me the opportunity to reciprocate this favour.	*Ich bin Ihnen sehr dankbar für Ihre Hilfe und bitte Sie, mir die Gelegenheit zu geben, diese Gefälligkeit zu erwidern.*
I would like to offer my sincerest thanks for your hospitality. I had a most enjoyable evening.	*Ich möchte mich herzlich für Ihre Gastfreundschaft bedanken. Ich habe einen sehr angenehmen Abend verbracht.*
It was really an interesting meeting.	*Es war ein höchst interessantes Treffen.*
Thank you for devoting so much of your precious time to me.	*Vielen Dank, dass Sie mir so viel Ihrer kostbaren Zeit gewidmet haben.*

I am writing to convey my warm congratulations on your appointment to Chairman of the Board / President of your Company / Corporation.	*Ich möchte Ihnen zu Ihrer Ernennung zum Vorstandsvorsitzenden Ihrer Gesellschaft herzlichst gratulieren.*
I was happy to learn that you have been appointed Chief Executive Officer.	*Ich habe mich gefreut, dass Sie zum Chief Executive Officer (Leiter der Verwaltung) ernannt worden sind.*
May I offer my sincere congratulations on the occasion of your 60th birthday.	*Darf ich Ihnen meine herzlichsten Glückwünsche anlässlich Ihres 60. Geburtstages aussprechen.*

16.3.6 Letter of sympathy and condolence; replies

I have heard of your accident and send you my best wishes for a speedy / swift recovery.	*Ich habe von Ihrem Unfall gehört und sende Ihnen meine besten Wünsche für eine baldige Genesung.*
I hope that your convalescence will be rapid.	*Ich hoffe, dass Ihre Rekonvaleszenz rasche Fortschritte machen wird.*
I am relieved to hear that you are making good progress and will be able to leave the hospital next week.	*Es freut mich zu hören, dass Sie gute Fortschritte machen und nächste Woche das Krankenhaus verlassen können.*
It was with deep / profound regret that I learned this morning of …	*Heute Morgen erfuhr ich zu meiner großen Bestürzung vom …*
It is only today that we have received the sad news of … the sudden / unexpected / untimely death of Mr … / the Chairman of your company.	*Erst heute erhielten wir die traurige Nachricht vom … plötzlichen / unerwarteten / viel zu frühen Tod von Herrn … / des Vorstandsvorsitzenden Ihrer Gesellschaft.*
We would like to express / Please accept the expression of our heartfelt sympathy.	*Wir möchten unser herzliches Beileid zum Ausdruck bringen.*
We wish to convey to you our deepest sympathy on the death of …	*Zum Tode von … übermitteln wir Ihnen unser tiefes Mitgefühl.*
We appreciate / We most sincerely thank you for your kind expression of sympathy on the occasion of the sudden death of our Managing Director, Mr …	*Wir danken Ihnen für die freundliche Anteilnahme anlässlich des plötzlichen Ablebens unseres Geschäftsführers, Herrn …*
On behalf of the Board of Directors, I wish to thank you for your kind letter of sympathy upon the death of the President of our Company.	*Im Namen des Vorstands möchte ich Ihnen für Ihren freundlichen Kondolenzbrief anläßlich des Todes des Präsidenten unserer Gesellschaft danken.*

16.4 Exercises
Please translate:

16.4.1 Antwort auf Memorandum 16.2.1 des Mutterhauses per Intranet

Gemäß dem Muster Ihres Memos vom … haben wir den von Ihnen gewünschten Briefkopf mit unserer Anschrift, Telefon- und Faxnummer sowie unserer E-Mail-Adresse im Computersystem gespeichert, so dass in Zukunft alle Schreiben und Formulare wie Rechnungen etc. mit diesem Briefkopf gedruckt werden. Als Attachment senden wir Ihnen ein Muster dieses Briefkopfes.

Wir haben einen Verbesserungsvorschlag: Das von Ihnen gewählte Logo unseres Firmenemblems ist unserer Ansicht nach zu sperrig (*bulky*). Es nimmt fast ⅓ des Briefkopfes auf der linken Seite ein. Wäre es nicht sinnvoller, es etwas zu verkleinern?

Bitte teilen Sie uns mit, ob Ihnen unser Muster zusagt und was Sie von unserem Vorschlag halten.

16.4.2 Antwort auf Besuchsankündigung und Reiseplan 16.2.9

E-Mail von: Hansjoerg.Fulda@miller.com
An: peter.cunningham@miller.ltd.uk

Lieber Peter,

Vielen Dank für die Zusendung Ihres Reiseplans.

Die beiden Termine, die wir in Leipzig für Sie arrangiert haben, habe ich nochmals telefonisch bestätigt. Ein Zimmer im Hotel Königshof ist für Sie reserviert.

Ich werde Sie, wie gewünscht, am 23. Mai 20.. am Hauptbahnhof Köln erwarten. Ich begleite Sie gern an diesem Tag zur Friedrich Lauch KG in Köln. Leider kann ich aber an dem Abendessen mit Frau Dr. Koch nicht teilnehmen, da ich bereits eine geschäftliche Einladung von Herrn Uhlenbruch von Meyer & Ritter habe, die für uns wichtig ist.

Die Termine am 24., 25. und 26. Mai gehen in Ordnung. Ich habe alle Termine noch einmal mit den entsprechenden Büros bestätigt. Am Freitag, den 26. Mai, werde ich Sie zum Flughafen fahren, damit Sie Ihren 16.15 h Flug nach London rechtzeitig erreichen.

Die Hotelbuchung im Rheinischen Hof ist uns vom Hotel per Fax bestätigt worden.

Ich freue mich auf Ihren Besuch und hoffe, dass wir eine erfolgreiche Woche haben werden.

Freundlichen Gruß,
Hansjörg

16.4.3 Gratulation zur Beförderung

Sehr geehrte Ms Morton,

wir danken für Ihr Schreiben vom 16. April, in dem Sie mitteilen, dass Sie ab 1. Juli als Nachfolgerin von Mr Collins den Posten des General Manager Ihrer Gesellschaft übernommen haben.

Wir möchten Ihnen unsere besten Wünsche für Ihre zukünftige Tätigkeit übermitteln und versichern Ihnen, dass wir alles tun werden, um die erfreuliche Zusammenarbeit zwischen unseren Gesellschaften aufrechtzuerhalten und in Zukunft noch weiter zu vertiefen.

Mit freundlichen Grüßen

16.4.4 Dank für gute Aufnahme und Bestätigung der Zusammenarbeit

Sehr geehrter Herr Tudor,

Am Mittwochabend bin ich wohlbehalten wieder aus New York zurückgekommen. Die dreitägige Sitzung dort hat mir sehr gefallen und mich in dem Gedanken bestärkt, dass unsere enge Zusammenarbeit lohnenswert und erfolgreich zu werden verspricht.

Ich möchte mich außerdem sehr herzlich für Ihre Gastfreundschaft bedanken. Ich habe einen sehr angenehmen Abend mit Ihnen verbracht.

Sobald ich meine Unterlagen durchgesehen habe, werde ich Ihnen einige Vorschläge über unsere nähere Zusammenarbeit zukommen lassen. Ich wäre Ihnen dankbar, wenn ich auch von Ihnen entsprechende Anregungen bekommen würde. Wir können diese dann vielleicht bei einem Besuch von Ihnen in unserem Hause durchsprechen.

Für heute darf ich mich nochmals bei Ihnen für Ihre Hilfe bedanken.

Mit freundlichen Grüßen

Please draft letters, faxes or e-mails from the following particulars:

16.4.5 Geschäftsfall:

Sie arbeiten bei der Hagenberg GmbH, Humboldtstr. 36, 91054 Erlangen, Fax-Nr.: +49 (9131) 745603, E-Mail-Adresse: hagenberg@firmlink.de, die die Powers Plc, Malet Street, London WC1E 7HU, Fax-Nr.: +44 (20) 7841084, E-Mail-Adresse: powers.plc@ac.uk vertritt. Sie schicken im Intranet eine Mitteilung an das Mutterhaus, in welcher Sie folgende Punkte berücksichtigen:

- Der beiliegende Bericht enthält die Verkäufe der letzten zwei Wochen (genauen Zeitraum angeben!)
- Der Gesamtumsatz beläuft sich auf € 40.980,00
- Ihr Lagerbestand der Produktserie „Alpha 2010" geht zur Neige, Sie brauchen dringend Nachschub
- Die Prospekte für den „Startrack 407" sind immer noch nicht da; Sie brauchen 100 Stück per Luftpost
- Ein Kunde interessiert sich für das in der Planung befindliche Modell „Sunshine 300". Kann man ihm einige Vorabinformationen geben?

- Bitten Sie höflich um baldige Gutschrift der Provision auf Ihr Konto, das letzte Mal hat die Überweisung mehr als 3 Wochen gedauert.

16.4.6 Geschäftsfall:

Sie sind persönliche(r) Assistent(in) von Herrn Richard Angenendt, Marketingchef der Völkel & Stichler AG, Moosdorfstr. 110, 12435 Berlin, Fax-Nr.: +49 (30) 2 09 84 15, E-Mail-Adresse: völkel.stichler@berlin.com. Ihr Chef ist soeben von einer USA-Reise zurückgekommen, wo er an einer Konferenz für Marktanalysen teilgenommen hat und bei einem der Lektoren, Professor Daniel Jermyn, eingeladen war.

Aufgabe: Schreiben Sie in seinem Namen ein Dankschreiben an Professor Daniel Jermyn, The Research Institute for Market Analyses, 204 Independence Ave, SE, Washington, DC 20540-4860, U.S.A., Fax-Nr: +1 (2 02) 59 08 72, E-Mail-Adresse: daniel.jermyn@research.us, und berücksichtigen Sie dabei folgende Punkte:

- Danken Sie Professor Jermyn für das höchst interessante Gespräch in seinem Hause und die Ihnen bezeugte Gastfreundschaft
- Sie waren von der Organisation und dem Inhalt der Konferenz sehr angetan
- Sie haben wertvolle Anregungen im Bereich der Marktanalysen mit nach Deutschland genommen, die Sie sicherlich verwerten können
- Laden Sie Professor Jermyn zu einem Gegenbesuch ein, wenn er in nächster Zeit einmal nach Berlin kommt
- Sie würden, falls ein solcher Besuch in der Zukunft erfolgt, auch einige interessante Persönlichkeiten ansprechen, die sich für das von Professor Jermyn vertretene Konzept interessieren.

16.4.7 Geschäftsfall:

In derselben Eigenschaft wie oben sollen Sie für Ihren Chef einen Brief an Mr Howard J. Lewis, Lewis & Partners, Solicitors, Sussex Place, Regent's Park, London NW1 4SA, Fax-Nr.: ++44 (20) 33 98 10, E-Mail-Adresse: lewis.partners@aol.com, senden, in dem folgende Punkte in seinem Namen berücksichtigt werden sollen:

- Ihr Chef hat soeben erfahren, dass Herr Lewis einen Autounfall hatte und sich einer Operation unterziehen musste
- Er bedauert dies sehr und wünscht Herrn Lewis gute und baldige Besserung
- Er hofft, dass Herr Lewis bald wiederhergestellt ist und Ihren Chef auch zur nächsten Herbstmesse in London begleiten wird
- Herr Lewis soll sich dennoch schonen und alles tun, was die Ärzte verordnen
- Ihr Chef wünscht ihm nochmals gute Besserung.

17. Job Applications

17.1 Introduction

Letters of application fall into two categories: solicited and unsolicited applications. A *solicited application* is written in response to an advertisement ("Situations Offered", "Situations Vacant", "Jobs Offered") or at the request of the prospective employer. Potential employers may also look for candidates through a private employment agency or an employment exchange (now called "Job Centre") run by the state. An *unsolicited application* is addressed to a firm on the off-chance that there is or will be an opening. Frequently, unsolicited applications are sent at the suggestion of a third party.

Sometimes companies use *head-hunters* in order to find executives who may be willing to leave their present employer and start a new position in exchange for better conditions and/or a higher salary.

When applying for a position, applicants are usually requested to submit a *curriculum vitae* or *personal data sheet/résumé* containing details about the applicant, his or her education, training and experience in tabular form.

Prospective employers also wish to see the applicant's school-leaving certificate, diplomas, and letters of recommendation (*references*). Copies of these documents may accompany the letter of application. Many firms send application forms to candidates for positions, requesting them to complete the forms and return them together with a curriculum vitae and copies of the necessary personal documents.

When candidates are shortlisted, they may be invited to one or several personal interviews during which they will talk to the *personnel manager*, who is very often assisted by a psychologist and/or other representatives of the company. There is no fixed range of questions asked at personal interviews. Many companies also use *assessment centres* in which candidates have to undergo a variety of *aptitude tests*. The best candidates are then invited to the *final interview*.

17.2 Model correspondence

17.2.1 Irish applicant sees advertisement on the Internet for post of tri-lingual receptionist

e-mail

Mail from: lydia.graham@compuserve.uk
to: hotel.poscher@sinzig.rhein.de cc:
Subject:
Attachment:

For the attention of the Personnel Manager

Dear Sir / Madam

I am writing with reference to your advertisement and am most interested in applying for the position of tri-lingual receptionist and booking clerk at your hotel.

I am 23 years old and currently employed at a call centre in Dublin, where I work for a German company. My job is to answer phone calls from all over the world in English, French and German. I have worked in this position for two years now and have been able to improve my knowledge of German considerably.

In 19.. I passed three A-levels, including French and German. Since leaving school, I have continued to study these two languages at the Oxford Institute. I can speak, read and write these languages nearly fluently.

To improve my knowledge of foreign languages I would very much like to spend some time abroad. The hotel trade is a field that interests me very much, and a position as tri-lingual hotel receptionist and booking clerk would be an attractive challenge for me.

My present salary is £... per annum.

I shall be happy to provide a full written application with CV and references if desired, and would be delighted to be invited to Germany for a personal interview.

Yours sincerely*

* Since in this case the letter is addressed to a specific person, ie the Personnel Manager, the complimentary clause should be "yours sincerely", which sounds more polite than the general clause "yours faithfully".

17.2.2 Advertisement published in an international newspaper

INTERNATIONAL BROKER HOUSE GERMAN DIVISION • P.O. Box 23 98 04 • 60327 Frankfurt/Main

For our German Division in Frankfurt, we are seeking an

ENGLISH TRANSLATOR.

Candidates must have a demonstrated ability to translate economic, financial, legal, banking and statistical material into native-level English from German.

Candidates must meet high standards of quality within tight production deadlines, and should hold an advanced degree in a language-related field, law, banking, and/or an economics-related field, and have at least 5 years of relevant experience, preferably with international companies or organizations. Additional language knowledge and/or administrative experience would be a plus.

Pre-selected candidates will be required to take written tests from the relevant source languages.

All candidates must be familiar with standard software applications.

Interested candidates should send their CV, by December 31, 20.., if possible by fax (fax no: +49-69-30 80 341). Please send only one copy, making explicit reference to
"Übersetzer Frankfurt – Stellenausschreibung 2400".

17.2.3 British candidate applies for position advertised under 17.2.2

FAO: International Broker House
German Division
P.O. Box 23 98 04
60327 Frankfurt / M
Germany

Fax No.: +49 (69) 30 80 341

From: Jane Beatrice Andrews
10 Victoria Square
Birmingham B1 1BD
Great Britain

Number of Pages: 2

Date: 10 December 20..

Re.: Übersetzer Frankfurt – Stellenausschreibung 2400

fax

Dear Sirs

I have seen your advertisement in the *Daily Telegraph* of .. and would like to apply for the position of English translator as described.

I think that I fulfil the high criteria required in your advertisement since I was born in Britain, but have a German mother, and grew up bilingual. After taking my A-levels in Birmingham, I went to Germany and studied languages at the *Fachhochschule* in Cologne.

I then applied for a job in my home city and came back to Britain, where I have been employed as a commercial clerk and translator in a large international company for the last 4½ years. I would, however, like to return to Germany for personal reasons and am therefore looking for a suitable position.

Please see my enclosed CV for further details about my education and qualifications.

I very much look forward to your reply and am, of course, prepared to travel to Frankfurt at any time for a personal interview or a written test.

I look forward to hearing from you.

Yours sincerely

J. B. Andrews

J. B. Andrews

Enclosure: Curriculum Vitae

17.2.4 British layout of CV as enclosure to 17.2.3

CURRICULUM VITAE

Name:	Jane Beatrice Andrews
Address:	10 Victoria Square Birmingham B1 1BD Great Britain Tel. no.: +44 (21) 33 06 Fax no.: +44 (21) 33 07
Date of birth:	2 February 19..
Marital status:	Single
Nationality:	British
Education:	– 7 years secondary school in Birmingham – A-levels in English, German, Mathematics – 8 semesters of language studies in German and French at the *Fachhochschule* in Cologne, Germany – Graduated from *Fachhochschule* Cologne as a qualified translator (*Diplom-Übersetzerin*) in German as a first and French as a second language
Employment:	
19..	6-week traineeship as a commercial clerk at Jumbo Department Store in Birmingham
July 19..	Assistant in the commercial department of Jumbo Department Store during my school and university holidays
Sept. 19..	idem
June 19..	idem
Since 19..	Permanently employed as a commercial clerk and translator with European Telecom plc, Birmingham
Interests:	Flying, travelling, languages
Additional qualifications:	– Full clean driving licence – Pilot's licence for small aircraft – familiar with software applications (Microsoft, Excel, Powerpoint)
Reference:	Prof. Gerald Bauerfeind Fachhochschule Köln Abteilung Moderne Sprachen Tel.no.: +49 (2 21) 37 09 84

17.2.5 American candidate applies for position advertised under 17.2.2

FAO: International Broker House
German Division
P. O. Box 23 98 04
60327 Frankfurt/M
Germany

Fax No.: + 49 (69) 30 80 341

From: Andrew P. Gordon
348 Teaneck Road
New Jersey
USA 07666

Number of Pages: 2

Date: 20.. Dec 9

Subject: Your advertisement in the *Wall Street Journal* of ..
"Übersetzer Frankfurt – Stellenausschreibung 2400"

Gentlemen:

In reply to your above-mentioned advertisement I am very interested in the position of English translator.

Although I have not worked directly as a translator so far, I am familiar with both languages, English and German, because I spent some years in Germany with my family and continuously correspond in German and English with my principals and customers.

Please see my résumé for details of my education and qualifications.

I am at present working as a commercial agent based in New Jersey for several German companies. For family reasons I am now seeking a position that does not involve a large amount of travelling. My wife being German, I would like to go back to Germany and live over there.

I am familiar with WinWord and Excel, which I use for my daily reports and business correspondence.

I am planning to be in Germany in the near future to visit my principals and on that occasion could come for a personal interview.

Thank you for an early reply.

Sincerely yours,

Andrew P. Gordon

Andrew P. Gordon

Enclosure: Résumé

17.2.6 American layout of CV as enclosure to 17.2.5

DATA SHEET

Name:	Andrew P. Gordon
Date of Birth:	19../5/18
Nationality:	American

Occupational Goal:
To use my commercial and language experience in a secure and interesting job in Germany

General Background:
5 years' experience as a commercial clerk in Germany
4 years' work as a commercial agent in the United States
Professional Experience

From 20..	Independent commercial agent for 3 German companies based in New Jersey, traveling all over the United States
20..–20..	Commercial clerk with Deutsche Pharmazeutische GmbH, Bayreuth, dealing mainly with exports to English-speaking countries
20..–20..	Employment with American subsidiary of Digital Equipment Inc., New York,in Munich, Germany, importing American digital devices to Europe Education
19..–20..	3-year traineeship obtaining a recognised qualification as a wholesale and export sales clerk with Spiller & Roll AG, Munich
19..	High School Diploma
19..–19..	High School
19..–19..	Primary education

Interests
Mountaineering, skiing, canoeing

References
Available on request

17.2.7 Letter of recommendation

To Whom it May Concern

Ms Johanna Schuster has been employed as my Personal Assistant at the Farland International Corporation from August 19.. to March 20.. . In addition to taking dictation and the minutes of company meetings, word processing and normal office routine, her responsibilities included receiving visitors, arranging business trips, organising in-house conferences and translating German and English correspondence.

Johanna has an excellent command of German and English and is thoroughly familiar with business and technical terminology in both languages. She is a very conscientious and accurate employee and has always performed her work to my entire satisfaction. She has a pleasant personality and a good sense of humour and is well-liked by both superiors and colleagues.

I regret Johanna's departure and recommend her to you without reservation. If you have any further questions with regard to her background or qualifications, please do not hesitate to contact me.

Farland International Corporation

E. D. McMartin

E. D. McMartin
Manager, Overseas Operations

17.2.8 Letter of recommendation from American company

AMERICAN SULPHUR INCORPORATED
NEW YORK CITY

Please let this letter serve as a general description of the duties performed by Clara Dunningale during her employment with AMERICAN SULPHUR INCORPORATED from 19../10/1 to 20../12/31.

1. Correspondence in English, German and French.
2. Translations in and from English, German and French, which she performed partly independently.
3. Complete and independent responsibility for salary records, calculations of payments and deductions.
4. Preparation of company reports to our administrative headquarters locations, and local authorities regarding social security, pension plan and tax matters as required.
5. Administrative work in connection with new hires, preparation of contracts, initial interviews, and independent preparation of certificates.
6. Processing of accounting officer expense statements, preparation of bookkeeping entries.
7. Normal secretarial tasks involving the preparation and typing of memos, faxes, e-mails, filing and telephone contacts.

Ms Dunningale was a dedicated worker and always concerned that her job was done quickly and correctly. She developed excellent working relationships with other staff members and was always cooperative. Her attitude was positive and optimistic.

We are indeed sorry to lose Ms Dunningale as a valuable member of our staff, but would highly recommend her for employment as a senior secretary. She is classified as re-employable by our company should the occasion ever arise.

AMERICAN SULPHUR INCORPORATED
Phil H. Roberts
Assistant Vice President

17.3 Terms and Phrases

17.3.1 Opening Phrases

In reply to / With reference to your advertisement in … of … I wish to apply for the position of …	*Ich beziehe mich auf Ihre Anzeige in … vom … und bewerbe mich um die Stelle als …*
I have been given the address of your company by …	*Ich erhielt die Adresse Ihrer Firma von …*
I see from your advertisement in … that you are looking for … with a good command of …	*Ihrer Anzeige in … entnehme ich, dass Sie nach einem / einer … mit guten …-Kenntnissen suchen.*
After … years' experience in the … trade I feel that I am qualified to fill the position of … advertised in today's edition of …	*Nach … Jahren in der … Branche bin ich der Ansicht, dass ich mich für die in der heutigen Ausgabe der … ausgeschriebenen Stelle als … eigne.*
Mr / Mrs / Ms … has told me that some time this year there will be an opening / a vacancy for the position of … in your office.	*Von Herrn / Frau … habe ich erfahren, dass im Laufe dieses Jahres in Ihrem Büro die Stelle eines / einer … frei wird.*
… that you are looking for an efficient salesman / agent.	*… dass Sie einen fähigen Verkäufer / Vertreter suchen.*
I found your interesting job offer on the internet.	*Ich habe Ihr interessantes Stellenangebot im Internet gefunden.*
On your website on the internet I saw that you are looking for suitable candidates for …	*Auf Ihrer Website im Internet habe ich gesehen, dass Sie geeignete Kandidaten für … suchen.*

17.3.2 Education, training and qualifications

I attended … Comprehensive School for five years.	*Ich besuchte fünf Jahre lang die … Gesamtschule.*
… I enrolled for a one-year course at … Commercial College.	*… schrieb ich mich für einen Jahreskurs am … Commercial College ein.*
In 20.. I graduated from … High School.	*Im Jahr 20.. schloss ich meine Ausbildung an der … High School (höhere Schule in den USA) ab.*
… I entered / enrolled at … University, where I studied business administration.	*… immatrikulierte ich mich an der … Universität, wo ich Betriebswirtschaft studierte.*

At … Commercial High School I studied business correspondence, learned how to use several computer programs such as … and took language courses in …	*Auf der … Commercial High School lernte ich das Erstellen von Geschäftskorrespondenz, die Bedienung mehrerer Computerprogramme wie … und nahm an Sprachkursen für … teil.*
I am conversant with internet applications including e-mail.	*Ich kenne mich mit Internetanwendungen einschließlich E-Mail aus.*
I am familiar with Windows / Microsoft Word / Excel / Powerpoint etc.	*Ich bin mit Windows / Microsoft Word / Excel / Powerpoint usw. vertraut.*
I served my apprenticeship as a wholesale and export clerk / office clerk with one of the leading companies in this city.	*Ich machte meine Lehre als Groß- und Außenhändler(in) / Bürokaufmann / -frau bei einem der führenden Unternehmen dieser Stadt.*
I passed an examination at the local Chamber of Commerce and Industry to become a qualified foreign language correspondent in … (language).	*Ich bestand eine Prüfung vor der örtlichen Industrie- und Handelskammer als anerkannte(r) Fremdsprachenkorrespondent(in) in … (Sprache).*
I sat for an examination of the London Chamber of Commerce and obtained a qualification in German / English Business Correspondence.	*Ich unterzog mich einer Prüfung der Londoner Handelskammer und erwarb eine Qualifikation in deutsch-englischer Geschäftskorrespondenz.*
I have a recognized qualification in …	*Ich habe eine anerkannte Qualifikation als …*

17.3.3 Practical experience

During my apprenticeship / traineeship with … I acquired a sound knowledge of bookkeeping and accounting.	*Während meiner Lehre / meiner Ausbildung bei … erwarb ich gute Kenntnisse in Buchhaltung und Rechnungswesen.*
I am thoroughly familiar with handling all kinds of exports and sales documents within the EU.	*Ich bin bestens vertraut mit der Handhabung aller Arten von Dokumenten für Export und Verkauf im EU-Gebiet.*
I speak French fluently and have a good (working) knowledge of Italian.	*Ich spreche fließend Französisch und habe gute Italienischkenntnisse.*
My proficiency in Spanish enables me to handle Spanish correspondence on my own.	*Auf Grund meiner sehr guten Spanischkenntnisse bin ich in der Lage, spanische Korrespondenz selbstständig zu erledigen.*
I have had … years' experience in selling …	*Ich habe … Jahre Erfahrung im Verkauf von …*

I have been working as P. A. (*Personal Assistant*) to the Managing Director / Marketing Executive / Sales Manager / Head of Exports / Team Leader in the … Section for … years.	*Ich arbeite seit … Jahren als Persönliche(r) Assistent(in) des Geschäftsführers / Marketingleiters / Verkaufsleiters / Exportchefs / Gruppenleiters in der … Abteilung.*

17.3.4 Reasons for wanting a change

My reason for seeking a change is the better opportunities offered in a large company like yours.	*Ich möchte mich verändern, weil mir eine Firma Ihrer Größe bessere Möglichkeiten bietet.*
I intend to leave my present job, as I see no possibility here of assuming greater responsibility.	*Ich habe vor, meine jetzige Stelle aufzugeben, da ich hier keine Möglichkeit sehe, eine verantwortungsvollere Tätigkeit zu übernehmen.*
My present employer is in the process of closing down his business and dismissing all the staff.	*Mein gegenwärtiger Arbeitgeber löst sein Geschäft auf und entlässt alle Angestellten.*
The downward trend in the … industry makes it necessary to think about looking for a position in a more dynamic sector.	*Die rückläufige Tendenz in der …-Branche lässt mich darüber nachdenken, einen Arbeitsplatz in einem dynamischeren Bereich zu suchen.*
Despite the fact that I have had considerable success in my present position, I am now looking for a position which gives me the chance to develop new skills / to earn a better salary.	*Obwohl ich in meiner jetzigen Stelle beträchtlichen Erfolg hatte, suche ich jetzt eine Stelle, die mir die Möglichkeit gibt, neue Fertigkeiten zu erwerben / ein höheres Gehalt zu bekommen.*
I am sure I will be able to open up this market successfully for your company.	*Ich bin sicher, dass ich diesen Markt erfolgreich für Ihre Firma erschließen kann.*
I have no doubt that I could be a valuable asset to your company.	*Ich bin mir sicher, dass ich eine wertvolle Kraft für Ihre Firma sein könnte.*

17.3.5 Availability for interview, request to be considered, references

I think that your company has the opening I am looking for.	*Ich glaube, dass Ihre Firma die Stelle hat, die ich suche.*
I hope that you will consider my application / shortlist me / put me on the waiting list.	*Ich hoffe, dass Sie meine Bewerbung berücksichtigen / mich in die engere Wahl ziehen / mich auf die Warteliste setzen.*

I would be grateful to be given the chance of a personal interview.	*Über die Einladung zu einem persönlichen Vorstellungsgespräch würde ich mich freuen.*
I am available for interview at any time / at short notice.	*Ich stehe jederzeit / kurzfristig für ein Vorstellungsgespräch zur Verfügung.*
I am prepared to sit for an aptitude test on …	*Ich bin bereit, am … an einem Eignungstest teilzunehmen.*
Should you require references, I will be pleased to provide you with any information you may need.	*Sollten Sie Referenzen benötigen, werde ich Ihnen gern jede gewünschte Information besorgen.*
For a reference please contact …	*Bezüglich einer Referenz wenden Sie sich bitte an …*

17.4 Exercises

Please translate:

17.4.1 Referenzschreiben

Sehr geehrte Frau O'Brien

Gern komme ich Ihrer Bitte nach, ein Urteil über Herrn Malloon abzugeben, der vom 1. Juli 20.. bis 30. September 20.., also ca. 3 Jahre, bei uns beschäftigt war.

Herr Malloon arbeitete zunächst in der Exportabteilung, wo er auf Grund seiner Sprachkenntnisse bei der Bearbeitung von Ersatzteilaufträgen, später auch von allgemeinen Exportaufträgen, eingesetzt wurde. Als Engländer fiel ihm die Betreuung englischsprachiger Kunden leicht. Er konnte sich gut in alle Exportfragen einarbeiten und lernte die Produktpalette unseres Hauses rasch kennen.

Nach 2 Jahren übertrugen wir ihm in steigendem Maß Marketingaufgaben. Im Zuge der Vergrößerung unseres Exports hatte Herr Malloon die Möglichkeit, unsere Marketingstrategien im europäischen und amerikanischen Raum zu implementieren.

Herr Malloon arbeitete stets zuverlässig und mit großem Eifer an seinen Aufgaben. Er brachte im Bereich Marketing neue Ideen ein und verwirklichte diese mit Elan und Interesse. Seine Kollegialität und sein Teamgeist sind hervorzuheben. Bei Kollegen und Vorgesetzten ist Herr Malloon sehr geschätzt. Er verhielt sich stets freundlich, loyal und war in seinem Auftreten zurückhaltend, aber bestimmt.

Nach einem Jahr beschloss Herr Malloon, sich beruflich nach Großbritannien zu verändern. Wir bedauern seinen Weggang, haben jedoch Verständnis für diese Entscheidung.

Ich habe keine Bedenken, Herrn Malloon für eine Position im Export- und/oder Marketingbereich zu empfehlen.

Ich hoffe, Ihnen mit dieser Auskunft geholfen zu haben.

Mit freundlichen Grüßen

17.4.2 Zeugnis

Stuttgart, den 27. November 20..

Ms Priscilla Jones trat im März 20.. als technische Übersetzerin in unsere Firma ein. Sie war in unserer zentralen Übersetzungsabteilung beschäftigt, wo sie technische Texte in ihre Muttersprache übersetzte. Nach einem hausinternen Schulungskurs in Textverarbeitung war sie in der Lage, ihre sämtlichen Übersetzungsarbeiten unter Zuhilfenahme verschiedener Programme am Bildschirm durchzuführen.

Ms Jones besitzt ein gutes Sprachgefühl im Englischen, technisches Verständnis und eine solide Kenntnis der deutschen Sprache. In den letzten drei Jahren gab Ms Jones auch einen englischen Konversationskurs für Fortgeschrittene in unserem Hause und wirkte an der Ausarbeitung von Unterlagen für unsere Englischkurse mit.

Wir waren mit den Leistungen von Ms Jones sehr zufrieden. Sie ist eine tüchtige und zuverlässige Kraft, die wegen ihres aufgeschlossenen Wesens und ihres Sinns für Humor bei ihren Kollegen und Vorgesetzten gleichermaßen beliebt war.

Ms Jones verlässt uns auf eigenen Wunsch. Wir können sie für eine anspruchsvolle Tätigkeit, bei der sie ihre sprachlichen Fähigkeiten einsetzen kann, uneingeschränkt empfehlen. Für ihre berufliche Zukunft wünschen wir ihr viel Erfolg.

M.K.M. AG
Personalverwaltung

Please draft letters, faxes or e-mails from the following particulars:

17.4.3 Geschäftsfall:

Sie sind in der Personalabteilung der International Broker House beschäftigt (Anschrift siehe 17.2.2). In Ihrer Anzeige suchten Sie eine(n) Übersetzer(in) für die englische Sprache.

Aufgabe: Antworten Sie auf Frau Andrews' Bewerbung unter 17.2.3 und den Lebenslauf unter 17.2.4 unter Berücksichtigung folgender Punkte:

- Bezugnahme auf Bewerbung
- Kandidatin erscheint Ihnen auf Grund ihrer Ausbildung geeignet
- Laden Sie sie zu einem Vorstellungsgespräch am 15. Januar 20.. 10.30 Uhr in Ihrem Hause ein
- Sie fügen eine genaue Wegbeschreibung vom Flughafen Frankfurt zu Ihrer Firma bei
- Wenn Frau Andrews der Termin passt, werden Sie die Flugtickets schicken
- An das Interview schließt sich ein Eignungstest an
- Nach dem Mittagessen werden die in die engere Wahl gekommenen Kandidaten noch einmal zu einem Gespräch eingeladen
- Sie sind bereit, eine Übernachtung in Frankfurt zu übernehmen
- Rückflug wird voraussichtlich am 16. Januar 20.. stattfinden.

17.4.4 **Geschäftsfall:**

Sie sind in der Personalabteilung der International Broker House beschäftigt (Anschrift siehe 17.2.2). In Ihrer Anzeige suchten Sie eine(n) Übersetzer(in) für die englische Sprache.

Aufgabe: Antworten Sie auf Herrn Gordons Bewerbung unter 17.2.5 und den Lebenslauf unter 17.2.6 unter Berücksichtigung folgender Punkte:

- Danken Sie für die Bewerbung
- Nach Durchsicht des Lebenslaufs von Herrn Gordon sind Sie der Meinung, dass er für die ausgeschriebene Stelle nicht die nötigen Voraussetzungen mitbringt
- Die Tätigkeit als Exportfachmann und Vertreter ist der eines Übersetzers nicht unbedingt vergleichbar
- Sie wissen aber, dass Leute mit seiner Berufserfahrung in Deutschland gute Chancen haben
- Sie sind gern bereit, Herrn Gordons Bewerbung an befreundete Unternehmen weiterzugeben, wenn er dies wünscht
- Höflicher Schluss

17.4.5 **Geschäftsfall:**

Die Meyer Personalberatung GmbH, Kavalleriestr. 10, 40213 Düsseldorf, Fax-Nr.: +49 (2 11) 45 09 83, E-Mail-Adresse: meyer.consult@t-online.de, hat auf einer Fachkonferenz in den Vereinigten Staaten Mr Ronald D. Jackson, den Chief Sales Executive der Fairthorne Inc., P.O. Box 30 415, Calgary, AB Canada T2N 1N4, Canada, Fax-Nr.: + 1 (403) 2 84 16 92, E-Mail-Adresse: fairthorne.inc@calgary.ca, kennen gelernt. Als Angestellte(r) der Meyer Personalberatung GmbH haben Sie den Auftrag, für die deutsche Niederlassung eines amerikanischen Konzerns einen geeigneten Kandidaten zu finden.

Aufgabe: Wenden Sie sich persönlich und vertraulich an Herrn Ronald D. Jackson und berücksichtigen Sie dabei folgende Punkte:

- Ihr Brief muss im Kopf den Vermerk „Private and Confidential" tragen
- Beziehen Sie sich auf Ihr Zusammentreffen auf der Fachkonferenz in Ohio, U.S.A.
- Erwähnen Sie die Vorzüge seiner Karriere (Führungsqualitäten, erfolgreiche Arbeit, hohe Umsatzsteigerungen in den vergangenen Jahren, guter Ruf und exzellente Presse)
- Beschreiben Sie kurz die deutsche Niederlassung Ihres amerikanischen Kunden (AG mit € 250.000,– Stammkapital, Sitz in deutscher Großstadt, verantwortlich für den EU-Raum)
- Beschreiben Sie die ausgeschriebene Position (Leiter des gesamten Exports, Aussicht auf Stelle im Vorstand nach Bewährung)
- Gehaltsvorstellung: € 100.000,– per annum, steigerungsfähig
- zusätzliche Vergünstigungen
- Bitte um Stellungnahme.

18. Vocabulary Lists

18.1 Progressive Vocabulary

List of the technical (commercial, economic, legal, engineering) terms and a few non-technical words and expressions used in the introductions and model letters (English-German) and the exercises (German-English). The terms are shown in the order in which they occur. Each term is mentioned only once; words for which a translation is given in "Terms and phrases" are not subsequently repeated here. The translations reflect the meaning of the terms in their respective context.

0. The Form of the Business Letter

letterhead	Briefkopf; Briefblattvordruck
reference	Referenz, Bezugszeichen
inside address	Empfängeranschrift
salutation	Anrede
body of the letter	Brieftext
complimentary close	Grußformel, Schlussformel

0.1.1

set rule	feste Regel
logo	Firmenzeichen
to be required by law	gesetzlich vorgeschrieben sein
limited company	Kapitalgesellschaft (Großbritannien)
registered office	eingetragener Sitz (einer Gesellschaft)
place of registration	Eintragungsort
registered number	Register-Nummer

0.1.2

initials	Initialen, Anfangsbuchstaben
typist	Schreibkraft
department	Abteilung
file number	Aktenzeichen
in the left-hand lower corner	am linken unteren Rand
letter sheet	Briefblatt
all-numeric forms	Formen mit ausschließlich Zahlen
as recommended	wie empfohlen
International Standards Organization (ISO)	Organisation für Internationale Normen
abbreviated form	abgekürzte Form
to avoid	vermeiden
confusion	Verwirrung

0.1.3

postal address	Postadresse

0.1.3.1

surname	Familien-, Nachname
forename	Vorname
distinct	eigen, unterschiedlich
firm name	Firmenname
sole-trader	Einzelkaufmann
sole-trader enterprise (AE sole proprietorship)	Einzelunternehmen, Einzelunternehmung
founder	Gründer
Protect Your Environment Store	Geschäft „Schütze Deine Umwelt"
partnership	Personengesellschaft, Sozietät
public limited company	(britische) Aktiengesellschaft
American corporation	amerikanische Gesellschaft
private limited company	Kapitalgesellschaft, die in etwa der deutschen GmbH entspricht

0.1.3.2

courtesy title	Höflichkeitstitel
academic degree	akademischer Grad
to designate	bezeichnen
corporate body	Körperschaft
official	Funktionär, offizielle Person

0.1.3.3

ZIP code	(amerikanisch) Postleitzahl
postcode	(britisch) Postleitzahl
country of destination	Bestimmungsland
addressee	Empfänger, Adressat
temporary address	vorläufige Anschrift

0.1.4

appropriate	geeignet
circular	Rundschreiben
to establish a friendly relationship	eine freundschaftliche Verbindung eingehen
to replace	ersetzen
to consist entirely of women	vollständig aus Frauen bestehen
to take account of	berücksichtigen, in Betracht ziehen

0.1.5

message	Botschaft
continuation sheet	Fortsetzungsblatt

0.1.6

to be consistent with	übereinstimmen mit
recipient	Empfänger
to precede	voranstehen
obsolete	veraltet
informal salutation	formlose Anrede

0.1.7

customary	üblich
signatory	Unterzeichner
on behalf of	für, im Namen von
absence	Abwesenheit

0.2

optional part	Teil zur Wahl
attention line	Zeile „zu Händen von“
subject line	Betreffzeile

0.2.1

to read	hier: lauten

0.2.2

optional feature	Merkmal zur Auswahl
to serve the reader's convenience	der Annehmlichkeit des Lesers dienen
to appear	erscheinen
introductory word	Einführungswort
to be put in bold print	fett gedruckt werden
to be capitalized	hier: mit Großbuchstaben anfangen
to be underlined	hier: unterstrichen werden

0.2.3

pro forma invoice	Proforma-Rechnung

0.2.4

to disappear	verschwinden
to be inserted	eingesetzt werden
a last-minute development	eine in letzter Minute erfolgte Entwicklung
to emphasize	betonen

0.3

sender	Absender
window envelope	Fensterbriefumschlag

0.4

layout	Layout
punctuation	Zeichensetzung
relevant	wichtig
paragraph	Absatz
left-hand margin	linker Rand
colon	Semikolon
to omit	weglassen
to apply to	hier: zutreffen auf

0.4.3

machine stand	Dämpfungsplatte für Maschinen
literature	Verkaufsliteratur, Prospektmaterial, Unterlagen
preliminary information	vorläufige Information
hardness of rubber	Gummihärte

particulars	Einzelheiten
to quote	anbieten
individual applications	individuelle Anwendungen
selector chart	Auswahltabelle
punch press	Stanzmaschine, Stanze
shopping facilities program	Programm für Einkaufsmöglichkeiten
application form	Anmeldeformular
regular customer	Stammkunde
to entitle	berechtigen

0.4.4

subject matter	Thema
fax transmission	Faxübertragung
to interrupt	unterbrechen
legally binding	gesetzlich bindend

0.4.5

screen	Bildschirm
to be prescribed	vorgeschrieben sein
attachment	Anlage (bei E-Mails)
VAT (value added tax)	MWSt (Mehrwertsteuer)

1. Enquiries

1.1

to establish contacts	Kontakte herstellen
potential agent	möglicher Vertreter
distributor	Verteiler, Vertriebsmann
licencee	Lizenznehmer
source of information	Informationsquelle
embassy	Botschaft
consulate	Konsulat
to browse through the internet	im Internet stöbern
customary	üblich
general enquiry	allgemeine Anfrage
specific enquiry	besondere Anfrage
bulletin board	Mitteilungsblatt
invitation to tender	Ausschreibung *(öffentliche Aufforderung zur Abgabe von Angeboten)*
government agency	staatliche Stelle
performance of construction work	Durchführung von Bauarbeiten
request for quotation	Bitte um (Preis-)Angebot
delivery date	Liefertermin, Lieferfrist
merely	lediglich
pattern	Muster
requirement	Bedarf
without obligation	unverbindlich

1.2.1

anti-friction bearings	Wälzlager
product range	Produktpalette
road vehicle	Straßenfahrzeug
agricultural machinery	landwirtschaftliche Maschinen
machine tools	Werkzeugmaschinen
particular applications	besondere Anwendungen
large-scale user	Großverbraucher

1.2.2

plywood	Sperrholz
veneer	Furnier
illustrated brochure	bebilderte Broschüre

1.2.3

purchasing department	Einkaufsabteilung
ad (advertisement)	Anzeige
standards	Normen

1.2.4

kitchenware	Küchengeräte
frame	Rahmen
turnkey town house	schlüsselfertiges Reihenhaus
drawing	Zeichnung
to be under construction	im Bau sein
size	Größe
property development company	Landentwicklungsgesellschaft
to be worthwhile	der Mühe wert sein
trade discount	(Groß-)Handelsrabatt
competitive	wettbewerbsfähig
substantial	umfangreich

1.2.5

digital watch	Digitaluhr
wholesale price	Großhandelspreis
suitable for	geeignet für
trial order	Probeauftrag
to have sth. in stock	etwas auf Lager haben
follow-up order	Nachfolgeauftrag

1.2.6

turbine generator and ancillary plant	Turbogenerator und dazugehörige Anlagen
steam power plant	Dampftriebwerk
head office	Hauptverwaltung
to comprise	einschließen, beinhalten
design	Design, Konstruktion
erection	Aufbau
commissioning	Inbetriebnahme
tenderer	Submittent, Bewerber
authorized representative	bevollmächtigter Vertreter
cash payment	Barzahlung
non-refundable	nicht rückzahlbar
to qualify for an award, tenderers must ...	nur Submittenten, die ..., können bei der Auftragsvergabe berücksichtigt werden
to apply for a loan	ein Darlehen beantragen
International Bank for Reconstruction and Development (World Bank)	Internationale Bank für Wiederaufbau und Entwicklung (Weltbank)
proceeds of a loan	ausgezahlter Darlehensbetrag
to reside	ansässig sein
eligible to tender	zur Ausschreibung zugelassen
to reserve the right	sich das Recht vorbehalten
to waive minor irregularities and informalities	geringfügige Abweichungen und Formfehler nicht berücksichtigen

1.4.1

Pullover	jumper, sweater, pullover
erfolgreich absetzen	to sell successfully
Herbstkollektion	autumn collection
ein Zahlungsziel gewähren	to grant account terms

1.4.2

Hannover-Messe	Hanover Fair
erfahren	to learn
Verkaufsleiter	sales manager
Spezialanfertigungen übernehmen	to manufacture to specification
vollautomatische Bohrmaschine	fully automatic drilling machine

1.4.3

computergestütztes Lernprogramm	computer-aided learning programme
Vorabinformation	preliminary information
bei Eignung	if it is suitable
zugänglich machen	to make available
vor Ort	locally

1.4.4

Gerät	hier: device, apparatus
EU-Normen	EU standards
Nachbestellung	subsequent order, follow-up order
Probelieferung	trial delivery

1.4.5

Ballen Seide	bale of silk
Kleidungsstück	garment
Damenkleid	lady dress
detailliertes Angebot	detailed offer
regelmäßiger Auftrag	regular order

2. Offers

2.1

offer	Angebot
sales letter	Werbebrief
to submit	unterbreiten
inevitable	unvermeidlich
acknowledgement	(Empfangs-)Bestätigung
to refer to	hier: richten an

source of supply	Lieferquelle
solicited offer	verlangtes Angebot
unsolicited offer	unverlangtes Angebot
offeror	Anbieter
firm offer	Festangebot
to revoke	widerrufen
legislation	Gesetzgebung
to embrace	hier: umfassen
to enforce	in Kraft setzen
reservation clause	Vorbehaltsklausel
to release	hier: befreien
acceptance	Annahme
without engagement	unverbindlich
confirmation	Bestätigung
subject to prior sale	Zwischenverkauf vorbehalten
as long as stocks last	solange der Vorrat reicht
offeree	Angebotsempfänger
to lapse	hier: verfallen
to conclude a contract	einen Vertrag abschließen
online advertising	Online-Werbung
applicable	anwendbar
validity	Gültigkeit
essential point	wichtiger Punkt
services rendered	geleistete Dienstleistungen
discount	Nachlass
to be supplemented	ergänzt werden
to fail to produce	nicht führen zu
follow-up letter	Nachfassbrief
circular	Rundschreiben
to prepare the ground	den Weg ebnen

2.2.1

to receive attention	hier: bearbeitet werden
engineer	Techniker, Ingenieur

2.2.2

sales manager	Verkaufsleiter
to proceed to	sich daran machen
to fill in a form	ein Formular ausfüllen
to return	hier: zurückschicken

2.2.3

laboratory equipment	Laborausrüstung(en)
distributor	Großhändler, Vertreiber
specific applications	spezifische Anwendungen
to appreciate	schätzen

2.2.4

line	hier: Produktpalette
no doubt	zweifellos
to give an outline	einen Überblick geben
to be in the market	hier: suchen

2.2.5

milling machine	Fräsmaschine
sole distributor	Alleinvertreiber
to be delighted	erfreut sein
principal	hier: Mutterhaus
to be ideally suited	ideal geeignet sein
to cover your requirements	Ihren Bedarf decken
a representative selection	eine repräsentative Auswahl
components	Teile

2.2.6

by banker's transfer	durch Banküberweisung
to place an order	einen Auftrag erteilen
balance	hier: Rest
cash against documents	Kasse gegen Dokumente
deposit	Anzahlung
to become forfeited	verfallen, verwirkt sein
to be taken up	hier: abgenommen werden
remittance	Überweisung
asap = as soon as possible	so bald wie möglich
accuracy	Genauigkeit, Präzision

2.2.7

to hold discussions	Gespräche führen
computer desk	Computertisch
to fit	hier: passen zu
furniture	Möbel
adjustable	einstellbar
height	Höhe
length	Länge

the Continent	das europäische Festland
reference list	Referenzliste
brochure	Broschüre, Prospekt
desk options	hier: Computertisch-optionen
invoice amount	Rechnungsbetrag
account	Konto
irrevocable letter of credit	unwiderrufliches Akkreditiv
to be opened in our favour	zu eröffnen zu unseren Gunsten
bank charges	Bankgebühren
to incur	entstehen
for the opener's account	zu Lasten des (Akkreditiv-) Eröffners
despatch	Versand
to grant open account terms	ein offenes Zahlungsziel gewähren
staff	Belegschaft, Personal
installation	Einbau, Aufstellung
to prove necessary	sich als notwendig herausstellen

2.2.8

General Conditions of Sale	Allgemeine Verkaufsbedingungen
printed on the back	auf der Rückseite gedruckt
to supersede	ersetzen, hier: überflüssig machen
in-line wrapper	integrierte Folieneinschlagmaschine
polyethylene film	Polyäthylenfolie
shuttle feeder	Zuführung für Einsteckprodukte
spares	Ersatzteile
air fare	Flugpreis
living expenses	Unterbringungs- und Verpflegungskosten
mate's receipt	Steuermannsquittung
bill of lading	Konnossement
on your premises	in Ihrem Hause
crating	Verpackung im Holzverschlag
seaworthy packaging	seemäßige Verpackung
clarification of all technical details	Klärung aller technischen Einzelheiten
sealing speed of 100 cycles per minute	Schweißgeschwindigkeit von 100 Takten pro Minute
pillowpack	rechteckige Packung
with a long seam on the overlap	mit einer langen Schweißnaht auf der Überlappung
port charges	Hafengebühren
clearance costs	Zollabfertigungskosten
customs duties	Zollgebühren
off-loading	Abladen, Ausladen
de-crating	Auspacken (Entfernen des Holzverschlags)
on site	am Aufstellungsort
3 phase, 50 cycles	Drehstrom, 50 Perioden
infeed	Zufuhr, Beschickung
take-off	Abtransport
wrapping material	Verpackungsmaterial

2.2.9

exchange rate	Wechselkurs
currency adjustment	Ausgleich für Kursschwankungen
on notification of dispatch	bei Versandbenachrichtigung

2.2.10

special flexible frame protecting laptop travel bags	Laptop-Reisetaschen mit besonderem, flexiblen Rahmenschutz
to be forthcoming	hier: anstehen

2.2.11

customer-designed programs	auf den Kunden zugeschnittene Programme
individual company needs	individuelle Firmenbedürfnisse
to count among	zählen zu
upon receipt	bei Erhalt
tailor-made	maßgeschneidert

2.2.12

up-to-date information	auf den neuesten Stand gebrachte Informationen
up-market	anspruchsvoll, exklusiv
network operators	Netzwerkbetreiber
application developers	Anwendungsentwickler
on-line shopping facilities	Online-Einkaufsmöglichkeiten
innovations	Neuerungen
to subscribe	hier: abonnieren

2.4.1

in Verbindung setzen	to contact
keinen Anspruch auf Vollständigkeit erheben	not to claim to be complete
kostenlos	free of charge

2.4.2

Fachhandel	specialized trade
die Preise verstehen sich	prices are to be understood
pro Position	per item
andernfalls	otherwise
nach Vereinbarung	according to special agreement
jmd. zur Verfügung stehen	to be at so.'s disposal

2.4.3

nach gesonderter Spezifikation	made to specification
abändern	to modify
Ihren Bedürfnissen anpassen	to adapt to your requirements
technische Einzelheiten	technical details

2.4.4

bei Erstaufträgen	in case of initial orders
Frachtsätze	freight rates
Präzision	precision
Zuverlässigkeit	reliability
sich einen Namen machen	to become known

2.4.6

Haftung bei Streik oder höherer Gewalt ist ausgeschlossen	liability is excluded in case of strike or force majeure
Montage	hier: installation
Gerichtsstand	venue, place of jurisdiction

2.4.7

das Sommerlager räumen	to clear the summer stocks

3. Orders

3.1

order cancellation	Auftragsstornierung
acceptable	annehmbar
firm offer	Festangebot
without qualifications	ohne Vorbehalt
counter-offer	Gegenangebot
out of courtesy	aus Höflichkeit
first order, initial order	Erstauftrag
repeat order	Nachbestellung
marketability	Marktfähigkeit
advance order	Vorausbestellung
standing order	Dauerauftrag
at certain intervals	in bestimmten Abständen
merchandise on call	Waren auf Abruf
storage times	Lagerungszeiten
indent	Indent, Auftrag
contractual obligations	vertragliche Verpflichtungen
to pave the way	den Weg ebnen
to suffice	genügen
to prevent fraud	Betrug vermeiden
to register with the supplier	sich beim Lieferanten registrieren lassen
virtual signatures	virtuelle Unterschriften
legal proceedings	gesetzliche Verfahren(sweisen)

3.2.1

water treatment	Wasserbehandlung
suitability	Eignung
application	hier: Anwendungsbereich

3.2.2

electrical switches	elektrische Schaltungen
to incorporate	einbauen
keen competition	scharfer Wettbewerb

3.2.5

deposit	Anzahlung
to become forfeited	verfallen
to ensure	sicherstellen
with the utmost care	mit größtmöglicher Sorgfalt

3.2.6

application software	Anwendungssoft- ware
an ordinary transport agency	eine gewöhnliche Transportfirma
to monitor	überwachen
inadequate	ungeeignet
to compensate	entschädigen

3.2.7

demonstration	Vorführung
dependability	Zuverlässigkeit
board = board of directors	Vorstand
mutually agreed upon	beiderseitig ver- einbart
warranty period	Garantiezeit
"down" condition	Ausfall
service engineer	Kundendienst- techniker
due allowance for	unter gebührender Berücksichtigung

3.2.8

optional feature	wahlweise Aus- stattung
to operate to a sufficient standard to ...	so einwandfrei arbeiten, dass ...
operating environment	Arbeitsumfeld, hier: räumliche Voraus- setzungen
accessories	Zubehör
engineering manager	technischer Leiter
eight-hour shift	8-Stunden-Schicht
maintenance agreement	Wartungsvertrag

3.2.9

to draw at 60 d/s (= days sight)	auf 60 Tage Sicht ziehen
D/A (documents against acceptance)	Dokumente gegen Akzept
to mark	beschriften, markieren
light-weight bicycle	Leichtrad
21-speed gear	21-Gangschaltung
chrome-plated headlight	verchromte Lampe
warning bell	Klingel
rear light / reflector	Schlusslicht / Strahler
transfer	Abziehbild
trim	Verzierung
saddle bag	Satteltasche

3.4.1

Toner	toner
Tintenpatrone	ink cartridge
recyclebar	recyclable
Einheitspreis	unit price
frei unseren Geschäftsräumen	free our premises

3.4.2

kundenbezogene Daten	customer-related data
Nutzung	utilization
Zielgruppeninfor- mationen	target group information
Verfahren	process

3.4.3

Nutzfahrzeug- Konstruktion	construction of commercial vehicles
komplette Montage	complete installation
Inbetriebnahme	start-up
Einweisung	training, instruction
Bedienungspersonal	operating staff
betriebsfertige Übergabe	hand-over in working condition
Werk	works
Betriebs- und Bedienungsanlei- tungen	operating and service instruc- tions
Typenschild	identification plate
metrisches System	metric system

Verladung	loading
sich vorbehalten	to reserve the right
Nichtbeachtung	non-observance
Garantiezeit	guarantee period
Anerkennung	hier: acceptance
umseitig	overleaf

3.4.4

Badarmaturen	bathroom fittings
Großhändlerrabatt	wholesale discount, trade discount
90-Tage-Wechsel nach Sicht	bill of exchange payable 90 days after sight

3.4.5

Analysewaagen	analytical scales
abholen	to collect
Begleitpapiere	accompanying documents

3.4.6

Vorzugspreis	preferential price

3.4.7

Sonnenkollektoren	sun collectors
Auftragsannullierung	order cancellation
Stilllegung	shutdown, closure
Baustelle	(building) site
offizielle Freigabe	official release
angeblicher Grund	alleged reason
ungeklärte Grundstückrechte	unclarified property rights
unvorhergesehene Kosten	unforeseen costs
Nichteinhalten des Vertrages	non-compliance with the contract, non-fulfilment of the contract
Schadensersatzansprüche stellen	to claim damages

4. Acknowledgements

4.1

acknowledgement	Auftragsbestätigung (Bestätigung der Bestellungsannahme)
sales agreement	Kaufvertrag
customary	üblich
to be legally valid	rechtsgültig sein
to constitute	hier: darstellen
to refuse the order outright	den Auftrag direkt ablehnen
substitute	Ersatz
to place on file	vormerken
middleman	Mittelsmann, Vermittlungsagent
legal significance	rechtliche Bedeutung
to bring about	zustandebringen
advice of dispatch	Versandanzeige
sales contract, contract of purchase	Kaufvertrag

4.2.1

subscription order	Abonnementsauftrag
topical	hier: aktuell
payment form	Zahlungsformular
top portion	oberer Teil

4.2.2

textile mill	Textilfabrik
shirting	Hemdenstoff
composition	Zusammensetzung
design	hier: Dessin
force majeure	höhere Gewalt
strike	Streik
lockout	Aussperrung
packing house	Spezialfirma für Exportverpackung
settlement of accounts	Rechnungsausgleich
to apply	gelten
bill of exchange	Wechsel

4.2.3

tyre	(Auto-)Reifen

4.2.4

to discontinue production	die Produktion einstellen
sample cutting	Muster

4.2.5

letter of intent	(Kauf-)Absichtserklärung
confidential	vertraulich
invitation to bid	Einladung zur Angebotsabgabe
to award	hier: zuteilen
vendor	Verkäufer, Lieferer

as stipulated	wie festgesetzt
issuance	Ausstellung
bill of material	Materialliste
pending	hier: bis zu
to authorize	ermächtigen
to proceed with the necessary action	die nötigen Schritte unternehmen
to contain	enthalten
scope of supply	Lieferumfang
in compliance to	in Übereinstimmung mit
amendment	Änderung
delivery schedule	Lieferzeitplan
cancellation charges	Stornierungskosten
notwithstanding	ungeachtet
to affix	anbringen

4.4.1

Gültigkeit	validity
gewährleisten	to guarantee

4.4.2

mit getrennter Post	by separate mail
in doppelter Ausfertigung	in duplicate
mit Aufträgen überhäuft sein	to be flooded with orders

4.4.3

Taschendiktiergerät	portable dictating machine
flach	slim
handlich	easy to handle
Markierungstaste (zum sofortigen Auffinden der gewünschten Textstelle)	fast-forward button (for forward scanning)
Diktat / Konferenz-Schalter	dictation / conference switch

4.4.4

zusammenklappbare Servierwagen	collapsible trolleys
stoßfeste Kunststoffbeschichtung	shock-resistant plastic coating
Tragfähigkeit	load capacity
Mengenrabatt	quantity discount
nicht mehr verfügbar	no longer available
unverändert	unchanged

4.4.5

Fahrrad-Sturzhelm	crash helmet for cyclist
Technischer Überwachungsverein (TÜV)	German technical surveyance body
schärfste Preiskalkulation	keenest price calculation

4.4.6

Kaffeeservice	coffee service
Essservice	dinner service

4.4.7

Bohrmaschine	drilling machine
Werkzeugmaschine	machine tool
Bedienungsanleitung	operator's manual
Bildschirm-Steuerung	display-screen control
Versandort	point of dispatch
Übernahmespediteur	forwarder's correspondent
Folgemonat	following month
Gefahrenübergang	transfer of risk
Aufstellungsversicherung	installation insurance
Exemplar	copy
Landtransport	overland transport

5. Credit Letters

5.1

credit enquiry	Kreditanfrage
creditworthy	kreditwürdig
source of information	Auskunftsquelle
court judgement	Gerichtsurteil
credit application form	Kreditantragsformular
balance sheet	Bilanz
bank reference	Bankreferenz
explicit	ausdrücklich
credit enquiry (credit reference) agency (AE commercial agency)	Auskunftei
fee	Gebühr
a free-of-charge favour	eine kostenlose Gefälligkeit
to reciprocate a favour	eine Gefälligkeit erwidern

to take for granted	als selbstverständlich ansehen
to hold responsible	verantwortlich machen
to treat confidentially	vertraulich behandeln
strictly confidential	streng vertraulich
to arouse suspicion	Verdacht wecken
common-law countries	Länder des angelsächsischen Rechtssystems
defamation	Verleumdung
to be couched	abgefasst sein
tantamount to	gleichbedeutend mit
credit rating	Bewertung der Kreditwürdigkeit
financial papers	Finanzzeitungen

5.2.1

financial status	Vermögenslage

5.2.2

credit standing	Kreditwürdigkeit

5.2.3

volume of business	Geschäftsumfang
to facilitate	erleichtern

5.2.4

to meet obligations	Verpflichtungen nachkommen

5.2.5

to collect bills	Rechnungen einziehen

5.2.6

to charter	*(durch Gründungsurkunde)* errichten
antiques	Antiquitäten
principal	hier: Mitglied der Unternehmensleitung, Vorstandsmitglied
chairman	Vorsitzender
to maintain an account	ein Konto unterhalten
balance	Saldo, Kontostand
a medium six-figure line of credit	Kreditlinie im mittleren sechsstelligen Bereich
a low five-figure aggregate	Gesamtbetrag im unteren fünfstelligen Bereich
outstanding	offen(stehend)
facilities	(Kredit-)Fazilitäten
(financial) statement	Finanznachweis
net worth	Eigenkapital
sustained	anhaltend
business commitments	geschäftliche Verpflichtungen

5.2.8

officer	Mitglied der Unternehmensleitung, Vorstandsmitglied
rating	Beurteilung, Bewertung
to incorporate	gründen (Kapitalgesellschaft)
native-born	im Land geboren
to operate a partnership business	eine Personengesellschaft betreiben
to succeed	nachfolgen
wholly-owned subsidiary	100%ige Tochtergesellschaft
to decline	ablehnen
parent company	Muttergesellschaft
current assets	Umlaufvermögen
current liabilities	kurzfristige Verbindlichkeiten
to maintain a liquid condition	die Liquidität aufrechterhalten
on a sight draft basis	auf Sichtwechsel-Basis
depository	hier: Bank
advance	hier: kurzfristiges Darlehen

5.4.1

sich bewerben um	to apply for
Vertretervertrag	agency agreement
Konsignationswaren	consignment goods
Vermögenslage	assets / net worth position
Geschäftsverbindung	business connection

5.4.2

Warenwert	merchandise value

5.4.4

Handelsregister	commercial register *(Germany)*
Amtsgericht	lower court *(Germany)*
Komplementär	general partner
Kommanditist	limited partner
Geschäftsgegenstand	purpose, object
Formen für die Kunststoffindustrie	moulds for the plastics industry
Kontokorrent- und Diskontkredite	overdraft and discount facilities
Grundbesitz	real property, real estate
belastet	encumbered

5.4.5

Hypothek aufnehmen	to raise a mortgage
Verschwiegenheit	discretion

5.4.6

Kreditrahmen	credit line

5.4.7

oHG (offene Handelsgesellschaft)	ordinary partnership according to German law
GmbH (Gesellschaft mit beschränkter Haftung)	private limited company according to German law
GmbH-Anteile	Ltd shares
Mangel an liquiden Mitteln	lack of liquid funds

6. Delivery

6.1

execution of orders	Auftragsausführung
adequate packing	geeignete Verpackung
caution marks	Vorsichtsmarkierungen
marking instructions	Markierungsanweisungen
to comply with	beachten
environmental protection	Umweltschutz
to adhere to	einhalten
forwarding agent	Spediteur
carrier	Frachtführer
parcel	Paket
despatch, dispatch	Versand
dispatch advice	Versandavis, Versandanzeige
shipping advice	Versandanzeige, Verschiffungsanzeige
certificate of origin	Ursprungszeugnis
to lodge with a bank for collection	einer Bank zum Inkasso übergeben
to notify	benachrichtigen
to be ready for dispatch	versandbereit sein
progress report	Zwischenbescheid
unit price	Einzelpreis, Stückpreis
extension	hier: Gesamtpreis
miscellaneous	verschieden
on approval	auf Probe, zur Ansicht
to consign to an agent for sale	einem Vertreter in Konsignation geben
import licence	Importlizenz
statement of account	Kontoauszug
to balance	ausgleichen
balance	Saldo
debit note	Lastschrift
credit note	Gutschrift
entry	Buchung
records	Aufzeichnungen, Geschäftsbücher
omission	Auslassung
vice versa	umgekehrt

6.2.1

engraving machine	Graviermaschine
to stencil	mittels Schablone anbringen
storage space	Lagerraum

6.2.2

turnover tax identification number	Umsatzsteuer-Identifikationsnummer

6.2.3

airway bill	Luftfrachtbrief

6.2.4

non-negotiable	nicht begebbar, nicht übertragbar

shipping documents	Versanddokumente, Warenbegleitpapiere
commercial invoice	Handelsrechnung
in triplicate full set of clean on-board bills of lading	3-fach voller Satz reiner Bordkonnossemente
certificate of insurance	Versicherungszertifikat
report of findings	Inspektionszertifikat

6.2.5

draft	Tratte
to furnish with an acceptance	mit Akzept versehen

6.2.6

after verification	nach Prüfung

6.2.7

to reject	zurückweisen
to cancel	stornieren

6.2.8

electrical switches	elektrische Schaltungen

6.2.9

by order of	im Auftrag von
for account and risk of	auf Rechnung und Gefahr von
E. & O.E. (= errors and omissions excepted)	Irrtümer und Auslassungen vorbehalten

6.2.10

remittance advice	Zahlungsanzeige

6.4.1

Nachricht geben	to advise

6.4.3

Jahrgang	vintage
palettenweise Abnahme	order by pallet
Euro-Paletten	euro-pallets
tauschen	to exchange
in Rechnung stellen	to invoice
Leerpalette	empty pallet

6.4.5

Klimaanlage	air conditioner
Abflugdatum	date of departure

6.4.6

Etikett	label
grüner Punkt	green dot
Vorlage	model, pattern
Lizenzgebühr	licence fee

7. Payment

7.1

advice of payment	Zahlungsavis
discrepancy	Abweichung, Diskrepanz
remittance	Überweisung, Übermittlung (einer Zahlung)
banker's draft	Bankscheck
documentary bill	dokumentärer Wechsel
clean bill	nichtdokumentärer Wechsel
international postal giro	internationale Postüberweisung
international money order	internationale Zahlungsanweisung
retail customer	*im Bankwesen:* Privatkunde
corporate customer	*im Bankwesen:* Geschäftskunde
order data	Auftragsdaten
electronic data transfer	elektronische Datenübertragung
account balance	Kostensaldo
by data carrier	durch Datenträger
for further processing	zur weiteren Bearbeitung
travellers' cheques	Reiseschecks
foreign exchange	Devisen
to convert	umtauschen
rate of exchange	Wechselkurs
to solicit further business	hier: um weitere Aufträge bitten
to take unearned discounts	unberechtigterweise Skonto abziehen
incompatible	unvereinbar

7.2.1

to channel payments	hier: Zahlungen abwickeln

7.2.3

crossed cheque	Verrechnungsscheck

7.2.5

to honour a bill	einen Wechsel einlösen, bezahlen

7.2.6

marine and war risk insurance certificate	See- und Kriegsrisiko-Versicherungszertifikat
in compliance with	in Übereinstimmung mit
complete set	vollständiger Satz
clean shipped-on-board bills of lading	reine an Bord verschiffte Konnossemente
made out to order	an Order ausgestellt
advance copy	Vorabkopie

7.2.8

quarterly statement	vierteljährlicher Kontoauszug
to deduct	abziehen

7.2.9

disagreement	Unstimmigkeit
item	Position
sweater	Pullover

7.4.2

berücksichtigen	to take into consideration
gegeneinander aufrechnen	to counterbalance
per Einschreiben	by registered mail

7.4.3

Klang	sound
Mengenrabatt	quantity discount
Zahlungsziel	account terms

7.4.4

Quartalsabrechnung	quarterly statement, account
Provision	commission

7.4.5

verlängern	to prolong, extend
alle zusätzlichen Kosten	all additional costs
disponieren	to dispose of

8. Delays in Delivery

missing consignments	fehlende Sendungen

8.1

to constitute a breach of contract	einen Vertragsbruch darstellen
earthquake	Erdbeben
to demand compensation	Entschädigung verlangen
to bring action for damages	Schadenersatzklage einreichen
to sustain a loss	Schaden erleiden
failure	Versäumnis
delayed performance	verspätete Erfüllung
non-performance	Nicht-Erfüllung
penalty	Strafe
liquidated damages	Konventionalstrafe
reminder	Mahnung
deadline	letzter Termin
allowance	hier: Gewährung
to dispense with sth.	auf etwas verzichten
balance	hier: Restmenge
to release so. from the contract	jmd. aus dem Vertrag entlassen
to commit a breach of contract	einen Vertragsbruch begehen
legal action	Klage
to reveal	zeigen
to misdirect	fehlleiten
in-house stock control system	firmeninternes Lagerkontrollsystem

8.2.1

digital camera	Digitalkamera

8.2.2

stockist	Lagerhalter
to bear extra costs	zusätzliche Kosten tragen

8.2.3

to cause great concern	große Sorgen bereiten
delivery status	Lieferstand
imprecise indications	ungenaue Angaben
to suffer serious damage	ernsthaften Schaden erleiden
to be on the subject of ...	beim Thema von ... sein
spare parts	Ersatzteile
annoyance	Verärgerung
unsatisfactory state of affairs	unzufriedenstellender Stand der Dinge
loss of confidence	Vertrauensverlust

8.2.4

shipment overdue	überfällige Lieferung
serviceability	hier: Leistungs-, Betriebsfähigkeit

8.2.6

prior to the holiday closure	vor den Betriebsferien
to ascertain	feststellen
wine carafe	Weinkaraffe
candleholder	Kerzenhalter
query	Frage, Rückfrage
aggrieved	verärgert

8.2.7

to be relieved	erleichtert sein
handled and unhandled decanter	Karaffe mit und ohne Griff
whereabouts	Aufenthaltsort, Verbleib
to await collection	auf die Abholung warten
to stage an exhibition	eine Ausstellung veranstalten

8.2.8

in the pressure of business	unter dem Druck des Arbeitsanfalls

8.2.9

was scheduled to sail on ...	sollte fahrplanmäßig am ... auslaufen

8.2.10

heavy-duty compressor	Hochleistungskompressor
debris	Schutt
to resume production	die Produktion wieder aufnehmen

8.4.1

Wollpullover	woollen sweaters
Lagerleitung	stock / warehouse manager
verspätet sein	to be delayed
Herbstmodenschau	autumn (AE fall) fashion show
Ensemble	ensemble
unvermeidlich	unavoidable
kurzfristig Ersatz beschaffen	to get a substitute at short notice
etwaige Kosten	possibly arising costs
in Rechnung stellen	to charge

8.4.2

Studie	(market) survey
Geschäftsimmobilien	commercial properties
einen Termin einhalten	to meet a deadline
eigenes Verschulden	one's own fault
Anfrage richten an ...	to direct an enquiry to ...
trotz mehrmaliger Erinnerung	in spite of several reminders
behördliche Auskunft	official information
vorsorglich	as a measure of precaution

8.4.3

Bohrmaschine	drilling machine
der zum Antrieb erforderliche Elektromotor	the electric motor required to drive the machine
unbenutzt im Lager stehen	to lie idle in stock
angewiesen sein	to depend on
Unmut verstehen	to understand the annoyance
einsatzbereit sein	to be ready for use
eine Nachfrist setzen	to grant a final deadline

die Annahme ablehnen	to reject acceptance
zu Ihren Lasten	at your cost
Anzahlung	deposit

8.4.4

Teppichfliesen	carpet tiles
Lieferrückstände	order backlogs
Gewinnausfall	loss of profits

8.4.5

Konstruktionsleiter	construction manager

8.4.6

aus stautechnischen Gründen	for technical reasons relating to stowage
entladen werden	to be unloaded
auslaufen	to sail
Anlegestop	landing, docking stoppage
keinen Einfluss nehmen	to have no influence

9. Complaints and Adjustments

complaint	Beschwerde, Reklamation
adjustment of complaint	Bereinigung der Beschwerde

9.1

services rendered	erbrachte Dienstleistungen
deficiency	Mangel
to rescind the contract	vom Vertrag zurücktreten
to refund	ersetzen, erstatten
replacement	Ersatz (ähnliches Produkt)
substitute	Ersatz (gleiches Produkt)
allowance	(Beanstandungs-) Nachlass
to remedy defects	Mängel beheben
misinterpretation	Missverständnis
guarantee, warranty	Garantie, Gewährleistung
to undertake	sich verpflichten
free of charge	kostenlos
to prove defective	sich als fehlerhaft herausstellen
faulty material or workmanship	Material- oder Verarbeitungsfehler
to receive attention	hier: bearbeitet werden
to accept a claim	einer Beschwerde stattgeben
to find oneself at fault	seinen Fehler eingestehen
to blame	hier: verantwortlich machen
to accommodate a good customer	einem guten Kunden entgegenkommen
erroneously	fälschlicherweise
unfounded complaints	unbegründete Beschwerden
to take advantage of sb.	jmd. ausnutzen, übervorteilen
to be properly packed	vorschriftsmäßig verpackt sein
to take up with	regeln mit
compensation for loss or damage	Ersatz für Verlust oder Schaden
policy	(Versicherungs-) Police
negligence	Fahrlässigkeit
subrogation	(Rechts-)Abtretung
to give rise to a dispute	einen Streitfall auslösen
to maintain	hier: behaupten
through the good offices of	durch Vermittlung von
to refer to	verweisen an
court of law	(ordentliches) Gericht
court of arbitration	Schiedsgericht
litigation	Rechtsstreit, Prozess
to be liable	haftbar sein

9.2.1

industrial sewing machine	Industrie-Nähmaschine
drive belt	Antriebsriemen
to disintegrate	sich auflösen
to be indispensable	unerlässlich sein
a tolerable minimum	ein erträgliches Mindestmaß

9.2.2

to lie idle	brach liegen, unbenutzt bleiben
to process orders	Aufträge bearbeiten

at your cost and expense	auf Ihre Kosten
to provide for a guarantee	eine Garantie vorsehen
to hold so. liable	jmd. haftbar machen

9.2.3

copying machine	Kopiergerät
installation engineer	Montagetechniker
to put into operation	in Betrieb nehmen
selenium-coated aluminium cylinder	selenbeschichtete Aluminiumwalze
to disconnect	Netzstecker ziehen, stillsetzen
purchasing manager	Einkaufsleiter
staple	Heftklammer
paper clip	Büroklammer
perfect operating condition	einwandfreier Betriebszustand
head of the repair department	Leiter der Reparaturabteilung
to be exhausted	erschöpft sein
operational	betriebsbereit
to repair to "as new" condition	durch Reparatur in einen Zustand versetzen, der dem eines Neugeräts entspricht
failing that action on your part	falls dies von Ihrer Seite aus nicht geschieht
to place the matter in the hands of our solicitors	die Angelegenheit unseren Rechtsanwälten übergeben

9.2.4

cutting	(Stoff-)Muster
oversight	Versehen

9.2.5

re-run	Neudruck
proof	Korrekturabzug

9.2.6

shortage	Fehlmenge
copy	hier: Exemplar
to check with sb.	mit jmd. Rücksprache nehmen
despatch department	Versandabteilung
pallet	Palette
to check	(nach-)prüfen, kontrollieren

9.2.7

service engineer	Kundendiensttechniker
unsatisfactory performance	nicht zufriedenstellende Leistung
printer	Drucker
approved paper manufacturer	anerkannter Papierhersteller
malfunction	Funktionsstörung

9.2.8

jar	(Marmelade-)Glas
shipping company	Reederei
survey report	Havariezertifikat
Lloyd's agent	Lloyd's-Agent *(für Lloyd's tätiger Havariekommissar)*

9.2.9

arbitrator	Schiedsrichter
silk textiles	Seidenstoffe
to dispute	Vorbehalte geltend machen
contention	Behauptung, Vorbringen
variation in quality	Qualitätsabweichung
to refer to an umpire	einen Obmann *(dritten Schiedsrichter)* hinzuziehen

9.2.10

to warrant sth.	Garantie für etwas übernehmen
to prove defective	sich als fehlerhaft herausstellen
faulty workmanship	fehlerhafte Verarbeitung

9.2.11

warranty clause	Garantieklausel
letter of intent	Kaufabsichtserklärung
vendor	Verkäufer, Lieferant
expeditiously	schnell, prompt
for incorporation into the goods	hier: zur Verarbeitung in die Waren
sub-orders	untervergebene Aufträge

to have appropriate provisions	geeignete Maßnahmen vorsehen
to be of merchantable quality	von marktgängiger Qualität sein
free of liens	frei von Pfandsicherheiten
encumbrance	(dingliche) Belastung, Schuldenbelastung
remedy	hier: Gegenmaßnahme
offshore commissioning	hier: Inbetriebnahme im Ausland
to notify	benachrichtigen
in the event	falls
to exercise the option	hier: sich für die Option entscheiden
to reimburse	entschädigen
whether direct or incidental	hier: ob (die Kosten) direkt oder zufällig entstanden sind
without limitation	ohne Einschränkung
costs of removal	Umzugskosten
customs duties	Zollgebühren
consequential damages	Folgeschäden
without prejudice of the foregoing	ungeachtet des Vorstehenden
to reserve the right	sich das Recht vorbehalten
a non-performance adjustment in the purchase price	eine Berichtigung des Einkaufspreises wegen Nichterfüllung
pursuant to	gemäß, in Übereinstimmung mit
to continue to apply to	weiterhin gültig bleiben für
to expire	auslaufen, ungültig werden
witness of tests	Bezeugen der Tests
final release	Endabnahme
certification	Zertifizierung
to relieve	befreien
to extend to	sich beziehen auf
to cover failure	Fehler abdecken

9.2.12

to prejudice	beeinträchtigen
at buyer's request	auf Wunsch des Käufers
to comply with	übereinstimmen mit
shortfall	Differenz, Fehlmenge

9.2.13

controversy	Kontroverse, Streitigkeit
under the auspices of	unter der Schirmherrschaft von

9.4.1

Antriebsriemen	drive belt
Vorfall	incident
Zulieferant	sub-supplier
den Anforderungen entsprechen	to meet the requirements
Industrie-Nähmaschine	industrial sewing machine

9.4.2

Gummiblase	rubber bag
Gummiball	rubber bulb
zur Begutachtung vorlegen	to present for a check-up
Gerät	device

9.4.3

Seidenstoffe	silk materials
zu Beanstandung Anlass geben	to give reason for complaint
zu lose gewebt sein	to be too loosely woven
sich verziehen	to get out of shape
verarbeitet werden zu	to be processed to
Sommerkollektion	summer collection

9.4.4

unzulänglich	inadequate, insufficient
Kundendienstleiter	head of after-sales service
Speicherkapazität	storage capacity

9.4.5

Hamburger freundschaftliche Arbitrage	Hamburg Amicable Arbitration

ranzige Ware	rancid merchandise
Ernte	harvest, crop
Minderwert	reduction in value
Minderung des Kaufpreises	abatement of the purchase price
Schiedsklausel	arbitration clause
Wohnsitz	(place of) residence
Aufenthaltsort	place of abode

10. Delays in Payment

reminder	Zahlungserinnerung
collection letter	Mahnbrief
debtor's response	Reaktion des Schuldners

10.1

credit period	Zahlungsfrist
insolvency	Insolvenz, Zahlungsunfähigkeit
failure to take up documents	Nichtaufnahme von Dokumenten
government action	staatliche Maßnahmen
the last resort	der letzte Ausweg
lawsuit	Prozess
to lodge an objection	Widerspruch erheben
to declare enforceable by execution	für vollstreckbar erklären
to levy execution on the debtor's property	in das Vermögen des Schuldners vollstrecken
court hearing	Gerichtsverhandlung
commercial risk, buyer risk	wirtschaftliches Risiko
del credere	Delkredere
political risk	politisches Risiko
imposition of new import restrictions	Einführung neuer Einfuhrbeschränkungen
Export Credits Guarantee Department	staatl. Exportkreditversicherung *(Großbrit.)*
hidden reminder	versteckte Mahnung
dunning letter	Mahnbrief
to suspend deliveries	Lieferungen einstellen
to withdraw credit privileges	den Lieferantenkredit entziehen
diplomatic or consular mission	diplomatische oder konsularische Vertretung
collection agency	Inkassobüro
extension	Stundung, Aufschub
payment on account	Abschlag-, Akontozahlung
amount owing	geschuldeter Betrag
to supply on a draft basis	auf Wechselbasis beliefern, gegen Akzept beliefern
prolongation	Verlängerung, Prolongation
interest	Zins(en)

10.2.3

application for payment	Zahlungsaufforderung, Mahnung
overdue balance	überfälliger Restbetrag

10.2.4

to clear a balance	einen Saldo ausgleichen

10.2.5

settlement on an amicable basis	gütliche Regelung, außergerichtliche Regelung
to institute legal proceedings	gerichtliche Schritte einleiten, Klage erheben

10.2.6

respite	Frist, Zahlungsaufschub

10.2.7

collection series	Mahnbriefreihe
to disregard	hier: als gegenstandslos betrachten
past-due account, overdue account	offenstehende Rechnung

10.2.9

slackness of trade	schlechter Geschäftsgang, Flaute
to dispose of	hier: verkaufen

10.2.10

short of cash	knapp bei Kasse
to negotiate a settlement of a strike	die Beilegung eines Streiks aushandeln
to accommodate sb.	jmd. entgegenkommen

10.4.1

mechanische Spielwaren	mechanical toys
sich eindecken	to stock up
Neuheit	novelty
überfällig	overdue
als gegenstandslos betrachten	to disregard

10.4.2

eine letzte Frist setzen	to fix a deadline
Leiter der Rechnungsabteilung	Head of the Accounts Department

10.4.3

unerwarteter Konkurs	unexpected bankruptcy
Liquiditätsprobleme bereiten	to cause liquidity problems
zuversichtlich sein	to be confident
in absehbarer Zeit	in the foreseeable future
Überziehungsperiode	overdraft period
Verständnis	understanding

10.4.9

Elektrowerkzeuge	electric tools
die Dokumente aufnehmen	to take up the documents
Gegenwert	countervalue
Zolllager	bonded warehouse
Bestimmungshafen	port of destination

11. Agencies and Distribution

foreign branch	ausländische Filiale
subsidiary	Tochtergesellschaft

11.1

foreign agent	Auslandsvertreter
foreign distributor	selbständiger Importeur, Vertragshändler im Ausland
commission agent	Handelsvertreter
consignee	Konsignatar, Verkaufskommissionär
principal	Prinzipal, Auftraggeber
on a commission basis	auf Provisionsbasis
to solicit orders	Aufträge einholen
to enter into contracts	Verträge schließen
after-sales service	Kundendienst
to settle disputes	Streitigkeiten schlichten
buying agent	Einkaufsvertreter
consignor	Konsignant
consignment stock	Konsignationslager
to render an account	eine Abrechnung vorlegen
account sales (A/S)	Verkaufsabrechnung
sales proceeds	Verkaufserlös
del credere commission	Delkredereprovision
solvency	Solvenz, Zahlungsfähigkeit
sole / exclusive agent	Allein-, Exklusivvertreter
agency agreement	Vertretervertrag
exclusive right of sale	Alleinverkaufsrecht
distributorship agreement	Händlervertrag
delegate	Delegierter
to be headed	geführt werden
branch manager	Filialleiter
to appoint	ernennen, bestimmen
legal entity	Rechtspersönlichkeit
to be set up	gegründet werden
majority of shares	Mehrheit der Geschäftsanteile, *bei AG auch:* Aktienkapital

parent company	Muttergesellschaft
assembling	Montage
production facilities	Produktionseinrichtungen
tariffs	hier: Zölle
import restrictions	Einfuhrbeschränkungen
aggregate duty	hier: Gesamtzoll
locational advantages	Standortvorteile
tax benefits	Steuervorteile
proximity	Nähe
to shift	verlagern
low-wage countries	Niedriglohnländer
to entail	nach sich ziehen
capital expenditure	Kapitalauslagen
treaty	(Staats-)Vertrag
export-credit insurance	Exportkreditversicherung
relief	(Steuer-)Erleichterung
income earned abroad	im Ausland verdientes Einkommen
double taxation agreements	Doppelbesteuerungsabkommen

11.2.1

Continental Europe	Kontinentaleuropa
weighing systems	Wiegevorrichtungen
authorized dealer	Vertragshändler
adequate maintenance and repair facilities	geeignete Wartungs- und Reparatureinrichtungen

11.2.2

to take into consideration	in Betracht ziehen
warehouse facilities	Lagereinrichtungen
staff	Belegschaft
backup services	Unterstützungsdienstleistungen
spares (spare parts)	Ersatzteile
replacement parts	Austauschteile

11.2.3

to get a foothold in the market	eine sichere Position im Markt bekommen
reputable	mit gutem Ruf, angesehen

11.2.4

traveller	Reisender
to insert	einschalten, inserieren
publication	Veröffentlichung
to furnish	hier: liefern, bereitstellen

11.2.5

cutlery	Schneidwaren, Essbesteck
tableware	Tischgeschirr

11.2.6

fruitful cooperation	fruchtbare Zusammenarbeit

11.2.7

registered office	eingetragener Firmensitz
hereinafter	im Nachfolgenden
term	hier: Dauer
terms and conditions	Bedingungen
notwithstanding the foregoing	ungeachtet des Vorstehenden
to reserve the right	sich das Recht vorbehalten
it being understood	wobei davon ausgegangen wird
confidentiality	Vertrauen
affiliate	hier: Tochtergesellschaft
without the prior written consent	ohne vorherige schriftliche Genehmigung
to disclose	bekanntmachen
promotional material	Werbematerial
on a case-by-case basis	auf der Basis von Fall zu Fall
to bear all expenses	alle Spesen tragen
for the benefit of	zum Nutzen von
to have no express or implied authority	keine ausdrückliche oder stillschweigende Befugnis haben
to assume or create any obligation	irgendeine Verpflichtung übernehmen oder schaffen
to misrepresent	falsch darstellen

independent contractor	unabhängiger Vertragspartner
to be deemed sb.	für jmd. gehalten werden
approval	Zustimmung, Genehmigung
remuneration	Entschädigung, Bezahlung
claim to commission	Provisionsanspruch
to become effective	gültig werden
all payments due	alle fälligen Zahlungen
without any reserve	ohne jede Einschränkung
cancellation	Stornierung
portion	Teil
termination	Beendigung
expiration	Auslaufen
prior to the date	vor dem Datum
the performance of his obligations hereunder	die Erfüllung seiner hierunter eingegangenen Verpflichtungen
out-of-pocket expenses	eigene Auslagen
initial period	Anfangszeitraum
thereafter	danach
with twelve months' prior notice	mit zwölfmonatiger vorheriger Kündigung
governing law	anwendbares Recht
disputes	Streitigkeiten
to settle amicably	gütlich regeln
controversy	Streitigkeit, Kontroverse
Rules of Arbitration	Schiedsgerichtsvorschriften
arbitration proceedings	Schiedsgerichtsverfahren
enforceable	vollstreckbar
award	(durch Schiedsspruch gefälltes) Urteil
mandatory provisions	zwingende Vorschriften
EU legislation	EU-Gesetzgebung
applicable	anwendbar

11.2.8

economic recovery	wirtschaftliche Erholung
compressor	Kompressor
revival in sales	Absatzbelebung
business upswing	Konjunkturaufschwung
recovery phase	Erholungsphase
minimum annual turnover	Mindest-Jahresumsatz
upsurge	Aufschwung
marginally higher	geringfügig höher, unwesentlich höher
comments	hier: Stellungnahme

11.2.9

price competition	Preiswettbewerb
to leave our stock temporarily depleted	unser Lager vorübergehend leerstehen lassen
to turn to other suppliers	sich an andere Lieferanten wenden
to lose sb.'s custom	jmd. als Kunden verlieren
for good	für immer
tardy	verspätet
hitch	Panne

11.2.10

to be on the spot	an Ort und Stelle sein
accessories	Zubehörteile
multi-lingual after-sales service	mehrsprachiger Kundendienst
skilled personnel	Fachpersonal

11.4.1

Fachverband für Sportartikel	Sports Equipment Trade Association
Golfausrüstung	golf equipment
Fuß fassen	to get a foothold
einschlägiger Großhandel	relevant wholesalers
Warenhäuser	department stores
Versandhäuser	mail order houses
Geschäftsführer	managing director
persönlich haftender Gesellschafter	personally liable shareholder
Ehrenmitglied	honorary member

11.4.2

Akkreditiveröffnung	opening of the L/C
Probleme lösen	to solve problems
kurzfristig	at short notice

unnötige Verzögerungen vermeiden	to avoid unnecessary delays
Gültigkeit	validity, duration
Quartalsabrechnung	quarterly account sales

11.4.3

Mindestumsatzvolumen	minimum sales volume
Rahmenauftrag	blanket order
abrufen	to call forward
bis auf Widerruf	until further notice
Verkaufsprognose	sales estimate

11.4.4

Warenwirtschaftssystem	material management system
Bestandsmeldung	stock report, inventory report
Datenübertragung	data transmission
Altbestände	old stocks
scannerfähig ausgezeichnet	to be scanner-readable

11.4.5

Transport- und Fördergeräte	transport and conveyor equipment
Gabelstapler	forklift truck

11.4.6

Camping- und Freizeitartikel	camping and leisure articles
Wanderstiefel	hiking boots
Rucksack	rucksack
Nachschub	new supplies

11.4.7

Segelboot	sailing boat
Motorboot	motorboat

11.4.8

Handelsregister	Registrar of Companies (GB)
Gesellschaftervertrag	Articles of Association
Zolllager	bonded warehouse
Zoll-Nummern	nomenclature numbers
Geschäftsräume	premises
Kaution	security deposit
Antrag	application form

12. Cooperation; Joint Ventures ...

cooperation	Zusammenarbeit, Kooperation
joint venture	Joint Venture
licensing	Lizenzvergabe
merger	Fusion
acquisition	Akquisition, Erwerb

12.1

obstacle	Hindernis
plant and machinery	Maschinen und Anlagen
with the appropriate skills	mit den geeigneten Fähigkeiten
intellectual property	geistiges Eigentum
across national boundaries	über nationale Grenzen hinweg
research and development	Forschung und Entwicklung
to share expenditure	Ausgaben teilen
licence holder	Lizenzinhaber
licensor	Lizenzgeber
licensee	Lizenznehmer
licence agreement	Lizenzvertrag
licence fee	Lizenzgebühr
royalty	Lizenz-, Nutzungsgebühr
patent attorney	Patentanwalt
Patent Office	Patentamt
cross-licensing arrangement	gegenseitiger Lizenzvertrag
marked increase	erheblicher Anstieg
amicable takeover	freundliche Übernahme
hostile takeover	feindliche Übernahme
leveraged buyout	*(mit Fremdkapital finanzierter)* Aufkauf
buy-in's	Einkauf *(in eine Firma)*
acquisition of majority shareholdings	Erwerb von mehrheitlichen Gesellschaftsanteilen
to spread risks	Risiken streuen
to cut down on staff	die Belegschaft reduzieren
to outsource parts of the production	Teile der Produktion ausgliedern
lay-offs	Freistellungen
disregard	hier: Missachtung
to accrue	hier: sich ergeben

standardized products	genormte Produkte
to endanger jobs	Arbeitsplätze gefährden

12.2.1

marketing arrangement	Vertriebsvereinbarung
reciprocal	gegenseitig
process automation	Verfahrensautomatisierung
stabilized power supplies	stabilisierte Stromversorgungsaggregate
microprocessor-based process monitoring and control systems	mit Mikroprozessoren ausgerüstete Regelungs- und Überwachungssysteme für Fertigungsabläufe
electronics assembly	Elektronikmontage
sheet-metal working	Blechverarbeitung
machining	hier: spanabhebende Bearbeitung
to be quality-approved to British Telecom and Ministry of Defence	den von BT und dem (brit.) Verteidigungsministerium aufgestellten Qualitätsnormen entsprechen
sales engineer	Verkaufsingenieur
collaborator	hier: Kooperationspartner
batch manufacturing	Serienfertigung
high-calibre	erstklassig
to circulate	durch Rundschreiben zur Kenntnis bringen
to reveal	preisgeben
consultation	hier: Rücksprache
assessment	hier: Auswertung

12.2.2

to license	hier: Lizenzen erwerben
economics	hier: die wirtschaftlichen Gegebenheiten
fire-alarm system	Feuermeldeanlage
signal	Signalgerät
timer	Zeitgeber
security equipment	Sicherungssysteme
national sales organization	hier: eine sich über das gesamte Gebiet der Vereinigten Staaten erstreckende Vertriebsorganisation
light industry	Leichtindustrie
annual sales	Jahresumsatz
medium and large-volume series	Mittel- und Groß-serien

12.2.3

to set up a plant	eine Fertigungsanlage errichten
self-sufficiency	Selbstversorgung
fuel efficiency	sparsamer Kraftstoffverbrauch
aggregate	Aggregat
power train	Kraftstrang
axle	Achse
ancillary industry	Zulieferindustrie
forgings	Schmiedeteile
castings	Gussteile
valve	Ventil
piston	Kolben
financial viability	Rentabilität

12.2.4

CKD kit (CKD = completely knocked down)	CKD-Bausatz (CKD = vollständig zerlegt)
component	(Einzel-)Teil
start-up phase	Anlaufphase
to fit out	ausrüsten
to signify one's agreement	sich bereit erklären
feasibility study	Durchführbarkeitsstudie
to capitalise	hier: in eine Kapitaleinlage umwandeln

12.2.5

to renegotiate the terms	die Bedingungen neu verhandeln
publicity activities	Werbeaktivitäten

12.4.1

Aktienmehrheit	majority of shares
Neuordnung	restructuring

12.4.2

Jahresbericht	annual report
„Außenwirtschaftsinformationen“	Foreign Trade Bulletin
Kammerbezirk	district of the Chamber of Commerce

12.4.3

Papierfabrik	paper mill
Impregnieranlage	paper-impregnating plant
Grammgewicht	weight in grammes
Rollenbreite	width of reel
Hülsendurchmesser	core diameter
Luftdurchlässigkeit	air permeability

12.4.4

rustikale Bauernmöbel	country-style furniture
in zerlegtem und verpacktem Zustand	in dismantled and wrapped condition
Schreinermeister	master cabinetmaker
Aufkleber	sticker

12.4.5

Solaranlagen	solar heating systems
Mindestlizenzgebühr	minimum license fee
Unterlizenz	sublicense
Nachfolgeerfindungen	subsequent inventions
Geheimhaltung	secrecy

13. Banking

13.1

financial intermediary	finanzieller (Ver-)Mittler
to safeguard money on deposit	deponiertes (hinterlegtes) Geld aufbewahren
borrower	Kreditnehmer
bearer cheque	Inhaberscheck
order cheque	Orderscheck
open cheque	Barscheck
crossed cheque	Verrechnungsscheck
giro or current account	Giro- oder laufendes Konto
standing order	Dauerauftrag
direct debiting	Lastschrifteinzug, Bankabbuchung
to withdraw money	Geld abheben
teller machine	Bankautomat
cash dispenser	Bargeldautomat
bill of exchange (B/E)	Wechsel
drawer	Wechselaussteller
at sight	auf Sicht
drawee	Wechselbezogener
to domicile	domizilieren, zahlbar stellen
day of maturity	Fälligkeitstag
to endorse	indossieren
endorser	Indossant
endorsee	Indossatar
letter of credit (L/C)	Akkreditiv
issuing bank	ausstellende (emittierende) Bank
to comply with	übereinstimmen mit
advising bank	avisierende Bank
confirmed L/C	bestätigtes Akkreditiv
irrevocable documentary L/C	unwiderrufliches Dokumentenakkreditiv
payment by collection	Zahlung durch Inkasso
documents against payment (D/P)	Zahlung gegen Dokumente
documents against acceptance (D/A)	Dokumente gegen Akzept
to grant an overdraft	einen Überziehungskredit gewähren
personal loan	persönlicher (privater) Kredit
corporate loan	Firmenkredit
mortgage	Hypothek
real estate	Immobilie(n)
retail customer	Privatkunde
corporate customer	Firmenkunde, Geschäftskunde
Stock Exchange	Börse
bonds	festverzinsliche Werte, Anleihe (titel)
debentures	(Industrie-)Obligationen
futures trading	Terminhandel
leasing and factoring transactions	Leasing- und Factoringgeschäfte
credit risk	Kreditrisiko

credit insurance	Kreditversicherung
performance bond	Erfüllungsgarantie
to check balances	Salden prüfen
to transfer funds	(Geld-)Mittel überweisen
internet portal	Internet-Portal
to automate the entire information flow	den gesamten Informationsfluss automatisieren
procurement	Beschaffung

13.2.1

convenience	Bequemlichkeit
to take the necessary steps	die notwendigen Schritte unternehmen

13.2.2

equivalent	hier: Gegenwert
as of today	mit dem heutigen Stand
asap (as soon as possible)	sobald wie möglich
whereabouts	Verbleib

13.2.3

to be domiciled	hier: ansässig sein
exchange risks	Devisenrisiken
to raise funds	(Geld-)Mittel aufbringen
to call	hier: vorbeikommen

13.2.4

credit line	Kreditlinie
unconditional	bedingungs-, vorbehaltslos
Security Bond	Sicherheitsgarantie
accrued interest	aufgelaufene Zinsen

13.2.5

credit enquiry agency	Auskunftei
consent	Einwilligung
nominal share capital	Nennwert-Stammkapital
outstanding debts	ausstehende Verbindlichkeiten
payment record	Zahlungsmoral
man of impeccable standing	Mann mit untadeligem Ruf
charitable institution	Wohlfahrtseinrichtung

13.2.6

beneficiary's draft at 60 days	Wechsel des Begünstigten mit 60-tägiger Laufzeit

13.2.7

partial shipment	Teilverschiffung
transshipment	Umladung
inflatable boat	Schlauchboot
commercial invoice	Handelsfaktura
full set of clean on-board bill of lading	voller Satz reiner Bordkonnossemente
master of the vessel	Kapitän des Schiffes
for onward delivery	zur weiteren Lieferung
to call at a port	einen Hafen anlaufen
on its current voyage	auf seiner gegenwärtigen (Schiffs-) Reise
indelible mark	unauslöschliche Markierung
reimbursement claim	Erstattungsforderung
discrepant documents	abweichende Dokumente
notwithstanding any instructions to the contrary	ungeachtet aller anders lautenden Anweisungen
to bear a date prior to the L/C date	ein Datum vor dem Datum des Akkreditivs aufweisen
date of issuance	Ausstellungsdatum
non-utilization	Nicht-Inanspruchnahme

13.4.1

Forfaitierung	non-recourse financing
ohne Rückgriff auf Sie	without recourse to you
zahlungsverpflichtete Bank	bank obliged to pay
Ankaufsbetrag	purchase amount
Gegenwert	countervalue
Höchstbetrag	maximum amount
Aufnahme von Dokumenten	acceptance of documents
Fälligkeit der Forderung	maturity of claim
Zahlstelle	place of payment

Diskontsatz	discount rate
Zinsfälligkeit	interest maturity
Bereitstellungsprovision	commitment commission
anfallende Zinsen	interest accrued
ausstehende Forderungen	outstanding claims
Nachzinsverpflichtung	obligation to pay extra interest
Akkreditivabwicklung	L/C transaction
Abtretung der Rechte und Ansprüche	assignment of rights and claims
Abtretungserklärung	declaration of assignment
offen legen	to disclose
Unstimmigkeitsprovision	discrepancy commission
Reimbourskosten	reimbursement costs
zu dem vollen geschuldeten Betrag	to the fully owed amount
ausdrückliche Zustimmung	explicit consent
Gewährleistungsverpflichtung	warranty obligation
Einrede	plea
Einwendung	objection
aufrechnen	hier: to set off
Zurückbehaltungsrecht	right of retention
geltend machen	to claim, to put forward
Rüstungsgüter	arms
verlängerter Eigentumsvorbehalt	prolonged reservation of title (ownership)
verpfändet	pledged
gerichtlicher und außergerichtlicher Art	of judicial and extrajudicial kind
zur Durchsetzung unserer Ansprüche	for the enforcement of our claims
Offenlegung der Abtretung	disclosure of assignment
Arrest	seizure
einstweilige Verfügung	injunction
zurückübertragen	to re-assign
zurückerstatten	to refund
rechtsverbindlich unterzeichnet	signed in legally binding form

13.4.2

in voller Höhe	to the full amount
mit allen damit verbundenen Neben- und Vorzugsrechten	with all accessory and preferential rights
Zusicherung	promise
Allgemeine Geschäftsbedingungen	General Conditions of Business
Einheitliche Richtlinien und Gebräuche für Dokumentenakkreditive der Internationalen Handelskammer (Publ. 500)	ICC Uniform Customs and Practice for Documentary Credits (UCP 500)

13.4.3

harte Patronatserklärung	hard letter of comfort
Eintragung einer Grundschuld	registration of a land charge
Grundbesitz	real estate
Bilanzen	balance sheets
Gewinn- und Verlustrechrechnungen	profit and loss accounts

13.4.4

notariell beglaubigt	authenticated by a notary public
Gründungsurkunde	Memorandum of Association
Satzung	Statutes
Registrierungsbestätigung	Certificate of Incorporation
verfügungsberechtigt	authorized to dispose
unterschriftsberechtigt	authorized to sign

14. Transport and Forwarding

forwarding	Versand, Beförderung

14.1.

forwarding agent	Spediteur
carrier	Verfrachter, Beförderungsunternehmer
to collect goods	Waren abholen
grouped consignment, consolidated shipment	Sammelladung
shipping charges	Versand-(Verschiffungs-)gebühren
freight	Fracht, Frachtgebühr
shipping company	Reederei, Schifffahrtsgesellschaft, Seespediteur
shipping documents	Versand-(Verschiffungs-)dokumente
bill of lading	Konnossement
consular invoice	Konsulatsfaktura
certificate of origin	Ursprungszeugnis
certificate of value and weight	Wert- und Gewichtsnota
insurance policy	Versicherungspolice
customs formalities	Zollformalitäten
bonded warehouse	Warenzollverschlusslager
perishable	verderblich
to imply certain risks	gewisse Risiken mit sich bringen
peak hour traffic	Verkehr zu Spitzenzeiten
haulage	Lkw-Transport
haulier	Lkw-Spediteur
over-congested roads	überfüllte Straßen
motorway	Autobahn (BE)
highway	Autobahn (AE)
containerisation	Container-Transport
harbour	Hafen
transport by inland waterways	Transport auf dem Binnenschifffahrtsweg
in bulk	in großen Mengen
liner	Linienschiff
tramp ship	Trampschiff
roll-on-roll-off ferry	Ro-Ro-Fähre
consignment note (waybill)	Frachtbrief
airway bill	Luftfrachtbrief
document of title	Besitz-, Eigentumsurkunde, Traditions-, Übergabepapier
charter party	Charterpartie
voyage	(See-)Reise
voyage charter	Reisecharter
time charter	Zeitcharter
unitized freight	in Einheiten verpackte Fracht
pallet	Palette
cargo policy	Frachtpolice
insurable interest	versicherbares Interesse
contract of sale	Kaufvertrag
Lloyd's underwriter	Lloyd's-Versicherer
premium	Prämie
to compensate	entschädigen
damage or loss caused to the insured property	dem versicherten Besitz zugefüger Schaden oder Verlust
insurance certificate	Versicherungszertifikat
valued policy	Police mit Wertangabe
floating policy	Abschreibe-, Pauschalversicherung
to take out insurance	eine Versicherung abschließen
marine insurance	Seeversicherung
free of particular average	ohne besondere Havarie
with particular average	mit besonderer Havarie
general average	allgemeine Havarie
major perils	größere Gefahren
minor perils of the sea	geringere Gefahren auf See
ship's sweat	Schiffsschweiß
theft	Diebstahl
rough handling	rauhe Behandlung
burglary	Einbruch(sdiebstahl)

14.2.1

vineyard	Weingut

14.2.2

metric tonne	metrische Tonne
at steamer's option	hier: nach Option der Reederei

lay days	Liegetage
sailing card	Schifffahrtsplan
to commence	beginnen
demurrage	Überliegegeld
charter party	Charterpartie

14.2.3

to rank (among)	gehören, zählen (zu)
expertise	Sachkenntnis
door-to-door delivery	Lieferung von Haus zu Haus
general cargo	Stückgüter
to consolidate	hier: Sammelladungen zusammenstellen, konsolidieren
consolidation	hier: Sammelverkehr

14.2.4

lamp-bulb making plant	Anlage zur Herstellung von Glühlampen
conveyance	Beförderung
rate structure	(Fracht-)Tarifstruktur, Ratenstruktur
mode of conveyance	Beförderungsart
to entail costs	Kosten verursachen

14.2.5

ID (= Immediate Delivery) Entry	Antrag auf Abfertigung zur sofortigen Auslieferung
bond fee	Gebühr für die Zolllagerung
import duty	Einfuhrzoll
as per outlay	gemäß Auslage
special messenger	Eilbote
customs examination charge	Zollprüfungsgebühren
trucking charge	Lkw-Fracht, Gebühr für die Lkw-Beförderung

14.2.6

fertiliser	Düngemittel, Kunstdünger
in bulk and in bags	lose und in Säcken
to fix a time charter	eine Zeitcharter abschließen
... should, fully loaded, be capable of steaming ... knots	... sollte bei voller Beladung eine Fahrtgeschwindigkeit von ... Knoten erreichen
classification society	Klassifikationsgesellschaft

14.2.7

through container service	direkter (durchgehender) Containerdienst
slots	hier: freier Stauraum
sailing	Abfahrt
agency network	Agenturnetz
trades	hier: Relationen, Fahrtgebiete
cargo bookings	Frachtbuchungen
to avail ones. of sth.	sich einer Sache bedienen

14.2.9

bill of lading	Konnossement
commercial invoice	Handelsfaktura
packing list	Packliste
master of the vessel	Schiffskapitän
for onward delivery	zur Weiterleitung

14.2.10

to commission	beauftragen
rolling stock	rollendes Material
signalling equipment	Signalgerät(e)
steel rail	Stahlschiene
freight wagon	Güterwagen
since ... will make up the bulk of the total amount ...	da ... den größten Teil des Gesamtbetrages ausmacht
to provide cover	Deckung gewähren
rust and oxidation	Rost und Oxydation
SR & CC (= strikes, riots and civil commotions)	Streik, Aufruhr und innere Unruhen
discharge	Entladung, Löschen

14.2.11

sea water	Seewasser
survey	hier: Schadensbericht
average adjuster	Havariekommissar
to place a claim	eine Schadensforderung anmelden
ship broker	Schiffsmakler

14.2.12

cubicles for communication equipment	Standschränke für Kommunikations-einrichtungen
claim report	Schadensmeldung
survey feeds	Schadenbesich-tigungsgebühren
insurance declaration	Versicherungs-meldung

14.2.13

swing frame	Schwenkrahmen
module	Modul
to commission	in Betrieb nehmen
holding rack	Haltegestell

14.2.14

blank parts	leere Stellen
sea voyage	Seereise

14.4.1

Prüfzertifikat	call-forward notice
Speditionsauftrag	forwarding order

14.4.2

Gemeinschaftsdienst	joint service
Verlader	shipper
Ablader *(Seehafen-spediteur)*	shipping forwarder
Ladehafen	loading port
Umladung	reloading
Ladungsangebot	loading capacity

14.4.3

Seeversicherungs-schaden	sea average
Schadensmeldung	average claim
Elektrokabel	electrical cable
Havariezertifikat	average certificate
Gutachter	hier: average adjuster
unsachgemäß	inappropriately
Laderaum des Schiffes	ship's hold
Schadensregulierung	settlement of the claim

14.4.4

chemische Apparatur	chemical apparatus
zollamtliche Abfertigung	customs clearance
Zollabfertigungs-gebühren	clearance charges

14.4.5

Folie	foil
Bänder	strapping
Handhabung der Dokumente	handling of the documents

14.4.6

Deckung aller Risiken	coverage of all risks
Versicherungs-deckung	insurance cover
Rechnungswert	invoice amount

15. Trade Fairs and Exhibitions

trade fair	Handelsmesse
exhibition	Ausstellung
hotel accommo-dation	Unterbringung im Hotel

15.1

to cater for	hier: bedienen, beliefern
trade buyer	Facheinkäufer
industry	hier: Branche
the Motor Show	Automobilaus-stellung
to display	ausstellen
hotel and catering trade	Hotel- und Gast-stättengewerbe
GDP (gross domestic product)	BIP (Bruttoinlands-produkt)
convention	Zusammenkunft, (Fach-)Kongress
vicinity	Nähe, Nachbarschaft
venue	hier: Ort, Platz

15.2.1

single room	Einzelzimmer
groupage rate	Gruppentarif

15.2.2

on departure of the guests	bei Abreise der Gäste

15.2.3

to put the finishing touches on ...	letzte Hand anlegen an ...
pavilion	Pavillon

biennial trade fair	im zweiährigen Turnus stattfindende Fachmesse
space	(Ausstellungs-) Fläche

15.2.4

to reserve prime space	Ausstellungsfläche in erstklassiger Lage reservieren
British Ceramic Plant and Machinery Manufacturers Federation	Verband der britischen Hersteller von Maschinen und Anlagen für die keramische Industrie
to back financially	finanziell unterstützen
British Overseas Trade Board (BOTB)	staatliche britische Außenhandelsförderungsstelle
to prejudice	beeinträchtigen
plan of the layout of stands	Übersichtsplan
rates	(Gebühren-)Sätze
exhibition contractor	Messebaufirma, Standbaufirma
to design	konstruieren
to erect a stand	einen (Messe-)Stand errichten

15.2.5

trade section	Handelsabteilung
organizer	Veranstalter
Overseas Import Fair "Partners for Progress"	Übersee-Import-Messe „Partner des Fortschritts“
craftsman	Handwerker
pottery	Töpferwaren
wood sculptures	Holzschnitzereien
genuine	echt
artisan	(Kunst-)Handwerker

15.4.1

Ausstellungshalle	exhibition hall
Rohstoffe	raw materials
Farben	dyes
Glasuren	glazes
Anmeldeformular	application form
Platzwunsch	wish for a specific location
Einzelaussteller	individual exhibitor
Gemeinschaftsstand	joint stand
Mietpreis	rental price
Lieferantennachweis	list of suppliers
Standbaufirma	stand builder

15.5.2

Anmeldeschluss	registration deadline
Brancheneinteilung	division into industrial sectors

15.5.3

Eilanfrage	urgent enquiry
Luxussuite	luxury suite
Marmorbad	marble bathroom
Badewanne	bathtub
Arbeitsraum	study

15.5.4

Pauschal-Messe- und Kundenrabatt	all-inclusive fair and customer discount
Büfettfrühstück	buffet breakfast
Nichtraucherraum	non-smoking room

15.5.5

Sammelbestellung	collective order

15.5.6

Bühne	stage
Flutlicht	floodlight(s)
Bühnenbeleuchtung	stage lighting
Teppichfliesen	carpet tiles
ovaler Tisch	oval chair
gepolsterte Stühle	upholstered chairs
fließendes warmes und kaltes Wasser	running hot and cold water
Steckdosen	sockets
Bürokommunikationsanschlüsse	office communication connections
Prospektständer	literature rack
Überwachungskamera	security camera

16. Office Communication

office communication	Bürokommunikation

16.1

in-house communication	innerbetriebliche Kommunikation

to record information	Informationen aufzeichnen
to gather statistical data	statistische Daten sammeln
graph	Grafik
to duplicate	hier: kopieren, vervielfältigen
to extract data	hier: Daten abrufen
commercial clerk	Sachbearbeiter(in)
EDP (electronic data processing)	EDV (elektronische Datenverarbei-tung)
redundant	hier: überflüssig
to monitor	überwachen
security	Sicherheit
stock control	Lagerkontrolle
foreign language correspondent	Fremdsprachen-korrespondent(in)
P.A. (personal assistant)	persönliche(r) Assistent(in)
company executive	leitende(r) Mitar-beiter(in) in einer Firma
comprehensive	umfassend, umfang-reich
letters of appreciation	hier: Dankschreiben
sympathy	Mitgefühl
condolescence	Beileid, Kondolenz
in-house memorandum	innerbetriebliche Aktennotiz
to be confined to	beschränkt sein auf

16.2.1

survey	Studie
printing requirements	Druckbedarf
form	hier: Formular
to be fed into the computer writing program	in das Computer-Schreibprogramm eingespeist werden
to cut costs	Kosten sparen

16.2.3

to call on so.	jmd. besuchen

16.2.5

impending	bevorstehend
acquaintance	Bekanntschaft
to make other arrangements	anders disponieren
schedule	Terminplan

16.2.9

presentation	Präsentation, Vorführung
device	Gerät
overnight stay	Übernachtung
return flight	Rückflug
surroundings	Umgebung

16.2.10

to be due for dispatch	versandbereit sein
to take steps	Schritte unter-nehmen
to get sth. crated	etwas in Kisten ver-packt bekommen
to look after the paper work	sich um den Papier-kram kümmern
top priority	höchste Priorität

16.2.11

to be appointed to the managing board	in den Vorstand (einer deutschen AG) berufen werden

16.4.1

Muster	sample
im Computersystem speichern	to store in the computer system
Verbesserungs-vorschlag	proposal for improvement
das von Ihnen gewählte Logo unseres Firmen-emblems	the version of our company logo selected by you
sperrig	bulky
sinnvoll	sensible

16.4.3

Nachfolgerin	successor
den Posten übernehmen	to take over the position
unsere besten Wünsche über-mitteln	to convey our best wishes
aufrechterhalten	to maintain

16.4.4

gute Aufnahme	friendly reception
lohnenswert	worthwhile
Anregung	idea
durchsprechen	to discuss

16.4.5

Gesamtumsatz	total sales
Lagerbestand	stocks
zur Neige gehen	to run low
Nachschub brauchen	to need new supplies
Vorabinformationen	preliminary information
Provision	commission

16.4.6

Lektor	lecturer
Gastfreundschaft	hospitality
sehr angetan sein	to be favourably impressed
verwerten	hier: to make good use of
jmd. ansprechen	to contact sb.

16.4.7

Autounfall	car accident
sich einer Operation unterziehen	to undergo an operation
sich schonen	to look after ones.
nochmals gute Besserung wünschen	to wish a speedy recovery once more

17. Job Applications

job applications	Bewerbungen um einen Arbeitsplatz

17.1

letter of application	Bewerbungs-schreiben
(un)solicited application	(un)verlangte Bewerbung
private employment agency	private Arbeitsver-mittlungsagentur
employment exchange (job centre)	(Vermittlungsstelle beim) Arbeitsamt
executives	Führungskräfte
off-chance	hier: Möglichkeit
opening	offene Stelle
CV = curriculum vitae (personal data sheet / résumé)	Lebenslauf
applicant	Bewerber(in)
training	Ausbildung
to be shortlisted	in die engere Wahl kommen
personal interview	persönliches Vor-stellungsgespräch
personnel manager	Personalchef
psychologist	Psychologe
aptitude test	Eignungstest

17.2.1

tri-lingual receptionist	dreisprachige Empfangsperson
booking clerk	Buchungsange-stellte(r)
"A" level	etwa: Abitur (GB)
challenge	Herausforderung

17.2.2

a demonstrated ability	eine nachgewiesene Fähigkeit
native-level English	Englisch auf mutter-sprachlichem Niveau
within tight production deadlines	innerhalb von engen Produktionstermi-nen
administrative experience	Verwaltungserfah-rung
pre-selected candidates	in die Vorauswahl gelangte Kandida-ten
to make explicit reference to	sich ausdrücklich beziehen auf

17.2.4

secondary school	höhere Schulbildung
to graduate (from)	die Abschluss-prüfung bestehen, absolvieren
traineeship	hier: Praktikum
commercial clerk	Sachbearbeiter(in)
department store	Kaufhaus
permanently employed	fest angestellt

17.2.6

occupational goal	Berufsziel
commercial agent	Handelsvertreter(in)
traineeship	hier: Lehre
a recognised qualification	eine anerkannte Qualifikation
wholesale and export sales clerk	Groß- und Außenhandelskaufmann
high school	höhere Schule (AE)
mountaineering	Bergsteigen
canoeing	Kanu fahren

17.2.7

to take minutes	Protokoll aufnehmen
to organise in-house conferences	innerbetriebliche Konferenzen organisieren
to have an excellent command of	ausgezeichnet beherrschen
to be thoroughly familiar with	genau vertraut sein mit
conscientious	gewissenhaft
departure	hier: Ausscheiden

17.2.8

salary records	Gehaltsaufzeichnungen
deductions	hier: abzugsfähige Beträge
company reports	Firmenberichte
administrative headquarters locations	Standorte der Hauptverwaltung
local authorities	Kommunalbehörden
social security	Sozialversicherung
pension plan	Pensionsplan
tax matters	Steuersachen
new hires	hier: Neueinstellungen
processing of accounting officer expense statements	Bearbeiten von Spesenabrechnungen der Rechnungsführer

17.4.1

ein Urteil abgeben	to give one's opinion
Ersatzteilaufträge	order for spare parts
Produktpalette	product range
im Zuge von	in the course of
Kollegialität	loyalty to one's colleagues
Gruppenverhalten	group behaviour

17.4.2

hausinterner Schulungskurs	in-house training course
Textverarbeitung	word processing
ein gutes Sprachgefühl besitzen	to have a good feeling for languages

17.4.3

Wegbeschreibung	route description
Eignungstest	aptitude test
die in die engere Wahl gekommenen Kandidaten	the shortlisted candidates

17.4.5

Führungsqualitäten	management qualities
Stammkapital	capital stock
nach Bewährung	after a probation period
zusätzliche Vergünstigungen	additional fringe benefits

18.2 Alphabetical Vocabulary

Alphabetical list (English-German) of the most important commercial, economic and commercial-law terms used in this book.

A	
acceptance	Annahme
account	Konto, Rechnung, Abrechnung
account sales (A/S)	Verkaufsabrechnung
account terms	Zahlungsziel
acknowledgement	Auftragsbestätigung *(Bestätigung der Bestellungsannahme)*
acquisition	Akquisition, Erwerb
act of God	unabwendbares Naturereignis
adjustment	Berichtigung, Korrektur, Beilegung (eines Streitfalls); (Schadens-) Regulierung
adjustment of complaint	Bereinigung der Beschwerde
advance	Vorschuss; kurzfristiges Darlehen
advance order	Vorausbestellung
to advertise	inserieren, werben (für)
advertisement (ad)	Anzeige, Inserat
advertising	Werbung
advice	Rat, Mitteilung
~ note, ~of despatch	Versandanzeige
~ of payment	Zahlungsavis
shipping ~	Versandanzeige, Verschiffungsanzeige
after-sales service	Kundendienst
agency agreement	Vertretervertrag
agency report	Bericht einer Auskunftei
agent	Agent, Vertreter
airway bill	Luftfrachtbrief
allowance	(Beanstandungs-) Nachlass; Gewährung
amendment	Änderung
annual report	Jahresbericht
annual sales	Jahresumsatz
applicant	Bewerber
application	Bewerbung
appointment	Ernennung; Termin
arbitration clause	Schiedsklausel
arbitrator	Schiedsrichter
Articles of Association	Gesellschaftervertrag
assignment	Abtretung
to authorize	ermächtigen
authorized dealer	Vertragshändler
authorized to dispose	verfügungsberechtigt
authorized to sign	unterschriftsberechtigt
B	
balance	Saldo, Kontostand
to balance	ausgleichen
balance sheets	Bilanzen
bank charges	Bankgebühren
bank reference	Bankreferenz
banker's draft	Bankscheck
by banker's transfer	durch Banküberweisung
bankruptcy	Konkurs
bill	Wechsel
clean ~	nichtdokumentärer Wechsel
documentary ~	dokumentärer Wechsel
to honour a ~	einen Wechsel einlösen, bezahlen
bill of exchange (B/E)	Wechsel
bill of lading	Konnossement
board (board of directors)	Vorstand
bonded warehouse	Warenzollverschlusslager
bonds	festverzinsliche Werte, Anleihe(titel)
borrower	Kreditgeber
branch	Filiale

buyer risk	wirtschaftliches Risiko
buying agent	Einkaufsvertreter

C

cancellation	Stornierung
cancellation charges	Stornierungskosten
carrier	Frachtführer
caution marks	Vorsichtsmarkierungen
certificate of insurance	Versicherungszertifikat
certificate of origin	Ursprungszeugnis
chairman of the board	Vorstandsvorsitzender
to charge	in Rechnung stellen
cheque (AE check)	Scheck
bearer ~	Inhaberscheck
crossed ~	Verrechnungsscheck
open ~	Barscheck
order ~	Orderscheck
to claim damages	Schadenersatzansprüche stellen
clearance costs	Zollabfertigungskosten
collection agency	Inkassobüro
collection letter	Mahnbrief
collective order	Sammelbestellung
commercial invoice	Handelsfaktura
commercial risk, buyer risk	wirtschaftliches Risiko
commission	Provision
commission agent	Handelsvertreter
to compensate	entschädigen
competitive	wettbewerbsfähig
complaint	Beschwerde, Reklamation
adjustment of ~	Bereinigung der Beschwerde
confidential	vertraulich
consequential damages	Folgeschäden
consignee	Konsignatar, Verkaufskommissionär
consignment goods	Konsignationswaren
consignment note	Frachtbrief
consignment stock	Konsignationslager
consignor	Konsignant
consular invoice	Konsulatsfaktura
contract	Vertrag
breach of ~	Vertragsbruch
cooperation	Zusammenarbeit, Kooperation
corporate body	Körperschaft
corporation (AE)	Gesellschaft
court of arbitration	Schiedsgericht
court of law	(ordentliches) Gericht
court hearing	Gerichtsverhandlung
court judgement	Gerichtsurteil
credit	Kredit
~ application form	Kreditantragsformular
~ enquiry	Kreditanfrage
~ enquiry agency (AE commercial agency)	Auskunftei
~ insurance	Kreditversicherung
~ line	Kreditrahmen
~ note	Gutschrift
~ period	Zahlungsfrist
~ rating	Bewertung der Kreditwürdigkeit
~ risk	Kreditrisiko
~ standing	Kreditwürdigkeit
creditor	Gläubiger
creditworthy	kreditwürdig
currency	Währung
current assets	Umlaufvermögen
current liabilities	kurzfristige Verbindlichkeiten
customer	Kunde
corporate ~	Firmenkunde, *im Bankwesen:* Geschäftskunde
retail ~	*im Bankwesen:* Privatkunde
customs clearance	Zollabfertigung
customs duties	Zollgebühren
CV (curriculum vitae)	Lebenslauf

D

date of issuance	Ausstellungsdatum
deadline	letzter Termin
debit note	Lastschrift
debtor	Schuldner
del credere	Delkredere
delegate	Delegierter
delivery schedule	Lieferzeitplan
deposit	Anzahlung
despatch, dispatch	Versand

despatch advice	Versandavis, Versandanzeige
discount	Nachlass
dispute	Streitfall
distributorship agreement	Händlervertrag
document of title	Dispositionspapier
documents against payment (D/P)	Zahlung gegen Dokumente
documents against acceptance (D/A)	Dokumente gegen Akzept
double taxation agreements	Doppelbesteuerungsabkommen
draft	Tratte
drawee	Wechselbezogener
drawer	Wechselaussteller
dunning letter	Mahnbrief

E

E. & O. E. (errors and omissions excepted)	Irrtümer und Auslassungen vorbehalten
encumbrance	(dingliche) Belastung, Schuldenbelastung
to endorse	indossieren
endorser	Indossant
endorsee	Indossatar
entry	Buchung
estate agent	Immobilienmakler
exchange rate	Wechselkurs
exhibition	Ausstellung
to expire	auslaufen, ungültig werden
export-credit insurance	Exportkreditversicherung
extension	Stundung, Aufschub

F

fair	Messe
feasibility study	Durchführbarkeitsstudie
finacial status	Vermögenslage
force majeure	höhere Gewalt
foreign agent	Auslandsvertreter
foreign distributor	selbständiger Importeur, Vertragshändler im Ausland
foreign exchange	Devisen
forwarding agent	Spediteur
free of charge	kostenlos

G

general cargo	Stückgüter
General Conditions of Business	Allgemeine Geschäftsbedingungen
grouped consignment	Sammelladung

H

haulage	Lkw-Transport
haulier	Lkw-Spediteur

I

import licence	Importlizenz
import restriction	Einfuhrbeschränkung
indent	Indent, Auftrag
in-house communication	innerbetriebliche Kommunikation
injunction	einstweilige Verfügung
insolvency	Insolvenz, Zahlungsunfähigkeit
insurance certificate	Versicherungszertifikat
intellectual property	geistiges Eigentum
interest	Zins(en)
internet portal	Internet-Portal
invoice	Rechnung, Faktura

J

joint venture	Joint Venture

L

lawsuit	Prozess
legal action	Klage
legal entity	Rechtspersönlichkeit
letter of application	Bewerbungsschreiben
letter of credit (L/C)	Akkreditiv
confirmed ~	bestätigtes Akkreditiv
irrevocable documentary ~	unwiderrufliches Dokumentenakkreditiv
letter of intent	Kaufabsichtserklärung
liability	Haftung
to be liable	haftbar sein
licence agreement	Lizenzvertrag
licence fee	Lizenzgebühr
licence holder	Lizenzinhaber

to license	Lizenzen vergeben oder erwerben
licensee	Lizenznehmer
licensing	Lizenzvergabe
licensor	Lizenzgeber
liquidated damages	Konventionalstrafe
litigation	Rechtsstreit, Prozess
Lloyd's agent	Lloyd's-Agent *(für L. tätiger Havariekommissar)*
loan	Darlehen, Kredit
personal ~	persönlicher (privater) Kredit
corporate ~	Firmenkredit
location	Standort

M

maintenance	Wartung
majority of shares	Mehrheit der Geschäftsanteile, *bei AGs auch:* Aktienkapital
marking instructions	Markierungsanweisungen
marine and war risk insurance certificate	See- und Kriegsrisikoversicherungszertifikat
mate's receipt	Steuermannsquittung
maturity	Fälligkeit
merger	Fusion
mortgage	Hypothek

N

negligence	Fahrlässigkeit
net worth	Eigenkapital
nominal share capital	Nennwert-Stammkapital
non-negotiable	nicht begebbar, nicht übertragbar
non-performance (of a contract)	Nicht-Erfüllung (eines Vertages)
non-recourse financing	Forfaitierung

O

offer	Angebot
firm ~	Festangebot
solicited ~	verlangtes Angebot
unsolicited ~	unverlangtes Angebot
offeree	Angebotsempfänger
offeror	Anbieter
officer	Mitglied der Unternehmensleitung, Vorstandsmitglied
omission	Auslassung
order	Bestellung, Auftrag
advance ~	Vorausbestellung
first ~, initial ~	Erstauftrag
repeat ~, follow-up ~	Nachbestellung
standing ~	Dauerauftrag
to place an ~	einen Auftrag erteilen
to solicit ~s	Aufträge einholen
order data	Auftragsdaten
ordinary partnership according to German law	oHG (offene Handelsgesellschaft)
overdraft period	Überziehungsperiode

P

parent company	Muttergesellschaft
partner	Partner, Gesellschafter
general ~	Komplementär
limited ~	Kommanditist
past-due account, overdue account	offen stehende Rechnung
patent attorney	Patentanwalt
Patent Office	Patentamt
penalty	Strafe
performance	Leistung, Ergebnis, Erfolg; (Vertrags-)Erfüllung
delayed ~	verspätete Erfüllung
non-performance	Nicht-Erfüllung
plant and machinery	Maschinen und Anlagen
policy	(Versicherungs-)-Police
political risk	politisches Risiko
port of destination	Bestimmungshafen
principal	Prinzipal, Auftraggeber
private limited company (plc)	*etwa:* GmbH
procurement	Beschaffung
prolongation	Verlängerung, Prolongation

Q

quantity discount	Mengenrabatt
quotation	(Preis-)Angabe, Angebot

R

rating	Beurteilung, Bewertung
real estate	Grundbesitz, Immobilien
records	Aufzeichnungen, Geschäftsbücher
to refund	ersetzen, erstatten
registered office	eingetragener Firmensitz
Registrar of Companies (GB)	Handelsregister
reimbursement	Erstattung
reminder	Mahnung
remittance	Überweisung, Übermittlung *(einer Zahlung)*
~ advice	Zahlungsanzeige
remuneration	Entschädigung, Bezahlung
replacement	Ersatz (ähnliches Produkt)
research and development	Forschung und Entwicklung
reservation clause	Vorbehaltsklausel
respite	Frist, Zahlungsaufschub
résumé (AE)	Lebenslauf
roll-on-roll-off ferry	Ro-Ro-Fähre
royalty	Lizenz-, Nutzungsgebühr

S

sales agreement, sales contract	Kaufvertrag
sales proceeds	Verkaufserlös
schedule	Terminplan
seaworthy packaging	seemäßige Verpackung
Security Bond	Sicherheitsgarantie
shareholdings	Gesellschaftsanteile
shipment	Lieferung
shipping company	Reederei, Schifffahrtsgesellschaft, Seespediteur
shipping documents	Versand- (Verschiffungs-)dokumente
shortfall	Differenz, Fehlmenge
sole / exclusive agent	Alleinvertreter
sole distributor	Alleinvertreiber
solvency	Solvenz, Zahlungsfähigkeit
statement of account	Kontoauszug
Stock Exchange	Börse
stock control system	Lagerkontrollsystem
stockist	Lagerhalter
stocks	Lagerbestand
strike	Streik
subrogation	(Rechts-)Abtretung
subsidiary	Tochtergesellschaft
substitute	Ersatz (gleiches Produkt)
supplier	Lieferant
supply and demand	Angebot und Nachfrage
survey report	Havariezertifikat

T

takeover	Übernahme
amicable ~	freundliche Übernahme
hostile ~	feindliche Übernahme
tariffs	hier: Zölle
tax	Steuer
tax benefits	Steuervorteile
trade buyer	Facheinkäufer
transfer of risk	Gefahrenübergang
turnover tax identification number	Umsatzsteuer-Identifikationsnummer

U

unit price	Einzelpreis, Stückpreis

V

validity	Gültigkeit
VAT (value added tax)	Mehrwertsteuer
vendor	Verkäufer, Lieferant
venue, place of jurisdiction	Gerichtsstand

W

warehouse facilities	Lagereinrichtungen
to warrant sth.	Garantie für etw. übernehmen
warranty	Garantie
warranty clause	Garantieklausel
waybill	Frachtbrief
wholesale price	Großhandelspreis

Abbreviations

AE	American English
BE	British English
ones.	oneself
sb.	somebody
so.	someone
sth.	something
etw.	etwas
jmd.	jemandem; jemanden

19. Glossary of Commercial Terms

acceptance
See *bill of exchange* and *documents against acceptance*.

agent
A person with authority to act for a principal.

airway bill. See *bill*.

arbitration
The settlement of commercial disputes between the parties to a contract by one or more arbitrators, whose decision – called the award – is final. A well-known court of arbitration is that of the International Chamber of Commerce in Paris.

asset and liability statement
American expression for the British *balance sheet*.

automated cash dispenser
(or **automated teller machine**)
Computerised terminal providing cash dispensing and deposit acceptance for banking transactions. ATM terminals provide individuals with 24-hour electronic access to their banking accounts without a bank cashier or bank teller.

average
Loss or damage incurred in a transport by sea. Experts who deal with such cases are called **average adjusters**.

B2B – business to business
Communication among businesses or companies, as opposed to customers or consumers.

B2C – business to consumer
Communication between companies and their customers.

balance sheet
Financial statement that gives an accounting picture of the position of a company on a specific date for a specific period, usually a financial year. It is divided into assets and liabilities.

bank or **banker's transfer**
A transfer of money from one bank account to another. This is mostly done by **SWIFT** (Society for Worldwide Interbank Financial Telecommunications), an interbank telecommunications network for confirming international funds transfers.

bankruptcy
Insolvent debtors, or their creditors, may file a petition in bankruptcy with the proper court. If the court finds sufficient proof of insolvency, the debtor is adjudged a bankrupt. The bankrupt's assets are placed under the control of the official receiver, pending the appointment of a trustee in bankruptcy by the creditors.

bill
In commercial law, an account for goods sold, services rendered and work done. Another word for *invoice*.

In the law of negotiable instruments, any form of paper money.

In legislation, a draft of proposed statute submitted to the legislature for enactment.

airway bill. Document of transport for goods transported by air.

bill of exchange (B/E). Defined in the Bills of Exchange Act as follows: "An unconditional order in writing, addressed by one person to another, signed by the person giving it, it requiring the person to whom it is addressed to pay on demand, or at a fixed or determinable future time, a sum certain in money to or to the order of a specified person or to bearer." This definition covers both cheque and draft, but in practice the term "bill of exchange" or "bill" is applied to drafts only.

A bill of exchange has three parties: the drawer (the person making out the bill), the drawee (the person directed to pay) and the payee (the person who is to get the money). The payee may be the drawer himself or a third party. The drawee has to accept the bill (unless it is a sight bill) by writing his name across its face. He thus becomes the acceptor, and the draft is turned into an acceptance.

A **sight bill** is payable when it is presented to the drawee. **Time bills** are payable on a fixed future date, the date of maturity.

Bills can be used in the following ways: They can be kept until they are due for payment; they can be discounted at banks; they can be endorsed, ie passed from the endorser to the endorsee by means of an endorsement. You can domicile a B/E eg with a bank, which means the bank presents the B/E to the drawee on its date of maturity. Should the drawee be unable to pay, the bill "bounces", is protested or dishonoured.

bill of lading (B/L). A document issued when goods are entrusted to a shipping company for conveyance by sea. It has three principal characteristics: 1. it is a formal receipt issued by the carrier for the goods in question; 2. it is a document of title giving the authorized holder the right to claim the goods on arrival; 3. it is a document evidencing the contract of carriage. Bills of lading are issued in a set, usually consisting of three originals signed by the master of the ship or another authorized person on behalf of the shipping company. The master is instructed to deliver the goods on presentation of any of the originals. When the goods have been released on the strength of one of the originals, the others become void.

There are "shipped" bills of lading and "received for shipment" bills of lading. A "shipped" bill of lading states that the goods in question have been loaded on board the vessel, it is therefore an on-board B/L. A "received for shipment" bill of lading, on the other hand, merely states that the goods have been received for subsequent loading. After the goods have been loaded, the "received for shipment" B/L can be converted into an on-board B/L by means of an appropriate notation.

A bill of lading stating – without qualification – that the goods are in "apparent good order and condition" is a clean B/L (the word "apparent" is used because the examination of the packages is necessarily confined to their outward condition). If the B/L bears a clause indicating any defect in the condition of the packages, it is called foul, dirty, unclean or claused.

Since in international transactions on the basis of payment by a letter of credit, bills of lading are always required to be clean, banks usually refuse foul B/Ls so that the seller is likely to run into trouble receiving payment.

Most B/Ls are issued to order and can thus be transferred by endorsement. Order bills of lading usually include a notify clause giving the name and address of the person to be notified on arrival of the shipment.

Special kinds of B/Ls are, for example, **through bills of lading** which are issued if a shipment has to be transferred en route from one ocean carrier to another or from an ocean carrier to a land carrier. **Multi-modal** and **combined transport B/Ls** refer to consignments for the transport of which several carriers (by land, sea or air) will be used. **Groupage** (AE **consolidated**) **bills of lading** cover grouped or consolidated shipments; they are addressed to the forwarding agent's correspondent in the port of destination, who will then distribute the individual shipment to their respective consignees.

An interesting novelty for the B/L is referred to in Point 19 of the *Introduction to Incoterms 2000* published by the International Chamber of Commerce in Paris, which reads as follows:

"In spite of the particular legal nature of the bill of lading it is expected that it will be replaced by electronic means in the near future. The 1990 version of Incoterms had already taken this expected development into proper account. According to the A8 clauses, paper documents may be replaced by electronic messages provided the parties have agreed to communicate electronically. Such messages could be transmitted directly to the party concerned or through a third party providing added-value services. One such service that can be usefully provided by a third party is registration of successive holders of a bill of lading. Systems providing such services, such as the so-called BOLERO service, may require further support by appropriate legal norms and principles as evidenced by the CMI 1990 Rules for Electronic Bills of Lading and articles 16–17 of the 1996 UNCITRAL Model Law on Electronic Commerce."

waybill or **consignment note**
Document of transport for goods transported by road or rail.

bonded warehouse
A stock or warehouse in which goods are kept under bond until customs duties have been paid.

cash against documents (CAD)
Condition of payment where documents are only released against cash payment (see 2.3.5).

cash on delivery (COD)
Condition of payment where goods are paid for on delivery (see 2.3.5).

cash with order (CWO)
Condition of payment where goods have to be paid when the order is placed (see 2.3.5).

certificate of origin
A document showing the origin of goods. It is prepared by the exporter on the prescribed printed form and signed by a chamber of commerce or customs officer in the exporting country. Proof of origin may be necessary because the treatment of foreign goods by the importing country frequently differs according to the country in which the goods originate. In particular,

preferential treatment regarding tariffs (duty-free entry or entry at a reduced rate of duty) is usually accorded on the basis of origin.

chamber of commerce
A voluntary association of business-people, formed for the purpose of promoting the interests of its members and the trade of the country as a whole. (In Germany, chambers of commerce are public-law corporations). In addition to the national chambers of commerce, there are binational chambers of commerce, such as the German-American or the Anglo-German Chamber of Commerce, whose specific function it is to further trade between the respective countries.

cheque
A cheque (AE check) is drawn on a bank and payable on demand. An **order cheque** is payable to a specified person or order and can be transferred by endorsement. A **bearer cheque** is payable to bearer, it can pass freely from hand to hand without endorsement. An **open cheque** is paid in cash by the bank on which it is drawn. A **crossed cheque** is not paid over the counter but credited to a bank account.

collateral
The property offered as security, usually as an inducement to another party, to lend money or extend credit.

collection agency
A company which collects outstanding accounts against payment of a fee.

collection order
An order usually given to a bank or financial institution to collect an outstanding sum or accounts receivable. In export orders documents of title are usually only released against cash payment or acceptance of a bill of exchange.

commercial disputes
Such disputes may arise in connection with sales contracts and other agreements. There are three possibilities of settling them: *conciliation*, *arbitration* and *litigation*.

commission
Fee paid to an employee, broker or agent for services performed, especially as a percentage of a total amount received in a transaction, as distinguished from salary.

commission agent
Agent working on a commission basis (see 11.1.).

company
A formal association of persons for business purposes, eg a corporation or group of persons legally incorporated under company law. The synonym in the USA is corporation. In the USA "company" is used for any organization engaged in business as a proprietorship, partnership, corporation or other form of enterprise.

joint stock company. In Britain, a form of business organization called a corporation, which has its capital divided into many small units of stock or shares.

private limited company (Ltd). It has at least two, but usually not more than fifty private members. They are not allowed to transfer their shares without the agreement of the other shareholders. Its shares and debentures are not available to the public.

public limited company (plc). There must be at least seven members. It can offer its shares and debentures to the public. There is normally no limit to the right of its members to transfer their shares to other persons. Shares of plc's which are listed on the Stock Exchange can be bought or sold to shareholders who in return for their investment receive a dividend if the company has made a profit.

conciliation
Settlement of *commercial disputes* by the parties themselves. A third party, such as a chamber of commerce, may help them to come to terms.

consignment note. See *waybill*.

credit enquiry agency. See 5.1.

credit rating
Formal evaluation of an individual's or company's credit history and capability of repaying obligations. Most large companies and lending institutions assign credit ratings to existing and potential customers.

current account
(also called **giro account**)
An account for recording current transactions between two parties. In banking, an account on which cheques can be drawn and from which money can be withdrawn on demand. No interest is usually paid on such an account.

deposit account
A bank account which is usually subject to a period of notice and on which interest is paid. It may also be a fixed deposit repayable on an agreed future date.

direct debit
A customer can arrange for his bank to pay money to certain organisations or suppliers when they present their bills directly to the bank, and to debit the amounts to his account.

discount
1. A deduction from an invoice or list price (rebate). 2. The deduction made from the face amount when a *bill of exchange* is discounted.

documentary collection
Under *documents against acceptance* (D/A) and *documents against payment* (D/P) terms, the task of presenting the shipping documents to the buyer and releasing them to him after he has paid or accepted the draft drawn on him is usually entrusted to a bank.

The exporter has to give his bank detailed instructions and to inform it whether the documents are to be surrendered on payment or acceptance of the draft, whether the documents are to be presented immediately or after arrival of the steamer, whether the importer is to be allowed to inspect the goods first, how the collection proceeds are to be remitted, what is to be done if the draft is dishonoured, etc. The exporter's bank forwards the draft and the documents, together with the exporter's instructions, to its branch office or correspondent in the importer's country. To avoid loss of documents in transit, the draft and the documents are usually made out in duplicate, the original being sent by first air mail, the duplicates by the following air mail. The banks in most countries handle documentary collections according to the Uniform Rules for Collections established by the International Chamber of Commerce.

documentary credit
A documentary credit (or **letter of credit**) is a promise made by a bank (issuing or opening bank) at the request of a customer (applicant for the credit) to pay a certain sum of money to a third party (beneficiary) on presentation of specified **shipping documents** within the validity of the credit. Documentary credits may be revocable or irrevocable. A **revocable credit** can be modified or cancelled at any time without notice to the beneficiary. An **irrevocable credit** cannot be modified or cancelled except with the beneficiary's consent. There are irrevocable and confirmed credits and irrevocable and unconfirmed credits; revocable credits are always unconfirmed. When a credit is **confirmed** by a bank in the beneficiary's country, this bank also commits itself to paying the L/C amount; the beneficiary is thus given a double assurance of payment. An **unconfirmed credit** is merely advised to the beneficiary by the bank in his country without any engagement on the part of the advising bank. The documents which the beneficiary presents to the advising or confirming bank must be in strict conformity with the terms of the credit, as otherwise the bank will reject them. It should be clearly understood that documentary credits deal with documents and not with goods. The banks assume no responsibility for the description, quantity, quality, weight or condition of the goods. If the importer wants to make sure that the goods are in accordance with the contract, he will arrange for the inspection of the goods prior to shipment and make sure that the documents to be presented by the exporter under the credit include the certificate made out by the inspection company.

The amount of the credit can be made available to the beneficiary in any of the following forms:

1. The beneficiary is authorized to draw a sight draft on the advising or confirming bank, which the bank pays on presentation of the documents.
2. The beneficiary is authorized to draw a time draft on the advising or confirming bank, which is accepted by the bank on presentation of the documents.
3. The beneficiary is authorized to draw a draft in foreign currency on the opening bank or the buyer, which is negotiated (ie purchased) by the advising or confirming bank on presentation of the documents.

The banks in practically all countries of the world apply the Uniform Customs and Practice for Documentary Credits prepared by the International Chamber of Commerce.

documents against acceptance (D/A)
Under D/A terms, the shipping documents relating to a shipment of goods are released to the importer on acceptance of a documentary draft drawn on him by the exporter. The exporter has control over the documents (and thus over the goods) only until

the buyer has accepted the draft (and not – as in the case of *documents against payment* – until payment has been made). See also *documentary collection*.

documents against payment (D/P). Also called **cash against documents (CAD)**. Under D/P terms, the shipping documents relating to a shipment of goods are released to the importer on payment of a documentary draft drawn on him by the exporter (or on payment of the invoice amount).

The exporter's security lies in the fact that he retains full control over the documents (and thus over the goods) until the importer has effected payment. Nevertheless, there is a risk for the exporter: the possibility of the importer's failure to take up the documents. In the event of such a failure, the exporter usually has no other choice than to have the goods sold by auction. Also see *documentary collection*.

draft. See *bill of exchange*.

ECGD – Export Credit Guarantee Department
A British government department responsible for encouraging exports by providing British companies with export credit insurance. In the USA this service is provided by the Export-Import Bank.

e-commerce
Online shopping of all kinds including purchase of tangible goods, online stock and bond transactions, buying and downloading of software. It includes business-to-business connections that make purchasing easier for big companies as well as e-banking, where banks provide traditional banking products via the internet (see 13.1).

electronic data interchange (EDI)
The process of transferring data between and within companies electronically.

exchange rate
The price at which one country's currency can be converted into another's at a specific time.

endorsement (indorsement)
Instruments issued to order, for example, *bill of exchange*, order *cheque*, promissory note and order *bill of lading*, are transferable by endorsement and delivery. Endorsements are placed on the back of the instrument. The person who writes the endorsement is called the endorser (indorser), the person to whom the instrument is endorsed is the endorsee (indorsee). The most common endorsement is the blank endorsement, which consists only of the endorser's signature. (Endorsements on *bills of lading*, for example, are always blank endorsements). A special endorsement includes the endorser's signature and the name of the endorsee. A blank endorsement turns an order paper into a bearer paper negotiable by delivery only; in the case of a special endorsement, the endorsee has to add another endorsement if he wishes to pass on the instrument.

factoring
Type of financial service, whereby a firm sells or transfers the title of its accounts receivable to a factoring company or a bank providing factoring services, which then acts as a principal. The receivables are sold without recourse, ie the factor

cannot turn to the seller if the accounts cannot be collected.

floating policy. See 14.1.

force majeure
A cause or event such as action by a government in time of war, strikes, lockouts or Acts of God which neither party to a contract can control. If this clause is used in a contract, it usually means that either or both parties are excused from performing their part of the agreement in such an event.

forfaiting transaction (**non-recourse financing transaction**)
Transaction in foreign trade financing, in which *bills of exchange* or accounts receivables are bought from the exporter without recourse if good securities have been offered. See also 13.4.1.

franchise
Licence given by a company (**the franchisor**) to an individual or firm (**the franchisee**) to use its name and sell its goods or services in a specific territory against payment of a fee. This usually includes the right to use the franchisor's promotion material, selling, distribution and display methods.

Free from Strikes, Riots and Civil Commotions (SR&CC)
A clause in a policy of marine insurance exempting the insurer from liability for loss or damage due to strikes, riots and similar disturbances.

haulage
Road transport organized by hauliers.

Hermes
German export credit insurance scheme, counterpart of the British *ECGD*.

import licence
A government permit for which an importer must apply if the goods he wants to import are subject to quantitative restrictions. Import licences are granted only until the import quota is exhausted.

import quota
The maximum quantity of a certain commodity allowed to be imported by a government during a certain period of time.

INCOTERMS
(International Commercial Terms)
Uniform definitions of terms of delivery used in foreign trade, prepared by the International Chamber of Commerce. When a contract is concluded on the basis of the Incoterms, the seller and the buyer know exactly what their duties are, a fact which helps to avoid misunderstandings in international law. See Chart of the Incoterms 2000 (p. 356) and 2.3.3.

Institute Cargo Clauses
The clauses used by insurers defining marine insurance cover for goods. They comprise three clauses: A, B, and C. See 14.1.

insurance certificate
When a floating policy has been taken out for insurance, a certificate of insurance will be issued to represent the insurance contract, eg in a consignment for which payment has been arranged on a *letter of credit* basis.

insurance policy
Insurance contract between the insured and the insurance company specifying what risks are insured and what premiums must be paid to keep the policy in force. The policy is the written document which determines whether or not a claim is covered. For types of policy see 14.1.

International Chamber of Commerce (ICC)
A federation of national chambers of commerce, business organisations and business firms from all over the world. The ICC acts as a spokesman for the international business community and has an important advisory position with the UN. It has done much to standardize international business practices by creating and regularly revising uniform rules, eg the Uniform Customs and Practice for Documentary Credits, the Uniform Rules for Collections and the Incoterms.

invoice
A bill used in commerce which is prepared by a seller of goods or services and sumitted to the purchaser. The invoice lists all the items bought and their respective unit price as well as the total price. In business, there are four types of invoices:

commercial invoice. This invoice constitutes the basis for payment. It usually includes: names and addresses of seller and buyer or consignee; place and date of issue; number of invoice; date when order was placed, reference numbers, exact description, quantity and quality of goods delivered; unit and total price; discounts; net and gross weight; packing and markings; conditions of delivery and payment; mode and costs of transport; in some cases VAT or other taxes.

consular invoice. An export invoice which has been legally attested or formally signed by the Consul of the country to which the goods are being sent. He thus confirms that all the details of the invoice are correct. Consular invoices are usually accepted by the Customs in the buyer's country as a true basis for charging import duty.

customs invoice. It is prepared by the exporter especially for customs purposes on an official form indicating the value of the goods in the exporting and the importing countries. In some cases where goods pass borders but are not actually sold to a customer in a foreign country (eg goods to be exhibited at a fair or exhibition), the customs invoice serves as a document in which the goods which pass the customs authorities are listed.

pro forma invoice. In British home trade, it is an invoice sent to a buyer who has to pay for the goods before they are delivered. In export trade, it is a detailed statement of costs which is sent to a potential buyer for information, practically taking the place of a quotation. In countries where an import licence is required, the buyer usually asks for a pro forma invoice to apply for the import licence.

invoicing department
The department of business in which invoices are prepared, produced and sent to customers (AE **billing department**).

IOU ("I owe you")
A written acknowledgement of a debt which has been signed by the debtor.

joint stock company. See *company*.

joint venture
Agreement by two or more parties to work on a project or provide a service together.

letter of comfort
A letter to a bank or other lender of money in which the writer supports a person who wishes to borrow money, and recommends that a loan be given to him. See 13.4.3.

letter of credit. See *documentary credit*.

letter of intent
A formal letter declaring it to be the writer's intention to negotiate an important deal or arrangement. See 4.2.5.

letter of subrogation
Transfer of a claim to another person or institution, the subrogee, in the place of the creditor, to whose rights to the debt the subrogee succeeds. See 13.4.2.

liquidation
Procedure in which shareholders surrender all of their shares in a company and receive, after all credits have been paid, their pro rate share of any remaining assets and accumulated earnings and profits.

litigation
Recourse to legal action, for example in a commercial dispute.

Lloyd's of London
The Society of Lloyd's in London does not itself transact insurance business, this is done by the underwriters, who accept insurance. They are grouped in so-called syndicates. Originally, Lloyd's underwriters were only concerned with marine insurance, but today they handle almost every type of insurance business. Lloyd's underwriters used to have unlimited liability, but after its reorganization, underwriting members and companies enjoy limited liability to a certain extent.

Lloyd's List and Shipping Gazette
Newspaper which is published daily by the Corporation of Lloyd's and gives news of all movements of ships and aircraft.

Lloyd's Register of Shipping
A survey which classifies British and foreign ships and publishes this information in the annual Lloyd's Register Book. It is also concerned with defining and maintaining standards for the building, upkeep and repair of ships.

merger
Amalgamation of two companies.

mortgage
A long-term loan on real estate by which the borrower gives the lender (usually a bank or building society) a lien on property as security for repayment.

multimodal transport (integrated transport; AE **intermodal traffic**)
Transport of unitized freight such as containers, pallets and trailers, by a combination of two or more carriers. Multimodal transport includes containerization, piggyback and roll-on/roll-off services. Containerization permits any combination of transport

modes. Piggyback is a combination of transport by rail and road: trucks and trailers are loaded on railway cars for long-distance hauls. Roll-on/roll-off, a combination of sea and road transport, involves the transport of trucks and trailers aboard ferry boats and ships. The advantages of multimodal transport are faster loading and unloading, savings of freight and packing costs, and reduced risk of pilferage and of damage in transit.

negotiable instrument
An unconditional order or promise to pay an amount of money which is easily transferable from one person to another, eg cheques, promissory notes or bills of exchange. The bill of lading as it is used in export trade is also negotiable, giving the owner the right to collect the goods.

overdraft
A credit arrangement by which banks allow their customers to overdraw their accounts up to a specified amount within a specified period of time. It is not advisable to make use of an overdraft credit over longer periods, since the rate of interest charged by the banks is usually high.

overheads
Regular fixed and variable costs for running a business.

parent company
Holding company which owns and controls a number of subsidiaries.

partnership
An association of two or more persons who carry on together a business for profit. There are ordinary (or general) partnerships and limited partnerships. The partners of an ordinary partnership have unlimited liability. A limited partnership consists of at least one partner with unlimited liability (general partner) and at least another with limited liability (limited partner). Limited partners do not participate in the management.

premium
An amount which is paid by the insured to the insurer to cover certain risks.

principal
A person or company who authorizes another person or company to be his agent or broker, ie the person for whom an agent or broker acts.

private limited company (Ltd)
See *company*.

profit and loss account
Accounting summary which is usually part of the balance sheet to calculate the net profit or loss of a business before taxation.

promissory note
An unconditional promise to pay a certain sum of money to the order of someone. It differs from a bill of exchange in that in a promissory note the drawer is identical to the drawee.

public limited company (plc).
See *company*.

R & D (Research & Development)
Two closely related activities in a company by which new products and processes are developed and checked before entering the production line.

rebate
In consumer marketing, payment made to a consumer after a purchase is completed. See *discount*.

retail trade.
The sale of goods to consumers and the general public, eg in shops, markets, by direct-mail, online, etc. The link between the wholesale trade and the end consumer.

shipping documents
Documents relating to a shipment of goods. See 6.3.3 and 14.1.

standing order
An order in writing by customers to their bank to pay a stated sum of money to a named party at certain stated dates until further orders. It is mainly used for fixed amounts which are payable on known dates, such as insurance premiums, rents, subscriptions, etc.

subsidiary
A company of which more than half the share capital is owned by another company, the holding or parent company. The subsidiaries of the same holding or parent company are said to be affiliates.

SWIFT
Abbreviation for "Society for Worldwide Interbank Financial Telecommunication", an interbanking computer system linking the banks of the major industrial and trading countries. These banks are connected to one of several systems and pass their transfer orders to their headquarters by computer.

stock corporation
A type of business organization in the United States which is similar to a limited company in Britain. There are close corporations and open corporations. In contrast to open corporations (or publicly owned corporations), close corporations (or privately owned corporations) do not offer their shares and bonds to the public and do not have to publish their balance sheets. State statutes require the name of corporations to indicate the fact that they are incorporated. The most commonly used words are Corporation (Corp) and Incorporated (Inc).

surveyor
Representative of the insurer in marine insurance whose duty it is to inspect damaged cargo and to issue a survey report summarizing the results of the inspection.

takeover
Change in the controlling interest of a company or corporation. A takeover may be a friendly acquisition (friendly takeover) or an unfriendly bid (hostile takeover). A hostile takeover aims to replace the existing management and is usually attempted by a public tender offer.

takeover bid
An offer made by one company to the shareholders of another with the aim of gaining control of the company or corporation.

trade association
An association of firms engaged in a particular trade, formed for the purpose of protecting and advancing the interest of its members.

trade discount
A discount on the list price granted to a middleman who buys goods for resale.

VAT (value added tax)
An indirect tax levied by the government as a percentage of the selling price of a product or service. It is added to the invoice as output tax at each stage of production and distribution, from manufacturer to wholesaler and retailer. At each stage, the taxable person must account to the government for the output tax but is allowed to set against it the input tax, ie the tax charged to him/her by his/her suppliers.

warranty
A guarantee given by the seller to the buyer concerning the quality of goods.

waybill. See *bill*.

wholesale trade
The sale of goods in large quantities, especially to retailers, not to consumers.

Incoterms 2000

EXW *ex works (named place)*
The seller makes goods available at his premises. He bears all costs and risks until the goods have been handed over to the first carrier.

FCA *free carrier (named place)*
The seller pays the transport costs and bears the risk until the goods have been delivered into the custody of the first carrier.

FAS *free alongside ship (named port of shipment)*
The seller pays the transport costs up to the port of shipment. He bears the risk until the goods have been delivered alongside the ship or are placed on the quay in the port of shipment.

FOB *free on board (named port of shipment)*
The seller pays the transport costs up to the port of shipment. He bears the risk until the goods have passed the ship's rail in the port of shipment.

CFR *cost and freight (named port of destination)*
The seller pays the transport costs up to the port of destination. He bears the risk until the goods have passed the ship's rail in the port of shipment.

CIF *cost, insurance and freight (named port of destination)*
The seller pays the transport costs, including marine insurance, up to the port of destination. He bears the risk until the goods have passed the ship's rail in the port of shipment.

CPT *carriage paid to ... (named place of destination)*
The seller pays the transport costs up to the named destination. He bears the risk until the goods have been delivered into the custody of the first carrier.

CIP *carriage and insurance paid to (named place of destination)*
The seller pays the transport costs, including transport insurance, up to the named destination. He bears the risk until the goods have been delivered into the custody of the first carrier.

DAF *delivered at frontier (named place)*
The seller pays all costs and bears the risk until the goods have been delivered on his side of the border.

DES *delivered ex ship (named port of destination)*
The seller pays the transport costs and bears the risk until the goods arrive at the port of destination.

DEQ *delivered ex quay (named port of destination)*
The seller pays the transport costs and customs duty and bears the risk until the goods are on the quay in the port of destination.

DDU *delivered duty unpaid (named place of destination)*
The seller pays all costs, excluding customs duty, and bears the risk until the goods have been delivered to the buyer.

DDP *delivered duty paid (named place of destination)*
The seller pays all costs, including customs duty, and bears the risk until the goods have been delivered to the buyer.

Application for an International Moneymover payment

Lloyds TSB

Lloyds TSB Bank plc
Please make the following payment
(tick the appropriate box)
Please complete by typewriter or in block capitals using a ball point pen.
For guidance to sending money abroad including types of payments please read leaflet PL706
NOTE for economy payments the application must be completed in accordance with information sheet form 55NI

BUSINESS CUSTOMERS
APPLICATION FOR AN INTERNATIONAL MONEYMOVER PAYMENT

55NB 0699c Bank Copy

☐ EXPRESS ☐ STANDARD ☐ ECONOMY — Low value and limited countries only. See note † below

Date ______

BRANCH	Title ______ Sorting code Number 3 0
REMITTER NAME	
	Account to be debited — Sterling account number ______ or Currency account number ______
Address	
Town/City/Post Code	
AMOUNT OF PAYMENT (please tick the appropriate box. RE see note 2 overleaf)	☐ Remit in foreign currency the sum of — Amount — Currency ☐ Remit the foreign currency equivalent of sterling — £ ☐ Remit the sterling amount of (not available for Economy International Moneymover) — £
AMOUNT AND CURRENCY IN WORDS	
BENEFICIARY NAME	
Address (note address if payment is being made to a Bank A/c)	
Town/City/Country	
BENEFICIARY BANK	
Address	
Town/City/Country	
Account number	
Bank Clearing Code	For Economy International Moneymovers – use numerics only
DETAILS FOR BENEFICIARY (See note 3 overleaf)	
CHARGES (please tick the appropriate box) (See note 5 overleaf)	Usually, Lloyds TSB Bank plc charges are paid by the Remitter and the foreign bank's charges ar paid by the beneficiary (,split charges'). ☐ Split charges ☐ All charges to be paid by the remitter ☐ All charges to be paid by the beneficiary Account number Charges to be debited to (if different from Remitter section).
METHOD OF PAYMENT	Payment will be made direct to Beneficiary/Beneficiary's account unless the box below is ticked. ☐ Pay to Beneficiary on Application and Identification (Not available for Economy International Moneymovers)

FOREIGN EXCHANGE DETAILS (if appropriate)			
	Date Booked/Agreed	Rate	If to be applied against a forward contract also quote:
	Value Date	Corres. Bank	Contract No. ______
	F.E. Ref.	Position Ref.	Maturity/Option dates ______

Please check: Has the type of payment box been ticked?
Please advise daytime telephone nummer, in case of need. ______

I/We* confirm the details quoted above and have read and agree to the Conditions of Payment overleaf. Please debit the account quoted above. (*Delete as appropriate)

Customer's Signature(s) ______ **Date** ______

FOR BANK USE ONLY	Market segment code	Special instructions CBD*/LBCS*	Hold entries Y*/N*
Lloyds Bank charges: Ccy & Amount		Cross Rate	F.E. Code B*/F*/X*
Authorised Signatory(ies) confirmed ______			Confirmed with customer (if appropriate)
For Lloyds TSB Bank plc (GRB.INL 4.1) ______			

Input by	Authorised by	Released by	Earmarked	Date	Payment No.	Funds Transfer No.	Code

Your application to issue a

Documentary Credit

Guidance notes for customers

Lloyds TSB

This Page consists of guidance notes to assist you to complete this application form and which you may find helpful to detach.

The references to article numbers in the following notes refer to the Articles of the "Uniform Customs and Practice for Documentary Credits", 1993 Revision, ICC Publication No. 500 ("UCP500"). Copies of this and the "Uniform Rules for Bank to Bank Reimbursements under Documentary Credits", ICC Publication No. 525 ("URR 525") are available from International Chamber of Commerce, United Kingdom, 14/15 Belgrave Square, London SW1X 8PS.

Specific Notes

1 An irrevocable credit cannot be cancelled or amended without the consent of the Issuing Bank, the Beneficiary and, where appropriate, the Confirming Bank (Article 9). An irrevocable and transferable credit gives the Beneficiary the right to request the transfer of all or part of the credit to one or (where partial shipment is allowed) more second Beneficiary(ies) (Article 48), although such transfer is at the discretion of the Transferring Bank.

2 A confirmed Credit is sometimes requested where the Beneficiary requires an irrevocable credit to be confirmed by another bank, normally in the Beneficiary's Country. The Confirming Bank will charge confirming commission which is payable by the applicant unless otherwise stipulated. The Confirming Bank's undertaking constitutes a definite undertaking to the Beneficiary in addition to that of the Issuing Bank, provided that the stipulated documents are present to it and that the terms and conditions of the credit are complied with. A bank will not usually be willing to add its confirmation **unless** the credit is expressed to be available with that bank.

3 Where a credit is available with the Advising Bank by payment, debit interest will be charged to the Applicant from the date of payment abroad until the date on which we are reimbursed by the Applicant, including instances where discrepancies are identified and waived. The rate of interest charged will be that applicable to the account of Lloyds TSB Bank plc debited in reimbursement for the payment made. For example, where the Paying Bank obtains US Dollar reimbursement for a payment made to a Beneficiary in Japan, debit interest will be charged at the rate applied to the Lloyds TSB Bank plc US Dollar Account from which reimbursement is obtained.

Where a credit is both **available with any bank by negotiation** and **transferable** a Transferring Bank must be nominated in the credit. Unless you indicate your choice of Transferring Bank (Under 'Additional Instructions'), we will nominate the Advising Bank as the Transferring Bank. Where a credit is to be **"freely negotiable"** (ie available with any bank by negotiation) unless you indicate otherwise we will stipulate that the credit is to expire in the Beneficiary's country.

4 If either the wording shown is not required or additional documents are to be called for please state your precise requirements under 'Other Documents'. Please also bear in mind that sub-Articles 20b and c set out what is acceptable as an original or copy document.

If the blanks within this section are not completed the appropriate words will be omitted from the credit. In the case of the insurance document sub-Article 34f of UCP 500 states that unless otherwise stipulated, insurance cover must be effected for

5 UCP 500 concentrates on the specific requirements of a transport document rather than how it is named. (Articles 23 to 30 cover the generic types of transport documents.)

6 The provisions of UCP 500 allow for transhipment to take place in some circumstances even where a credit expressly stipulates "transhipment is prohibited" (sub-Article 23(d) and similar sub-Articles). If you wish to restrict transhipment beyond the provisions of UCP 500 either partially or fully, please state your requirements under "Additional Instructions" specifying the nature of the documentary evidence of compliance required.

7 If a latest date for shipment / dispatch is not specified, this date will be deemed to be the same as the expiry date (see note 10).

8 The goods (or services) description should be brief (Article 5). In addition, it is not the practice of Lloyds TSB Bank plc to issue credits which do not include a specific description of the underlying goods or services, eg terms such as "goods", "services", "merchandise", "materials as per proforma ..." etc. by themselves would not usually be acceptable.

9 The price basis must be consistent with the documents required (eg for CIF or CIP, an insurance document would usually be required) and the relative port / airport / place named (eg CIF or CIP Southampton).

10 If no period is inserted, we will stipulate a period of 21 days for presentation of documents (sub-Article 43a). Where a latest date for shipment (see note 7) is specified the number of days allowed for presentation of documents should be **at least** as great as the difference between that latest date for shipment / dispatch of goods and the expiry date.

11 **If a credit contains conditions without stating the document(s) to be presented to evidence compliance with those conditions ("non-documentary conditions") banks will deem such conditions as not stated and will disregard them** (sub-Article 13c). Therefore, please ensure that where you include a condition to be met by the Beneficiary you also state the document required to evidence its fulfilment. You should also state who is to issue the document and what, if anything, it should say (Article 21).

12 Where Lloyds TSB Bank plc and other Bank charges are payable by the Beneficiary, we would incorporate such a condition into the terms of the credit; however if these are not forthcoming we will look to you for settlement (sub-Article 18(c) ii).

General notes

13 Lloyds TSB Bank plc has formal business links with a large number of banks throughout the world ("Correspondent Banks") and consequently we would prefer that the choice of the Advising Bank be left to us. However, if you wish to choose the Advising Bank, for example if you know the details of the Beneficiary's bankers, please indicate your choice under "Additional Instructions".

14 Where the Beneficiary is in the UK, we will not use an Advising Bank unless specifically requested to do so.

Specimen

Lloyds TSB Bank plc 71 Lombard Street, London EC3P 3BS Registered in England no. 2065.
Lloyds TSB Bank plc, which is regulated by the Personal Investment Authority and IMRO, represents only the Scottish Widows and Lloyds TSB Marketing Group for life assurance, pensions and investment business.
A Member of the Banking Ombudsman Scheme and a signatory to the Banking Code.

Acknowledgements

The authors and publishers are grateful to the following copyright owners for permission to reproduce illustrations and texts. It has not been possible to identify the sources of all the material used and in such cases the publishers would welcome information from copyright owners.

pp. 40–41:	Norpak Plastics Ltd, Bradford, England
p. 42:	Deckel Ltd, Stratford-on-Avon, England
p. 73:	The McGraw-Hill Publications Companies, Hightstown, USA
pp. 106–109:	Macmillan Publishers Ltd, Oxford, England
p. 151:	Macdonald & Evans, Plymouth, England
pp. 222–225:	Stadtsparkasse Köln, Köln
pp. 228–232:	Stadtsparkasse Köln, Köln
pp. 245–248:	Stadtsparkasse Köln, Köln
pp. 358–359:	Forms repruduced by courtesy of Lloyds TSB Bank plc, London, England

Illustrations:

pp. 16, 21, 36, 53, 85, 99, 101, 128, 129, 145, 164, 179, 202, 216, 236, 260, 278, 288: Daniela Eisenreich, München

p. 112: Reinhard Blumenschein, München